教員採用試験「全国版」過去問シリーズ ⑥

全国まるごと

過去問題集

英語科

#分野別　　#項目別

協同教育研究会 編

2025
年度版

協同出版

はじめに

　本書は，全国47都道府県と20の政令指定都市の公立学校の教員採用候補者選考試験を受験する人のために編集されたものです。

　教育を取り巻く環境は変化しつつあり，学校現場においても，教員免許更新制の廃止やGIGAスクール構想の実現などの改革が進められており，現行の学習指導要領においても，「主体的・対話的で深い学び」を実現するため，指導方法や指導体制の工夫改善により，「個に応じた指導」の充実を図るとともに，コンピュータや情報通信ネットワーク等の情報手段を活用するために必要な環境を整えることが示されています。

　一方で，いじめや体罰，不登校，教員の指導方法など，教育現場の問題もあいかわらず取り沙汰されており，教員に求められるスキルは，今後さらに高いものになっていくことが予想されます。

　協同教育研究会では，現在，626冊の全国の自治体別・教科別過去問題集を刊行しており，その編集作業にあたり，各冊子ごとに出題傾向の分析を行っています。本書は，その分析結果をまとめ，全国的に出題率の高い分野の問題，解答・解説に加えて，より理解を深めるための要点整理を，頻出項目毎に記載しています。そのことで，近年の出題傾向を把握することでき，また多くの問題を解くことで，より効果的な学習を進めることができます。

　みなさまが，この書籍を徹底的に活用し，教員採用試験の合格を勝ち取って，教壇に立っていただければ，それはわたくしたちにとって最上の喜びです。

協同教育研究会

教員採用試験「全国版」過去問シリーズ⑥

全国まるごと過去問題集　英語科＊目次

●学習指導要領・学習指導法

本書について

　本書には，各教科の項目毎に，出題率が高い問題を精選して掲載しております。前半は要点整理になっており，後半は実施問題となります。また各問題の最後に，出題年，出題された都道府県市及び難易度を示しています。難易度は，以下のように5段階になっております。

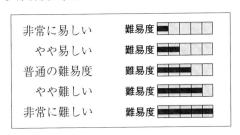

非常に易しい	難易度
やや易しい	難易度
普通の難易度	難易度
やや難しい	難易度
非常に難しい	難易度

　また，各問題文や選択肢の表記については，できる限り都道府県市から出題された問題の通りに掲載しておりますが，一部図表等について縮小等の加工を行って掲載しております。ご了承ください。

出題傾向と対策

出題傾向

　学習指導要領に関する問題は頻出である。出題形式としては，学習指導要領や学習指導要領解説の一部の空所補充問題や，記載されていない内容を選択する問題，中学・高校の学習指導要領の内容の違いなど，かなり詳細な内容で出題されることもある。日本語版・英語版の学習指導要領をしっかりと読んでセクションごとの内容をよく頭に入れておくことが必要である。

　学習指導要領以外では，出題傾向にあまり大きな変化はみられない。語彙，文法を問う問題，英作文，英文解釈は，ほぼ従来どおりである。ただし最近は，英作文に関しては和文英訳が減少し，課題作文が増加の傾向にある。英文解釈に関しては，長文が増え，論理的思考力が問われる文章の出題が目立つようになってきた。以下，どの都道府県を受験するにせよ必ず出題され，また配点の高い英文読解問題を中心に，その傾向と対策を述べることにする。

　英文読解問題に使用される文章は，物語文と説明文に分けることができる。最近の傾向としては，このうち後者の説明文，その中でも論説型の文章が多く出題されている。この試験によく出る論説型の文章を効率よく理解する方法はあるのであろうか。言語学研究の成果から，文章を理解するにあたり読者はスキーマを利用していることがわかっている。スキーマは過去に蓄積した経験を抽象化した知識構造と定義されている。スキーマを基盤とした文章理解の理論によると，文章の内容を理解するための仕組みには，ボトムアップ処理とトップダウン処理がある。文章を細部から徐々に大きな構成へと発展させて理解するのがボトムアップ処理であるのに対し，文章の全体から細部へと理解を深めていくのがトップダウン処理である。試験対策としては，この2つの処理過程を同時並行して行える優れた読解力を身に付けていなくてはならない。

　言い換えれば，英文に使われている個々の単語の意味を理解するといったボトムアップ処理だけでは十分な読解力とはいえない。ボトムアッ

プ処理に加え，文章全体の構造に注意を向け，主要な部分と細部を分けて文章全体の意味を理解するトップダウン処理を上手に行えるかどうかが優れた読解力を身に付けられるかの鍵といえる。

スキーマには基本的にフォーマル・スキーマ(formal schema)とコンテント・スキーマ(content schema)の2つがある。フォーマル・スキーマとは構造に関するスキーマであり，コンテント・スキーマとは内容に関するスキーマである。試験に多く出題される論説型の文章の読解では，英語におけるフォーマル・スキーマの1つとしてパラグラフがどのように構成されているかの知識を習得することにより文章理解の効率を飛躍的に高めることが可能となる。このパラグラフの構成については後述の「受験対策」の項で詳しく述べることにする。

英文読解問題として論説型の文章の要約問題が出題されることがある。英文要約問題は出題されない都道府県もあるが，出題された場合，点数の差がつきやすいのでここで少し触れておきたい。要約問題は，日本文に要約するにせよ英文に要約するにせよ，「受験対策」の項で解説するフォーマル・スキーマとして持っているパラグラフ構成の知識を活用すれば，さほど難しいことはない。

一般的に文章を要約する場合，6つの方法が考えられる。それらは，

(1) 不要な部分は省略する

(2) 余剰的な部分は省略する

(3) 同類に属する語は上位の語で代表させる

(4) 個々の行動は上位の行動に統合する語

(5) 主題文を与えられた文章から取り出して入れる

(6) 主題文が文章内に明示されていない場合は自分で主題文を作る

である。(3)は例えば，dogs, cats, goldfish, parrots と列挙してあればpetsで代表するということである。(4)は例えば，バス，電車，飛行機，レンタカーを使いはるばる来たのであれば，単純にさまざまな交通手段を使ってやって来たと表現するということである。要約は原文の3分の1程度に短縮することが多いが，試験では字数が指定されているのでそれに従い，概要を主題文と支持文を中心に簡潔かつ的確に表現することである。

■■■■■■■■■■■■■■■■■■■受験対策■■■■■■■■■■■■■■■■■■

　受験対策として，文章理解の効率を高めるために英語のパラグラフ構成の知識を身に付けることは不可欠である。日本語を母語とする我々にとって，英語の文章構成は明示的に学ばなければ獲得することがむずかしい知識である。しかし，この知識をいったん身に付ければ，フォーマル・スキーマとしてその知識を活用しトップダウン処理をすることにより，英文読解の大きな助けとなるのである。そこで，ここではパラグラフ，そしてパラグラフの集合体としてのエッセーの構成及び展開について解説をする。

　論説型の英語の文章構成は，日本語の文章構成とは異なる。英語のパラグラフは日本語の「段落」とは同義ではない。パラグラフは，主題をもって統一された文の集合体として，1つのまとまりのある思想を表している。まず1つのパラグラフの構成についての解説からはじめよう。

　パラグラフは主題文，支持文，結語文から成り立っている。主題文は冒頭に置かれ，パラグラフで論じられる主題を示す。主題文はパラグラフの中で最も統括的で重要な文である。英語の論説型の文章では日本語の文章によくあるような結論が最後になってはじめてわかるような構成をとることはまずない。主題文に続く支持文では主題文で述べたことを読み手に納得してもらうために，主題をサポートする文がつづく。支持文は主題を詳しく論じたり説明したりする文であり本論といえる。支持文につづくのが結語文である。結語文はパラグラフが終わることを示し，主題についてのメッセージを再び与える。その方法としては，主題文を別の表現で言いかえたりパラグラフ全体の要点をまとめたりする。

　なお，パラグラフの構成につづきパラグラフの展開法について確認しておくと，論説型で書かれたパラグラフの典型的な展開法としては，

(1)　時間的順序　　(2)　過程　　(3)　比較対照
(4)　原因，結果　　(5)　例示　　(6)　分類
をあげることができる。

　以上，1つのパラグラフについて述べてきたが，いくつものパラグラフが集まったエッセーとの対応関係を最後に解説しよう。パラグラフの主題文は主題を示し，その主題をどのように説明するのかについて述べ

るエッセーの最初のパラグラフに相当し，パラグラフの支持文はエッセーの本編に相当し，パラグラフの結語文はエッセーの結論を述べる最後のパラグラフに相当する。

　以上，パラグラフ及びエッセーの構成と展開について述べてきた。実は，このように多くの誌面を割いて解説してきたのは，この知識が読解問題を解く時に役立つだけでなく，自由英作文形式の課題作文を書く時，また2次試験のスピーキングテストとしてスピーチをする時，演説などの比較的長めのまとまった内容を聞き取るといったリスニングテストを受ける時にも十分に役立つからである。

　これからの英語教員には，単語や文法の知識を超えた真の英語力が求められる。4技能を統合したバランスのよい英語力，英文を理解したり表現したりする時に役立つ情報処理力と論理的思考力を身に付けるよう，日々努力を怠らないでいただきたい。

語彙・文法

要点整理

音声に関しては，発音，アクセント，発音記号，Sentence, Stress, Intonation, Punctuation, Breath-Group などについて考えてみることが基本である。

このうち今回は発音について考えてみることにする。英語は生きたことばである以上，その正しい学習は正確な発音をもって始めなければならず，正しい音読が大切である。音読の効果というものは，自分の耳に英語の音を聴き分ける力を与える上で，大きな効果がある。またそれは Dictation およびListening にも大いに役立つ。

音読というものは，英語の内容を理解する上にも大きな影響がある。日本の諺にも「読書百遍意(義)おのずから通ず」（Repeated reading makes the meaning clear.）というのがある。また音読をすれば耳から印象を与えて，記憶を確実にするという利点もある。正しい発音と正しい spelling がお互いに関連して，単語の知識を正確にし，同音異義語，類音異義語などの類似語の混同を少なくすることもできる。会話の練習の上で，正しい音読が基礎になることは言うまでもない。

次にぜひ実行することを勧めたいのは以下のようなことである。

① 1日に少しでもよいから，毎日欠かさず英文を朗読して，口と耳の練習をすること。

② 予習，下調べの際に，ひと通り調べたら朗読する習慣をつけること。

③ 復習するときにも音読を必ず行うようにしたい。意味が分かって音読すれば，より正しい音読ができるはずである。

④ 教室では，先生やテープの音読，あるいは友人の音読に耳を傾け鋭敏にしなければならない。

⑤ ネイティブ・スピーカーの読み方，話し方に十分注意して，できるだけそれらを真似るようにすること。

以上のことを実行していけば，正しい発音も身につくであろう。

次に文章を読むときに区切るところ（Breath-Group）について注意すべきところを2, 3述べる。(1) 形容詞が名詞の次にあるときは，形容詞の前で切る。(2) 名詞以外の主語は切る。(3) 強意のための転倒語句は

その前後で切る。(4) 語句の省略のあるところでは切る。(5) 同格語句の前後では切る。(6) 接続詞，関係代名詞などと，それに従う句とは切ってはならない。

▼アクセントの規則

1. ―ion, ―ian, ―eon, ―eous, ―ious, ―ient, ―ience, ―iency で終わる語は，この語尾のすぐ前の音節にアクセントがある。

   státion, musícian, pígeon, courágeous, relígious, impátient, pátience, effíciency

2. ―ican, ―itan, ―ial, ―ical で終わる語は，この語尾のすぐ前の音節にアクセントがある。

   Américan, metropólitan, artifícial, económical

3. ―ety, ―ity, ―ify で終われば，この語尾のすぐ前の音節にアクセントがある。

   anxíety, possibílity, idéntify

4. ―mble で終わる語は，すぐ前の音節にアクセントがある。

   rámble, resémble, assémble

5. 次の語尾をもつ語は，すぐ前の音節にアクセントがある。

   rémedy, geógraphy, geólogy, mónarchy, demócracy, sýmpathy, philósophy, acádemy, astrónomy, geómetry, barómeter, twéntieth, mínister

6. ―ula, ―ular で終わる語は，すぐ前の音節にアクセントがある。

   península, partícular

7. 次の語尾をもつ語は，すぐ前の音節にアクセントがある。

   encyclopédia, stúdio, famíliar, supérior, gymnásium

8. ―sive で終わる語は，すぐ前の音節にアクセントがある。

   expénsive, exclúsive, pássive

9. ―ful, ―ness, ―ous, ―tive, ―some, ―le, ―ing, ―est および ―ed [id] で終わる2音節の語は，はじめの音節にアクセントがある。

   úseful, cálmness, nérvous, mótive, tíresome, stáble, pláying, stróngest, éducated [édjukeitid]

10. any―, by―, every―, some― で始まる語は，はじめの音節にア

クセントがある。

ánywhere, býstander, éverybody, sómething

11. 形容詞と名詞が結合して1語となっているものは，はじめの音節にアクセントがある。gréen-house「温室」，bláck-bird「つぐみ」。ただし形容詞と名詞が結合して1語となっていないで，2つの独立の単語として並んでいるときは，各語にアクセントがある。bláck bírd「黒い鳥」，gréen hóuse「緑色の家」

12. —eer, —oon, —oof で終わる語は，この語尾，つまり後の音節にアクセントがある。

voluntéer, pionéer, typhóon, afternóon, repróof, alóof

13. —esque, —ique, —ese で終わる語は，この語尾，つまり最後の音節にアクセントがある。

picturésque, uníque, techníque, Japanése

14. 最後の音節の i が ［i:］と発音され e で終わる語は，最後の音節にアクセントがある。

po-líce, ma-chíne, mag-a-zíne, fa-tígue, tech-níque

15. —self, —selves で終わる語は，この語尾，つまり最後の音節にアクセントがある。

my-sélf, it-sélf, our-sélves, them-sélves

16. —ish で終わる2音節の語は，終わりから2つ目の音節に，多音節の語は，動詞の時は終わりから2音節目に，形容詞の時は終わりから3つ目の音節にアクセントがある。

〈2音節の語の場合〉fín-ish, pún-lish, púb-lish, sélf-ish

〈多音節の語の場合〉1. 動詞 ac-cóm-plish, dis-tín-guish, es-táb-lish

2. 形容詞 bá-by-ish, yél-low-ish, fé-ver-ish

17. —gen, —tude で終わる多音節の語は，終わりから3つ目の音節にアクセントがある。

óx-y-gen, hý-dro-gen, sól-i-tude, át-ti-tude

18. —ever で終わる語は，ev にアクセントがある。

what-év-er, how-év-er, wher-év-er

19. —ental を語尾とする語は en にアクセントがある。

el-e-mén-tal, ac-ci-dén-tal

20. —ness, —ism, —ist で終わる語は，もとの語のアクセントのまま
　　である。

　　háppy→háppiness, héro→héroism, ecónomy→ecónomist

▼慣用語句

　英文解釈上，単語と同じように大切なのは，慣用語句の知識である。
数学では1＋1＝2，2－1＝1となるが，英語の慣用語句は，油断できな
い。たとえば「少し」という意味の表現に，a bit というのがある。こ
れに打消の not をつけると，「少しではない」とはならず，「まったく
ない」＝ not at all の意味になる。a little, a fewはともに「少し」で，
これを not a little, not a few とすると，「少なからずの，多くの」とな
る。

　英語の慣用句とは，常識的に，英語に特有な言いまわしと定義でき
るが，日本語に直訳しただけでは，意味の通じないものを慣用語句と
考える。by and large「概して」，time and again「しばしば」，go to the
dogs（話）「零落する，だめになる」などはその例。その他 inquire
about～「～について問い合わせる」，inquire into～「～を調査する」，
inquire after～「～の安否をたずねる」，behind time「遅刻して」，behind
the times「時代遅れになって」，with a child「子どもをつれて」，with
child（文語）「妊娠して」というように，注意しないと間違いやすいも
のもある。また文脈の中で at once A and B の at once は「～と同時に」
の意味で「Aであると同時にB」の意味。「直ちに」ではない。慣用句
については，熟語集などでまとめて整理しておくことをすすめたい。

▼同意語，反意語

　同意語（Synonym）は他の語と意味が同一の語あるいは語の集団を
いう。refuse と reject「拒絶する」，on the other hand と on the contrary
「これに反して」，in case of と in the event of「～の際には」のようなも
のである。なお，広義には Synonym は，同一の意味でなくとも，類似
した意味の場合にも適用することができる。tell「話す」と explain「説
明する」，establish「設立する」と found「建設する」，in error「間違っ
て」と at fault「迷って」のような場合である。

　反意語は，同じ品詞で反対の意味を持つ1対または1群の語（句）をいう。これは大別して次のように「反対」「打ち消し」を表す接頭辞（dis－, in－, im－, ir－, ig－, n－, un－など），接尾辞（－some, －less, －or, －essなど）などをつけて作るものと，全く別の語で示すものとの3通りのものがある。以下に例をあげておくので参照にしておくこと。

（接頭辞）appear－disappear, active－inactive, moral－immoral, regular－irregular, noble－ignoble, ever－never, happy－unhappy, など。

（接尾辞）tiresome－tireless, actor－actress, noise－noiseless, など。

（別の語を用いるもの）above－below, abstract－concrete, entrance－exit, borrow－lend, peace－war, など。

　なお成句としては，by day「昼は」－by night「夜は」, in front of「～の前に」－in the back of「～の後ろに」などがある。

▼語形変化

　語形変化は文字通り，ある語の品詞変化をつくることである。たとえば，courage の動詞はencourage，形容詞はcourageous, life の動詞はlive，形容詞は living, obedience の動詞は obey，形容詞は obedient となるように，その知識を問うものである。これは派生語についての知識を問うものと同じに考えてよい。

▼同音異義語（Homonym）

　これは発音が同じで，意味の異なる語をいう。たとえば，air と heir「相続人」のどちらも同じ発音である。これは日本人には苦手なところであるからふだん勉強の際に十分注意しておく必要がある。これに関して，類音異義語というものを考えておく必要があろう。他のいくつか例をあげておく。

fairy－hairy, revel－rebel, alight－aright, breeze－breathe, face－faith, mouse－mouth, wizard－withered, bath－birth, carriage－courage, flash－flush, soar－sow, owner－honour, were－war, worm－warm, word－ward

語彙・語句

実施問題

【1】次の(1)～(3)の日本語を英語で書け。

(1) 小テスト　　(2) 学期　　(3) 合唱コンクール

┃ 2024年度 ┃ 香川県 ┃ 難易度 ■■■■□□

【2】次の(1)～(5)の英語で説明される語を書きなさい。ただし，始まりは【　】内に指定された文字にすること。

(1) 【d　　】: period of ten years

(2) 【w　　】: colorless transparent liquid compound of oxygen and hydrogen

(3) 【h　　】: line at which the earth and sky appear to meet

(4) 【b　　】: amount of money needed or available

(5) 【h　　】: institution providing medical and surgical treatment and nursing care for ill and injured people

┃ 2024年度 ┃ 名古屋市 ┃ 難易度 ■■■□□□

【3】次の問1～問3に答えなさい。

問1　次の(1), (2)が説明する内容として，適切なものを選びなさい。

(1) the money that is available to a person or an organization and a plan of how it will be spent over a period of time

ア　site　　イ　colleague　　ウ　budget　　エ　upbringing

(2) to think about a problem or a situation and decide how you are going to deal with it

ア　leave　　イ　address　　ウ　expunge　　エ　ignore

問2　次の(1)～(4)の空欄に当てはまるものを選びなさい。

(1) Some of the [　　] English used in fourteenth-century texts would not be understandable to native English speakers today.

ア　sinister　　イ　muddy　　ウ　archaic　　エ　scenic

(2) A recent environmental concern is the [　　] decrease in the world's wild bee population. This huge loss could seriously affect plants' ability

15

to reproduce.

ア nosy　イ impaired　ウ secretive　エ drastic

(3) A: Do you think the economy will recover next year, Professor Martin?

B: Well, I'm a little worried. Fewer people are buying houses, and that usually [　] a worse economy in the future.

ア acts out　イ points to　ウ heads off　エ misses out

(4) A: Is everything ready for the restaurant's grand opening tomorrow?

B: I think so. There will [　] be some problems on the first day, but hopefully nothing major will go wrong.

ア inevitably　イ remarkably　ウ charitably

エ densely

問3　空欄に当てはまるものを選びなさい。

A: Did you hear? Grace isn't able to attend tomorrow's party.

B: Oh, no! I can't imagine a party without Grace! That's like a....

A: A day without sunshine?

B: [　]. She always makes parties exciting and enjoyable.

ア That's how she used to be.

イ That's what I was going to say.

ウ That's quite far from the truth.

エ That's not exactly what I meant.

| 2024年度 | 北海道・札幌市 | 難易度 ■■■■□ |

【4】Substitute the underlined phrase with the best alternative from the four choices.

(1) These absurd rules should have been done away with years ago.

A. looked up to　B. put up with　C. gotten rid of

D. dropped in on

(2) He had to account for his absence from the meeting.

A. explain　B. undergo　C. demand　D. inquire

(3) She thoroughly went over the house before deciding whether to buy it.

A. stopped　B. purchased　C. revealed　D. examined

(4)　Was it an accident or did Scott do it <u>on purpose</u>?

　　A．occasionally　　B．eventually　　C．immediately

　　D．intentionally

(5)　The writer decided to <u>leave out</u> those two lines in her book.

　　A．cease　　B．omit　　C．advocate　　D．revolt

┃ 2024年度 ┃ 京都府 ┃ 難易度 ▪▪▪▫▫

【5】Read each sentence and look at the underlined parts. Choose the word which is the closest in meaning to it.

1．The Non-Profit Organization <u>divides and distributes</u> food and clothing to refugees.

　①　assembles　　②　integrates　　③　discloses　　④　dispenses

2．According to a news article, the city held a fancy <u>opening</u> ceremony for a new hall.

　①　baptism　　②　coronation　　③　demolition

　④　inauguration

3．Economic experts worry if intersecting crises, such as natural disasters and increasing volatility in the cost of the necessities, happen <u>at the same time</u>, it could lead to catastrophic consequences.

　①　simultaneously　　②　consequently　　③　periodically

　④　spontaneously

4．The audience was disappointed because they thought there would be more <u>essential</u> discussion between the presidential candidates.

　①　irrelevant　　②　subliminal　　③　substantive　　④　statutory

5．So as not to be heard by the patient, the doctors spoke in <u>muted</u> voices.

　①　muffled　　②　tightened　　③　concealed　　④　dimmed

┃ 2024年度 ┃ 沖縄県 ┃ 難易度 ▪▪▫▫▫

【6】次の(1)，(2)の用語について，英語教育において用いられる際の意味を，それぞれ日本語で説明せよ。

(1)　communication strategy　　(2)　global error

┃ 2024年度 ┃ 山梨県 ┃ 難易度 ▪▪▪▫▫

17

【7】 Directions: There are blanks in the following definitions of technical terms in language teaching. Beneath each definition you will see four words or phrases, marked a to d.

Choose one word or phrase for 　ア　 ~ 　オ　 that best completes the definition. Then, mark your answer on your answer sheet.

(1) 　ア　 is the total number of words a person understands, either in reading or listening.

    a　Sight vocabulary   b　Receptive vocabulary

    c　Productive vocabulary   d　Academic vocabulary

(2) 　イ　 is, in testing, the positive or negative impact of a test on classroom teaching or learning. In some countries, for example, national language examinations have a major impact on teaching and teachers often "teach to the tests". In order to bring about changes in teaching, changes may have to be made in the tests.

    a　Washback   b　Transfer   c　Feedback   d　Reflection

(3) 　ウ　 is a method that integrates language instruction with subject matter instruction in the target language, for example, studying science, social studies or mathematics through the medium of English.

    a　Audiolingual method   b　Content-based instruction

    c　Task-based language teaching   d　Usage-based learning

(4) 　エ　 is, in conversation, what speakers do in order to achieve successful communication. For example, to make successful conversation, it may be necessary for speakers to indicate that they understand or do not understand, or that they want the conversation to continue.

    a　Output   b　Dictation   c　Recast   d　Negotiation

(5) 　オ　 is a process common in both first- and second-language learning, in which a learner extends the use of a grammatical rule of a linguistic item beyond its accepted uses, generally by making words or structures follow a more regular pattern.

    a　Fossilization   b　Cross-linguistic influence

    c　Overgeneralization   d　Interlanguage

▌2024年度 ▌ 高知県 ▌ 難易度 ▌■■■□□

18

【8】次の(1)～(3)で説明されている語として最も適切なものを以下のA
～Dから一つずつ選び，その記号を書け。

(1) used to say what normally happens in a particular situation, especially
because something different is happening this time

A apparently   B comfortably   C ordinarily   D purposely

(2) the fact that there is nothing or nobody in a place

A eloquence   B emptiness   C equator   D erosion

(3) to take something from a person, shop, etc. without permission and
without intending to return it or pay for it

A detach   B catch   C separate   D steal

▌2024年度 ▌愛媛県 ▌難易度 ▭▭▭▭▭

【9】英語教育に関する次の(1)，(2)の用語について，日本語で説明せよ。

(1) communication strategy

(2) global error

▌2024年度 ▌山梨県 ▌難易度 ▭▭▭▭▭

【10】Choose the most semantically appropriate word or phrase from among 1 to
4 in order to complete each sentence.

〔1〕 (   ) is a language that is used for communication between different
groups of people, each speaking a different language. It could be an
internationally used language of communication (e.g. English), it could be
the native language of one of the groups, or it could be a language which is
not spoken natively by any of the groups.

1 Filler   2 Lingua franca   3 Dialect   4 Babbling

〔2〕 (   ) is a close and harmonious relationship in which the people or
groups concerned understand each other's feelings or ideas and
communicate well.

1 Rapport   2 Attitude   3 Empathy   4 Interaction

〔3〕 (   ) is the way in which words are used together regularly. It refers to
the restrictions on how words can be used together, for example which
prepositions are used with particular verbs, or which verbs and nouns are

19

used together.

1　Plural　　　2　Syllable　　　3　Collocation　　　4　Minimal pair

┃ **2024年度** ┃ **東京都** ┃ **難易度** ┃▪▪▪▪▪▪┃

解答・解説

【 1 】(1)　quiz　　　(2)　term　　　(3)　chorus contest

○**解説**○　(1)　testは学期末などのある程度の節目の試験だが，いわゆる小テストはquizとなる。　(2)　学期はtermで表し，例えば「1学期」はthe first termとなる。　(3)「合唱」はchorusであるが，「コンクール」はフランス語由来の外来語であることに注意。英語ではcontest(もしくはcompetition)となる。

【 2 】(1)　decade　　　(2)　water　　　(3)　horizon　　　(4)　budget
(5)　hospital

○**解説**○　(1)　空欄の後に続く内容は「10年間」であり，decadeが正解。
(2)　空欄の後に続く内容は「酸素と水素の無色透明の液体化合物」であり，「水」を意味するwaterが正解。　(3)　空欄の後に続く内容は「地球と空が交わっているように見える線」であり，「地平線(水平線)」を意味するhorizonが正解。　(4)　空欄の後に続く内容は「必要または利用可能なお金」であり，「予算」を意味するbudgetが正解。
(5)　空欄の後に続く内容は「病気やけがをした人に医療的または外科的な処置や，看護のケアを提供する施設」であり，「病院」を意味するhospitalが正解。

【 3 】問1　(1)　ウ　　　(2)　イ　　　問2　(1)　ウ　　　(2)　エ　　　(3)　イ
(4)　ア　　　問3　イ

○**解説**○　問1　(1)「人や組織が使用可能なお金であり，それを一定期間内にどのように使用するかの計画」であり，「予算」を意味するウが正解。　(2)「問題や状況について考え，どのように処理するか決め

ること」であるから，「(問題などを)扱う，処理する」を意味するイが正解。なお，ウのexpungeは「抹殺する，削除する」の意味。

問2　(1)　空欄を含んだ英文は「14世紀に使用されていた(　　)な英語は，現在の英語の母語話者にも理解されないだろう」の意であり，「古風な」を意味するウが正解。　(2)　空欄を含んだ英文は「最近の環境問題で懸念されていることは世界の野生の蜂の(　　)な減少である」の意であり，「急激な」を意味するエが正解。　(3)　空欄を含んだ英文は「家を買う人が少なくなっていて，それは将来的な景気悪化を(　　)する」の意であり，「指し示す」を意味するイが正解。

(4)　空欄を含んだ英文は「初日は，いくつか問題は(　　)に起こるだろうが，大きな問題が起こらないことを願っている」の意であり，「必然的に，必ず」を意味するアが正解。　問3　AとBの1回目の発話から，BはGraceが明日のパーティに来られないことに驚いていることがわかる。Aの2回目の発話は，Bの「That's like a...」を受けたものであり，「日のささない1日だ」という意味である。これを受けたBは，空欄の直後に，Graceがいつもパーティを楽しいものにしてくれる存在であることを述べて同意している。従って，「まさにそれを言おうとしたんだ」を意味するイが正解。

【4】(1)　C　　(2)　A　　(3)　D　　(4)　D　　(5)　B

○**解説**○　(1)　do away with～「～を廃止する」に近いのはget rid of～「～を取り除く」となる。　(2)　account for～「～を釈明する」に近いのはexplain「説明する」となる。　(3)　go over～「～を詳細に調べる」に近いのはexamine「検査する」となる。　(4)　on purpose「わざと，故意に」に近いのはintentionallyとなる。　(5)　leave out～「～を省く」に近いのはomit「除外する」となる。

【5】1　④　　2　④　　3　①　　4　③　　5　①

○**解説**○　1　「NPOは難民に食料や衣類を分けて配っている」。dispense「分配する」。　2　「ニュース記事によると，市は新しいホールのオープニングセレモニーを派手に行った」。inauguration「落成式，除幕式」。　3　「自然災害や必需品の物価変動などの危機が交錯して同時に起これ

ば，破滅的な結末を招きかねないと経済専門家は懸念している」。simultaneously「一斉に，同時に」。　4　「聴衆は大統領候補の間でもっと本質的な議論がなされると思っていたのでがっかりした」。substantive「本質的な」。　5　「患者に聞こえないよう医師たちは声をひそめて話した」。muffled「音を消した，こもった」。

【6】(1)　学習者が自分の意思を相手に伝達できない場合に，不足している伝達能力を補うために意識的に用いる方略。　(2)　発話者の意図を伝えることが極めて困難になる，または全く不可能になってしまう全体的な誤りのこと。

○**解説**○　(1)　コミュニケーション・ストラテジー「伝達方略」。コミュニケーションにおいて，言語能力不足を補い意思疎通を図るための方法。具体的な手段として，パラフレーズ，身振り，母語の使用等がある。　(2)　global error(グローバルエラー)はコミュニケーションに支障をきたすレベルの誤用であるのに対し，local error(ローカルエラー)はコミュニケーションに支障をきたすほどではない誤用。なお，第2言語学習者の誤用には，エラーとミステイクがあり，ミステイクは学習者の不注意等による誤用，エラーは学習者が何度も繰り返して間違える誤用である。エラーには，他に，母語の干渉によって生じるinterlingual error(言語間エラー)や，学習の発達途上に起こるintralingual error(言語内エラー)がある。それぞれ定義と具体例を整理しておきたい。

【7】(1)　b　　(2)　a　　(3)　b　　(4)　d　　(5)　c
○**解説**○　(1)　文章を読み，話を聞く時に理解できる語彙。「受容語彙」。反対は，Productive vocabulary で，文章を書いたり，言葉を話したりする際に用いる「発信語彙」。　(2)　テストを行う授業で，そのテストに対する意識から授業時の教え方や学習に及ぼす何らかの影響のこと。良い面と悪い面がある。「波及(効果)」。　(3)　言語学習とその言語を使って科学，社会科学，数学などの科目学習を統合させて実施する教授法。「内容重視型教授法」。　(4)　会話時にお互いに同意し合えるように話し合う行為。その過程ではお互いが理解しているかいない

か，話し合いを継続するかしないかを伝え合うことが相互に必要となる。「交渉」。　(5)　第一言語，第二言語を学習する際に共通に見られ，文法ルールを必要以上に拡張的に適用すること。「過剰般化」。不規則的であっても一般的に定着した表現を文法ルールに当てはめることにより，かえって不自然な表現にしてしまったりする。

【8】(1)　C　　(2)　B　　(3)　D

○**解説**○ (1)　説明は「特に今回は別のことが起こっているため，特定の状況で通常起こることを言うために用いられる」の意味なので，Cのordinarily「通常は，いつもなら」が適切。　(2)　説明は「ある場所に物や人が全くない，いないという事実」なので，Bのemptiness「からっぽ，空虚」が適切。　(3)　説明は「許可なしに，返したりお金を払ったりする意図なく人や店などからものを取ること」なので，Dのsteal「盗む」が適切。

【9】(1)　学習者が，自分の意思を相手に伝達できない場合に，不足している伝達能力を補うために意識的かつ意図的に用いる方略。

(2)　発話者の意図が極めて困難になるか，または全く不可能になってしまう誤りのこと。

○**解説**○ (1)　コミュニケーション・ストラテジー「伝達方略」。コミュニケーションにおいて，言語能力不足を補い意思疎通を図るための方法。具体的な手段として，パラフレーズ，身振り，母語の使用等がある。　(2)　global error(グローバルエラー)はコミュニケーションに支障をきたすレベルの誤用であるのに対し，local error(ローカルエラー)はコミュニケーションに支障をきたすほどではない誤用。なお，第2言語学習者の誤用には，エラーとミステイクがあり，ミステイクは学習者の不注意等による誤用，エラーは学習者が何度も繰り返して間違える誤用である。エラーには，他に，母語の干渉によって生じるinterlingual error(言語間エラー)や，学習の発達途上に起こるintralingual error(言語内エラー)がある。それぞれ定義と具体例を整理しておきたい。

【10】〔1〕 2 〔2〕 1 〔3〕 3

○**解説**○ 〔1〕異なる母語話者間でのコミュニケーションに用いられ，英語など国際的にコミュケーションツールとして使われている言語とあるので，解答はリンガ・フランカ(共通語)。リンガ・フランカを知識として知っていれば1文目を読んだだけで解答可能だが，知らなくとも消去法で対応可能。Filler繋ぎ言葉，Dialect方言，Babbling喃語。

〔2〕「親密で調和の取れた関係」なので1のラポール。フランス語由来で，心から相手を理解し，相互に信頼している関係を表す。やや難度が高い。Attitude態度，Empathy共感，Interaction交流。

〔3〕「単語と単語のつながり」を指し，例として前置詞と動詞の組み合わせなどが挙げられているので，正答はコロケーション。Plural複数形，Syllable音節，Minimal pair最小対語。

実施問題

【1】次の(1)～(5)の英文の(　　　)に入る適切な語(句)をア～エからそれぞれ1つずつ選び，記号で答えなさい。

(1) The professor does not draw a (　　) between men and women.
　ア　desperation　　イ　distinction　　ウ　density　　エ　dissent

(2) The country's economy is in (　　) recession.
　ア　chronological　　イ　immortal　　ウ　indignant
　エ　chronic

(3) Eastern Europe (　　) historic transformations.
　ア　underwent　　イ　undertook　　ウ　overdosed
　エ　overlooked

(4) Our company has the (　　) of accessing confidential files.
　ア　assortment　　イ　proportion　　ウ　assumption
　エ　privilege

(5) My father is afraid he's (　　) the flu.
　ア　making up to　　イ　getting away with　　ウ　coming down with
　エ　catching on to

■ 2024年度 ■ 名古屋市 ■ 難易度

【2】Answer the following questions. Choose the best answer from the choices provided to complete the sentences. Answer using the characters from A to D.

(1) (In the classroom)
　A : I have a quiz. What is the animal (　　) the fastest?
　B : Well, is it a cheetah?
　A : Yes. You're right.
　　A．run　　B　which ran　　C．which run　　D．which runs

(2) (At home)
　A : Look! (　　) a new watch.
　B : That's nice. Where did you buy it?
　　A．I've got　　B．I get　　C．I'm getting　　D．I'm going to get

● 語彙・文法

(3) (On the school trip)

A : (　　) a big temple!

B : It's 46 meters high. It's more than 1000 years old.

　　A.　How　　B.　What　　C.　How old　　D.　What's

2024年度 ▎ **長野県** ▎ **難易度** ■■□□

【3】次の各英文の(　　)内に入れるべき最も適当な語(句)を1〜4から一つ選び，番号で答えよ。

(1) (　　) that we miss the last train, what should we do?

　　1　Suppose　　2　Supposed　　3　Supposing to　　4　To suppose

(2) John apologized (　　).

　　1　her for his rudeness　　2　her his rudeness

　　3　his rudeness to her　　4　to her for his rudeness

(3) (　　), the simplest explanation is the best.

　　1　Being equal to other things　　2　Being other things equal

　　3　Other things being equal　　4　Other things equal being

(4) If our luck holds, we will reach London in (　　) two hours or so.

　　1　another　　2　far　　3　more　　4　still

(5) Have you considered (　　) out of the city?

　　1　for moving　　2　moving　　3　to move　　4　to moving

2024年度 ▎ **愛知県** ▎ **難易度** ■■□□

【4】次のAとBの問いに答えなさい。

A　次の(1)〜(4)の[　　]に入る最も適当なものを以下のア〜エの中から1つずつ選び，その記号を書きなさい。

(1) When you see [　　] in a dictionary, it means you should compare the word to another.

　　ア　i.e.　　イ　etc.　　ウ　e.g.　　エ　cf.

(2) Before applying for a promotion, employees [　　] to notify their Assistant Manager.

　　ア　had required　　イ　must require　　ウ　are required

　　エ　will be requiring

26

(3)　X: Excuse me. Do you mind if I sit here?

　　Y: [　　] The seat is vacant.

　ア　Oh, you do?　　イ　No, go ahead.　　ウ　Yes, here we are.

　エ　Yes, I do mind.

(4)　X: It suddenly started raining heavily on my way home, and I got completely wet.

　　Y: You should have [　　] and taken an umbrella with you.

　ア　heeded my advice　　　　　　イ　molded my plan

　ウ　contemplated your direction　　エ　reasoned about your problem

B　次の(1)〜(3)において，ア〜オの語句を並べかえて意味が通るように文を完成させるとき，それぞれ[　①　]と[　②　]に入る語句の記号を書きなさい。

(1)　It is this question [　　][　①　][　　][　②　][　　] solve.

　ア　I　　イ　you　　ウ　want　　エ　that　　オ　to

(2)　We have to keep trying, no [　　][　①　][　　][　②　][　　].

　ア　tired　　イ　matter　　ウ　we　　エ　are　　オ　how

(3)　This year's wheat crop is estimated to be [　　][　①　][　　][　②　][　　] a normal year.

　ア　of　　イ　than　　ウ　20 percent　　エ　less　　オ　that

┃ 2024年度 ┃ 福島県 ┃ 難易度 ┃■■■■□□┃

【5】Choose the most appropriate answer for each blank.

(1)　Jack silently [　　] the room.

　①　entered　　②　entered in　　③　entered into　　④　entered to

(2)　When I told Meg the news, she seemed [　　].

　①　surprising　　②　to surprise　　③　to have surprised

　④　surprised

(3)　Some young Japanese people do not feel that chopsticks are easy [　　].

　①　to pick up food　　②　to pick up food with

　③　to pick up with it　　④　to pick up food with it

(4)　The veterinarian treated the hawk's injury to the point [　　] it could get food.

① where   ② which   ③ of   ④ as

(5) I can never see this photo without [   ] my happy days in the countryside.

① reminding   ② reminding of   ③ being reminding

④ being reminded of

┃ **2024年度** ┃ 千葉県・千葉市 ┃ 難易度 ▰▰▰▱▱

【6】次の(1)~(5)の英文の(   )に入る適切な語(句)をア~エからそれぞれ1つずつ選び、記号で答えなさい。

(1) Michael appears (   ) no sense of humor.

　ア　by having　　イ　it has　　ウ　like having　　エ　to have

(2) Some neighbors watched the children (   ) the tree.

　ア　climbing　　イ　to climb　　ウ　to be climbed　　エ　climbed

(3) (   ) had I begun to eat dinner than the telephone rang.

　ア　No longer　　イ　No sooner　　ウ　As soon　　エ　No better

(4) What (   ) our mother say if she were still alive?

　ア　shall　　イ　does　　ウ　will　　エ　would

(5) This is the painting (   ) I referred in my letter.

　ア　to which　　イ　that　　ウ　with that　　エ　in which

┃ **2024年度** ┃ 名古屋市 ┃ 難易度 ▰▰▰▱▱

【7】次の各英文について、(   )に当てはまる最も適当な語句を、以下の選択肢からそれぞれ1つ選び記号で答えなさい。

(1) This is the aquarium (   ) my grandmother visited fifty years ago.

　ア　where　　イ　which　　ウ　at which　　エ　to which

(2) Daigo (   ) it a rule to get up early in the morning.

　ア　gives　　イ　does　　ウ　performs　　エ　makes

(3) If you had taken your father's advice at that time, you (   ) more successful now.

　ア　are　　イ　would be　　ウ　will have been

　エ　would have been

┃ **2024年度** ┃ 宮崎県 ┃ 難易度 ▰▰▰▱▱

28

【8】 Choose the most appropriate word or phrase from among 1 to 4 in order to complete each sentence.

〔1〕 His voice was shaking (　　) all his efforts to control it.

1　in spite　　2　although　　3　despite　　4　regardless

〔2〕 A：Shall I give you a check?

　　B：I'd rather (　　).

1　you paid cash　　2　you will not　　3　not to pay by check

4　being paid cash

2024年度 ┃ 東京都 ┃ 難易度 ▰▰▱▱▱

【9】 (1)〜(5)は，教師(T)と外国語指導助手(ALT)との会話である。空欄に当てはまる最も適切な語を，次のア〜エから，それぞれ1つ選んで記号を書きなさい。

(1)　ALT : My parents are scheduled to arrive at Takasaki station tomorrow evening at 6:30 p.m.

　　　T : Okay. Please (　　) me if there are any changes. I don't want to keep them waiting.

　ア　spoil　　イ　vary　　ウ　notify　　エ　immigrate

(2)　ALT : She is my favorite artist.

　　　T : Really? I like her, too. Her paintings always tend to (　　) a positive message.

　ア　omit　　イ　mimic　　ウ　predict　　エ　convey

(3)　T : I heard you work as a volunteer after school every day. What do you do?

　　ALT : I read English picture books to children at some nursery schools.

　　　T : You are a highly (　　) teacher.

　ア　bearable　　イ　dedicated　　ウ　incapable　　エ　reluctant

(4)　ALT : Your English is so good!

　　　T : Thank you, but I think I need to (　　) my grammar, for instance.

　ア　refine　　イ　reject　　ウ　recruit　　エ　replicate

(5)　ALT : She gave a speech about the importance of working as a team at

29

the speech contest.

T : I was there, too. It was excellent. Her speech was very (　　).

ア　incoherent　　イ　eloquent　　ウ　perspective　　エ　unstable

▌2024年度 ▌ 群馬県 ▌ 難易度 ▌

【10】Complete the following sentences with the most appropriate word/phrase for the blank.

(1)　Creating a daily habit is the easiest thing to do. On the other hand, it is extremely difficult to (　　) bad habits.

ア　get rid of　　イ　keep up with　　ウ　make up for

エ　take advantage of

(2)　Student-oriented classes will (　　) students' interest in class and develop critical thinking abilities.

ア　assert　　イ　derive　　ウ　oppose　　エ　stimulate

(3)　An *irori*, a sunken fireplace, had served the (　　) functions of heating and lighting until the power supply system became widespread in Japan.

ア　decayed　　イ　dense　　ウ　dismal　　エ　dual

(4)　(　　) bias is a cognitive bias that causes someone to believe that they themselves are less likely to experience a negative event.

ア　Criticism　　イ　Optimism　　ウ　Pessimism　　エ　Realism

(5)　There is a risk of technology being (　　) in a way that rewards young people in richer countries and leaves others in low-income countries lagging behind when it comes to getting the skills needed for the new economies.

ア　confounded　　イ　deployed　　ウ　excavated　　エ　fabricated

▌2024年度 ▌ 宮崎県 ▌ 難易度 ▌

【11】In the following English sentences (1) to (3), choose the most appropriate word in parentheses from ① to ⑤ below.

(1)　The growing of corn and other vegetables (　　) Mesoamericans to settle down in permanent communities.

①　gave　　②　had　　③　enabled　　④　served

⑤　supposed

(2) I found (　) difficult to tell what he thought just then.
① this　② that　③ what　④ it　⑤ which

(3) I am (　) to chicken pox because I had it when I was young.
① immune　② keen　③ senior　④ disobedience
⑤ peripheral

2024年度 | 岐阜県 | 難易度

【12】 Choose the best answer from the four choices (A), (B), (C) and (D) beneath each question. Write the appropriate letter on your answer sheet.

1 Laura bought a stylish table at a new furniture shop last week. After she purchased it, she found that it was very sturdy and could (　) weights of 200 kg.
(A) catch　(B) jump　(C) lift　(D) stand

2 (　) you don't have a membership for the program, you are still able to use the trial version for twenty days.
(A) As if　(B) Even though　(C) As soon as
(D) In order that

3 Ellie was about to get her cellphone from the couch, when she noticed that her baby was sleeping nearby. So she walked near her baby softly (　) waking him.
(A) for fear of　(B) for the purpose of　(C) in charge of
(D) in spite of

4 My husband often goes with me when I go food shopping, but hates going with me when I go clothes shopping, because I always spend too much time (　) my clothes.
(A) breaking up　(B) keeping up　(C) picking out
(D) taking out

5 Tomorrow's sunshine is expected to be quite (　). Please refrain from exercising outdoors to prevent heatstroke.
(A) comfortable　(B) delicate　(C) intense　(D) strict

6 When the big sports competition was held in this area last month, it was impossible to find a hotel with a (　). Most of the hotels filled up

31

quickly.

(A) comment (B) redundancy (C) segment

(D) vacancy

7 Ben wrote an essay on science last weekend and had it evaluated by a professor. The professor said that, apart from a few (　) errors, his essay was perfect.

(A) ambitious (B) criminal (C) numerous (D) trivial

8 The boy broke a vase with a ball. He tried to blame the dog for the broken vase. His mother did not (　) the lie because she had seen the whole thing.

(A) fall for (B) figure out (C) hang on (D) see off

9 A : Hello, Linda. I've got plenty of meat for the barbecue party!

B : Thank you, Mike! But we need more vegetables. Will you get some on the way tomorrow?

A : Sure! But you know I have a bad memory, so (　)

B : OK, thanks for your help! I'll give you a call in the morning.

(A) can you grow vegetables for me?

(B) will you remind me tomorrow just in case?

(C) can you get them for me instead?

(D) will you mind my getting vegetables?

10 A: Hi, Jeffry. I heard you walk to work. Is something wrong with your car?

B : No, I recently started a diet because I've just been putting on a bit of weight.

A : Good for you. And (　)

B : Definitely! So now I'm planning to buy new walking shoes with the money I'm saving.

(A) walking will save you a lot of time.

(B) repairing your car can cost you a lot of money.

(C) I bet walking is easier on your wallet too.

(D) I guess driving to work is safer than walking.

2024年度 ┃ 栃木県 ┃ 難易度

【13】 次の(1)〜(6)の英文の(　　)に入る最も適当な語句を，ア〜エからそれぞれ一つ選び，記号で記せ。

(1) Scientists have discovered that our sense of smell is surprisingly (　　), capable of distinguishing thousands of chemical odors.

　ア　rigid　　イ　erratic　　ウ　insolent　　エ　keen

(2) There are still several issues to talk about, so I want everyone to regroup in the conference room after lunch so that we can (　　) the meeting.

　ア　shrink　　イ　postpone　　ウ　resume　　エ　terminate

(3) Jim sometimes loses his temper with his children and speaks (　　) to them. He regrets it when his children begin to cry.

　ア　harshly　　イ　skeptically　　ウ　hesitantly　　エ　gloomily

(4) It is a beautiful vase, but it is not (　　) the price that I paid for it.

　ア　deserve　　イ　valuable　　ウ　reasonable　　エ　worth

(5) (　　) the prisoner's motivation may be understood, his actions certainly cannot be condoned.

　ア　Despite　　イ　Only if　　ウ　Even though　　エ　At least

(6) Our aircraft was caught in some heavy (　　), so we were required to remain in our seats with our seatbelts on.

　ア　promotion　　イ　turbulence　　ウ　interchange
　エ　commotion

▌ 2024年度 ▌ 山梨県 ▌ 難易度 ▌

【14】 次の各文の(　　)に入る最も適切なものを以下のア〜エの中からそれぞれ一つ選び，記号で答えよ。

1　He can speak English well, because he is (　　) online learning to talk with foreigners.

　ア　making fun of　　イ　running short of　　ウ　coming out of
　エ　taking advantage of

2　I tried to solve this question, but I couldn't. It was (　　) me.

　ア　beside　　イ　before　　ウ　beyond　　エ　behind

3　It is important for teachers to guide students in a long-term (　　) for their future.

ア perspective　　イ habitat　　ウ opponent　　エ experiment

4 （　　） the lottery then, I could travel around the world now.

　ア If I won　　イ Had I won　　ウ I had won

　エ Should I win

5 （　　） is the method of teaching English as a foreign language to non-native English speakers.

　ア CEFR　　イ TESL　　ウ CLIL　　エ TEFL

▎2024年度 ▎鹿児島県 ▎難易度 ▇▇▇▇▇▇

【15】次の(1)〜(10)の英文の(　　)に入る最も適切な単語または語句を(ア)〜(エ)からそれぞれ一つずつ選び，記号で答えなさい。

(1) John thinks that it is more important to form the (　　) of children's future learning than to provide them with specialized knowledge at elementary school.

　(ア) classification　　(イ) foundation　　(ウ) delegation

　(エ) transportation

(2) The number of students is decreasing in this school. The (　　) to this problem should be sought not only by the teachers but also by everyone involved in this town.

　(ア) illusion　　(イ) objection　　(ウ) relation　　(エ) solution

(3) Children learn adult behavior by (　　) their parents. For instance, my daughter watches me feed her baby sister, then she feeds her dolls in the same way.

　(ア) mimicking　　(イ) inciting　　(ウ) fabricating

　(エ) producing

(4) Firefighters come to the nursery school in a fire engine and (　　) a fire drill three times a year.

　(ア) conduct　　(イ) represent　　(ウ) imitate

　(エ) summarize

(5) Naomi (　　) about her grades so much she cannot sleep well at night. She feels she must get perfect scores and is upset if she ever receives less than 100 percent.

（ア）　imparts　　（イ）　transmits　　（ウ）　obsesses

（エ）　reminisces

(6)　Tom was very good at (　　) children. He sang songs well and taught us fun games, and he always told us interesting stories before going to sleep.

（ア）　donating　　（イ）　entertaining　　（ウ）　interpreting

（エ）　upsetting

(7)　The cafe is not a good place to go if you're on a diet because the desserts are (　　).

（ア）　relevant　　（イ）　complaisant　　（ウ）　irresistible

（エ）　superficial

(8)　Sara was admitted to three universities, but she is (　　) about which one to choose because she really likes all three of them.

（ア）　illicit　　（イ）　irreverent　　（ウ）　indiscriminate

（エ）　indecisive

(9)　Tomoki is a very popular instructor at the dancing school because his instructions are always clear and (　　).

（ア）　to the point　　（イ）　along the way　　（ウ）　in use

（エ）　on the average

(10)　Phillip just (　　) the full report because he did not have time to read it before the meeting.

（ア）　handed down　　（イ）　flipped through　　（ウ）　poured over

（エ）　indulged in

| 2024年度 | 鳥取県 | 難易度

【16】次の(1)〜(6)の英文の(　　)に入る英語として最も適切なものを，それぞれ1〜4から1つずつ選べ。

(1)　It was (　　) of him to offer to pay for us both.

　1　skeptical　　2　generous　　3　frantic　　4　gross

(2)　The film paints a depressing picture of life in (　　) Britain.

　1　insane　　2　contemporary　　3　transparent　　4　fluorescent

(3)　The government has raised the (　　) of increasing taxes next year.

　1　burglar　　2　orbit　　3　faith　　4　prospect

(4) The company has recently acquired a new (　　).

　1　subsection　　2　suburb　　3　subsidiary　　4　subcontinent

(5) Our school prohibits us (　　) bills on the wall.

　1　to post　　2　posting　　3　from posting　　4　by posting

(6) I (　　) know what he is going to say.

　1　am curious to　　2　am curious about　　3　am curious as to

　4　am curious at

▌ 2024年度 ▌ 奈良県 ▌ 難易度 ▌■■■■□□□

【17】次の(1)〜(3)の英文や対話の(　　)に当てはまる語として最も適切なものを以下のA〜Dから一つずつ選び，その記号を書け。

(1) Erika has always wanted to settle (　　) in Paris since she traveled to France in her childhood.

　A　permanently　　B　tactfully　　C　ruthlessly

　D　uneconomically

(2) Tom has been a man of artistic (　　) and his paintings have been admired by a lot of people.

　A　opponent　　B　precaution　　C　captivity　　D　temperament

(3) [in the airplane]

Passenger　　　　　：Hi, it's too cold in here.

Flight attendant　：Would you like a blanket? I'll have it brought to you.

Passenger　　　　　：Umm, sure. But (　　) it two. I'll need one for me and one for my friend.

　A　get　　B　make　　C　take　　D　have

▌ 2024年度 ▌ 愛媛県 ▌ 難易度 ▌■■■■■□□

【18】Choose the most grammatically appropriate word or phrase from among 1 to 4 in order to complete each sentence.

〔1〕It wasn't long after arriving on the show floor last week (　　) I began to feel — how to put this delicately? — bored out of my mind.

　1　that　　2　which　　3　where　　4　what

〔2〕Chileans are used to dry years periodically; 2010 was one such year. But in 2011, and then in 2012 and 2013, there was still (　　) rainfall. "Then came 2014," which was also dry, "and that was suspicious," says René Garreaud.

1　few　　2　little　　3　several　　4　a number of

〔3〕　This curry is too spicy for me to (　　).

1　ate　　2　eaten　　3　eat　　4　eating

┃ 2024年度 ┃ 東京都 ┃ 難易度 ┃■■■■□□

【19】 次の(1)〜(7)の(　　)に入る適切な語句をア〜エの中から一つずつ選び，記号で答えよ。

(1)　A : How about driving somewhere for a change?

B : Sorry, I'm not (　　) for it.

ア　feeling　　イ　mood　　ウ　condition　　エ　up

(2)　A : It's on me.

B : No. You treat me whenever we eat out.

A: Well, OK. Then, let's (　　) the check.

ア　draw　　イ　split　　ウ　have　　エ　pay

(3)　A : It's not my title that (　　). That's for sure!

B : I definitely think your title is very important. With it, everyone will recognize you.

ア　does　　イ　counts　　ウ　sells　　エ　appears

(4)　A : What's the matter, Bob? You look so miserable.

B : Leave (　　). It's none of your business.

ア　it behind　　イ　it at that　　ウ　me alone　　エ　me cold

(5)　A : The government launched a campaign to (　　) physical exercise among children.

B : That's a great initiative. Encouraging kids to be active and healthy is so important for their development.

ア　promote　　イ　manipulate　　ウ　moderate　　エ　suppress

(6)　A: He got ahead (　　) his colleagues. He should be ashamed of himself.

B : Yeah, it's really disappointing when someone advances their career

37

by undermining others.

ア　at the expense of　　イ　for the sake of　　ウ　on behalf of

エ　at the mercy of

(7)　A: I felt utterly out of place among those (　　) people.

B : Don't worry about it. Everyone feels that way sometimes. Just be yourself and people will appreciate your authenticity.

ア　stubborn　　イ　pessimistic　　ウ　sophisticated

エ　outdated

┃ 2024年度 ┃ 島根県 ┃ 難易度 ▰▰▰▱▱

【20】 Choose the most appropriate word(s) for each sentence and mark ①, ②, ③, ④ or ⑤ on the answer sheet.

(1)　A : Did you hear anything about the examination?

B : No. The teacher has not yet informed me (　　) that.

A : I see. I will go to the teachers' room and ask about it.

B : Thank you.

①　for　　②　of　　③　to　　④　in　　⑤　by

(2)　A : There's only a month left until the upcoming school festival.

B : Speaking of which, I made a sample brochure for the festival. What do you (　　) of it?

A : I really liked it! You did a great job.

B : I'll print the final version based on the sample.

①　speak　　②　feel　　③　call　　④　know　　⑤　think

(3)　A : It is nice to see you after such a long time. How have you been?

B : I've been fine. Sorry for visiting you suddenly.

A : No, thank yon for coming all the way here. Please have a seat.

B : Thank you, but I would (　　). I won't be staying long.

①　rather stand　　②　rather standing　　③　rather not stand

④　rather sit　　⑤　like standing

(4)　A : I think we have already bought everything on our shopping list.

B : Wait! We are making pizza tonight, right? Should we buy some cheese?

A : I don't think so. My mother has bought (   ).

B : Okay. Then let's go home.

① plenty ② applicable ③ compatible ④ disastrous

⑤ dreamy

(5) A : I went to Hawaii last month.

B : Really? That (   ) have been nice.

A : It had been a long time since I had traveled abroad, so I enjoyed it. Here is some Hawaiian coffee for you.

B : This is my favorite one. Thank you.

① Can ② should ③ might ④ must ⑤ may

(6) A : What happened to your face?

B : My face is swollen because I have just had a tooth (   ) out.

A : Did you have a wisdom tooth?

B : Yes, I don't want to go through this again.

① passed ② carried ③ pulled ④ handed

⑤ backed

‖ 2024年度 ‖ 神戸市 ‖ 難易度 ‖■■■□□‖

【21】次の(1)～(3)の英文の(   )に当てはまる語(句)として最も適切なものを以下のA～Dから一つずつ選び，その記号を書け。

(1) I don't know the extent to (   ) it will be applied.

A what B that C which D those

(2) If he had followed my advice, he (   ) in it.

A succeed B succeeded C would have succeeded

D has succeeded

(3) Ken's presentation on environmental issues was excellent. He must have read (   ) books on the issues.

A not a little B not a few C only a little D only a few

‖ 2024年度 ‖ 愛媛県 ‖ 難易度 ‖■■■□□‖

● 語彙・文法

【22】To complete each item, choose the best word or phrase from among the four choices.

1 Betty's job involved mostly (   ) work such as making copies and entering data.
　ア　parental　　イ　clerical　　ウ　nutritional　　エ　radical

2 The mayor presented the man with a Good Citizen Award as a (   ) to his efforts to help the homeless in his area.
　ア　testament　　イ　foundation　　ウ　bureau　　エ　deficiency

3 Mr. Grieg went to a school that (   ) good manners and self-discipline.
　ア　harvested　　イ　cultivated　　ウ　blossomed　　エ　planted

4 A major accident caused serious (   ) on the highway, as two lanes of traffic were closed for over two hours.
　ア　testimony　　イ　visibility　　ウ　congestion　　エ　drainage

5 Many students complained the book was too difficult to understand in places, so the teacher tried to (   ) those sections using simpler language.
　ア　paraphrase　　イ　contradict　　ウ　obstruct　　エ　scorn

6 A fire broke out on Bloor Street last night. It took firefighters almost eight hours, but they eventually managed to get the (   ) under control.
　ア　clamp　　イ　drizzle　　ウ　comet　　エ　blaze

7 Richard is extremely busy with his job, but he always makes sure to (   ) time for his children in the evening.
　ア　roll up　　イ　stay off　　ウ　miss out　　エ　set aside

8 Glen realized his long years of service to the company did not (   ) anything when he was suddenly fired as part of a cost-cutting measure.
　ア　count for　　イ　go back on　　ウ　sell out　　エ　do away with

2024年度 | 岩手県 | 難易度 ■■■□□

【23】次の(1)～(4)の各組において，a)とb)がほぼ同じ意味になるように，b)の(　　)内にあてはまる最も適切な一語をそれぞれ書け。

(1) a) He is responsible for this project.
　　b) He is (　　) charge (　　) this project.

(2) a) I have never seen such a beautiful sunset.

40

　b)　This is the (　　) beautiful sunset I have (　　) seen.

(3)　a)　I'm sorry that I can't go with you.

　　b)　I (　　) I (　　) go with you.

(4)　a)　While he was staying in Japan, he studied electronics.

　　b)　(　　) his (　　) in Japan, he studied electronics.

▌2024年度 ▌香川県 ▌難易度 ▰▰▱▱▱

【24】次の問1〜問4の英文の[　　]の中に入る最も適切なものを，以下のそれぞれ①〜④のうちから選びなさい。

問1　White Factory deliveries have been [　　] two months owing to lack of semiconductors.

　　①　broken down　　②　gone through　　③　held back

　　④　taken on

問2　After Sue enjoyed visiting the Zen temple in Kyoto, she started to [　　] time for meditation every day.

　　①　roll up　　②　miss out　　③　set aside　　④　stay off

問3　I'd like to hire more staff in order to work only four days a week. But that's just a [　　] in the sky at the moment.

　　①　thought　　②　pie　　③　cloud　　④　drawing

問4　[　　] his wishes, the inheritance was split evenly between the three children.

　　①　In accordance with　　②　In front of　　③　In order that

　　④　In the event that

▌2024年度 ▌神奈川県・横浜市・川崎市・相模原市 ▌難易度 ▰▰▰▱▱

【25】Choose the answer that best completes the sentence from the four choices.

(1)　Our teacher's enthusiasm is (　　). In other words, you just can't help feeling inspired when you are with her.

　　A．confining　　B．concise　　C．contagious　　D．compliant

(2)　The case was (　　) candies, and Bob took some. He hoped that his mother would not notice that there were fewer candies.

　　A．pleased with　　B．full of　　C．absent from　　D．based on

41

(3) Mary remained ( ) despite failing her driving test for the first time. She said she would definitely pass on her second attempt.

    A. allied   B. misty   C. parallel   D. resolute

(4) The politician's comments were so ( ) that reporters didn't understand what he was actually going to do.

    A. ambiguous   B. credulous   C. analogous   D. infectious

(5) My mother opened the mail, which ( ) that morning.

    A. delivered   B. is delivered   C. had delivered

    D. had been delivered

(6) Susan ( ) moving to a new house in the countryside, but in the end, she decided to keep living in the same house.

    A. released   B. solved   C. considered   D. promoted

(7) ( ) at the company all day long, she was completely worn out.

    A. Worked   B. Not working   C. Being working

    D. Having worked

(8) Melissa studied so hard ( ) well on the test.

    A. that she had not done   B. that she should not have done

    C. that she must have done   D. that she had to be done

(9) Sarah wanted to keep swimming in the river. However, ( ) it was getting dark, her father told her that it was time to go home.

    A. as   B. unless   C. though   D. until

(10) When he was invited to the party, he was ( ) himself with pleasure.

    A. at   B. beside   C. for   D. over

(11) This morning, train services throughout the area were ( ) for several hours due to heavy rain overnight. Thousands of people were affected.

    A. descended   B. deployed   C. discerned   D. disrupted

(12) I have a lot of friends, many of whom ( ).

    A. I was at school together   B. I was at school with

    C. I was at school with them   D. I was together at school

(13) Although Makoto had spent a few years in Australia when he was a teenager, he still had to ( ) his English skills before applying for the

job.

   A．shake up   B．sign off   C．brush up   D．knock off

(14) Computer supplies are very expensive in Japan. Just this keyboard ( ) me 20,000 yen.

   A．charged   B．cost   C．owed   D．paid

(15) Although Monica tried to ( ) a book on the top shelf, she was not tall enough to get it. She asked her brother to do it.

   A．come out   B．turn off   C．reach for   D．result in

(16) My sister and I ( ) often play tennis in the park when we were young.

   A．can   B．may   C．should   D．would

(17) The fans were ( ) into silence because their national soccer team lost the important game.

   A．stunned   B．dulled   C．hassled   D．penalized

(18) Without your ( ) advice, I would have failed in my attempt to climb the mountain.

   A．valueless   B．invaluable   C．invalid   D．vain

(19) ( ) since she went over to France to study French.

   A．It was three years   B．Three years are passed

   C．Three years passed   D．Three years have passed

(20) Mary has been reading a book about Germany for two months. She is now on the ( ) chapter of the book and has a few pages left.

   A．final   B．common   C．foreign   D．national

| 2024年度 | 京都府 | 難易度 |

解答・解説

【1】(1) イ　　(2) エ　　(3) ア　　(4) エ　　(5) ウ

○**解説**○ (1)　空欄を補充した英文は「その教授は男性と女性を区別しない」の意である。draw a distinctionで「区別する」の意味である。
(2)　空欄を補充した英文は「その国の経済は長期にわたり不況である」の意である。　(3)　空欄を補充した英文は「東ヨーロッパは歴史的変容を経験した」の意である。　(4)　空欄を補充した英文は「当社には機密ファイルにアクセスできる特権がある」の意である。　(5)　空欄を補充した英文は「私の父はインフルエンザにかかることを恐れている」の意である。come down withで「(病気に)かかる」の意味である。

【2】(1) D　　(2) A　　(3) B

○**解説**○ (1)　空欄を含んだ文の直前にある発話に着目すると，空欄を含んだ文は「最も早く走る動物は何か」を尋ねるクイズを出していることがわかる。空欄後にある情報が空欄前にあるthe animalを修飾しており，the animalは単数である。　(2)　Bの2つ目の発話「どこでそれを買ったの？」に着目すると，空欄を含んだ文は「新しい時計を手に入れたよ」という意になることがわかる。完了形の時制が適切である。
(3)　Bの1つ目の発話「高さは46メートルあります」に着目すると，空欄を含んだ文は「なんて大きなお寺だろう」の意になることがわかる。名詞が続く感嘆文はWhat (＋冠詞)＋形容詞＋名詞＋主語＋動詞の形になるが，今回は最後の主語＋動詞が省略されている。

【3】(1) 1　　(2) 4　　(3) 3　　(4) 1　　(5) 2

○**解説**○ (1)　Suppose (Supposing) that〜でIf〜と同じ意味になる。
(2)　apologizeは謝る相手を示す前置詞としてto，そして謝る内容を示す前置詞としてforを用いる。　(3)　Other things being equalは「他の条件が同じなら」の意であり，いわゆる独立分詞構文である。(4)　空欄部は「さらに2時間くらいで」の意である。似たような意味になるmoreはtwo more hoursの形でないと使えない。(5)　considerの目的語は

動名詞のみであり，to不定詞を取ることができないことに注意したい。

【4】A (1)　エ　　(2)　ウ　　(3)　イ　　(4)　ア　　B (1)　①　ア　②　イ　(2)　①　オ　②　ウ　(3)　①　エ　②　オ

○**解説**○ A　(1)　英文は「辞書でcf.を見たら，その単語を別の単語と比較すべきだの意味である」の意である。cf.は「参照しなさい」を意味するラテン語の略語である。　(2)　英文は「昇進を申請する前に，従業員はアシスタント・マネージャーに報告することが求められている」の意である。be required to～は「～することが求められている」の意味である。　(3)　英文は「X：すみません。ここに座ってもいいですか」，「Y：どうぞ。その席は空いていますから」の意である。Do you mind～に対しては許可を出す場合はNo(私は気にしない)」で答える必要がある。　(4)　英文は「X：家に帰る途中で急に激しく雨が降り出して，びしょぬれになってしまった」，「Y：私のアドバイスを聞いて傘を持っていけばよかったのに」の意である。heedは「(助言などを)聞き入れる」の意味である。　B　(1)　完成した英文はIt is this question that I want you to solve.である。空欄前にあるIt is this questionと，選択肢にあるthatから強調構文であることに気づけるとよい。

(2)　完成した英文はWe have to keep trying, no matter how tired we are.である。no matter how＋形容詞で「どんなに～でも」の意になる。空欄前にあるnoと選択肢にあるmatterと疑問詞に着目するとよい。

(3)　完成した英文はThis year's wheat crop is estimated to be 20 percent less than that of a normal year.である。that of＋名詞は，前述の名詞句を指すときに使用する表現である。また，選択肢にあるlessとthanに着目するとよい。

【5】(1)　①　　(2)　④　　(3)　②　　(4)　①　　(5)　④

○**解説**○ (1)　enterは他動詞であるため前置詞は不要である。

(2)　surpriseは「驚かす」という他動詞であるため，主語が「驚いた」という意味になるのは受動態の形になる④である。　(3)　元の形はIt is easy to pick up food with chopsticksであることを踏まえればよい。難易を表す形容詞の後に不定詞が続いて「～するには…である」という

意味を表す，いわゆる「tough構文」である。 (4) 空欄の直前にあるto the pointに着目する。to the point where～で「～の程度まで」という意味である。 (5) remindは「思い出させる」という他動詞であるため，主語が「思い出す」という意味になるのは受動態の形になる④である。

【6】(1) エ　　(2)　ア　　(3)　イ　　(4)　エ　　(5)　ア

○**解説**○ (1) 空欄を補充した英文は「マイケルはユーモアのセンスがないように見える」の意である。appearは，主語＋appear to doの形で「主語が～するように見える，思われる」の意味になる。 (2) 空欄を補充した英文は「その子どもたちが木に登っているのを見た近所の人もいた」の意である。知覚動詞を用いた第5文型の形になっており，この時の動詞は原形，現在分詞または過去分詞のいずれかである。「子どもたち」と「木」の関係から，現在分詞が正解となる。なお，原形の場合は動作が全て終わるまで知覚している一方，現在分詞の場合は，動作の一部分のみを知覚しているというニュアンスがある。
(3) 空欄を補充した英文は「私が夕食を食べ始めたらすぐに電話が鳴った」の意である。No sooner～than…で「～するやいなや…」の意になる。 (4) 空欄を補充した英文は「私の母がまだ生きていたとしたら，何と言っただろう」の意である。if節から仮定法の文であることがわかる。 (5) 空欄を補充した英文は「これは私が手紙の中で言及した絵である」の意である。「言及する」はrefer toであり，このtoが関係代名詞の前に移動した形になっている。

【7】(1)　イ　　(2)　エ　　(3)　イ

○**解説**○ (1) 関係詞の問題。This is the aquarium.とMy grandmother visited it fifty years ago.の2文を関係詞でつなげた形を考える。visitは他動詞で目的語を取る動詞であることに注意。 (2) イディオムmake it a rule to (do)「(信念として)～することにしている，～するように努めている」の意。itは形式目的語で後続のto不定詞を指す。 (3) 仮定法過去完了の基本形は，If S had過去分詞～, S' would have過去分詞….で，「もし(過去に)～したら，(過去に)…しただろうに」と過去の事実

に反する事柄や仮定を表す。問題文は，主節にnowがあり現在の事実に反することを述べているため，If S had 過去分詞〜, S' would 動詞原形….「もし(過去に)〜したら，(現在は)…だろう」という，if節が仮定法過去完了，主節が仮定法過去の混合型となる。

【8】〔1〕 3　　〔2〕 1
○**解説**○ 〔1〕「〜にも関わらず」という意味になる前置詞は3のみ。名詞であるeffortにつなげる必要があるため，接続詞ではなく前置詞が正しい。なお，"in spite of"と同じ意味であるが，今回は括弧の後にofがないため，文法的に1は不適切。　〔2〕「小切手をお渡ししましょうか(小切手でお支払いしましょうか)」というAのセリフに対し適切な返答は，1の「現金の方が良いのですが」のみ。would rather＋仮定法過去で「むしろ〜していただきたいのですが」という丁寧な依頼となる。

【9】(1)　ウ　　(2)　エ　　(3)　イ　　(4)　ア　　(5)　イ
○**解説**○ (1)「何か変更があれば，私に知らせてください」。notify「知らせる」。　(2)「彼女の絵画はいつもポジティブなメッセージを伝える」。convey「伝える」。　(3)「あなたはとても熱心な先生だ」。dedicated「ひたむきな，献身的な」。　(4)「でも私は，例えば文法に磨きをかける必要があると思う」。refine「洗練する」。　(5)「彼女のスピーチはとても説得力があった」。eloquent「雄弁な，人を動かす力のある」。

【10】(1)　ア　　(2)　エ　　(3)　エ　　(4)　イ　　(5)　イ
○**解説**○ (1)「悪習を取り除くことは非常に難しい」の意。get rid of「取り除く」，keep up with「遅れずについていく」，make up for「補う，埋め合わせをする」，take advantage of「利用する，活用する」。
(2)「生徒主導型の授業では生徒の授業への好奇心が刺激され，クリティカル・シンキング(批判的思考)が育成される」の意。assert「断言する，主張する」，derive「由来する，得る」，oppose「反対する」，stimulate「刺激する」。　(3)「日本で給電システムが広がるまでは囲炉裏が熱源と光源の二重機能を果たしていた」の意。decay「腐った，

破損した」, dense「密集した」, dismal「陰気な，荒涼とした」, dual「二重の」。　(4)「楽観性バイアスとは，自分が否定的な出来事を経験する可能性が低いと信じるようになる認知バイアスである」の意。criticism「批判」, optimism「楽観主義」, pessimism「悲観主義」, realism「現実主義」。　(5)「新経済で必須のスキルを習得するという点からすれば，より豊かな国の若者には報酬に結び付くが，低所得国の方では立ち遅れたままになるというテクノロジーの導入リスクがある」の意。confound「混乱させる，困惑させる」, deploy「配備する，展開する，効果的に使われる」, excavate「掘り返す」, fabricate「製造する，捏造する」。

【11】(1)　③　　(2)　④　　(3)　①

○**解説**○　(1)　enableの用法は S enable O to doで「SはOが〜するのを可能にする，SのおかげでOは〜できるようになる」の意。　(2)　find it C to doで第5文型を取り「〜することはCである」の意。このitは形式目的語と呼ばれ，to以下を指している。　(3)　chicken poxは「水疱瘡」で問題文より「若いころにかかったことがあるので」とある。ここから空所は「免疫がある」という意味の語が来ることがわかり，immuneが入る。

【12】1　(D)　　2　(B)　　3　(A)　　4　(C)　　5　(C)　　6　(D)
　　　7　(D)　　8　(A)　　9　(B)　　10　(C)

○**解説**○　1　空所の前にsturdy「頑丈な」とあるので200kgにも「耐えられる」のstandが適切。　2　カンマの後でyou are still able to use〜「なお〜を使うことができる」とあるので逆接のEven thoughが適切。
3　空所直前のShe walked near her baby softly「赤ちゃんの近くを静かに歩いた」とあるので「起こさないように」といった意味が空所に入る。よってfor fear of〜「〜することを心配して」が適切。　4　買い物に時間がかかりすぎるという文であるためpicking out「選ぶ」が適切。
5　空所の次の文が熱中症を避けるために外での運動を避けるように，という意味なので空所はintense「強烈な」が適切。　6　空所の次の文で「ほとんどのホテルがすぐに埋まってしまった」とある。空所を含

む文は「～のあるホテルを見つけるのは不可能だ」の意味なので空所はvacancy「空室」が適切。　7　空所の後でhis essay was perfect「彼のエッセイは完璧だった」とあるので空所はtrivial「些末な」が適切。apart from～は「～は別として」の意味。　8　because以下で「彼女の母親はすべてを見ていた」とあるのでfall for～「～にだまされる」が適切。　9　空所の前でAが「記憶力が悪い」と，空所の後でBが「朝に電話する」と言っていることから(B)の「念のため明日忘れないよう連絡してくれますか」が適切。　10　空所の前でダイエットのために歩いて通勤していること，空所の後でためたお金で新しいウォーキングシューズを買うという会話をしていることから，(C)の「歩くことは間違いなくお財布に優しいですしね」が適切。

【13】(1)　エ　　(2)　ウ　　(3)　ア　　(4)　エ　　(5)　ウ　　(6)　イ
○解説○　(1)「私たちの嗅覚は驚くほど鋭く，何千種類もの化学物質の匂いを嗅ぎ分けることができる」。keen「(感覚などが)鋭い」。
(2)「まだいくつかの議題が残っているので，会議を再開できるよう昼食後，みなに会議室に集まってもらいたい」。resume「再び始める」。
(3)「ジムは時々，子供たちに腹を立ててきつい言葉をかけることがある。子供が泣き出すと，彼はそれを後悔する」。harshly「厳しく」。
(4)「きれいな花瓶だが，私が支払った値段の価値はない」。be worth～「～に値する」。　(5)「受刑者の動機は理解できるが，彼の行動を容認することはできない」。even though～「～だけれども」。　(6)「私たちの飛行機は激しい乱気流に巻き込まれたため，シートベルトをしたまま座席に留まるよう求められた」。turbulence「乱気流，大荒れ」。

【14】1　エ　　2　ウ　　3　ア　　4　イ　　5　エ
○解説○　1「外国人と話すためにオンライン学習を活用しているので，彼は上手に英語を話すことができる」。take advantage of～「～をうまく利用する」。　2「私はこの問題を解こうとしたが，できなかった。それは私の理解を超えていた」。beyond me「理解不能で」。　3「教師は生徒の将来を長期的な視点で指導することが重要だ」。perspective「見通し」。　4「あのとき宝くじが当たっていたら，今頃は世界中を

旅していただろうに」。仮定法のIfの省略。後ろのSVに倒置が起こる。If節は仮定法過去完了，主節は仮定法過去。　5　「TEFLとは英語を母国語としない人々に外国語として英語を教える方法である」。

ア　CEFR(Common European Framework of Reference for Languages)は「外国語の学習・教授・評価のためのヨーロッパ言語共通参照枠」のこと。外国語の運用能力を同一基準で評価する国際標準である。

イ　TESL(Teaching English as a Second Language)は、「第2言語としての英語教授法」で、英語圏の国で留学生や移民など英語を母語としない人々に英語を教えること。　ウ　CLIL(Content and Language Integrated Learning)は「内容言語統合型学習」のことで、言語と教科内容を同時に教えることを目的とした指導法のこと。

【15】(1)（イ）　(2)（エ）　(3)（ア）　(4)（ア）　(5)（ウ）　(6)（イ）　(7)（ウ）　(8)（エ）　(9)（ア）　(10)（イ）

○解説○ (1)「ジョンは、小学校で専門的な知識を教えるよりも子供たちの将来の学習の基礎を形成することの方が重要だと考えている」。foundation「基礎」。　(2)「この学校では生徒数が減少している。この問題の解決は、教師だけでなく、この町に関わるすべての人に模索されるべきである」。solution「解決」。　(3)「子どもは親の真似をして大人の行動を学ぶ」。mimic「真似る」。現在分詞はmimickingとなる。(4)「消防士が消防車で保育園に来て、年に3回消防訓練をする」。conduct「実施する」。　(5)「ナオミは成績にこだわって、夜もよく眠れない」。obsess about～「～を心配する」。　(6)「トムは子供たちを楽しませるのがとても上手だった」。entertain「楽しませる」。　(7)「そのカフェはデザートがたまらなく美味しいので、ダイエット中の人は行かない方がいい」。irresistible「抑えられない」。　(8)「サラは3つの大学に合格したが、3つともとても気に入っているからどの大学にするか迷っている」。indecisive「優柔不断の、決定的でない」。　(9)「トモキはダンススクールの人気インストラクターである、というのも彼の指示はいつも明確で、的を得ているからだ」。to the point「的確で」。(10)「フィリップは会議の前に報告書を読む時間がなかったので、パラパラと目を通しただけだった」。flip through「ざっと読む」。

【16】 (1) 2 (2) 2 (3) 4 (4) 3 (5) 3 (6) 1

○**解説**○ (1) It is … of (人) to (do) の構文。「私達2人のために支払うことを申し出てくれるとは彼は気前が良かった」の意で2を選択。skeptical「懐疑的な」, generous「気前が良い」, frantic「取り乱した, 死に物狂いの」, gross「気持ち悪い, 非常に不快な」。 (2) 「その映画は, 現代イギリスの憂鬱な暮らしを描いている」の意で2を選択。paint a picture「描写する」, insane「正気でない」, contemporary「現代の」, transparent「透明な, 見え透いた」, fluorescent「蛍光の, 鮮やかな」。 (3) 「政府は, 翌年には増税の公算を強めた」の意で4を選択。raise the prospect of～「～の公算を強める」, burglar「強盗」, orbit「軌道, 活動範囲」, faith「信念, 信仰」, prospect「見通し」。 (4) 「その会社は最近になって新たに子会社を買収した」の意で3を選択。acquire「買収する」, subsection「下位区分」, suburb「郊外」, subsidiary「子会社」, subcontinent「亜大陸」。 (5) 「私たちの学校では壁面にポスターを張ることが禁止されている」の意で3を選択。prohibit (人) from～ing「(人)が～するのを禁止する」, post a bill「ポスターを張る」。 (6) 「彼が何を言おうとしているのかぜひ知りたい」の意で1を選択。be curious to know「知りたい」。2と4は, knowという動詞の原形があるので, その直前に前置詞は置けない。3は, as to＋(主に疑問詞)で「～に関して」となる。

【17】 (1) A (2) D (3) B

○**解説**○ (1) A permanently「ずっと, 永遠に」, B tactfully「巧みに」, C ruthlessly「冷酷に」, D uneconomically「不経済に」から文意に合うのはAとなる。 (2) Dのtemperamentは「気質, 気性」でartistic temperament で「芸術的気質」となる。 (3) make it twoで「2つ持ってきてください, 私も同じものをください」といった意味になる。

【18】 〔1〕 1 〔2〕 2 〔3〕 3

○**解説**○ 〔1〕 It wasn't long after～の基本形は, it is～that…(…なのは～である)の強調構文。「私が退屈し始めたのは, 会場に到着したあと長く経たないときだった」→「会場に到着してまもなく, 私は退屈しは

じめた」の意味となる。　〔2〕2　rainfall降雨量は不可算名詞なので
littleをつけて降雨量が少ないという意味にする。fewは可算名詞に用い
る。　〔3〕too形容詞to不定詞で「～すぎて…できない」という意味
になる。toの後は動詞の原型にする必要がある。

【19】(1)　エ　　　(2)　イ　　　(3)　イ　　　(4)　ウ　　　(5)　ア　　　(6)　ア
(7)　ウ

○**解説**○ (1)　I'm up for itは，誘いに対して「喜んで，ぜひ」という返答
である。　(2)　It's on me, treatは，いずれも「おごる」という意味で
ある。Aがおごろうとしたところ，Bがいつもおごってもらっていると
反論したので，「割り勘にしよう」という文脈である。　(3)　that
countsで「重要だ」という意味。それ以外は意味不明。　(4)　「どうか
したのか」と尋ねるAに対して，Bが「君には関係ない」と冷たくあし
らっている。答えは「放っておいてくれ，一人にしてくれ」。
(5)　BのEncouraging kidsから子供に運動を勧める文脈だとわかる。
promote「促進する」，manipulate「操作する」，moderate「やわらげる」，
suppress「抑圧する」。　(6)　Bの台詞から，誰かが他者を踏み台にし
て出世したことがわかる。よってat the expense of「～を犠牲にして」
が適切。　(7)　Aは，このような人たちに囲まれているのは場違いだ
と言っているので，空欄にはプラスの言葉が入る。ウ以外では人をけ
なすことになる。

【20】(1)　②　　　(2)　⑤　　　(3)　①　　　(4)　①　　　(5)　④　　　(6)　③
○**解説**○ (1)　inform＋O(人)＋of～「～について(人)に知らせる」。
(2)　What do you think of it?「それについてどう思いますか」。日常会
話での定型表現である。Bの冒頭の発言Speaking of which,～は，「そう
いえば，ちなみに」の意で，Speaking of～「～と言えば」＋関係代名
詞which(前述の内容を受ける)の組合せ表現。「そのことについて言え
ば～」の意。　(3)　would rather＋動詞の原形「むしろ～したい」。文
脈を考えて，「長く留まっていられない」ということなのでsitは適さ
ない。　(4)　「私の母がたくさんチーズを買ってあるから今は買う必要
がない」という文脈から，副詞plenty「かなり，たくさん」を選択。

plenty of cheeseのof cheeseを省略したと考えてもよい。 (5) Aさんが「先月，ハワイに行った」という過去の事実から，その出来事に対して確信をもって推量する表現としてmust have＋過去分詞「～だったに違いない」を選択。この表現を使うときは，必ず根拠となる過去の出来事が何なのかを確認すること。 (6) have＋O＋C(過去分詞) 「Oを～してもらう」。SVOCの文型なので，OとCは「主語・述語の関係」を反映させるようにCに来る動詞の形を考える。ここでは「OがCするのを経験する」のではなく「OがCされるのを経験する」というイメージを持てれば，「歯が1本抜かれるのを経験した」→「ちょうど抜歯したばかりなんだ」と意味が取れる。pull out「引き抜く」。

【21】(1) C (2) C (3) B
○**解説**○ (1) to the extentで「その程度まで」の意で，関係代名詞whichを組み合わせてthe extent to whichとすることで「それはどの程度適用されるか私はわからない」という文意になる。 (2) If節が仮定法過去完了であることから適切なのはCのみとなる。 (3) 1文目「彼の環境問題に関するプレゼンテーションは非常によかった」より「多くの本を読んだに違いない」というのが空所を含む文の意味になる。これに当てはまるのはBのnot a fewとなる。bookは可算名詞のためAは不適切。

【22】1 イ 2 ア 3 イ 4 ウ 5 ア 6 エ 7 エ
8 ア
○**解説**○ 1 「ベティの仕事はコピーやデータ入力などの事務的な仕事がほとんどであった」。clericalは「事務的な」の意味である。 2 「市長は，その地区のホームレスの支援に尽力してきた証として，その男性を善良な市民賞で表彰した」。testamentは「証」の意味である。3 「グリーグは作法と自制心を養う学校に通っている」。cultivateは「養う，育てる」の意味である。 4 「その大事故によって，2車線が2時間以上も封鎖となり，その高速道路に深刻な渋滞が引き起こされた」。congestionは「渋滞」の意味である。 5 「多くの生徒が，その本はところどころ難しすぎて理解できないところがあると苦情を言

ったので，教師はより易しい言葉を使って該当箇所を言い換えるようにした」。paraphraseは「言い換える」の意味である。　6　「ブロア通りで昨晩火事が起き，約8時間かかったが，最終的に，消防隊はなんとか鎮火することができた」。blazeは「炎」の意味である。　7　「リチャードは仕事で非常に忙しいが，夕方に子どもたちとの時間を確保するようにしている」。set asideは「確保する，取っておく」の意味である。　8　「グレンは，コストカットの一環として突然解雇された時，会社に対する自分の長年の貢献が何にもならなかったと気がついた」。count forは「価値がある，ものを言う」。

【23】(1)　in, of　　(2)　most, ever　　(3)　wish, could　　(4)　During, stay

○**解説**○　(1)　be responsible for～は「～に責任がある，～の担当である」の意でin charge of～がほぼ同様の意味になる。　(2)　「私が～した中で最も…なものである」という意味にするために，最初の空所には最上級のmost，次の空所にはeverを用いる。　(3)　「あなたと一緒に行けなくて残念だ」という現実を示すa)の文に対し，仮定法を用いるのがb)の文になる。「～であればよいのに」と願望を表すwishを最初の空所に，仮定法過去のcouldを次の空所に入れる。　(4)　While～「～する間」の副詞節はDuring～で言い換えられる。次の空所は名詞のstay「滞在」を入れれば直前のhisとうまくつながる。

【24】問1　③　　問2　③　　問3　②　　問4　①

○**解説**○　問1　「White Factoryの出荷は半導体不足のために2か月遅れている」。hold back「引き留める」。　問2　「…彼女は毎日瞑想のための時間を取り始めた」。set aside「取っておく」。　問3　pie in the sky「絵に描いた餅，実現性のないもの」。　問4　「彼の願い通り，遺産は3人の子供の間で平等に分けられた」。in accordance with～「～に従って，～の通りに」。

【25】(1)　C　　(2)　B　　(3)　D　　(4)　A　　(5)　D　　(6)　C
(7)　D　　(8)　C　　(9)　A　　(10)　B　　(11)　D　　(12)　B

(13)　C　　(14)　B　　(15)　C　　(16)　D　　(17)　A　　(18)　B

(19)　D　　(20)　A

○**解説**○　(1)　空所の後の「彼女と一緒にいると必ず触発される」より contagious「(感情・態度が)人から人へ広がりやすい」が適切。

(2)　full of〜で「〜でいっぱいの」の意味。　(3)　2文目「彼女は2回目の挑戦で絶対に合格すると言った」よりresolute「固く決意している」が適切。　(4)　空所の後の「レポーターは彼が実際に何をしようとしているのか理解できなかった」よりambiguous「あいまいな」が適切。

(5)　whichの先行詞がthe mailであることから受動態でなければならず，whichの前の節が過去形であるため現在形のBは不適切であり，「すでに届いていた」を表す過去完了のDが適切。　(6)　consider doingで「〜することを検討する」の意味。　(7)　分詞構文Having workedを用いて「1日中働いていたので」という意味を表す。　(8)　must have doneで「〜したに違いない」の意味でstudied so hardとつながる。

(9)　as it was getting dark「暗くなってきたので」とasを理由の接続詞として用いる。　(10)　beside oneself with〜で「〜に我を忘れて，夢中で」の意味。　(11)　夜の大雨で電車を用いる数千人に影響があったという文なのでdisrupt「中断する，邪魔する」の受動態を用いる。

(12)　I have a lot of friends.とI was at school with many of them.の2文を関係詞でつないだ形。　(13)　brush up〜「〜を磨き上げる，ブラッシュアップする」が適切。　(14)　cost＋A(人)＋B(金額)で「AにBの金額をかける」の意味。　(15)　reach for〜で「〜を取ろうと手を伸ばす」の意味。　(16)　would often doで「よく〜したものだ」と過去の習慣を表す。　(17)　be stunned into silenceで「驚きのあまり静まりかえる」の意味。　(18)　invaluableは「極めて貴重な」の意味。valuableの意味が強調された語である。　(19)　時間 have passed since〜で「〜から…が経った」を表す。　(20)　final chapterで「最終章」の意味。

対話文

【1】 次の各問いに答えよ。

問1　A群の発話に対する応答として最も適当なものをB群から一つず
つ選ぶとき，一つだけ余るものがある。その英文を1〜5から一つ選
び，番号を答えよ。

[A群]

(1)　Let's make a list and decide what to do next.

(2)　Did you open a business bank account yet?

(3)　Can we at least look at a few more places?

(4)　What do you think of the articles?

[B群]

1　Good idea.

2　That might be true.

3　I agree with most of them.

4　Fine, but we won't find anything better than this.

5　No, I need to register the company beforehand.

問2　次の(1)及び(2)の対話の内容について，それぞれ以下の問いに対
する答えとして最も適当なものを1〜4から一つ選び，番号で答えよ。

(1)　Man:　　What did you think of Aya's speech?

Woman: It was good overall. She remembered everything, and her
pronunciation and grammar were just about perfect.

Man:　　Yeah, but her facial expressions still didn't match her
message, so she came across as flat and unemotional.

Woman: I know. It's too bad because the experience she talked about
is so unique and influential.

(問い)　What do we learn about Aya's speech?

1　She made several grammar errors.

2　Her intonation was poor.

3　It lacked sufficient feeling.

4　The topic was not interesting.

(2) Woman: My publisher has just given me another book project.

Man: But you just said this morning you're feeling stressed out and can barely keep up with things.

Woman: Yeah, but the reason I'm getting all this work is that I'm always willing to take it on, and I'm dependable.

Man: So where do you draw the line? Are you going to take anything that comes your way until you break down?

Woman: You're right. I should start prioritizing more and learn to say no.

(問い)　What does the man imply?

1　She should turn down some projects.

2　She needs to be more professional.

3　She needs to be more reliable.

4　She complains too much.

▌2024年度 ▌ 愛知県 ▌ 難易度 ▮▭▭▭

【2】次の(1)〜(6)の会話文が成り立つように，それぞれの(　　)に入る最も適当な一語を記せ。

(1)　A : Will you come to our party tonight?

B : No, I'm (　　) not. I already have another appointment.

(2)　A : Kathy didn't come to school today. I wonder if something happened to her.

B : I'm a little worried, too. I'll get in (　　) with her at home tonight.

(3)　A : I'm sorry to be late. Let me (　　) up for it by treating you to lunch.

B : Really? That's very kind of you.

(4)　A : My husband always finds (　　) with my cooking or cleaning.

B : That's terrible! Then let him do all the housework.

(5)　A : Why don't you wear more fashionable clothes?

B : (　　) your own business! Leave me alone!

(6)　A : We have so much homework! I don't know how I'll write a 500-word essay.

B : I know! In (　　) to that, we need to prepare for a speaking test.

▌2024年度 ▌ 山梨県 ▌ 難易度 ▮▭▭▭

【3】 For each conversation, choose the answer that best fills in the blank.

1 *A:* I have no idea where we can have a farewell party for Bob.

B: You always ask me for help, Ken.

A: ( )

B: It's OK. Leave it to me. I'll find a nice restaurant.

　ア　Who else can I depend on?

　イ　Where can I find out?

　ウ　How can I take off?

　エ　When can I talk with you?

2 *A:* Have you lived here long?

B: About five years. Come in. ( )

A: Wow! You have a great view from up here.

B: Yes. It's amazing, isn't it?

　ア　I've just checked in.

　イ　I'm not allowed to have guests.

　ウ　I made a reservation for you.

　エ　I'll show you around.

3 *A:* I did some volunteer work over the summer break. It was such an invaluable experience.

B: ( )

A: Sure. Why don't we have a seat and chat?

　ア　Why did you do that? That's expensive.

　イ　I see. What's next?

　ウ　That's great! Tell me more, about it!

　エ　I'm sorry to hear that. You should have done something else.

4 *A:* When is the assignment due?

B: Next Monday. ( )

A: Yes, I am really overworked now.

B: OK. How about Wednesday? I look forward to receiving it.

　ア　Can you get it in on time?

　イ　Have you already turned it in?

　ウ　Do you need an extension?

　　エ　Have you already finished?

5　*A:*　Emily, do you want to go to the new movie theater this weekend?

　　B:　Sorry, but I can't. I have to work all weekend to get ready for a big presentation on Monday.

　　　　It's really important.

　　A:　That's too bad. Do you have time for dinner Sunday evening?

　　B:　(　　) Sorry.

　　ア　I'll finish working as soon as possible.

　　イ　I may not be working late on Sunday.

　　ウ　I'll be there.

　　エ　I may not be finished by then.

┃ 2024年度 ┃ 岩手県 ┃ 難易度 ┃

【4】次の1〜4の各場面について，AとBの会話の(　　)に入る最も適当なものを選びなさい。

1　A: Masa, I have some feedback on your speech practice.

　B: I'm grateful for any advice, Ms. Smith.

　A: Well, you obviously made a big effort, and the story was interesting, but you should think about pacing. You seemed to rush.

　B: I see. It was my first public speaking, so I think I got pretty tense.

　A: True, but the more you go over the speech beforehand, (　　).

　B: OK, I'll do that.

　A: Considering your knowledge of the subject, you can make it better, Masa.

　B: Thank yon, Ms. Smith.

　ア　the more you'll get stage fright in public

　イ　if it helps, you can practice on me

　ウ　you've taken quite a few lessons before

　エ　the easier it'll be to deliver it at a reasonable pace

2　A: The weather forecast says it will be warm and sunny by next week, Amy.

　B: That sounds good.

A: Where are you planning to take our exchange student this weekend?

B: We're visiting the new ballpark on Saturday. And she wants to go to the shopping mall on Sunday. Can you come with us?

A: OK. I can come along tomorrow, but on Sunday, you're on your own.

B: I know you're not into shopping, but I was hoping you could drive us.

A: All right. But I need to finish a report, so I'll just bring my laptop and work in a nearby coffee shop (　　).

B: Great! Thanks, Tom.

ア　while you guys go shopping
イ　while you guys go to the ballpark
ウ　until the weather improves
エ　until you get a taxi

3　A: Emma, my computer isn't working properly. It slows to a crawl.

B: Well, perhaps it's spyware?

A: What's spyware?

B: It's spy software. Spyware can get into your computer and steal information, including your ID.

A: That's OK because I never shop online.

B: Even so, (　　). You don't want someone else snooping around inside your machine.

A: Then, I'll ask Liam to help.

B: Unfortunately, he's not here today. You'll have to call someone in the Technology Department.

ア　they should get it online
イ　it's been protected by antivirus software
ウ　you should get it looked at
エ　recent online shopping is credible

4　A: Hi, Chloe. How's the job in Hokkaido going?

B: Hi, Dad. It's going well, thanks.

A: Great. By the way, I'm calling about your old books.

B: Don't tell me you sold them at the yard sale!

A: No. They're still in the garage, but I may have to throw some things away.

B: Why? I want to hang on to them.

A: Well, your mom and I will move to a smaller house in a couple of months, so what are you going to do with them before then?

B: Oh, I see. Well then, I'll just drop by your house next month, and ( ).

ア set them up and let people know

イ have them sent to my place

ウ find them at the yard sale

エ park my car in there

┃ 2024年度 ┃ 北海道・札幌市 ┃ 難易度 ▰▰▰▱▱

【5】次の会話文を読み，(1)～(4)の問いに答えなさい。

A: Jake, you've been in advertising for what—thirty-five years? How have things changed over that time?

B: Well, there have been huge changes in where and how we advertise, but many of the basic principles of marketing are the same, for example, how consumers choose brands.

A: (①)

B: Yes, let's imagine a coffee shop in a town centre somewhere, anywhere, and it sells a thousand cups of coffee a day. Now, if another coffee shop opened next door …

A: … the first owner would be furious.

B: (②) How many cups of coffee would each shop sell?

A: I don't know. Five hundred?

B: ┃ I ┃, but no. They'd sell at least a thousand cups each.

A: Incredible. Why's that?

B: Choice makes people want things more. With one coffee shop, the question is, "Shall I get a coffee or not?" but with two, the question becomes "Which coffee shall I get?"

A: Fascinating. (③)

B: Pricing is still important. People still like a bargain. But they also like to

61

treat themselves.

A: What do you mean?

B: Well, (Ⅱ) (and your / of chocolate / to sell / supposing / competitor's / wanted / you / a new brand) price was €2, what price would you set?

A: Mmm, I'd reduce the price. Maybe 1.80?

B: Why?

A: Because consumers want to save money.

B: True, to a certain extent. But experience shows that if the price is higher people think your product is better.

A: (④)

B: Indeed.

A: How about advertising a product? It's all video now, isn't it?

B: (⑤) One thing hasn't changed though, which is the way we respond to colour.

A: Oh, you mean like red means danger?

B: Yes, that kind of thing. We have built-in associations for every colour. Red is associated with energy, so it's good for energy drinks, cars, sports equipment and things like that. Green suggests safety, so it's often used for medical products. Apparently, yellow and orange stimulate the appetite, so they're used for food ads; blue on the other hand 　Ⅲ　 the appetite. It's linked more to intellect and precision, so it's used to promote high-tech products.

(1)　本文中の会話が成り立つように, (①)～(⑤)に当てはまる最も適切なものを, 次のa～eの中からそれぞれ一つ選びなさい。なお, 同じものを2回以上使用してはいけません。

　　a　So what else hasn't changed?

　　b　Well, not completely, but much more.

　　c　Don't be so sure.

　　d　Can you give me an example?

　　e　So 2.50 would be better?

(2)　文が成り立つように, 　Ⅰ　に当てはまる最も適切な語を, 次のa～eの中から一つ選びなさい。

a Skeptical　　b Ethical　　c Radical　　d Logical

e Practical

(3) 下線部(Ⅱ) において，適切な文になるように(　　)内の語や語句を並べ替えたとき，前から5番目にくる語や語句を，次のa〜eの中から一つ選びなさい。

a to sell　　b competitor's　　c a new brand　　d and your

e of chocolate

(4) 文が成り立つように，　Ⅲ　に当てはまる最も適切な語を，次のa〜eの中から一つ選びなさい。

a depresses　　b compresses　　c oppresses　　d impresses

e suppresses

2024年度 ┃ 茨城県 ┃ 難易度

【6】次の英文及び英語の対話文の(　　)に当てはまる語句や文として最も適当なものを(ア)〜(エ)からそれぞれ一つ選び，記号で答えよ。

1 Please finish lunch by noon at the very (　　). We must get on the train at 12:30.

(ア) late　　(イ) latter　　(ウ) latest　　(エ) last

2 The next Olympic Games are planned to be held in Paris. It will (　　) me. I'm looking forward to table tennis games!

(ア) disappoint　　(イ) amuse　　(ウ) blame　　(エ) accuse

3 A : It's hot.

B : Would you care for some drinks?

A : (　　)

(ア) Take it easy.

(イ) I know your favorite. You like milk tea.

(ウ) You are very fond of orange juice.

(エ) I'd like something cold.

4 A : I was invited to Kate's birthday party last night. I ate a lot.

B : Sounds fun! (　　) that tasted the best to you?

(ア) What was it　　(イ) What would be　　(ウ) What might

(エ) What could

63

5 A : How was the concert yesterday?

   B : It was (   ) due to illness of the singer.

   A : Oh, that's too bad!

   (ア) called in   (イ) called up   (ウ) called away

   (エ) called off

6 A : (   ) it snows, go home earlier than usual.

   B : OK. I'll bring my umbrella.

   (ア) As far as   (イ) What is more   (ウ) In case

   (エ) If it were not for

▌2024年度 ▌岡山市 ▌難易度 ▇▇▇▢▢

【7】Read the following passage and choose the best sentence for each of [1]〜[4] from the six choices below.

A: Hello. How are you?

B: I'm good. I heard you stayed at school to finish your assignments.

A: That's right. I had a lot of things to write yesterday, and [1].

B: OK. Can I see it?

A: Sure. Wait. Where is my file? I saved something on this computer yesterday, but [2].

B: When you turn off the school computers, all files get deleted.

A: Why?

B: The school doesn't want students to leave unwanted things on them.

A: My file was not an unwanted thing. It was my report!

B: I think [3].

A: It looks like it.

B: When is the deadline for the paper?

A: Well, [4].

   A. it's gone

   B. it's going very well

   C. I have to submit it in two weeks

   D. I saved them in a file on this computer

   E. you are out of luck

F. you don't have to write your report

┃ 2024年度 ┃ 京都府 ┃ 難易度 ▪▪▪▪▫

【8】次の(1)～(3)の対話の(　　)に当てはまる文として最も適切なものを以下のA～Dから一つずつ選び，その記号を書け。

(1)　Takuya：Hi, Ali, I want to ask a favor of you.

　　　Ali　　：Sure. What can I do for you?

　　　Takuya：Could you lend me your geography notebook? (　　)

　　　Ali　　：OK. Why don't we go to the library and copy my notebook?

　　A　Why don't you go over the lessons?

　　B　That will be a load off your shoulders.

　　C　I'm sure I can get you back on track.

　　D　I missed a couple of classes, and now I'm totally lost.

(2)　Andy　：Hello. Is this Keiko?

　　　Hina　：No, this is Hina, her sister. She's not home now. Did you call her on her smartphone?

　　　Andy　：Yes .(　　)

　　　Hina　：Oh, I found she left her smartphone on her desk. I'm sorry. Can I take your message?

　　　Andy　：Yes, please.

　　A　But I couldn't get through to her.

　　B　So did you tell her to help you?

　　C　But can I ask what with?

　　D　So that's a good idea.

(3)　Mike　：Hi, Junko. (　　)

　　　Junko　：I'm looking for accommodation for my business trip to New York next week.

　　　Mike　：I see. What websites are you using?

　　　Junko　：This one's called ABC hotel.com. I enter my dates and the area I want to stay in, and it gives me a list.

　　A　Have you found anywhere that you like?

　　B　What are you up to?

65

C Can I crash at your place?

D You were busy yesterday, weren't you?

┃ 2024年度 ┃ 愛媛県 ┃ 難易度 ▨▨▨□□

【9】次の対話文を読んで，(1)～(5)に入る適切な語(句)を以下のア～セか
らそれぞれ1つずつ選び，記号で答えなさい。

Alexander : Welcome to today's program where we are discussing famous partnerships. Bruno, who would you like to mention, first?

Bruno : Well, I love their product and I respect their values, so I would like to talk about Ben Cohen and Jerry Greenfield.

Alexander : And we know them better as?

Bruno : Ben and Jerry, the world's best ice-cream makers.

Alexander : (　1　) about their early days?

Bruno : Of course. They actually met in a gym class at the age of 12. They were friends at school, but then went on to different colleges. They met up again in the late 70s and decided to go into business together. At first, they thought of the bagel business, but the equipment for making bagels is very expensive so instead they decided on ice cream.

Alexander : If they had started a bagel business, they mightn't have been so successful.

Bruno : Possibly, but we'll never know.

Alexander : (　2　) about ice cream?

Bruno : Ben had worked as an ice-cream seller before going to college, but they both decided to take a correspondence course in ice-cream making at Penn University. It cost $5 and was a great investment.

Alexander : And were they immediately successful?

Bruno : (　3　). They chose a college town, which meant there were a lot of potential customers. There was no ice-cream shop, so there was no competition, and they made different ice creams every day depending on what was available.

66

Alexander : (　4　) about their ice cream?

Bruno 　　 : Because Ben had a rare condition which means he has very limited taste and smell, he put big chunks in the ice cream, of cookie and fruit, and so on. This made the taste unique.

Alexander : So it would have been a completely different story if he hadn't had this condition.

Bruno 　　 : (　5　).

Alexander : And are they still involved in the business?

Bruno 　　 : They sold it to Unilever in 2000, but 7.5％ of profits goes to the Ben and Jerry Foundation which donates money to good causes.

Alexander : An interesting pair.

　ア　Could you show us something
　イ　Could you tell us a little
　ウ　What did they do
　エ　What did they know
　オ　When did their business become
　カ　Did their parents teach them
　キ　Pretty much
　ク　Not really
　ケ　Yes, they did
　コ　What did people think
　サ　What was the problem
　シ　What was different
　ス　Exactly
　セ　It was difficult for him

| 2024年度 | 名古屋市 | 難易度 ■■■□□ |

【10】次の対話を読んで，その内容を表す以下のA～Dのイラストを対話中の出来事が起こった順に左から右に並べ替え，記号で書け。

Kathy ：Danny, I thought you'd come home much later. Did the party end early?

Danny ：Well, as a matter of fact the party's still going on. I left it halfway.

What happened is that I started feeling nauseous as soon as I had a
sip of the red wine, and I had to lie down a little.

Kathy ：That's too bad. I wonder what was wrong with the wine. I think you
must be tired from watching dramas all last night.

Danny ：I should have gone to sleep yesterday. Anyway, the food was good,
though. And I really enjoyed the first part of the party. I only wish I
could have stayed longer and socialized more.

| 2024年度 | 愛媛県 | 難易度 |

解答・解説

【1】問1　2　　問2　(1)　3　　(2)　1

○**解説**○　問1　A群の(1)がB群の1，A群の(2)がB群の5，A群の(3)がB群の
4，そしてA群の(4)がB群の3と対応するため，余るのはB群の2である。
問2　(1)　男性の2つ目の発話に，Ayaはflat and unemotional「平板で感
情がなかった」とある。　(2)　男性は2つ目の発話で「君は身体をこ
わすまで仕事を引き受けるつもりか」と言っている。

【2】(1)　afraid　　(2)　touch / contact　　(3)　make　　(4)　fault
(5)　Mind　　(6)　addition

○**解説**○　(1)　I'm afraid not.は，「～ではない(notである)ことを残念に思
う，残念ながら～ない」という意味。　(2)　get in touch[contact] with～
「～に連絡をとる」。　(3)　make up for～「の埋め合わせをする」。
(4)　find fault with～「～のあら探しをする」。　(5)　Mind your own

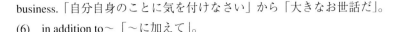

business.「自分自身のことに気を付けなさい」から「大きなお世話だ」。
(6)　in addition to〜「〜に加えて」。

【３】1　ア　　2　エ　　3　ウ　　4　ウ　　5　エ
○**解説**○　1　空欄の前後のBの発話に着目する。空欄の前では「ケン，いつも僕に助けを求めるよね」と言っており，空欄の後では「わかったよ。まかせて。素敵なレストランを探すよ」と言っている。「他のだれを頼ればいいの」を意味するアが正解。　2　空欄の前後のAとBの発話に着目する。空欄の前でBは「どうぞ入って」と言っており，空欄の後でAは「わぁ。ここからすごく良い景色が見えるね」と言っている。「案内するよ」を意味するエが正解。　3　空欄の前後のAの発話に着目する。空欄の前では「夏休みのボランティアはかけがえのない経験だったよ」と言っており，空欄の後では「いいとも。座って話をしよう」と言っている。「それはすごいね。もっと教えてよ」を意味するウが正解。　4　空欄の前後のAとBの発話に着目する。空欄の前でBは「次の月曜だよ」と言っており，空欄の後でAは「うん。いま本当にオーバーワークなんだ」と言っている。「延期が必要かな」を意味するウが正解。　5　空欄の前後のAとBの発話に着目する。空欄の前でAは「日曜に夕食を食べる時間はあるかな」と聞いており，空欄の後でBは「ごめん」と言っている。「その時までに準備が終わっていないかもしれない」を意味するエが正解

【４】1　エ　　2　ア　　3　ウ　　4　イ
○**解説**○　1　Aの2つ目の発話に着目すると，Bのスピーチは話す速度がやや早いことをアドバイスしている。さらにAの3つ目の発話の空欄前には「the more」という表現があるため，「the ＋比較級, the＋比較級」の形になると判断できる。この形に該当するのはアとエであるが，アは「もっと人前であがるようになるだろう」の意味なので，エの「ほどよいペースでスピーチできるようになるだろう」が適切。　2　Bの3つ目の発話に着目すると，Aが買い物に行く気はなくても車で送ってくれると助かると述べている。それを受けたAの4つ目の発話では，車で送ることを承諾した上で，レポートを終えないといけないので，B

たちが買い物をしている間に，ノートパソコンを持参して近くのコーヒーショップで作業をしていると述べている。 3 Bの2つ目の発話に着目すると，Aのパソコンにスパイウェアが入っている可能性があり，スパイウェアは個人情報等を盗むと述べている。それを受けた，Aの3つ目の発話では，オンラインショッピングをしないからその可能性はないと言っているが，Bの3つ目の発話にて，オンラインショッピングをしていなくても，見てもらった方がいいとアドバイスをしている。 4 Aの2つ目と4つ目の発話に着目すると，Bの父親であるAは，数か月以内に引っ越しをするので，Bの本を捨てるなどしないといけないと述べている。Bは2つ目または3つ目の発話から，それらの本を手放したくないことがわかる。これらを踏まえると，Bの4つ目の発話では，来月に家に立ち寄って，それらの本を自分の家に送るというイが正解。

【5】(1) ① d ② c ③ a ④ e ⑤ b (2) d
(3) c (4) e
○**解説**○ (1) ① 空所直後でBが「1日1,000杯を売り上げる町の中心にあるコーヒーショップを想像してみてください」と言っていることから，何か例を挙げてほしいと言っているdが適切だと判断できる。
② 空所直前でAが「(別のコーヒーショップが隣に開店したら)最初の店主は激怒するだろう」と言っているのに対し，Bは空所の後で特にこのことには触れずに別の話をしている。ここからcのDon't be so sure.「結論を急がないで，そう決めつけないで」であると判断できる。
③ 空所直後でBがPricing is still important. People still like a bargain.「値段はやはり重要で，人々はやはりお買い得品が好きだ」と返答していることから，aのSo what else hasn't changed?「では何か他に変化しないことはありますか」という質問が適切だと判断できる。 ④ 空所直前のBのBut experience shows that if the price is higher people think your product is better.「もし値段がより高ければ，人はその製品がより良いと考えるということを経験は示しています」と，空所直後のIndeed.「その通りです」から，具体的な費用を示しているeが適切。2.50の単位が省略されているが，空所の少し前の会話から €だと読み取れる。
⑤ 空所直前でHow about advertising a product? It's all video now, isn't it?

「製品の宣伝はどうですか。今は映像による宣伝がすべてですよね」に対して残った選択肢bを検討すると、「いや、全部ではないですが、以前よりははるかに多いですね」とつながることが判断できる。

(2) 空所の前で「1日1,000杯を売り上げる町の中心にあるコーヒーショップの隣に別のコーヒーショップが開店したらそれぞれの店の売れ行きはどうなるか」という話をBがしている。Aが半分の500杯かと答えており、2つの店が客を取り合うと予想したこの答えは妥当でありdのLogical「論理的ですね」が適切。その後でBはAの答えは誤りであることも述べている。　(3)　正しい語順はsupposing you wanted to sell a new brand of chocolate and your competitor'sである。冒頭のsupposing「もし〜ならば」とprice was €2の直前にand your competitor'sを置くことがポイントとなる。　(4)　空所前文の yellow and orange stimulate the appetiteと、空所直前のon the other hand「一方で」より、stimulate「刺激する」の反対の意味を持つ語が空所に入ることがわかり、eのsupresses「抑圧する」が適切。

【6】1　(ウ)　　2　(イ)　　3　(エ)　　4　(ア)　　5　(エ)　　6　(ウ)
〇解説〇 1 「どんなに遅くとも正午までには昼食を済ませてください」。2 amuse〜「(人)を楽しませる」。　3 Would you care for some drinks? 「飲み物はいかがですか」に対して応答する文を選ぶ。　4 〈What is it＋that節〉「〜なのは何ですか」。「あなたにとって一番おいしかったのは何ですか」。　5 call off〜「〜を中止する」。　6 in case〜「〜の場合には」。

【7】1　D　　2　A　　3　E　　4　C
〇解説〇 1 空所の後でコンピュータに保存したファイルの話をしているためDが適切と判断できる。　2 I saved something on this computer yesterday, butの後に来るのはAのit's gone.「なくなってしまいました」が適切となる。　3 意図せずファイルが削除されてしまったAに対してBがかける言葉としてE「運が悪かったね」が適切となる。　4 レポートの期限をBから聞かれており、Aの返答としてCが適切となる。

● 語彙・文法

【8】(1)　D　　(2)　A　　(3)　B
〇**解説**〇 (1)　Aliの2回目の発話より，Takuyaの頼みを快諾して図書館で
ノートのコピーを取らせてくれることが読み取れる。その前に来る空
所の内容はノートを貸してほしい理由を述べたD「2，3回授業を欠席
して全く授業がわからなくなってしまった」が適切。　(2)　Hinaは2
回目の発話で，Keikoがスマートフォンを机の上に置き忘れてしまっ
たことを謝っている。ここから空所は電話がつながらなかったという
内容のAが適切。　(3)　空所の次にJunkoが来週の出張の宿の予約をし
ているという現在の行動を述べている。ここから空所に適切なのは口
語表現であるB「今何しているの？」となる。

【9】(1)　イ　　(2)　エ　　(3)　キ　　(4)　シ　　(5)　ス
〇**解説**〇 (1)　空欄の前後にあるBrunoの発話に着目すると，世界最高の
アイスクリームメーカーであるBenとJerryは12歳の時に体育の授業で
出会ったと述べられている。そのため，「もうちょっと教えてもらえ
ませんか」を意味するイが正解。　(2)　空欄の後にあるBrunoの発話
に着目すると，Benは大学入学前，アイスクリーム販売の仕事をした
ことがあり，ペンシルベニア大学でアイスクリーム製造の通信講座を
受講することに決めたと述べられている。そのため，「彼らはアイス
クリームのことについて何か知っていたのですか」を意味するエが正
解。　(3)　空欄の直前にあるAlexanderの発話に着目すると，Benと
Jerryがすぐに成功したのかと尋ねており，空欄の直後にあるBrunoの
発話では，彼らは，多くの潜在的な顧客がいて競合するアイスクリー
ム店がない大学街を選び，毎日違ったアイスクリームを提供した，と
成功の理由が述べられている。従って，「かなりね」を意味するキが
正解。　(4)　空欄の直後にあるBrunoの発話に着目すると，Benの味覚
と嗅覚が乏しかったために，アイスクリームにクッキーや果物の大き
な塊を入れたことから，独特な味ができたと述べられている。そのた
め，「彼らのアイスクリームは何が違っていたのか」を意味するシが
正解。　(5)　空欄の直前にあるAlexanderの発話に着目すると，「では，
もしBenの味覚と嗅覚に問題がなければ，完全に違う話になっていた
んでしょうね」と述べられている。そのため，「その通り」を意味す

るスが正解。

【10】 C→A→D→B

○**解説**○ Kathyの2回目の発話I think you must be tired from watching dramas all last night.より，昨晩のDannyの行動を示しており起こった順としては一番早いことがわかる。watching dramasより，遅い時間までテレビを見ているCが最初に来る。Dannyの1回目の発話I started feeling nauseous as soon as I had a sip of the red wine, and I had to lie down a little. より，ワインを一口飲んで気分が悪くなり横になったとありA→Dと続く。Bはややわかりにくいが，I left it halfway.より途中でパーティーを退出して帰宅したイラストと判断し，時系列の最後とする。

【1】Complete each sentence by arranging the words within each {   } bracket. Then choose the appropriate words to fill in the blanks indicated with numbers, (1) and (2). Answer the most appropriate combination from ① to ⑤.

(1) Our editor called us more than a year ago to point out that this book would soon be 10 years old. We suspected that he was telling us this because on several occasions he had hinted that (1) (   ) (   ) (   ) (2) (   ) second edition.

{ be / for / it / a / would / time }

① 1 time   2 for
② 1 time   2 be
③ 1 time   2 a
④ 1 it   2 for
⑤ 1 it   2 be

(2) This study examines how teaching active listening and questioning skills can improve English language students' speaking skills, and how the effects (   ) (   ) (   ) (1) (   ) (2) individual affective factors.

{ this / on / depending / of / differ / approach }

① 1 this   2 of
② 1 this   2 on
③ 1 this   2 approach
④ 1 differ   2 on
⑤ 1 differ   2 of

▎2024年度 ▎岐阜県 ▎難易度■■■■■

【2】次の各英文の(   )内に, [   ]内の語(句)を入れて英文を完成するとき, (A)及び(B)に入れるべき語(句)の組合せとして正しいものを1〜5から一つ選び, 番号で答えよ。なお, 選択肢のカナ記号は

74

A−Bの順に示されている。

(1) A worker ( ) (A) ( ) (B) ( ) the rules regarding safety and society.

[ア be　イ fired　ウ for　エ may　オ violating]

1 ア−ウ　2 イ−ア　3 ウ−ア　4 ウ−エ

5 オ−エ

(2) With ( ) (A) ( ) (B) ( ) see or do, we decided to go out into the garden.

[ア else　イ for　ウ nothing　エ to　オ us]

1 ア−ウ　2 ア−オ　3 イ−エ　4 エ−ア

5 エ−オ

(3) I am in ( ) (A) ( ) (B) ( ) will work.

[ア as　イ doubt　ウ this method　エ to

オ whether]

1 ア−イ　2 ア−オ　3 ウ−イ　4 ウ−オ

5 エ−オ

(4) The media have a ( ) (A) ( ) (B) ( ) appropriate information.

[ア provide　イ responsibility　ウ the public　エ to

オ with]

1 ア−ウ　2 イ−オ　3 ウ−エ　4 エ−ア

5 エ−ウ

(5) The film's annual results ( ) (A) ( ) (B) ( ) be.

[ア aren't　イ ought　ウ they　エ to　オ what]

1 ア−イ　2 ウ−ア　3 ウ−エ　4 オ−イ

5 オ−エ

2024年度 ┃ 愛知県 ┃ 難易度

【3】次の(1)〜(5)の〔　〕内の単語または語句を並べ替えてそれぞれ正しい英文を作るとき，(①), (②)に入る単語または語句を(ア)〜(オ)からそれぞれ一つずつ選び，記号で答えなさい。ただし，英文のはじめにくる単語または語句の頭文字も小文字にしてある。

(1) The camera my father gave me was (　　) (①) (　　) (②)
(　　). I had to consider the light and the distance from the object and
carefully adjust the lens to take a good picture.

〔 (ア) easy 　　 (イ) but 　　 (ウ) use 　　 (エ) to
(オ) anything 〕

(2) Lisa didn't like (　　) (①) (　　) (②) (　　). The other day
she said to her mother that she knew what she should do.

〔 (ア) to 　　 (イ) do 　　 (ウ) being 　　 (エ) what
(オ) told 〕

(3) Cathy received an email from her boss(　　) (①) (　　) (②)
(　　) put off until next Friday.

〔 (ア) been 　　 (イ) saying 　　 (ウ) had 　　 (エ) that
(オ) the sales meeting 〕

(4) (　　) (①) (　　) (②) (　　) time to play baseball, Shohei
did quite well even though he didn't get any hits.

〔 (ア) first 　　 (イ) it 　　 (ウ) was 　　 (エ) his
(オ) considering 〕

(5) When Takeshi entered the restaurant, he (　　) (①) (　　)
(②) (　　). While eating a pizza, he realized that his mother had
taken him there when he was a small boy.

〔 (ア) having 　　 (イ) before 　　 (ウ) there 　　 (エ) been
(オ) remembered 〕

2024年度 ▌ 鳥取県 ▌ 難易度■■■■□

【4】 Complete each sentence by arranging the given words in the correct order.
Then, mark the number of the word(s) in each blank.

(1) Many people say that the younger we are, ＿＿ [1] ＿＿ [2]
＿＿ learn a foreign language.

① easier 　② is 　③ it 　④ the 　⑤ to

(2) In ＿＿ [1] ＿＿ [2] ＿＿ properly, it must have a command
system.

① function 　② to 　③ for 　④ order

76

⑤　an organization

(3)　What he ____ [1] ____ [2] ____ the matter.

①　little　②　has　③　said　④　with　⑤　to do

(4)　Those ____ [1] ____ [2] ____ to a new plan for consolidation of two high schools.

①　at　②　opposed　③　present　④　the conference

⑤　were

2024年度 ┃ 千葉県・千葉市 ┃ 難易度

【5】次の(1)〜(4)の英文について，意味の通る英文になるように，[　]内のa〜eの英語を並べ替えるとき，2番目と4番目にくる最も適切な組合せを，それぞれ1〜5から1つずつ選べ。ただし，組合せの左側を2番目，右側を4番目とする。

(1)　They [$_a$source $_b$a $_c$me $_d$reliable $_e$considered].

1　a−d　2　c−d　3　b−d　4　b−a　5　b−c

(2)　The Big Dipper [$_a$the $_b$as $_c$to $_d$is $_e$referred] Great Bear.

1　c−b　2　d−a　3　d−b　4　e−a　5　e−b

(3)　He has [$_a$six $_b$less $_c$than $_d$no $_e$dogs].

1　a−b　2　b−a　3　a−c　4　d−a　5　b−c

(4)　Today [$_a$every $_b$out $_c$three $_d$of $_e$four] Americans live in cities.

1　b−c　2　b−a　3　e−b　4　e−c　5　e−d

2024年度 ┃ 奈良県 ┃ 難易度

【6】次の(1)〜(5)について，[　]内の語(句)を並べ替えて，日本文の意味を正しく表す英文を作るとき，[　]内の語(句)の中で前から2番目と5番目にくる語(句)をア〜キからそれぞれ1つずつ選び，記号で答えなさい。ただし，文頭にくるものも小文字で表記されています。

(1)　私がどんなに心配したかあなたには分からないよ。

[was / how / have / I / you / no idea / worried].
　ア　　イ　　ウ　　エ　オ　　カ　　キ

(2)　この仕事以外なら何でもします。

[but / will / this / anything / job / do / I].
　ア　　イ　　ウ　　エ　　オ　カ　キ

77

(3) 昨年出版されたすべての本が賞の対象となる。

[are / the prize / eligible / last year / all books / published / for].
　ア　　イ　　ウ　　　エ　　　　オ　　　　カ　　キ

(4) 子供のころパイロットになることを思い描いたものです。

I [was / to / a pilot / becoming / when I / used / imagine] a kid.
　ア　イ　　ウ　　　エ　　　オ　　　カ　　キ

(5) 私があなたの健康をどれだけ気遣っているか分かりますか。

Do [anxious / about / you / the way / your health / know / I'm]?
　　ア　　　イ　　ウ　　　エ　　　　オ　　　カ　　キ

▎2024年度 ▎名古屋市 ▎難易度 ■■■■□□

【7】次の(1)〜(5)の〔　〕内の語句を日本語の内容にあうように並べかえ，全文を記せ。

(1) What 〔 whether, is, best, you, or, matters, your, do 〕 not.
大事なのは，全力を尽くすか否かだ。

(2) I 〔 into, where, of, I, an old friend, ran, least, mine 〕 expected to see him.
思いがけないところで昔の友人に会いました。

(3) I'll tell 〔 being, you, your, it's, with, angry, good, no 〕 me.
言っておくが，私に怒ってもはじまらないよ。

(4) Never 〔 I, terrifying, this, as, have, read, so, a novel 〕.
こんな怖い小説ははじめてだ。

(5) The problem 〔 how to, solved, prevent, be, remains, to, war, of 〕.
戦争をいかにして防止するかという問題は，いまだ解決されていない。

▎2024年度 ▎山梨県 ▎難易度 ■■■□□□

【8】次の各問いの日本文と意味がほぼ同じになるように，〔　〕内の語を正しく並びかえたときの，(A)と(B)に当てはまる最も適当な語句を記号で答えなさい。ただし，〔　〕内にはそれぞれ不要な語が，1つある。また，文頭にくる語も小文字となっている。

(1) この家は私たちが住めるだけの広さがある。

This house is 〔 ア　enough　イ　for　ウ　in　エ　too

オ　large　　カ　us　　キ　live　　ク　to〕．

This house is （　A　）（　　）（　B　）（　　）（　　）（　　）（　　）．

(2)　本に書いてあるからといって，何でもすぐに信用してはいけない。

Don't believe everything 〔ア　in books　　イ　it's　　ウ　because

エ　however　　オ　immediately　　カ　just　　キ　written〕．

Don't believe everything （　　）（　　）（　A　）（　　）（　B　）（　　）．

(3)　貴子はいつも宿題をするのに2時間を費やす。

Takako usually 〔ア　hours　　イ　her　　ウ　doing

エ　spends　　オ　for　　カ　two　　キ　homework〕．

Takako usually （　　）（　A　）（　　）（　B　）（　　）（　　）．

▌2024年度 ▌宮崎県 ▌難易度 ▒▒▒▒▒□□

【9】 Complete the following sentences by putting the most appropriate word(s) in each space. Then, mark on the answer sheet the corresponding numbers for words in the blanks （　a　） and （　b　）. The same word(s) cannot be used twice.

(1)　A : Look, there's that actor. You've been a fan of his for years, right?

B : Yes, I still like the actor — but he （　　）（　a　）（　　）（　　）（　　）（　　）（　b　）（　　）．

① was　　② what　　③ ten　　④ not　　⑤ he

⑥ years　　⑦ is　　⑧ ago

(2)　A : I heard about the accident. I'm sorry to hear about it How long will it take for you to recover?

B : My doctor said, "You'll （　　）（　a　）（　　）（　　）（　　）（　　）（　b　）（　　）．"

① to　　② be　　③ week　　④ able　　⑤ about

⑥ in　　⑦ a　　⑧ get

(3)　A : How would you describe your 30 years of working as a newspaper reporter?

B : Well, （　　）（　　）（　a　） that （　　）（　　）（　　）（　b　）（　　） job when it was done.

① myself　　② bad　　③ it　　④ flatter　　⑤ wasn't

⑥ such ⑦ I ⑧ a

(4) A : Do you have a good relationship with your seniors in club activities?

B : One of my seniors had too much pride, but the ( ) (a)
( ) ( ) ( ) asked (b) ( ) ( ). I hope we can
develop a closer and better relationship.

① and ② pride ③ swallowed ④ for ⑤ senior
⑥ our ⑦ her ⑧ help

(5) A : Why did you talk with die president?

B : Since we ( ) ( ) ( ), ( ) (a)( ) (b)
( ).

① didn't ② called ③ to ④ she
⑤ account ⑥ us ⑦ the meeting ⑧ attend

┃ 2024年度 ┃ 神戸市 ┃ 難易度 ■■■□□

【10】 次の[ ]内の語(句)を意味が通るように並べかえ，英文を完成さ
せなさい。並べかえた英語のみ書くこと。ただし，文頭にくる語も小
文字にしてある。

(1) A : [are / matter / busy / how / you / no], you need to take care of your
health.

B : I will keep that in mind.

(2) A : I heard you were involved in a terrible traffic accident. Are you all
right?

B : [from / getting / prevented / the seat belt / hurt / me / fastening].

(3) A : How was the movie?

B : Never [terrifying / so / seen / as / have / I / a movie / this].

(4) A : Congratulations! You finally made it!

B : [help / been / had / if / not / it / for / your], I would have lost the
game.

┃ 2024年度 ┃ 佐賀県 ┃ 難易度 ■■■□□

【11】次の(1)～(3)の英文や対話の文脈に合うように,〔   〕内のA～Eの語(句)を並べ替えて(   )に入れ,英文を完成するとき,最も適切な語順になるよう,左から順に記号で書け。ただし,文頭に来る語(句)も小文字で表記している。

(1) David ：Hey, Craig! Do you want to grab some tempura for lunch?

Craig ：Actually, is there anything spicier around here?

David ：(   )(   )(   )(   )(   ) around our office. But if you are free this weekend, I know a good place in Osaka.

Craig ：OK. Let's eat tempura today and take me to Osaka for spicy food on Saturday.

〔A serve   B the restaurants   C anything   D don't

E spicy 〕

(2) We may not realize it, but oil is an essential part of our everyday lives. Oil, which is usually called petroleum, is a valuable world resource because (   )(   )(   )(   )(   ) from it.

〔A that   B useful products   C the many

D are manufactured   E of 〕

(3) For many years, the word "gig" has been mainly used by young people to talk about a live musical performance in a small venue. These days, (   )(   )(   )(   )(   ) all kinds of short-term jobs are said to be doing "gig work."

〔A but   B doing   C musicians   D not only

E people 〕

| 2024年度 | 愛媛県 | 難易度 |

【12】Put the words in the correct order, and answer with the numbers.

(1) この説明書を英語になおしてもらいたい。

I [① have   ② manual   ③ this   ④ to   ⑤ translated
⑥ want] into English.

(2) ボブは2, 3分歩いて,博物館に着いた。

A [① Bob   ② brought   ③ few   ④ walk   ⑤ to
⑥ minutes'] the museum.

(3) 大事なのは何をするかではなく，どのようにするかである。

It is not what you do but [① counts ② do ③ how ④ it ⑤ that ⑥ you].

(4) あのドアを開けていただけませんか？

Would you [① as ② be ③ kind ④ open ⑤ so ⑥ to] that door?

(5) 兄は私にコンピュータを貸したがらないと思いますが，説得して貸してくれるか確かめましょう。

I don't think my brother is willing to lend me his computer, but I'll [① can ② him ③ I ④ if ⑤ see ⑥ talk] into it.

┃ 2024年度 ┃ 京都府 ┃ 難易度 ▨▨▨□□

【13】 *Put the words in the parentheses from ① to ③ in the correct order.*

Through STEM, students develop key skills including problem-solving, creativity, critical analysis, teamwork, independent thinking, taking the initiative, communication, and digital literacy. These skills are necessary for students to be successful in their future careers.

Although STEM education empowers students with the various technical and practical skills to succeed, however, these disciplinary skills ①(to / to / not / are / sufficient / adapt) a fast-changing world. The skills learned today will soon be outdated due to fastchanging technology, industries, and other societal aspects. The jobs ②(after / exist / longer/ may / seen today / no) a few years, or at least it will not be sufficient with the same skill level that can be performed at the moment. In this context, we are preparing students for jobs that even don't exist at the moment. In this sense, we are at a critical point of ③(to / children / educate / that / a learning environment / in / time) is more dynamic, flexible, and relevant for the future.

【Modified from "At the dawn of science, technology, engineering, arts, and mathematics (STEAM) education : prospects, priorities, processes and problems (2021)"】

┃ 2024年度 ┃ 兵庫県 ┃ 難易度 ▨▨▨▨□

82

【14】 次の英文における〈問1〉〜〈問4〉の下線部にある(ア)〜(ケ)の語(句)を並べ替えて，意味の通る英文を作りなさい。その時4番目と7番目にくるものの組合せとして最も適切なものを，以下のそれぞれ①〜④のうちから選びなさい。(なお，文頭にくる語も選択肢の中では小文字となっている。)

In the Japanese e-waste management system the withdrawal is not free of charge, but consumers pay an amount of money when they return used electronic products to the traders. Japan has established a withdrawal system for four types of e-waste (air conditioners, televisions, refrigerators and washing machines) since 1998. The law specifies target rates and imposes strict penalties for non-compliance. Until 2004 there were 41 e-waste recycling facilities in Japan, partially financed by the ministries, municipalities or Japanese companies producing electronic products. Producers implement in their business strategy the e-waste management and have their own facilities or collaborate with other producers to create and operate such facilities. 〈問1〉(ア) are not　(イ) residencies (ウ) are collected　(エ) anymore　(オ) e-waste　(カ) these products　(キ) coming from　(ク) when　(ケ) used or when consumers buy new ones. The collected waste is transported to the intermediate 380 e-waste collection points and eventually to the facilities through a distribution system. A basic characteristic of the Japanese system is the use of the primary disassembly procedure of big parts initially 〈問2〉(ア) process　(イ) handle　(ウ) with　(エ) the residues　(オ) accurate and brief　(カ) a more　(キ) so (ク) they　(ケ) that in a more proper way. Therefore, the Japanese companies of electronic equipment were the first ones to evolve welding without insulation and the electrical panel board connections without bromide compounds in relation to the European guidelines of the Directive RoHS, 〈問3〉(ア) to be recycled　(イ) constantly　(ウ) the designing (エ) cheaper and easier　(オ) lighter products,　(カ) while (キ) of　(ク) aim at　(ケ) they. They plan the disassembly by reducing the number of the plastic resins in their products and reuse their

● 語彙・文法

parts.

  Equivalent legislation is in force also for the collection and recycling of used electronic computers since 2003. The legal framework provides for two different categories for the used electronic computers. For those bought before October 2001, recycling is financed with 20-30€, while for those bought after October 2001, 〈問4〉(ア) an additional (イ) the price (ウ) are included (エ) recycling tax (オ) as (カ) the product (キ) in (ク) the recycling costs (ケ) of. This legislation also directs on order the manufacturers to recover their corresponding products after they have been used by their last owners. This system is an example for the individual responsibility of producers, from the moment they have the natural and financial responsibility for their products recycling. Nevertheless, it should be noted that the e-waste recycling system success in Japan is based on social responsibility, environmental sensitivity and general discipline of Japanese people vis-à-vis regulations.

問1 (ア) are not (イ) residencies (ウ) are collected (エ) anymore (オ) e-waste (カ) these products (キ) coming from (ク) when (ケ) used
① 4番目(ケ)　7番目(イ)　② 4番目(ウ)　7番目(ア)
③ 4番目(ケ)　7番目(キ)　④ 4番目(ウ)　7番目(キ)

問2 (ア) process (イ) handle (ウ) with (エ) the residues (オ) accurate and brief (カ) a more (キ) so (ク) they (ケ) that
① 4番目(ア)　7番目(イ)　② 4番目(エ)　7番目(ア)
③ 4番目(ア)　7番目(ク)　④ 4番目(エ)　7番目(イ)

問3 (ア) to be recycled (イ) constantly (ウ) the designing (エ) cheaper and easier (オ) lighter products, (カ) while (キ) of (ク) aim at (ケ) they
① 4番目(ウ)　7番目(オ)　② 4番目(ウ)　7番目(ケ)
③ 4番目(ク)　7番目(ウ)　④ 4番目(ク)　7番目(オ)

問4 (ア) an additional (イ) the price (ウ) are included

84

(エ) recycling tax　(オ) as　(カ) the product　(キ) in (ク) the recycling costs　(ケ) of

① 4番目(イ)　7番目(オ)　② 4番目(イ)　7番目(カ)

③ 4番目(ア)　7番目(ケ)　④ 4番目(ア)　7番目(キ)

> 本文はG. Gaidajis et al. : E-waste : Environmental Problems and Current Management (2010, Journal of Engineering Science and Technology Review 3 193-199)から。一部表記を改めたところがある。

▌2024年度▌神奈川県・横浜市・川崎市・相模原市▌難易度 ▰▰▰▱▱

【15】次の(1)～(4)の日本語の文に合うように，英文の〔　〕内の語をそれぞれ適切に並べ替え，〔　〕内で2番目と5番目になる語の記号を書け。ただし，〔　〕内の語には，不要な語が1語含まれている。

(1) 私は家に帰る途中，バス発着所を歩いて通ったのを覚えています。

I remember walking through the bus〔A　home / B　which / C　on / D　station / E　way / F　my〕.

(2) コンピュータを使った実務経験はどのくらいありますか。

How much〔A　you / B　experience / C　have / D　do / E　practical / F　use〕of working with computers?

(3) 人は考え，話すことができる点で動物と異なる。

Human beings are different from〔A　animals / B　they / C　of / D　in / E　can / F　that〕think and speak.

(4) その火事の原因は，警察が調べているところです。

The cause of the fire〔A　by / B　into / C　being / D　looked / E　is / F　investigating〕the police.

▌2024年度▌愛媛県▌難易度 ▰▰▱▱▱

解答・解説

【1】(1) ④ (2) ④

○**解説**○ (1) it would be time for aが正しい語順となる。空所を含むhe had hinted that以下の意味は「第2版を出す時期ではないかと彼はほのめかしていた」となる。 (2) of this approach differ depending onが正しい語順となる。語群の中で動詞は自動詞のdifferしかなく，depending on「～次第で」とよくセットで用いられる。残りのof this approachをthe effectsの後ろに続けて「このアプローチの効果」としてhow節の主語とすればよい。

【2】(1) 1 (2) 2 (3) 2 (4) 5 (5) 4

○**解説**○ (1) 完成した英文はA worker may be fired for violating the rules regarding safety and society.である。the rules以下がviolatingの目的語になることに着目すればよい。 (2) 完成した英文はWith nothing else for us to see or do, we decided to go out into the garden.である。with nothing else to doで「他にすることがないので」の意である。ここに不定詞の意味上の主語のfor usと，動詞のseeが加わった形になっている。 (3) 完成した英文はI am in doubt as to whether this method will work.である。will workの主語になるのはthis methodのみであることに着目する。in doubt as to (about)～で「～について疑っている」の意である。 (4) 完成した英文はThe media have a responsibility to provide the public with appropriate information.である。have aに続くのが名詞のresponsibilityであることに着目する。また，provide A with Bは「AにBを与える」の意である。 (5) 完成した英文はThe firm's annual results aren't what they ought to be.である。最後のbeの前にought toが置かれることに着目する。また，今回のwhatは先行詞がない関係代名詞である。

【3】(1) ① (イ) ② (エ) (2) ① (オ) ② (ア)
(3) ① (エ) ② (ウ) (4) ① (イ) ② (エ)
(5) ① (ア) ② (ウ)

○解説○ (1) 「父からもらったカメラは使いやすいものではなかった」。anything but〜「決して〜でない」。整序すると，anything but easy to use となる。 (2) 「リサは指図されるのが嫌いだった」。整序すると，being told what to doとなる。 (3) 「キャシーは上司から，営業会議は来週の金曜日に延期されたというメールを受け取った」。整序すると，saying that the sales meeting had beenとなる。 (4) 「初めての野球だったことを考えれば，ショウヘイはヒットを打てなかったものの，とてもよくやった」。整序すると，Considering it was his firstとなる。

(5) 「タケシはレストランに入ると，以前にも来たことがあることを思い出した」。整序すると，remembered having been there beforeとなる。

【4】(1) 1 ① 2 ② (2) 1 ③ 2 ② (3) 1 ② 2 ⑤ (4) 1 ① 2 ⑤

○解説○ (1) 完成した英文はMany people say that the younger we are, the easier it is to learn foreign language.である。the 比較級, the 比較級の形になっていることに着目する。 (2) 完成した英文はIn order for an organization to function properly, it must have a command system.である。in order toに意味上の主語であるan organization が加わった形になっている。 (3) 完成した英文はWhat he said has little to do with the matter.である。have to do with〜で「〜と関係がある」という意味になる。

(4) 完成した英文はThose present at the conference were opposed to a new plan for consolidation of two high schools.である。those presentはthose who were presentだったものが省略された形になっている。

【5】(1) 2 (2) 5 (3) 2 (4) 2

○解説○ (1) They considered me a reliable source. 「彼らは私を信頼できる情報源と考えた」。consider＋O＋C 「OをCと考える，みなす」。

(2) The Big Dipper is referred to as the Great Bear. 「北斗七星は大ぐま座と呼ばれている」。the Big Dipper 「北斗七星」，the Great Bear 「大ぐま座」，refer to A as B 「AをBと呼ぶ」。 (3) He has no less than six dogs. 「彼は6匹も犬を飼っている」。no less than〜は 「〜も(多く)の＝as many as〜／as much as〜」。一方，not less than〜は 「少なくとも＝at least」。

混同しないように注意しよう。　(4)　Today three out of every four Americans live in cities.「今日では，アメリカ人の4人に3人が都市部に住んでいる」。数詞＋out of＋数詞＋名詞で割合を表す。例：nine out of ten students「学生の10人中9人」。

【6】(1)　2番目…ウ　　5番目…キ　　(2)　2番目…イ　　5番目…ア
(3)　2番目…カ　　5番目…ウ　　(4)　2番目…イ　　5番目…ウ
(5)　2番目…カ　　5番目…ア

○**解説**○ (1)　完成した英文はYou have no idea how worried I was.である。「どのくらい〜」の場合は，howの直後に形容詞が続く形になることに注意しよう。　(2)　完成した英文はI will do anything but this job.」である。anything but〜は「〜以外は何でも」の意味である。　(3)　完成した英文はAll books published last year are eligible for the prize.である。eligible for〜は「〜の資格がある」の意味である。　(4)　完成した英文はI used to imagine becoming a pilot when I was a kid.である。used to〜は「〜したものだった(今はしていない)」の意味である。　(5)　完成した英文はDo you know the way I'm anxious about your health?である。

【7】(1)　(What) matters is whether you do your best or (not.)　(2)　(I) ran into an old friend of mine where I least (expected to see him.)　(3)　(I'll tell) you it's no good your being angry with (me.)　(4)　(Never) have I read so terrifying a novel as this.　(5)　(The problem) of how to prevent war remains to be solved.

○**解説**○ (1)　matter「重要である，問題となる」という意味の動詞。What matters is〜「大事なことは〜だ」。　(2)　run into〜「〜に出くわす」。where I least expected to see him「私が彼に会うことを最も期待していなかった場所で」→「思いがけないところで」。　(3)　it's no good 〜ing「〜しても無駄だ」。yourはbeingの意味上の主語。　(4)　I have never read …のneverが強意のために文頭に置かれると，倒置が起きてhave Iの語順となる。soは副詞なので直後の形容詞を修飾する。「とても怖い小説」は〈so＋形容詞＋a＋名詞〉の語順となる。　(5)　the problem of how to prevent war「戦争をいかにして防止するかという問

題」。同格のof。〈remain to be＋過去分詞〉「～されないで残っている」。

【8】(1)　A　オ　　B　イ　　　(2)　A　ウ　　B　キ　　　(3)　A　カ
B　ウ

○**解説**○　不要な語が1つあることに注意。　　(1)　This house is large enough for us to live in. 形容詞／副詞＋enough for (人) to (do)「(人)が～するのに十分なほど(形容詞／副詞)」の構文に関する問題。　　(2) Don't believe everything immediately just because it's written in books.副詞justはonlyの意。　　(3)　Takako spends two hours doing her homework. イディオムspend (time) (in) doing「～して(時間)を費やす」(in)は省略されることが多い。

【9】(1)　a　④　　b　⑥　　　(2)　a　④　　b　⑦　　　(3)　a　①
b　⑧　　　(4)　a　③　　b　④　　　(5)　a　②　　b　③

○**解説**○　(1)　…but he is not what he was ten years ago. 「今の彼は10年前の彼とは違う」となる。主格の関係代名詞whatを使った表現，what＋S＋be「Sが～である状態」のパターンを覚えておこう。be動詞の時制に注意して，what he is「今の彼」，what she used to be 「過去の彼女」，what Japan was to the US「過去における日米関係」などがある。付随する表現があれば訳出には工夫が必要になる。また，what he isを「彼の人柄」と訳出することもある。似たパターンとして，what he hasを「彼が持っているもの」から文脈により「彼の財産」と訳出することもある。　　(2)　You'll be able to get about in a week. 「1週間もすれば動き回れるようになるでしょう」となる。未来形＋in＋「時間」で「～後に…だろう」。get about「歩き回る，出歩けるようになる」。

(3)　I flatter myself that it wasn't such a bad job when it was done. 「(記者として30年間働いてみて，)それほど悪い仕事ではなかったと我ながら自負している」となる。flatter oneself that～ 「～であるとうぬぼれる，自負する」。　　(4)　…but the senior swallowed her pride and asked for our help.「その先輩は自分のプライドを捨てて私たちに援助を求めた」となる。swallow one's pride「自分のプライドを捨てる，恥を忍ぶ」。

(5)　Since we didn't attend the meeting, she called us to account. 「会議に出

なかったので，叱られた」となる。call～to account「～に責任を問う，弁明を求める，～を叱責する」。

【10】(1) No matter how busy you are　(2) Fastening the seat belt prevented me from getting hurt　(3) have I seen so terrifying a movie as this　(4) If it had not been for your help

○**解説**○ (1) no matter how～「どんなに～でも」。　(2) prevent O from ～ing「Oが～するのを妨げる」。　(3) I have never seen…のneverが強調のために文頭に出て，以降に倒置が起きる。so terrifying a movieは〈so＋形容詞＋a/an＋名詞〉の語順。　(4) 過去の事実に反する仮定。If it had not been for～「～がなかったら」。

【11】(1) B→D→A→C→E　(2) E→C→B→A→D　(3) D→C→A →E→B

○**解説**○ (1) 正しい語順はThe restaurants don't serve anything spicyとなる。don'tの主語となるのは複数形のThe restaurantsしかない。something(anything)＋形容詞で「何か～なもの」の意味になる。
(2) 正しい語順はof the many useful products that are manufacturedとなる。becauseの後にS＋Vと続けようとするとうまく文が組み立てられないためbecause of～「～のために」とする必要がある。thatはmany useful productsを先行詞とする関係代名詞として用いる。　(3) 正しい語順はnot only musicians but people doingとなる。not only A but (also) B「AだけでなくBも」と，doing all kinds of short-term jobsがpeopleを修飾する用法に気づく必要がある。

【12】(1) ⑥→④→①→③→②→⑤　(2) ③→⑥→④→②→①→⑤
(3) ③→⑥→②→④→⑤→①　(4) ②→⑤→③→①→⑥→④
(5) ⑤→④→③→①→⑥→②

○**解説**○ (1) want to have this manual translatedが正しい語順となる。have＋O＋過去分詞「Oを～してもらう」を用いる。　(2) few minutes' walk brought Bob toが正しい語順となる。「数分歩くことがボブを～へ連れて行った」が直訳となる表現である。　(3) how you do it that countsが正しい語順となる。「どうやるか」はhow you do itで表す。「重要である」の部分は強調構文が使われており，countは自動詞「重要である」の意味で用いられている。　(4)　be so kind as to openが正しい語順となる。Would you be so kind as to～で「～してくださいますか」と物事を依頼する頻出の会話表現である。　(5)　see if I can talk himが正しい語順である。see if～で「～かどうか確かめる」，talk O into～で「Oに～するよう説得する」の意味。

【13】① are not sufficient to adapt to　② seen today may no longer exist after　③ time to educate children in a learning environment that

○**解説**○　トピックは，STEM教育すなわち科学(Science)，技術(Technology)，工学(Engineering)，数学(Mathematics)の4つの領域を統合的に学ぶ教育法についてである。　①「急速に変化する世界に適応するには，こうした学問的スキルだけでは不十分である」。adapt to～に適応する。　②「今日見られる仕事は，数年後にはもう存在しないかもしれず，…」。no longer～「もはや～ない」。　③「この意味で私たちは，よりダイナミックで，柔軟性があり，将来に関連した学習環境で子供たちを教育する重要な時期にある」。at the point of time to～「～する時期で」。

【14】問1　②　問2　③　問3　④　問4　①

○**解説**○　問1　整序すると，e-waste coming from residencies are collected when these products are not used anymore「居住により出る電子廃棄物はそれらの製品がもう使われたくなくなったとき回収される」。　問2　整序すると，with a more accurate and brief process so that they handle the residues「残留物を処理するのに，より正確で迅速なプロセスで」。

問3　整序すると，while they constantly aim at the designing of lighter products, cheaper and easier to be recycled「一方，彼らは，より軽く安く容易にリサイクルできる製品のデザインを常に目指している」。

問4　整序すると，the recycling costs are included in the price of the product as an additional recycling tax「リサイクル費用は，追加のリサイクル税として製品価格に含まれている」。

【15】(1)　2番目…C　　5番目…A　　(2)　2番目…B　　5番目…C

(3)　2番目…D　　5番目…E　　(4)　2番目…C　　5番目…A

○**解説**○ (1)　正しい語順はstation on my way homeである。on my way～で「～に行く途中に」の意味でhomeが来ると「帰宅途中に」となる。

(2)　正しい語順はpractical experience do you haveである。「どのくらい」という量を尋ねる疑問文を表すにはHow muchを文頭に用いる。

(3)　正しい語順はanimals in that they canである。in that S＋Vで「～という点で」という意味である。　(4)　正しい語順はis being looked intobyである。現在進行形の受動態が用いられていることと，look into「調査する」を用いて同じ意味のinvestigateは使わないことに注意する。

語彙・文法 | # 誤文訂正

実施問題

【1】以下の[問1]～[問5]の英文には，英文・語法的に誤っている箇所が1つずつある。次の(例)にならって，誤っている箇所を下線部①～④の中から1つずつ選び，その番号を書け。また，その箇所の語句を正しい形に直して書け。

(例)　Success is ①within ②reach if you ③are willed to ④put in the work.

番号：③　正しい形：are willing

[問1]　My brother ①is singing ②in ③a low voice with his eyes ④closing.

[問2]　We ①came to ②a fountain, ③which we rested ④for a short while.

[問3]　If I ①had not ②taken the pills this morning, I ③would have been suffering ④from carsickness now.

[問4]　The twins ①used to be so ②alike that even their friends found ③it difficult to tell one from ④other.

[問5]　①Since no one ②is at home ③during the day, our dog is ④taken care by our grandparents.

▌2024年度 ▌和歌山県 ▌難易度 ■■□□□

【2】次の英文1～5にはそれぞれ誤りや不適切なところがある。修正が必要な箇所を(ア)～(ウ)からそれぞれ一つずつ選び，適切な形に直しなさい。

1　Sam would (ア)appreciate very much (イ)if you (ウ)could show him how to cook your special paella.

2　For (ア)those of you who don't (イ)exercise regularly, it will probably be extremely difficult to (ウ)enjoy to run until you get used to it.

3　Anyone who has tried to study for an exam, (ア)write a report or read a book (イ)know how hard it is to concentrate (ウ)for significant chunks of time.

4　A record 10.3% of new graduate nurses in Japan (ア)quit from their jobs (イ)within a year of employment in fiscal 2021, (ウ)which ended in March last year, a survey by the Japanese Nursing Association showed.

語彙・文法

5 "$_{(ア)}$Compared to 20 years ago, there are fewer students in our school. Although a little sad about that, our homeroom teacher always says that we can realize our dreams if every one of us $_{(イ)}$are determined to never give up. So we should look forward to the school life that is about $_{(ウ)}$to begin."

2024年度 ┃ 岩手県 ┃ 難易度

【3】次の(1)～(3)の英文について，文法的・語法的な誤りを含むものを A～Dから一つずつ選び，その記号を書け。

(1) "Intonation" is the melody $_A$of language and is $_B$made up of pitches $_C$that $_D$rises and falls.

(2) $_A$However hard $_B$he tried, he $_C$could not make himself $_D$understand to the local people.

(3) One of the reasons $_A$the demand for sesame seeds is $_B$by the increase is that many people are starting $_C$to realize $_D$how beneficial they are for health.

┃ 2024年度 ┃ 愛媛県 ┃ 難易度

【4】For each question, choose the one underlined, word or phrase that should be corrected or rewritten.

1 I'm still in the middle $_ア$of lunch right now, $_イ$but I will be ready $_ウ$to leave $_エ$ten minutes later.

2 $_ア$While I $_イ$drive to Sendai, $_ウ$I was stopped by a policeman for $_エ$going over the speed limit.

3 If he $_ア$had stopped $_イ$to read the instruction manual before $_ウ$turning on the machine, I'm sure this $_エ$didn't happen.

4 Her telephone $_ア$wasn't functioning because her cat $_イ$had knocked $_ウ$a receiver off the hook without $_エ$her noticing it.

5 I could $_ア$rise public awareness about $_イ$animal abuse in America and many other countries $_ウ$as a result of your $_エ$wonderful research.

┃ 2024年度 ┃ 岩手県 ┃ 難易度

94

解答・解説

【1】問1　番号…④　　正しい形…closed　　問2　番号…③　　正しい形…where　　問3　番号…③　　正しい形…would be　　問4　番号…④　　正しい形…the other　　問5　番号…④　　正しい形…taken care of

○**解説**○　誤っている個所を指摘し，正しい形にする問題。　問1　付帯状況with＋O＋C　「OがCである状態で」の問題。O＋Cの関係は第5文型O＋Cの関係に準じる。Cに動詞が来る主な形として，現在分詞を使ったwith＋O＋〜ing「Oが〜している状態で」と過去分詞を使ったwith＋O＋p.p.「Oが〜されている状態で」を押さえておくこと。私の兄弟が歌を歌っているときに目をつぶっている状態なので，He is closing his eyes.の意味を，状況説明的にwithを使って表現する。その際に，受動態に変換し，His eyes are being closed.からOとCの要素を抽出し，with his eyes closedとまとめる。　問2　関係代名詞と関係副詞の違いに関する問題。ここではWe came to a fountain.とWe rested beside the fountain for a short while.の2文を，関係詞を使って接合する。rest「休息する」は他動詞ではなく自動詞なので，前置詞の存在に気づくことが大切である。　問3　仮定法過去完了の構文。①If S had 過去分詞〜，S' would have 過去分詞….「もし(過去に)〜したら，(過去に)…しただろうに」と，②If S had 過去分詞〜，S' would 動詞原形….「もし(過去に)〜したら，(現在は)…だろう」の2パターンある。主節にnowがあるので，ここは②で考える。　問4　The twinsから2人の人間が存在し，不定代名詞を使って一方と他方を区別する時は，oneとthe otherの組合せを使う。so〜that構文に注意。used to(動詞の原形)「過去に〜だった」，be alike「似ている」，tell A from B「AとBを区別する」。問5　群動詞の受動態の問題。能動態の文は，Our grandparents take care of our dog.である。take care ofを1つの動詞という視点でとらえれば，our dogはその群動詞の目的語となるので，our dogを主語にした受動態に変換できる。その際に前置詞ofを忘れないこと。

【2】1 記号…(ア) 修正…appreciate it 2 記号…(ウ) 修正…enjoy running 3 記号…(イ) 修正…knows 4 記号…(ア) 修正…quit 5 記号…(イ) 修正…is

○**解説**○ 1 appreciateは「(〜を)感謝する，正しく評価する」の意味の他動詞である。appreciate it if〜で「〜してもらえるとありがたい」の意になる。 2 enjoyの目的語となる動詞は動名詞のみである。 3 文の構造がやや複雑であるが，whoから始まる関係代名詞節がwho has tried to study for an exam, write a report or read a bookまでであり，study for an exam, write a report or read a bookがtriedの目的語のto不定詞であることがわかれば，この文の動詞となるknowは主語がAnyoneであるために三単現のsが必要になることがわかる。 4 「(仕事など)を辞める」場合，quitは他動詞として目的語を取る形で使うことができる。そのためfromは不要である。 5 「every one of us」は「私たち1人1人」の意であり単数であることから，動詞はisにする必要がある。

【3】(1) D (2) D (3) B

○**解説**○ (1) Cのthatはpitchesを先行詞とする関係代名詞であり，動詞は原形のrise and fallとなるためDが誤りである。 (2) make oneself understoodで「自分の言葉を相手に伝える」という用法のためDが誤りである。 (3) isの後にby the increaseと続くのは文法的に不適切で，現在進行形のincreasingとする必要がある。isの主語はthe demandとなる。

【4】1 エ 2 イ 3 エ 4 ウ 5 ア

○**解説**○ 1 該当箇所はten minutes laterではなくin ten minutesが正しい。未来のことを表現する際，具体的な時間を示すときにlaterは使用しない。 2 「車を運転しているとき，警察に止められた」の意。接続詞whileが「〜する間に」という「同時性」を表しているので，while I was drivingとなる。主節と主語が一致しているので，通常はwhile drivingと表せるが，本問では，Iが下線部に含まれていないので不可。 3 仮定法過去完了の文章。「もし機械の電源を入れる前に立ち止まって取扱説明書を読んでいたら，こんなことは起こらなかったに違いな

い」なので，wouldn't have happenedとなる。　4　該当箇所はa receiver
ではなくthe receiverが正しい。彼女の電話の受話器であることが特定
されている。　5　rise public awarenessではなくraise public awareness
「人々の意識を高める」が正しい。riseは主語が「上がる」を意味する
自動詞である。

英文作成

要点整理

　英文作成の根底となるものは，(1)まず英文の構造に通じていること，(2)次に単語の知識を豊富に持って，語句の運用になれていることが大切である。このうち(1)は，英文法の教えるところであるが，(2)のほうの単語の蓄積は主として，意識的にふだんの多読と精読の間に身につけるものである。

　なお英文作成は英作文(和文英訳)だけとは限らず，英語による表現全体を指すものである。日頃から，自分の考えなどを英語で表現する練習を積むことにより，自由英作文に対する対策もたてておきたいものである。

　次に英文作成の根底となる2つの要素を築いて行く上で，強調しておきたい点を挙げる。

①作文の種をしこんでおくこと。

　　基礎となる模範文を頭の中に蓄積することである。これは佳語・麗句をつらねた英文をいうのではなく，教科書の，特に文法の教科書の中に散在する基本的な構文形式の短文のことを指す。これらの模範文を1つでも多く，そして1日でも早く暗記し，いつでも自由に借用し，利用し，活用し，応用するのである。

②日英語法の相違を研究すること。

　　日英両語は全く系統を異にする語族に属するもので，単語自体の成り立ち，語句の組み合わせから，思想表現の様式にいたるまで，共通のものは極めて少なく，むしろ相違するものが大部分である。この異同の諸点は，細心の注意をはらって検討しなければならない。

③慣用語法の公式研究

　　英文解釈の研究において公式を使うことが便利であると同様に，英作文(和文英訳)の場合も公式が大切である。英作文(和文英訳)の学習は一方において，文法，idiom，日英語法の異同，その他作文上の諸現象を研究すると同時に，一方これらの語法で，英語の特徴を公式として研究し，それに習熟することが大切である。つまり，真の意味における和文英訳というものは，英語の達人にだけできる

高等技術なのである。しかし学生諸君の場合，むしろ与えられた日本文の内容だけを，英語の習慣にかなった言い回しで，すなわち英語の考え方に置き換えてみて，それから英語で表現するという習慣を養うことが必要である。

　以上述べたことを，別のことばで説明すれば，英作文(和文英訳)の場合，「上手な文」より「正しい文」であることが重要であり，単語，熟語を並べるだけが英作文ではなく，文法の応用力を養うこと，原文の内容を理解して，英文に訳しやすいようにいいかえてみること，やさしい文を利用することに気を配ることである。たとえば「通学」というと堅苦しくなるが，「学校へ行く」とすればわけなく英文になる。「彼には久しくごぶさたをしています」という文で「ごぶさた」に相当する語句をいくら考えてもむだである。その意味を他の語句を使って，1. いままで長い間彼に手紙を書いていない。2. いままで久しい間彼に会っていません。3. この前彼に会ってから，長くなります。などと，いいかえてみると，

1. I have not written to him for a long time.

2. I have not seen him for a long time.

3. It is a long time since I saw him last.

などという文が自然につくれるはずである。たとえば，Spring will come round again. In a few days flowers will be opening. というような文を覚えて応用すれば，「2，3週間たてば，また夏休みがやってくる」 The summer vacation will come round again in a few weeks. のような文がすぐできる。中学2，3年で習ったやさしい英文を，いかにうまく応用するかが，立派な英文を書くコツでもある。

　英文作成には，和文英訳のほかに，完成問題，整序問題，語句の選択，書き換え，適語挿入，誤文訂正，組み合わせ問題など，文法の知識を試されるものも含まれる。

　以上の知識は，高等学校の教科書，あるいは参考書などで自分の知識を整理しておくこと。文の要素，修飾語句，文型についての知識をしっかり身につけて，色々な問題にあたって知識を確実なものにしておくことが大切である。

【1】次は，ある中学校で英語担当教師(JTE)と外国語指導助手(ALT)が，次時の英語の授業を計画しているところである。会話文中の下線部①，②を英語にせよ。

JTE：①今度の英語の授業計画を立てるのを手伝ってくれますか。

ALT：いいですよ。環境問題をテーマにした内容でしたよね。

JTE：はい。②前回の授業では，関心をもっている生徒が予想以上に多かったことに驚きました。

ALT：そうですね。今回もいろんな意見が出るように生徒主体の授業を展開したいですね。

┃ 2024年度 ┃ 岡山県 ┃ 難易度 ■■□□□

【2】次の(1)，(2)の文中の下線部分を，それぞれ英文に直しなさい。

(1) 不確実な状況下で判断を下す時，私たちはある決まったルールや方程式に従っているわけではない。不確実な状況下における私たちの直観を支えているのは，私たちの感じるさまざまな感情のニュアンスである。

(茂木 健一郎 『脳と創造性』)

(2) すべての子供は生まれながらにして自ら進んで環境に関わり，環境との相互作用を通して「学び」を実現する能力を有しています。そして，乳幼児期から「学び」という営みを旺盛に展開しており，就学時にはすでにインフォーマルな知識とか素朴概念と呼ばれる膨大な知識を所有しています。

(奈須 正裕 『「資質・能力」と学びのメカニズム』)

┃ 2024年度 ┃ 新潟県・新潟市 ┃ 難易度 ■■■■□

【3】次の(1)〜(3)の日本文を英文にせよ。

(1) 月へ旅行できる日も遠くはあるまい。

(2) 外国人から日本のことを聞かれると，私たちは自分の無知なことに驚くことがよくある。

(3) あなたの言葉は必ずしもあなたの思い通りに理解されるとは限らないのだから，何を言うかだけでなく，どう言うかについても注意する必要がある。

┃2024年度┃山梨県┃難易度■■■□□

【4】次の(1)〜(4)の場面において，授業者は生徒に対して英語でどのように言うべきかを書け。
(1) 前回の授業を復習することを伝えるとき。
(2) ワークシートに自分の考えを書くように指示するとき。
(3) 残り時間があと5分であることを伝えるとき。
(4) 聞き手から発表者に対して質問をするように指示するとき。

┃2024年度┃香川県┃難易度■■■□□

【5】次の(1)，(2)を英語に直しなさい。
(1) 近年，「リスキリング(reskilling)」が世界的に注目されています。その言葉は，社会や技術の変化に適応するために，職務上必要なスキルを習得することを意味します。

(出典) VIEW next 2023 April

(2) 個性が大事といいながら，実際には，よその人の顔色をうかがってばかり，というのが今の日本人のやっていることでしょう。だとすれば，そういう現状をまず認めるところからはじめるべきでしょう。

(出典)『バカの壁』養老孟司著より一部変更
┃2024年度┃佐賀県┃難易度■■■■□

【6】次の文章の下線部①，②を英語にせよ。
　①ここ数年で，猫好きが多くなった気がする。ところが，だ。猫は犬のようには懐かない。飼い主がどんなに愛情を注いだとしても，愛情を返してくれるとは限らない。一体，猫の何に多くの人が魅了されているのだろうか。
　考えてみれば，日々世話をしては，飼い猫が一人遊びをするさまに何気なく目をやる。それだけでじゅうぶん。②だからこそ，猫が飼い主に甘えてきた喜びはひとしおである。猫はきまぐれでそうしている

● 英文作成

だけだとしても。これこそが人を惹きつけてやまない魅力なのだろう。

年度 ┃ 岡山県 ┃ 難易度 ■■■□□

【7】Translate the underlined sentence into English.

　(1)近年では，日本への観光客の数が劇的に増えている。観光客はその国の経済を助けるが，様々な問題も引き起こしている。

　京都を例にあげる。公共交通機関は観光客で混み合っていて，中には大きなスーツケースを持った人もいる。その結果，住民は公共交通機関を利用できないときがある。他の問題としては，観光客のマナーがある。地元の人々は，観光客が幅の狭いショッピングストリートでお菓子を食べながら歩くのを目にする。一部の観光客は写真を撮る許可もなく，私有地へ入る。

　地元の人々は，ますますいらだっている。今，(2)私たちは，観光公害の問題にどう対処すべきかを考えなければならない。

┃ 2024年度 ┃ 京都府 ┃ 難易度 ■■■□□

【8】次の文の下線部(1)，(2)を英語に直して書け。

　eスポーツは新しいビジネス分野かもしれませんが，そのルーツは遠くさかのぼります。(1)最初のeスポーツ競技大会の1つは40年以上前に米国で開催されました。そのときプレーヤーたちは，日本の有名なゲームであるスペースインベーダーで最高得点を競い合いました。しかし，状況は変わりました。今ではeスポーツのプレーヤーやチームは，大きな競技大会で1対1の勝負をします。(2)何千人ものファンがスタジアムで試合をライブで観戦し，さらに何百万人もの人たちがライブ配信を見ています。

┃ 2024年度 ┃ 香川県 ┃ 難易度 ■■□□□

【9】Translate the underlined parts below into English.

1　自由とならんで民主主義が最もたいせつにするのは，人間の平等である。民主主義は，すべての国民を個人として尊重する。

　　　　　文部省「民主主義　上」(1948)　＜一部改編＞

2　ペーパーテストだけでは生徒の英語力を測るのは難しいですよね。CAN-DOリストにある4技能5領域での目標のうち，話すことの2領

域の評価をペーパーテストでは測ることができないので，スピーキングテストは必ず必要です。

　　阿野幸一・太田洋「これからの英語授業にひと工夫」(2022)
　　＜一部改編＞

| 2024年度 | 栃木県 | 難易度 ■■■■□ |

【10】次の文は，授業で，教師が調べ学習の際に生徒に話した内容である。(1), (2)を英語に直しなさい。

(1)　クラスメートに紹介したいと思う人物について，インターネットで調べなさい。

(2)　例を取り入れて，聞き手にわかりやすい発表にしなさい。

| 2024年度 | 青森県 | 難易度 ■■■■□ |

解答・解説

【1】①　Could you help me plan the next English lesson?　②　In the last lesson, I was surprised more students were interested in the topic than I had expected.

○**解説**○　①は，〈help＋O＋動詞の原形〉を用いて英語にする。②は「予想以上に」を「私が予想していたより」と表せる。ALTと打ち合わせをしたり，授業後に評価をしたりする機会は日常的にあるので，教授法に関する専門用語等は身に付けておくとスムーズに業務が進む。

【2】(1)　When we make decisions under uncertain situations, we do not follow specific rules or equations.　(2)　All children, by nature, have the ability to willingly get involved with their surroundings and to realize "their learning" through their interaction with the surroundings.

○**解説**○　訳す和文内で主語(主部)と述語(述部)を確認し，また，修飾語句の箇所とその修飾語句がどの語句を説明しているのかも確認すること。理由や原因から何らかの結果を生じているというようなパターン

● 英文作成

の場合には，無生物主語にした方がすっきり訳せることも多いので，和文英訳演習の時に練習しておこう。時には，訳す和文の趣旨，ニュアンス，文脈を理解した上で，英語に変換しやすいように和文を書き換えることを考えてもよい。 (1)「判断を下す」はmake decisions，「不確実な」はuncertain，「ある決まった」はspecific，「方程式」はequations。文構造については主語，述語，修飾語句を押さえて英語にすればよい。和文で「従っているわけではない」と書かれていると，部分否定not～always などを考えてしまうかもしれないが，そうすると「ルールや方程式に従う可能性もある」という意味合いが出てきてしまう。ここはそうではなく全否定で表現すべきと考える。 (2) 最初に和文の構造を整理する。主語は「すべての子供は」，述語は「～する能力を有する」，さらにどのような能力かを説明する際に，「環境に関わる能力」と「学びを実現する能力」の2つを並列させたto不定詞で表現する。「生まれながらにして」はby nature，「自ら進んで」はwillingly，「～との相互作用」はinteraction with～。

【3】(1) It will not be long before we can take a trip to the moon.
(2) When a foreigner asks us things about Japan, we are often surprised to find out how ignorant we are of our own country. (3) You cannot always make yourself understood as you like, so you need to be careful about not only what you say but also how you say it.
○解説○ (1)「～できる日まで遠くはあるまい」は「～できるまで長く(かから)ないだろう」と表現できる。 (2) surprised at our own ignorance「無知さに驚いて」。 (3) 長くなるので，2文に分けて表現してもよい。not always～「いつも～とは限らない」，the way you want「あなたの思い通りに」。

【4】(1) Let's review our previous lesson. (2) Write your opinion on your worksheet. (3) Five minutes left. (4) Ask your presenter a question.
○解説○ (1)「復習する」はreview，「前回の」はpreviousやlastで表す。生徒への伝達のためLet's ～とする。 (2)「意見」はopinionで表す。

生徒への指示のため命令形でよい。　(3)　残り時間を表す場合は時間＋leftで短く簡潔に述べる。　(4)　「発表者」はpresenterで表す。(2)と同じく生徒への指示のため命令形を用いる。

【5】(1)　In recent years, "reskilling" has attracted worldwide attention. The word means acquiring the skills necessary for jobs in order to adapt to changes in society and technology.　(2)　Japanese people today may claim that individuality is important, but actually, they are always trying to read other people's feelings from their facial expressions. If so, we should start off by accepting this situation.

○**解説**○ (1)　adapt to changes「変化に適応する」。　(2)　問題文の第1文目は冗長な日本語なので，簡潔に簡単な英語で表現することを心掛ける。

【6】①　It seems that more and more people have become cat lovers in the past few years.　②　Therefore, owners feel even happier when their cats try to gain their attention and affection.

○**解説**○ 元の内容が損なわれない程度に英訳しやすい日本語の表現に置き換えたり，箇所によっては複文で表現する工夫をしたりすることも必要である。日本語にとらわれすぎないことが大切である。どの文法事項で表現するか，自分がストックしている英文の中で使えそうな構文に当てはめられるかなどを検討し，簡潔に表現することを心がけよう。　①「猫好きが多くなった」は，there are more and more cat lovers, the number of cat lovers has risen等も可。　②「だからこそ」は，文脈を考えて「それゆえに，それだから」と言い換えてthereforeとしている。「甘える」，「喜びはひとしおである」をどのように表現するかがポイント。be affectionate to～「～に愛情を抱く」，it's a great pleasure「大いなる喜びである」等も可。

● 英文作成

【7】(1)　The number of tourists to Japan has dramatically increased in recent years.　(2)　we need to think about how to deal with the problem of overtourism.

○**解説**○ (1)「～の数」はthe number of～,「近年では」はin recent years で表す。動詞の「増えている」は現在までのことを述べているため現在完了で表す必要がある点にも注意したい。　(2)　観光客が増えすぎて地元の人に悪影響をもたらす「観光公害」はovertourismで表す。「対処する」はdeal with～で表し,「どう対処すべきか」はhow to deal with ～とする。

【8】(1)　One of the first e-sports tournaments was held in America over 40 years ago.　(2)　Thousands of fans watch the games live in stadiums, and millions of people watch live streams.

○**解説**○ (1)「eスポーツ競技大会」はe-sports tournamentsで表す。「開催される」はholdの受動態heldを用いる。　(2)「～をライブ鑑賞する」はwatch～liveと表現する。「ライブ配信」はwatch live streamsとなる。

【9】1　Democracy respects every citizen as an individual.　2　Of the goals in the four skills and five areas on the CAN-DO list, two areas of the speaking skill cannot be assessed with paper tests, so speaking tests are necessary.

○**解説**○ 1「民主主義」はDemocracy,「AをBとして尊重する」はrespect A as Bで表す。「国民」はcitizen。　2「～のうち」はof～「～の中で」で表すことができる。「測る」は,assess「評価する」を受動態で用いて表せばよい。

【10】(1)　・By using the Internet, research the person you'd like to introduce to your classmates.　・Please use the Internet, and research the person you want to introduce to your classmates. から1つ　(2)　・Make your presentation understandable to the listeners by showing examples.　・Put some examples to make your presentation easy to understand to the listeners. から1つ

○**解説**○ 和文英訳では，一番伝えたい内容が何かを確認すること。(1)なら「インターネットで調べなさい」，(2)なら「わかりやすい発表にしなさい」という内容が伝わる表現を考える。その際に，SVOCの文型による表現にすると簡潔にまとまることも多く，その可能性を意識しておこう。残りの部分はどのような修飾表現(接続詞や前置詞，関係詞や準動詞，節にするか句にするかなど)にするとわかりやすいかを意識しよう。日本語にとらわれすぎて和製英語にならないようにすることにも要注意。

【1】以下に示したTOPICについて，自分の意見を英語で書きなさい。ただし，次の点を踏まえて書くこと。

○　あなたの意見と，その理由を2つ書くこと。

○　主張，展開，結論の構成で書くこと。

○　目安は80～100語とする。また，使用語数を最後に記入すること。(符号は，語数に含めない。)

TOPIC

Agree or Disagree: Schools should ban students from using translation applications in English classes.

2024年度 ▌ 福島県 ▌ 難易度

【2】コミュニケーションにおいて人工知能(AI)の活用が進む中，外国語を学ぶ意義について，あなたの考えを80語程度の英語で書け。なお，使用した語数を記入すること。

2024年度 ▌ 鹿児島県 ▌ 難易度 ■■■■■

【3】授業で「話すこと(やりとり)」の活動を実施する際，学習指導要領の内容を踏まえ，あなたはどのようなことに留意して指導するか，その理由も含めて70語以上90語以内の英語で書きなさい。また，使用語数を算用数字で記入しなさい。ただし，符号は語数に含まないものとする。

2024年度 ▌ 青森県 ▌ 難易度 ■■■■■

【4】Suppose that each student has their own tablet PC in English classes. What is the benefit to use tablet PCs in English classes in order to encourage students to use English? Write your opinion in about 130 words.

2024年度 ▌ 名古屋市 ▌ 難易度 ■■■■

【5】次の英文を読んで，以下の問いに120語程度の英語で答えなさい。

Imagine this situation. Your friend is trying to decide whether to become an English teacher or do something else for their career. You must encourage them to become an English teacher. Write a persuasive essay in which you explain to your friend the most important reason why they should become an English teacher, including supporting details, as well as specific examples.

▌2024年度 ▌岩手県 ▌難易度 ■■■■■□

【6】次の英文を読んで，指示に従い，解答を記述せよ。

What do you think about plastic pollution in the ocean? Write your answer in English. Your essay should have at least two points that you can do to stop it in our daily life.

▌2024年度 ▌山口県 ▌難易度 ■■■■■□

【7】パフォーマンステストを用いて，生徒の英語で「話すこと(やり取り)」の能力を評価したい。どのようなパフォーマンステストを実施するか。具体的な内容について，あなたの考えを100語程度の英語で書け。

なお，短縮形(I'mやdon'tなど)は1語と数え，符号(,や?など)は語数に含めない。

(例)　No,　I'm　not.【3語】

▌2024年度 ▌和歌山県 ▌難易度 ■■■■■■

【8】Imagine that in your English class, some of your students are reluctant to speak English in language activities. They say, "I don't want to speak English because I don't know how to express what I want to say in English." How would you deal with this situation? Write your opinions or ideas in about seven sentences, including reasons.

▌2024年度 ▌栃木県 ▌難易度 ■■■■■□

● 英文作成

【9】 Imagine that in your English class, some of your students are reluctant to speak English in language activities. They say, "I don't want to speak English because I'm afraid of making mistakes," How would you deal with this situation? Write your opinions or ideas in about seven sentences, including reasons.

| 2024年度 | 栃木県 | 難易度 ■■■□□ |

【10】 外国語の授業において，あなたが「話すこと[やり取り]」，「話すこと[発表]」，「書くこと」のいずれかの言語活動を設定する際，翻訳ソフト等の使用について，どのように指導するか。その言語活動を通して，生徒に身に付けさせたい力を明らかにして，100語程度の英語で書け。

| 2024年度 | 奈良県 | 難易度 ■■■■□ |

解答・解説

【1】 解答例①(agree)：I agree that schools should ban students from using translation applications in English classes for the following two reasons. To begin with, translation apps may discourage students from thinking independently. With these apps, students can easily make sentences without understanding them. So, students might be deprived of the chance to independently express themselves and be creative. In addition, some translation apps can't translate adequately well. Such poor translations only make students more confused.　For these reasons, I think it would be a good idea to ban students from using translation apps in English classes. (94 words)

解答例②(disagree)：I disagree that schools should ban students from using translation applications in English classes. I have two reasons to support this opinion.　Firstly, these apps will make students more motivated. Such apps make it easier for students to express what they want to say. This should encourage them to use English more. Secondly, students can quickly learn

112

various expressions by using those apps. These will make students faster at translating what they want to express. This makes it possible to set aside time to learn even more expressions.　Therefore, I disagree with banning translation apps in English classes. (98 words)

○**解説**○　英語授業における翻訳アプリの使用に関する意見について，2つの理由と併せて80～100語で書くことが求められている。一見すると難しいように思えるかもしれないが，主張，展開そして結論の形で構成が指示されているため，トピックセンテンスから始まる基本的なパラグラフ構成で書けばよい。展開に書く2つの理由から逆算して，賛成または反対のどちらの立場を取るか決めればよく，結論は理由を踏まえて主張を言い換えて表現すれば十分である。

【2】In human communication, it is essential to tell our ideas and feelings in our own words. Although we can communicate through the use of AI technology such as translation apps, I believe that relationships get stronger through communicating with others without AI. This is because real communication consists of not only words but also facial expressions, tones of voice, gestures, etc., which enables us to understand each other better. Therefore, learning foreign languages is still meaningful in the AI era. (80 words)

○**解説**○　採点基準は，①内容・論の展開の適切さ(24点)，②語彙・文法の適切さ(10点)，③分量(6点)となっている。解答例の文意は次の通り。「人間のコミュニケーションでは，自分の考えや感情を自分の言葉で伝えることが不可欠だ。翻訳アプリなどのAI技術を使ってもコミュニケーションはとれるが，AIを介さずに他者とコミュニケーションをとることで人間関係はより強固なものになると思う。なぜなら本当のコミュニケーションは言葉だけでなく，表情や声のトーン，ジェスチャーなどで構成され，それがお互いをより深く理解することを可能にするからだ。したがって，外国語を学ぶことは，AIの時代になっても意味があるのだ」。

【3】解答例1　When my students do speaking activities, many of them are afraid of making mistakes. So first of all, I'd like to create an atmosphere where my students can enjoy speaking. I always say to students, "Enjoy making mistakes," and encourage them to speak a lot. Second, it's important to give students a clear goal. If students feel the goal is necessary, they'll try hard to accomplish it. Finally, to speak on the spot, students have to practice enough through the activities like small talk. (84 words)　　解答例2　My students like talking in pairs, so it's effective for them to do small talk. I will give the students a clear goal when I do this activity. Through small talk, students can input enough expressions and will be able to speak on the spot by degrees. To make small talk more active, I'd like to make an atmosphere where students aren't worried about making mistakes and encourage them to speak a lot. (73 words)

○**解説**○　解答に当たってはparagraph writingを意識して，まずはmain idea を書き，それをsupportするために理由などを2～3つ述べていけば指定語彙数で収まるであろう。解答例では，生徒が失敗を恐れず楽しんで話せる雰囲気づくりに心がけ，明確な目標を与えて，できるだけ多く話させることを挙げている。中学校学習指導要領(第2章　第9節　外国語)，高等学校学習指導要領(第2章　第8節　外国語)の「話すこと[やり取り]」の項を念頭に置いて，自分なりの指導内容が書かれていればよい。生徒たちに，関心のある事柄，日常的な話題，社会的な話題について，基本的な表現を使って，即興で伝え合う，自分の考えや気持ちを整理する，論理的に伝え合うなどの作業を行わせていくという状況を想定できるようにしておくこと。

【4】The benefit to use tablet PCs in English classes is that students can be motivated to use English. Tablet PCs can connect students with people in the world on the Internet. If they have online meetings with native English speakers, they have good opportunities to talk with people in other countries. Even though students have difficulty in talking in English, they will struggle to make themselves understood. Through these experiences, probably they make some mistakes. However, both Japanese students and native English speakers will be eager to know each other and do their best to communicate with each other. In addition, both of them can learn different cultures. Therefore, students can feel excited in using English in the meetings. From the above, tablet PCs motivate students to use English. (129 words)

○**解説**○ 英語の授業において生徒に英語使用を促すためにタブレットを使用するメリットについて，130語程度の英語を書く問題である。生徒に英語使用を促すための具体的な方法としては，解答例にある，オンラインで様々な英語ネイティブと話す機会を設けるということの他にも，「書くこと」の活動において，生徒同士やクラス全体での意見の共有や交流を促すことなども可能であろう。従来，生徒が書いたものを読み合うのはペアやグループで行うことが現実的であったが，タブレット等のICT機器を使うことで，書いたものをクラス全体で共有できるようになった。どのような方法でも，ICT機器を使うことのメリットがわかるように書きたい。なお，130語程度であるということから，解答を作成する際には，パラグラフ構成を意識するとよい。例えば，タブレットを使用する方法をメインアイデアとして，その方法の具体的な内容やメリットを説明するようなパラグラフ構成にすると書きやすいだろう。

【5】 The most important reason you should become an English teacher is that you can change students' lives, making them into global citizens. Firstly, as an English teacher, by creating appropriate classroom settings, you can give students opportunities to develop their communication skills and learn to respect different ideas. Specifically, you can give them opportunities for opinion exchange and other interaction, both inside and outside the classroom. Also, you can help them cultivate a willingness to communicate proactively and autonomously, deepening their understanding of the underlying culture of English. Consequently, students may choose to study or work abroad, or engage in international affairs while working in Japan. Their way of living and thinking will be transformed and globalized, thanks to you. (120 Words)

○**解説**○ 友人に対し，英語の教員になるように勧めるという状況設定である。具体的な根拠や例を含めて，英語の教員を勧める最大の理由を

120語程度で説明する。基本的なパラグラフ構造として，勧める理由をトピックセンテンスとして書き，その根拠を具体的な例を挙げて書き，最後に結論を書くといった構成が書きやすいと思われる。トピックセンテンスとなる理由さえ決まれば，その理由について具体例を挙げつつ丁寧に説明すればよい。

【6】Plastic pollution in the ocean is an urgent and concerning issue that requires collective action. Improper disposal and excessive use of plastic have resulted in severe environmental consequences, endangering marine ecosystems. Here are three impactful actions that we can take to contribute towards stopping plastic pollution in the ocean.

The first step is to reduce the consumption of single-use plastics. Items such as plastic bags, bottles, straws, and packaging contribute significantly to ocean pollution. By carrying reusable bags and water bottles, refusing plastic straws, and choosing products with minimal packaging, we can minimize our reliance on single-use plastics.

Second, proper waste management is crucial to preventing plastic waste from entering the ocean. Recycling plastic whenever possible is essential. By familiarizing ourselves with local recycling guidelines, segregating waste correctly, and promoting responsible waste disposal in our communities, we can help ensure that plastic waste is properly managed and diverted from our oceans.

Finally, participating in beach and waterway cleanups is another effective way to combat plastic pollution. These initiatives help remove existing debris and prevent further harm to marine life. Joining local environmental organizations or community groups that organize cleanups provides an opportunity to directly contribute to preserving ocean health. Additionally, participating in cleanups raises awareness about the consequences of plastic pollution and encourages others to take action.

In conclusion, plastic pollution in the ocean is a pressing concern. By reducing single-use plastics, practicing proper waste management, and participating in cleanups, we can play a significant role in stopping plastic pollution. Each small action adds up, contributing to the protection of marine ecosystems and the preservation of our oceans for future generations. Let us take responsibility and work together to create a future free from plastic pollution.

○**解説**○ 設問の指示に沿って，海洋プラスチック汚染についての意見と，日常生活で汚染を止める方法を2つ記述する必要がある。解答例では5つの段落に分けて，第1段落で喫緊の問題であるという意見を述べ，第2〜4段落でそれぞれ1つずつ合計3つの対応策「プラスチックの消費量を削減する」「適切な廃棄物管理をする」「海辺や水路の清掃に参加する」を述べ，最後の第5段落で全体のまとめという非常に整った構成となっている。

【7】 First, I will tell my students about two goals in the conversation test. One is to give correct information about their school life to their FLT. The other goal is to get information about those in other countries. Then a student will have a conversation with their FLT. The FLT will begin with some questions about their timetable, school rules, or school events so that the student can answer to them based on facts, using easy words. Then, I will check if the student can exchange information with the FLT, if they can use proper vocabulary, and if they have a positive attitude to communicating with others in English. (109 words)

○**解説**○ 「話すこと[やり取り]」の能力評価のためにパフォーマンステストを実施するにあたり，その実施方法や内容を英文100語程度でまとめる問題である。この設問の配点は20点となっており，点数評価の詳細は不明だが，学習指導要領の「話すこと[やり取り]」の内容を意識した内容になっているか，英文として論理的に内容を整理して書いているか，文法的な間違いがないか，という点には注意すべきである。また，テスト内容は「話すこと[やり取り]」であって，プレゼンテーションやスピーチなどの「話すこと[発表]」ではないので誤解しないように注意すること。難しく考える必要はなく，自分が生徒に対して具体的にどのような作業をさせたいか，話題は何か，資料を活用するのか，評価者は誰か，評価のポイントをどこに置くかなどに思いを巡

● 英文作成

らせ，内容のアウトラインをまとめてから英文に仕上げることになる。解答例では，生徒に2つのテスト目標を示し，英語教員(FLT)との対話を行わせて，情報伝達力，語彙力，英語によるコミュニケーションにおける積極性を見ようとしていることが窺われる。英文を書く際には，ディスコースマーカーを十分駆使して分かりやすくまとめることを忘れないように。

【8】(解答例)　Some students are unable to express their thoughts due to a lack of vocabulary and sentence structure. To help students improve their vocabulary or sentences, I would like to repeat a small talk activity. I will choose a topic that is familiar to students and introduce some useful vocabulary and sentences. In pairs, they have their initial small talk about the topic. After the small talk, I will give students different vocabulary, sentences, phrases to convey their thoughts more accurately. Then, they have a second small talk on the same topic in different pairs. By repeating this process, students will be able to express their thoughts better. (7sentences, 107 words)

○**解説**○　解答例では，語彙力や文章力不足のため，自分の考えを表現できない生徒のために，継続的にsmall talk活動を行うことを挙げている。生徒にとって身近なトピックを挙げ，関連する語彙やセンテンスを提示して，ペアでトピックについて話しをさせる。その後，生徒が自分の考えをより正確に伝えられるように，さらに別の語彙やセンテンス，フレーズを挙げ，再び別のペアになって同じトピックについて話す。これを繰り返すことによって，生徒は自分の考えをよりよく表現できるようになると，small talk活動を提案する理由として述べている。

【9】(解答例)　Some students are too concerned about making mistakes in English. To solve this problem, I would like to ask them to complete a simple English task. Telling a foreigner how to get to the nearest station or assisting him in ordering food from a Japanese restaurant menu can be used as the task example. In this task, it is necessary to let students use any vocabularies and sentences freely. Students don't have to focus on using correct English during the task. The primary objective is to give students a successful experience in communicating with and helping foreigners using their English skills. This experience will lead them to have confidence in communicating with others in English. (7 sentences, 115 words)

○**解説**○ 解答例では，外国人に道を教えたり，レストランでの注文を手伝ったりするなどの，日常場面に即した簡単な課題解決型のタスクを生徒に与えている。使用語彙や文は限定せず生徒に自由に発言させ，正しい英語を意識させないようにする。外国人を手助けし，話が伝わった成功体験を与えることで，英語を通してコミュニケーションを取れるという自信につながることを，理由として挙げている。

【10】(解答例) When I design a teaching plan for students presenting their ideas in class, I'll focus on enhancing their self-expression and self-motivation skills. Students, who often fall short of words to express their feelings, will find reliable translation apps equipped with reading-out function so useful that they may gradually improve on their wording, they may internalize new words or phrases by imitating the voice heard from the reading-out tool repeatedly aloud, and eventually they may easily experience a sense of accomplishment in their in-class presentations. If they feel successful in speaking English, they will be proactive in sharing their thoughts about various topics in English.(104 words)

○**解説**○ 「話すこと[やり取り]」，「話すこと[発表]」，「書くこと」のいずれか1つを選び，簡潔にまとめる。翻訳ソフト等の使用，指導の方向性，生徒に身に付けさせたい力にも言及することになるので，具体的なイメージを心に描きながら，やさしい英語で表現することが大切である。指定語数は100語程度であり，具体例を多く盛り込むことができないため，議論を広げずに一点に絞り込んでみよう。解答例では，「話すこと[発表]」の言語活動として，翻訳ソフトの読み上げ機能を活用することを述べている。

英文解釈

要点整理

　英文解釈という形式は，英語を学習する場合の中心をなすものである。つまり，書かれてある英文の内容を正しく理解することである。そのためには，まず英文の構文に対して正しい知識を持つことである。英文の構文の基本知識というのは，主語，述語，目的語，補語という英文の要素をしっかりおさえることだ。主語についていえば，<u>文頭主語</u>，<u>分割主語</u>がある。<u>文頭主語</u>というのは，文頭にある名詞，代名詞，形容詞，不定詞，動名詞，名詞句および名詞節である。主語が長い場合には，述語動詞を見失うことがあるから注意を要する。主語があまり長い場合，形を整えるために<u>分割主語</u>（形式主語，仮主語）を文頭に出し，真主語を後にすることがある。分割主語の述語は，形式主語と真主語の間にくる。

　<u>目的語</u>になるものは，名詞，代名詞，不定詞，動名詞，名詞句，名詞節などである。次に<u>補語</u>には主格補語と目的補語とがある。主格補語は，主語を説明するもの，目的補語は，目的語を説明するものである。たとえば，He is our teacher of English. で teacher ＝ He で，teacher は，主語 He に対して主格補語である。補語になり得るものは，名詞，形容詞，不定詞，名詞句，名詞節である。目的補語は，Don't leave the door *open*. 「ドアを開けておくな」の open で the door ＝ open となり，You will find the dictionary *of great use*. 「その辞書がとても役に立つということがわかるでしょう」では，of great use が目的語である the dictionary を説明している。

　以上，文の要素についてその基本的なことを説明したが，これに修飾語句がつくことによって文は長く複雑になってくる。<u>修飾語句</u>となるものは，形容詞，形容詞句，形容詞節，副詞，副詞句，副詞節である。<u>不定詞</u>は，「to ＋動詞の原形」で，副詞的，形容詞的，名詞的な用法がある。述語動詞の<u>時制</u>（Tense）と<u>態</u>（Voice），つまり能動態（Active Voice）と受動態（Passive Voice），<u>法</u>（Mood），つまり命令法（Imperative Mood），仮定法（Subjunctive Mood）などに注意することが大切である。

▼文の骨格

(a) 文脈の検討は文の骨格を探ることから始まる。

　　英文の骨格は「主語＋述語動詞」であることは前にも述べた。ど
れほど修飾語句で飾られた文でも，またどれほど難語，難句でかた
められた文でも，裸にすれば，主語と述語動詞の2つが残る。だか
ら英文を読む時には，まずその主語をつき止め，次にその主語に対
する述語動詞をさがし出すことである。主語と述語動詞こそ文の核
心であり，文の頭脳と心臓にたとえられる。そしてその他の一切の
語句はこの核心を包む筋肉，または筋肉をおおう皮膚もしくは毛髪
のようなものである。

　　Not for a moment even must the traveller be off his guard. この文を読
み，主語は必ず名詞か名詞相当語句であることに注意して，名詞を
さがし出す。すると，moment と traveller と guard が名詞であるが，
moment は for a moment（一瞬間），guard は off his guard（警戒を離
れて）という句になっている。残っているのは traveller だけで，こ
れがこの文の主語だと見当がつく。

(b) 無生物の主語

　　日本語では主語になるものは大部分が生物で，無生物はきわめて
少ない。ところが英語では，無生物の主語がめずらしくない。
Urgent business called him all the way to San Francisco. は直訳すれば，
「緊急の用事が彼をはるばるサンフランシスコへ呼びよせた」とな
るが，これは自然な日本語ではない。主語を副詞化して「急用のた
め彼ははるばるサンフランシスコへ行った」と訳すと自然な日本語
になる。同様に _This_ enabled him to go there. は「彼はそのために，そ
こへ行くことができた」となる。

(c) どこで区切るか。

a. You have seen _how powerful an agent heat_ is.

b. It is a strange thing _how little people_ know about the sky.

　　上の2つの例文はともに「how＋形容詞＋名詞」の順に語句が並ん
でいるが，aの文では powerful は agent にかかる形容詞で，how
powerful an agent が意味の上で1単位になっている（agent は force の
意味）。bの文では，how little で切れ，little は副詞だから people には

123

かからない。このように文中にある語の働きを見違うと誤解の原因
になる。

(訳) a. 君たちは熱がどんなに強力な力であるかが分かっただろう。
b. 世間の人びとが空についてほとんど知らないということは不思
議なことだ。

また次の例を見よう。a. It matters comparatively little _what a healthy
man_ eats, so long as he does not eat so much.　b. _What a difference_ to
the world Columbus's discovery had made it is impossible to exaggerate.
aの文，bの文ともに「what＋冠詞＋名詞」の順に単語が並んでいる
が，what が動詞の目的になっているのか，あるいは名詞を修飾して
いるのか，その働きによって区切り方がちがってくる。aの文では
what a healthy man eats「健康な人は何を食べるか」，bの文では what
a difference to the world 「世界に対してどんなに大きな相違を」とい
う続きぐあいになる。なお what a difference to the world は，had
made の目的で，had made までの全体が exaggerate の目的で，強調
のために前に出たものである。

(d) その他の例

　She did _all_ the doctors made her do. では all の次に関係代名詞の that
が抜けている。All the doctors の all を形容詞に読むと誤りである。
All buds of necessity must be borne either terminally on the end of a shoot,
or on the sides of the shoot. で all bud of necessity / must ... と読んでは
いけない。of necessity が「必然的に，もちろん」という副詞句にな
ると見抜かねばならない。

124

英文解釈①

【1】次の文章の(①)～(⑩)に最も適する語句を，以下のア～エ
からそれぞれ1つ選び，その記号を書きなさい。

Japan is often in the world news for an unhappy reason: its sinking birthrate. The government, for example, wants to incentivize parenthood by upping its (①) of 420,000 yen on the birth of a child to 500,000 yen. Tokyo's governor, Yuriko Koike, promises the city will give children under 18 living in the capital 5,000 yen per month. Koike said the national baby drought "shakes the very (②) of society". Births were likely to have fallen below 800,000 last year for the first time since 1899.

I have three kids and, in my view, these small handouts are as likely to reverse the baby shortage as whistling into the wind. But it's important from the outset to make one point clear: this is not just Japan. Birthrates in advanced countries are (③) across the planet. Fertility rates average 1.67 in 38 OECD countries — that's well below what statisticians call the "replacement level" — the number of children (about 2.1) needed per woman to keep the population constant.

Japan's fertility rate of 1.3 (2020) is about the same as China, and higher than Taiwan (1.0) or South Korea (0.8). It is not that much lower than the largely Catholic countries Poland (1.4) and Italy (1.3). Surveying Europe's population drop, the Catholic News Agency notes fearfully that the (④) triggered by the covid pandemic has accelerated what it calls the continent's "demographic winter."

A 2020 survey in the Lancet, a prestigious medical journal, predicted a "jaw-dropping" fall in baby numbers with 23 nations — including Spain and Japan — "expected to see their populations (⑤) by 2100."

Pandemic aside, most of this is just progress. As countries modernize and women gain more control over their bodies, birthrates fall. Growing up in Ireland in the 1970s, it wasn't uncommon to see mothers stuck in small homes with eight children or more. The fertility rate there half a century later is 1.6

births per woman. In South Korea, women had four kids on average at the beginning of the 1970s; today they have fewer than their (⑥) in any other country.

Still, it is striking how Japan and South Korea (with China coming up the rear) are on the lowest end of the global baby-making spectrum. One reason, say (⑦), is the strong hold of marriage in those countries. Half or more of all births now occur outside marriage in France, Iceland, Norway and Sweden, says the OECD. The equivalent number in Japan and South Korea is negligible.

In my own discussions with female students, I find many are just not attracted to the prospect of having children with salarymen because the demands of corporate life leave wives at home alone for much of the week. In addition to the struggles of motherhood, there is the cost of raising children. Many women prefer to start their own careers first, which helps postpone marriage entanglements till later in life.

Among countries that have reversed slightly sagging fertility rates over the last decade, the key factor, says the OECD, was more equal sharing of household and parenting duties. Some surveys suggest that when men help out more at home (assuming they can), fertility rates rise.

Yet, what's clear is that this is a complex worldwide issue. Birthrates are often stubbornly resistant to government (⑧). Does anyone believe that throwing a bit of cash at young Japanese will persuade them to magically conjure up millions more babies? In the absence of that, there is another widely adopted way to boost populations: importing people. There is plenty of room for growth here: just 2％ of Japan's population is "foreign" compared to the 10.6％ of OECD countries.

It is not at all clear, however, that Japan will ever take this option. Despite former Prime Minister Shinzo Abe's much ballyhooed plans to bring in hundreds of thousands more foreign workers, the number of foreigners living here has actually fallen in the last few years.

(略)

In the meantime, Tokyo Gov. Koike and other policymakers might

(⑨) whether the obsession with propping up birthrates is not misplaced. We are, after all, in the midst of a climate crisis, where global resources seem stretched to the limit by our 8 billion inhabitants. By most (⑩), we'll add another 3 billion to that before the global population peaks. As science journalist Laura Spinney notes, "it's absurd to say that what's lacking is babies."

Japan may just have to make the best of its declining population.

From : The Mainichi Life in Japan：Will this country produce more babies?

By David McNeill　　February 16, 2023

① ア loan イ grant ウ scholarship
エ reward
② ア theories イ assumptions ウ justifications
エ foundations
③ ア booming イ tumbling ウ landing
エ adapting
④ ア aptitude イ uncertainty ウ elimination
エ assurance
⑤ ア halve イ double ウ divide
エ increase
⑥ ア companions イ colleagues ウ counterparts
エ representatives
⑦ ア psychologists イ sociologists ウ capitalists
エ biologists
⑧ ア influences イ inducements ウ placements
エ pavements
⑨ ア analyze イ disregard ウ overlook
エ ponder
⑩ ア calculations イ numbers ウ calibrations
エ evaluations

| 2024年度 | 青森県 | 難易度 ■■■□□ |

【2】 Read the following passage. Choose the most appropriate number(①～④)

127

to fill in each blank and complete the passage.

IT for Schools in the UK

Coding is on the curriculum for primary and secondary school pupils in the UK. Pupils as young as five learn about algorithms and computational thinking, as well as creating and debugging simple programs of their own, using a variety of tools. But parents are often surprised when their children come home from school and start using technical (1) from the world of computing. In 2013, the UK got kids coding, with changes to the national curriculum. ICT — Information and Communications Technology — was (2) a new "computing" curriculum including coding lessons for children as young as five.

The technology industry has wanted more kids to become familiar with coding for some time. If children can learn to program, in the future this could provide enough qualified people to fill vacant technology jobs. According to Bill Mitchell, education director at BCS, The Chartered Institute for IT, the UK has become the first country in the world where computing is a (3) school subject for all children from the age of five. But he adds, "We currently have, (4), 40 percent of schools able to teach it confidently, so there is a lot of work still to be done there."

Nearly 10 million people currently lack a minimum level of digital skills. The report by the House of Lords Digital Skills Committee warns the UK risks becoming "a branch economy, much less (5) and influential" if it doesn't try to educate children in this area. An expert has warned that 35 percent of jobs in the UK are likely to be automated over the next 20 years. It is important that children learn digital skills in school to prepare for future jobs. Educating children for the next industrial revolution has started in the UK.

(Yubune, E., Nakai, A., Arai, M., Hitomi, K., & Benfield, B. (2022). IT for schools in the UK. *Strategic Reading for Global Information*)

1. ① arms   ② terms   ③ customs
    ④ letters

2. ① alluded to   ② obsessed with   ③ deprived of

④ replaced by

3. ① temporary　② preliminary　③ compulsory

④ hereditary

4. ① in shape　② at best　③ on the blink

④ by far

5. ① prosperous　② indigenous　③ notorious

④ dubious

▎2024年度 ▎沖縄県 ▎難易度 ■■■■■■

【3】次の英文の(　　)内に入れるべき最も適当な英文を1〜5から一つ選び，番号で答えよ。

Do you know how many deaf sign languages there are in the world? Deaf sign languages have several thousand signs, which can be used in sequences to do the same job as the sentences of spoken and written language. And when we see signers on television, they're translating everything they hear into sign language.

There are two important things to remember about deaf sign languages. First, deaf people don't simply take the words from spoken language and translate them into signs: The signs directly express meaning. So if a signer heard me say, "The boy who won the long jump has also won the high jump," we wouldn't see signs for "the," then "boy," then "who," and so on. What we'd see is something like: boy ＋ win ＋ past time ＋ long jump ＋ also ＋ high jump. ___(1)___

The second thing to remember about deaf sign languages is that they're very different from each other. Just as we don't expect someone who speaks only English to understand Chinese, so we mustn't expect someone who knows only British Sign Language to understand Chinese Sign Language. ___(2)___ These two sign languages have gone in different directions over the past 200 years. There are a few similar signs, but they aren't enough to make the languages comprehensible to each other.

___(3)___ What about the sign for "elephant"? Surely that will always have a hand movement showing the distinctive trunk? But actually, there's more than one way in which we can show a trunk. There are obviously many possibilities, even in the case of something as easy to see as an elephant. And when we start to think of such notions as "garden," "blue," or "argue," it's clear that different sign languages will express them in many different ways.

All the important notions that we use in studying spoken and written language are needed in relation to sign language too. For instance, we'll find dialects and accents.　(4)　And if someone from Britain went to China, and started to learn Chinese Sign Language, they would make the Chinese signs but probably not in exactly the Chinese way. For instance, the sign for "father," which involves closing the fingers over the palm of the hand, might be made with fingers very straight and tense, or with the fingers slightly bent and relaxed. A British person would be likely to make it with the fingers relaxed, and that would be noticed by a Chinese deaf person as a foreign accent.

It all adds up to one thing.　(5)　It's as complex, useful, and beautiful as any spoken or written language.

1　You might think that at least some of the signs used by the deaf will be shared by all the sign languages of the world.

2　Never think of deaf signing as if it were simply a set of primitive gestures.

3　Nor, surprising as it seems, does someone who knows only British Sign Language even understand American Sign Language.

4　Nor would the signs need to come out in that particular order.

5　Deaf people from one part of a country will have a few signs that differ from those used in other places.

‖ 2024年度 ‖ 愛知県 ‖ 難易度 ▦▦▦□□ ‖

【4】 Read the passage below and choose the most appropriate answer for each blank.

Young kids' brains are very tuned in to their mothers' voices, science has shown. But as kids morph into teens, everything changes. Teenagers' brains are now more tuned in to strangers' voices than of their own moms', new research shows. "Adolescents have this whole other class of sounds and voices that they need to tune into," explains Daniel Abrams. He's a neuroscientist at Stanford University School of Medicine in California.

The researchers scanned the brains of 7- to 16-year-olds as they listened to things said by their mothers or by unfamiliar women. The words were pure gibberish: teebudieshawlt, keebudieshawlt and peebudieshawlt. Using such [　(1)　] words allowed the scientists to study voices on their own, not what they were saying. As the kids listened, certain parts of their brains became active. This was especially true in brain regions that help us to detect rewards and pay attention.

Abrams and his colleagues already knew that younger kids' brains respond more strongly to their mom's voice than to a stranger's. "In adolescence, we show the exact [　(2)　] of that," Abrams says. For teens, these brain regions respond more to unfamiliar voices than to their mom's. This shift in what voice piques interest most seems to happen between ages 13 and 14. That's when teenagers are in the midst of puberty, a roughly decade-long transition into adulthood.

These areas in the adolescent brain [　(3)　] responding to mom, Abrams says. It's just that unfamiliar voices become more rewarding and worthy of attention. Here's why: As kids grow up, they expand their social connections way beyond their family. So their brains need to begin paying more attention to that wider world.

That's exactly as it should be, Abrams adds. "What we're seeing here is just purely a [　(4)　] of this."

But mothers' voices still have special power, especially in times of stress, one 2011 study in girls showed. Levels of stress hormones dropped when these stressed-out girls heard their moms' voices on the phone. The same wasn't true for texts from the moms.

The brain seems to adapt to new needs that come with adolescence. "As we mature, our survival depends less and less on [　(5)　]," says Leslie Seltzer. She's a biological anthropologist at the University of Wisconsin-Madison. She was part of the team that carried out that 2011 study. Instead, she says, we rely more and more on our peers — friends and others closer to our own age.

So while both teens and their parents may sometimes feel frustrated by missed messages, that's okay, Abrams says. "This is the way the brain is wired, and there's a good reason for it."

(Adapted from *https://www.snexplores.org/article/mom-voice-kid-brain-teen-neuroscience*)

(1) ① nonsense   ② childish
     ③ sophisticated   ④ complicated

(2) ① continuation   ② description
     ③ opposite   ④ limit

(3) ① enjoy   ② avoid
     ③ don't stop   ④ don't keep

(4) ① responsibility   ② reflection
     ③ fantasy   ④ contradiction

(5) ① approval from others   ② care and affection
     ③ general acceptance   ④ maternal support

▌2024年度▐ 千葉県・千葉市 ▌難易度▐

【5】次の空所[(1)]～[(5)]に入る最も適切な文を，ア～キより一つずつ選び，その記号を書きなさい。ただし，同じ記号を複数回用いてはならない。

As artificial intelligence systems play a bigger role in everyday life, they're changing the world of education, too. OpenAI's ChatGPT, Microsoft's Bing and Google's Bard all come with both risks and opportunities. I am a literacy educator and researcher, and here are four ways I believe these kinds of systems can be used to help students learn.

Teachers are taught to identify the learning goals of all students in a class and adapt instruction for the specific needs of individual students. But with 20 or more students in a classroom, fully customized lessons aren't always realistic. Everyone learns differently. An AI system can observe how a student proceeds through an assigned task, how much time they take and whether they are successful. [(1)] This type of real-time feedback is often difficult for an educator or school to do for a single student, let alone an entire class or campus. AI adaptive learning tools have been shown to quickly and dynamically make changes to the learning environment, content, and tasks to help individuals learn more and quickly improve. For instance, researchers at the Human-Computer Interaction Institute at Carnegie Mellon University taught a system how to solve a math problem. The system can follow instructions from a human supervisor to understand mathematical rules and adapt its approach to problems it has never seen before. The system can also identify areas where it had to make multiple attempts before arriving at the correct answer, flag those for teachers as places human students may get confused, and highlight methods the system used to more efficiently arrive at the right answer.

Researchers at Stanford have been developing and testing a prototype of what's called an "intelligent textbook," titled "Inquire." [(2)] The interactive text includes definitions of key words accessible by touch or click and allows students to highlight and annotate while reading. The textbook can also suggest questions about the content and areas for future inquiry that are customized for each individual. It can change the reading level of the text and also include supplemental photos, videos and materials to help students understand what they're studying.

Educational assessment focuses on how an educator knows whether a student is learning what is being taught. Traditional assessments — essays, multiple-choice tests, short-answer questions — are little changed from a century ago. Artificial intelligence has the potential to change that by identifying patterns in learning that may not be apparent to individual teachers or administrators. [(3)] The tests start with a series of standard questions, but based on how the student does with those, the system will select harder or easier questions to more quickly identify a student's exact abilities and weaknesses. Another assessment project, Reach Every Reader, staffed by the Harvard Graduate School of Education, MIT and Florida State University, creates educational games for parents to play with their children while teaching them to read. Some of the games have adults and children role-play as characters based on real-life scenarios. [(4)]

Personalized learning occurs when the students' interests and goals guide learning. The teacher is more of a facilitator, while the what, why and how of learning are mostly dictated by the student. Artificial intelligence systems can provide individualized instruction tailored to each student's individual interests. AI adaptive learning systems can quickly identify when a student is struggling and then provide more or different support to help them succeed. As the student shows that they have mastered the content or skill, the AI tool provides more difficult tasks and materials to further challenge the learner. Chatbots have been used to respond to typed or spoken input. Many individuals interact with a chatbot when they ask Alexa or Siri a question. In education, chatbots with artificial intelligence systems can guide students with personalized, just-in-time feedback or assistance. These chatbots can answer questions about course content or structure. [　(5)　]

Much like an automated playlist of musical or video recommendations, an AI-powered recommender system can generate tailored assessment questions, detect misunderstandings and suggest new areas for a learner to explore. These AI technologies have the potential to help learners today and in the future.

＜選択肢＞

ア　This software would create more opportunities for both teachers and students to cooperate and interact with each other.

イ　For instance, the language-learning company Duolingo uses AI and machine learning to create and score tests of English proficiency for universities, companies and government agencies.

ウ　If students use these books, they will read at a level, which is appropriate for their grade.

エ　If the student is struggling, the system can offer help; if the student is succeeding, the system can present more difficult tasks to keep the activity challenging.

オ　It is an iPad app that monitors students' focus and attention while they read by paying attention to how students interact with the app.

カ　These games can help parents and teachers efficiently determine whether

children are reading at their appropriate grade level and get them on track if
they are not.

キ　This helps students keep track of their own learning while keeping them
motivated and engaged.

┃ 2024年度 ┃ 岩手県 ┃ 難易度 ■■■□□

【6】次の英文の[　　]の中に入る最も適切なものを，以下のそれぞれ問
1〜問5の①〜④のうちから選びなさい。

You can motivate them. You can direct their energies. You can teach them,
lead them, and guide them.

But you can't really control them. You shouldn't try. You shouldn't even
want to.

If you want to control employees, you have to watch them all the time. As
soon as you're not looking, they may rebel and go back to doing things their
way. That requires you to exercise "eternal vigilance" — which is a rotten
way to spend the day and will keep you from doing anything [　1　].

Don't control; coach for results, giving clear directions and defining the
goal. Then trust them.

When you evaluate their job performance and related workplace behaviors,
put your [　2　] to this test:

"Is what they're doing *wrong*, or is it just *different* from the way I'd do it?"

Too many supervisors manage by the "my way or the highway" standard.
They view a different approach as a threat to their [　3　].

You'll waste a lot of time and engender a lot of anger and resentment if you
make people undo and redo things they did competently the first time.

Part of your job as manager/coach is to learn your workers' individual work
styles and [　4　] them to do things their way whenever possible — as long
as they get the results you want, when you want them.

The same goes when you're called on to edit their written work. You must
of course edit for clarity and accuracy. You should help them achieve
concision. But when it comes to idiom and voice — the way an individual
"sounds" on paper — let them be them.

135

Let these three slogans guide you:

If it ain't broke, don't [5] it: This sounds simple, but it's worth keeping in the back of your mind when you're tempted to do something untoward.

If it is broke, let them [5] it: They'll take ownership and be more motivated because of it.

If they can't [5] it, [5] it with them: That's an essential part of leadership and teamwork.

> 本文はMarshall J. Cook : How to Be a Great Coach 24 LESSONS FOR TURNING ON THE PRODUCTIVITY OF EVERY EMPLOYEE (Lesson 11 : Celebrate the differences) 松本茂監訳 すぐれたコーチになる秘訣　社員の能力を引き出す24講座から。一部表記を改めたところがある。

問1　[1]　① respective　② sensitive　③ productive
　　　　　　④ destructive

問2　[2]　① fascinations　② predictions　③ portions
　　　　　　④ perceptions

問3　[3]　① majority　② authority　③ spontaneity
　　　　　　④ hospitality

問4　[4]　① say　② allow　③ wait
　　　　　　④ agree

問5　[5]　① fix　② call　③ support
　　　　　　④ show

┃ 2024年度 ┃ 神奈川県・横浜市・川崎市・相模原市 ┃ 難易度 ┃

【7】次の英文が筋道の通った一つの段落となるようにA～Dを[　　]に並べるとき，順序として最も適切なものを①～⑤の中からそれぞれ一つ選びなさい。

1

There are many researchers with fixed-term contracts at national universities. Of the total, 1,672 were hired under contracts that explicitly placed a 10-year limit on the period of their employment. [　　] Universities and research institutions should make all-out efforts to keep them on their payrolls.

A　Not all of them are facing the immediate risk of losing their jobs.

B　A 10-year limit is also included in the contracts for 317 researchers at research and development institutions.

C　But giving the boot to young researchers would deliver an immeasurable blow to Japanese academic research.

D　While many are believed to be young science researchers, researchers in the social sciences and liberal arts are facing the same fate.

①　B－C－A－D　　②　B－D－A－C　　③　B－D－C－A

④　D－A－B－C　　⑤　D－B－C－A

2

There are different stories about the origin of the iPad. [　　] He was so angry that he decided to make an Apple tablet to show that touch control was better.

A　The man talked for hours and hours about the tablet PC he was making.

B　Jobs thought people should use their fingers, not a stylus.

C　Some people say that Jobs had the idea for it when he went to dinner with a Microsoft engineer.

D　But the Microsoft tablet used a stylus.

①　B－C－A－D　　②　B－C－D－A　　③　C－D－A－B

④　C－A－D－B　　⑤　C－D－B－A

【8】次の問1，問2の書き出しの文に続いて1〜4の英文を，文意が通るように並べ替えなさい。その最も適切な配列を，以下のそれぞれ①〜④のうちから選びなさい。

問1

Few would deny that men and women differ physically: While tall, muscular women abound, men are, on average, taller than women and have much greater grip strength.

1　Increasingly, it seems, it is de rigueur to reject or downplay psychological differences between the sexes—despite substantial scientific evidence that they exist.

2　Men, on average, perform better on tasks in which they mentally rotate an object, while women can better remember the location of objects.

3　But their brains and behavior reflect no significant differences, argue many people, including some psychologists.

4　Women tend to engage in more altruistic behavior and rate higher on certain measures of empathy.

Evolutionary theorists postulate that sex differences arose because male and female hominids faced different reproductive and survival pressures.

※本文は10 Myths About the Mind by Matt Huston, *Psychology Today* (SEPTEMBER/OCTOBER 2019)から。一部表記を改めたところがある。

①　1−3−4−2　　②　4−2−1−3　　③　3−1−4−2
④　2−4−1−3

問2

Bats are known for using high-frequency acoustic signals to deftly snatch flying insects from the air at night, even amid dense forests.

1　By approaching the target along a specific trajectory, the common big-eared bat *Micronycteris microtis* treats the leaf as an acoustic mirror to reflect unwanted echoes away from its angle of attack.

2　But more than 40 percent of insectivorous bat species hunt by plucking prey resting on leaves or other surfaces.

3　Now, however, biologists Inga Geipel of the Smithsonian Tropical Research Institute, Ralph Simon of Free University Amsterdam and their colleagues have shown how some bats detect a still and silent insect on a leaf using echolocation alone.

4　Because the sound waves bats emit reflect off vegetation at all angles, the returning jumble of echoes should render a leaf-bound insect virtually imperceptible — so scientists have long suspected that bats use clues from vision, smells or prey-generated sounds to help find a motionless meal.

This makes the insect's signal stand out, according to a study published in August in *Current Biology*.

※本文はSound Judgment by Rachel Berkowitz, *Scientific American* (December 2019)から。一部表記を改めたところがある。

①　2－3－1－4　　②　1－2－4－3　　③　3－1－2－4
④　2－4－3－1

▌2024年度▌神奈川県・横浜市・川崎市・相模原市▌難易度

【9】次の英文の趣旨を180字以上200字以内の日本語で記せ。ただし，句読点も一語とみなす。

Researchers in the U.K. looked at more than 100,000 participants from studies in Europe to examine the link between the mental stimulation at work and dementia. They measured mental stimulation at work at the start of the study, then followed the participants for an average of nearly 17 years to see if they developed dementia. They defined a mentally stimulating job as one that includes demanding tasks and more decision-making freedom. Some examples of high-stimulation jobs include company executives and senior members of government. A low-stimulation job, in contrast, is not very demanding and lacks control over the work.

The researchers found that dementia was over 50% more likely in the low-stimulation group than in the high stimulation group. They also discovered that there were as many people in the low-stimulation group with dementia at age 78 as there were in the high-stimulation group at age 80. People with mentally stimulating jobs have a lower risk of dementia in old age than people who have non-mentally stimulating work. This supports the idea that mental stimulation as an adult could delay the onset of dementia. This pattern seems to be stronger for Alzheimer's disease than for other types of dementia.

This study's results might be important for policy, the researchers wrote, since they suggest that finding mentally stimulating work for everyone will be important for future brain health.

[出典：「英語ニュースを読める！語れる！技術」 一部改訂]

▌ 2024年度 ▌ 山梨県 ▌ 難易度 ▆▆▆▆▢▢

【10】次の英文を読んで，各問いに答えよ。

How does our body clock work, and how do we use that knowledge to get a baby to sleep through the night? Because of the earth's rotation around itself, which takes twenty-four hours, our (a)_____ clock has evolved to produce a circadian rhythm of approximately twenty-four hours. The length of one cycle is twenty-four hours, and this length is called a period.

What drives our body clock, and what tells us what time it is? Almost fifty years ago, scientists discovered that the clock is (b)governed by a set of genes in our bodies, the so-called clock genes. Working at the California Institute of Technology in the early 1970s, the geneticists Ron Konopka and Seymour Benzer asked the following question: are there genes that are required for certain behaviors that (c)_____? They were able to find an answer using the tiny fruit fly *Drosophila melanogaster* as a model system.

During normal development, fly eggs turn into larvae, which eat a lot and grow. Seven days later, during metamorphosis, each larva makes a little case for itself, called the pupal case. While in the pupal case, the larva transforms into an adult fly. The mature fly then breaks out of the case in a process called eclosion, ten days after the egg was (d)_____. Interestingly, eclosion usually only happens at a certain time of day—in the early morning—probably

$_{(e)}$(their wings / the newborn / the warm / flies / that / during / spread / so / can) day and get accustomed to their new bodies while it's light and warm out.

To find out if there were genes required for the flies' regular morning eclosion time, Konopka and Benzer exposed the flies to a DNA-damaging chemical, or mutagen, thereby randomly $_{(f)}$perturbing the function of individual genes, and then watched to see if this genetic perturbation altered the timing of eclosion. Indeed, a certain mutation rendered the flies' eclosion arrhythmic: $_{(g)}$———— all eclosing in the morning, the mutant flies eclosed at random times of day and night. Furthermore, the researchers found two other mutations that, $_{(h)}$————— rendering the flies arrhythmic, shortened or lengthened the flies' twenty-four-hour eclosion cycles to nineteen hours and twenty-eight hours, respectively.

1 下線部(a), (d)に入れるのに最も適当な組合せを次の(ア)～(エ)から一つ選び, 記号で答えよ。

(ア) (a) external (d) lied
(イ) (a) external (d) laid
(ウ) (a) internal (d) lied
(エ) (a) internal (d) laid

2 下線部(b), (f)の意味に最も近いものを次の(ア)～(エ)からそれぞれ一つ選び, 記号で答えよ。

(b) governed ： (ア) claimed   (イ) expressed
                 (ウ) justified   (エ) controlled
(f) perturbing ： (ア) restoring   (イ) disrupting
                  (ウ) allocating (エ) creating

3 下線部(c)に入れるのに最も適当なものを次の(ア)～(エ)から一つ選び, 記号で答えよ。

(ア) steadily improve the quality of sleep
(イ) are innately displayed at a specific place
(ウ) are directly affected by the amount of sleep
(エ) normally happen only at certain times of the day

4 下線部(e)の語句を全て用いて, 意味が通るように並べ替えよ。

5 下線部(g)と(h)に共通して入れるのに最も適当な語(句)を次の(ア)～
(エ)から一つ選び，記号で答えよ。
(ア) instead of   (イ) in spite of   (ウ) on   (エ) by

2024年度 ┃ 岡山県 ┃ 難易度 ■■■□□

【11】次のA，Bの問いに答えよ。

A 次の英文の①，②に入る最も適当なものの組合せを，以下の1～9
のうちから一つ選べ。

When you have a science question not covered in school, where can you
turn? Check out *Tumble*, a podcast for kids about scientific exploration and
discovery.

Hosted by Marshall Escamilla and Lindsay Patterson, *Tumble* takes
questions directly from kids, then finds scientists to help answer them.
(①), if you're wondering if aliens exist, you can listen to *Tumble* and
hear what an astrobiologist and a zoologist have to say about this
otherworldly matter.

"Growing up, I wasn't interested in science at all, (②) I thought that
everything there was to be known by science was already known,"
Patterson told TIME for Kids. "It was only after I talked to a scientist that I
learned I was totally wrong." She wants to share this sense of curiosity and
wonder with kids. Speak Spanish? Learning the language? You're in luck!
The podcast team also makes *Tumble en Español*.

① ア In addition   イ For example   ウ In short
② ア although   イ of course   ウ because

1 ①：ア   ②：ア   2 ①：ア   ②：イ
3 ①：ア   ②：ウ   4 ①：イ   ②：ア
5 ①：イ   ②：イ   6 ①：イ   ②：ウ
7 ①：ウ   ②：ア   8 ①：ウ   ②：イ
9 ①：ウ   ②：ウ

B 次の英文の [　　] に入る三つの文が，以下のア～ウに示されてい
る。論理的な文章にするために最も適当な配列のものを，あとの1
～6のうちから一つ選べ。

A man named Randy liked to hunt trees. He looked for big trees and old trees. He made maps to show where these trees were. He did not want to cut them down. He wanted people to take care of them.

Randy was told of a very tall tree on Vancouver Island. The tree was said to be 314 feet tall. That would make it the tallest tree in Canada. Randy set out to find the tree.

But someone else found it first. It was found by a logger. Loggers wanted to cut down Canada's tallest tree and all the trees around it.

Randy made a path in the forest so people could see the tall tree. ☐ Canada's tallest tree is still there.

There may still be a bigger tree out there. Maybe you will find it. But there are only a few old forests left in Canada. Many are still at risk of being cut down.

ア More and more people wanted to save that forest.

イ Thanks to these people, that forest is now a park.

ウ The tree was so big and beautiful it would fill them with awe.

1 アーイーウ　　2 アーウーイ　　3 イーアーウ
4 イーウーア　　5 ウーアーイ　　6 ウーイーア

2024年度 ┃ 大分県 ┃ 難易度

【12】次の☐の中に書かれているアメリカのニュース番組CNNで流れた4つのニュースについて，各問いに答えなさい。

(1) 次のニュースの(①)，(②)に入る最も適切な語を，それぞれ以下の(ア)〜(エ)から一つずつ選び，記号で答えなさい。

Japanese Cherry Trees in Washington

Decades before the war, the (①) between the Japanese and American people was demonstrated in mutual gifts of trees. In 1912, Japan sent more than 3,000 cherry trees across the Pacific. The Japanese gift bloomed into an (②) highlight on Washington, D.C.'s Tidal Basin. Every year, in late March and early April, visitors walk through a springtime wonderland of white and pink flowers.

(April 7, 2021)

---

① （ア） difference （イ） argument （ウ） confrontation
（エ） friendship

② （ア） amiable （イ） intense （ウ） annual
（エ） overwhelming

(2) 次の③，④のニュースのタイトルとして最もふさわしいものを，
それぞれ以下の(ア)～(エ)から一つずつ選び，記号で答えなさい。
また，それぞれの下線部を日本語に訳しなさい。

③ Barack Obama's hands may be memorable to some people, but
to eight sheep in England, it's his face that's unforgettable. Scientists
from the University of Cambridge found they could train the animals
to recognize human faces from photos. The sheep were shown
images of specific celebrities, including the former president. Then
the celebrity's face was shown next to an unknown person. It turns
out that the sheep could identify the familiar face about four times
out of five. (November 9, 2017)

③のタイトル
（ア） Barack Obama Identified the Sheep
（イ） Sheep Learn to Recognize Faces
（ウ） Celebrities Purchased Specific Sheep
（エ） Scientists in Cambridge Didn't Forget the Sheep

④ One group of pigeons is taking to the skies to tell Londoners
just how bad their air pollution has gotten. They're called Pigeon Air
Patrol. It's a flock of 10 brave birds, all equipped with tiny, backpack
sensors and assisted by Plume Labs. They've been flying over the
city this week, tracking the toxic air and then tweeting back their
readings. London has some of the world's dirtiest air.
(March 17, 2016)

④のタイトル
（ア） Pigeons Monitor Air Pollution
（イ） Air Pollution is Getting Worse

144

(ウ)　Brave Pigeons Died from Dirty Air

(エ)　Londoners Love Pigeons Flying Over their City

(3)　次のニュースについて下線部⑤は具体的にどうなることを意味しているのか，下線部中のthatの内容を明らかにして日本語で答えなさい。

AI News Anchor Unveiled in China

No, that's not a real person. It's a lifelike example of how artificial intelligence is developing in China. Xinhua News Agency reports that this news caster can work uninterrupted. That means no coffee breaks, no bathroom breaks, no coughing; just constant updates typed into its software. Cheap and efficient? Maybe. Missing a little personality? You bet. But, hey, ⑤that is what's to come.

(November 12, 2018)

| 2024年度 | 鳥取県 | 難易度 ■■■■□ |

【13】次の英文中の空欄(①)～(⑩)に最も適する単語を以下の語群から1つずつ選び，必要であれば適切な形に変えて書きなさい。なお，それぞれの単語は1回だけ使うものとする。

In the beginning of December the year I was thirteen, my father declared bankruptcy. That was the year we all made our Christmas presents. I remember (①) for Christmas with more than the usual anticipation, anxious to know if the muffler I had secretly knit for my father would (②) him and how the bracelet I had designed and made from copper wire would look on Mom. Despite the stress in the household, on Christmas morning the living room was much as always, the familiar decorations out and the coffee table heaped with presents, only wrapped this year in the sporting green section of the newspaper and tied with last year's red ribbon. Among them lay a small velvet box.

Even at thirteen, I knew that such a box was not likely to contain something homemade. I looked at it with suspicion. My father smiled. "It's for you," he told me. "Open it."

Inside were a pair of twenty-four-karat gold earrings. They were exquisite.

I stared at them in silence, bewildered, (③) the weight of my homeliness, my shyness, my hopeless difference from my classmates who easily joked and flirted and laughed. "Aren't you going to try them on?" prompted my father, so I took them into the bathroom, closed the door, and (④) them on my ears. Cautiously I looked into the mirror. My sallow, pimply face and lank hair, oily before it even dried from a shower, looked much as always. The earrings looked absurd.

(⑤) them from my ears, I rushed back into the living room and flung them on the floor. "How could you do this?" I shrieked at my father. "Why are you making fun of me? Take them back. They look stupid. I'm too ugly to wear them. How could you waste all this money?" Then I burst into tears. My father said nothing until I had (⑥) myself out. Then he passed me his clean, folded handkerchief. "I know they don't look right now," he said quietly. "I bought them because someday they will suit you perfectly."

I am truly grateful to have (⑦) my adolescence. At some of its lowest moments, I would get out the box and look at the earrings. My father had spent a hundred dollars he did not have because he believed in the person I was becoming. It was something to hold on to.

Behind my father's gift lay the kind of double vision which is the mark of every healer. He could have told me not to cry, that someday I would be a lovely woman. But that would have belittled my pain and (⑧) my experience, the truth of the moment. What he did was far more powerful. He acknowledged my pain and its appropriateness while backing my process. His belief that change would (⑨), naturally, in the course of things made all the difference. Wholeness was just a matter of time.

"Human being" is more a verb than a noun. Each of us is unfinished, a work in progress. Perhaps it would be most accurate to add the word "yet" to all our assessments of ourselves and each other. Jon has not learned compassion...yet. I have not developed courage...yet. It changes everything. I have seen the "yet" become real even at the very edge of life. If life is process, all judgments are provisional. We can't judge something until it is finished. No one (⑩) won or lost until the race is over.

〔Rachel Naomi Remen, *Kitchen Table Wisdom* より一部抜粋〕

語群

| cry | emerge | feel | have | invalidate | please | put |
| survive | tear | wait |

2024年度 ┃ 群馬県 ┃ 難易度 ■■■■□

【14】次の英文を読んで，(1)，(2)の問いに答えよ。

　The brain is a complex processing hub. It's the control center of your nervous system, the network of nerve (　ア　) that carry messages to and from your body and the brain. A healthy brain tries to make sense of the world around you and the constant information it receives, including sound and music.

　"Sound is an important and (　イ　) force in our lives," explains Northwestern University neuroscientist Dr. Nina Kraus. "The more we exercise our sound processing in the brain, the better the brain becomes at making sense of sound and the world around us. Music does this more than any other sound."

　Music and other sounds enter the ear as sound waves. ▢

　But music affects more than the brain areas that process sound. Using techniques that take pictures of the brain, like fMRI, scientists have found that music affects other brain areas. When music (　ウ　) the brain, it shows up on brain images as flickers of bright light. Studies have shown that music "lights up" brain areas (　エ　) in emotion, memory, and even physical movement.

(1) 本文中の(　ア　)～(　エ　)に入れるのに最も適切な語を次のA～Dから一つずつ選び，その記号を書け。

ア　A　cabins　　B　cavities　　C　cells
　　D　curbs

イ　A　indifferent　B　profound　C　racial
　　D　weary

ウ　A　illustrates　B　integrates　C　stimulates
　　D　translates

　　エ　A　embedded　　　B　entitled　　　C　immersed
　　　　D　involved

(2)　本文中の◻︎◻︎◻︎に入る次の①〜③の英文の順序として最も適切なものを以下のA〜Dから一つ選び，その記号を書け。

①　The electrical signals travel up the auditory nerve to the brain's auditory cortex.

②　These create vibrations on our eardrum that are transformed into electrical signals.

③　This brain area interprets the sound into something we recognize and understand.

A　③→②→①　　　B　③→①→②　　　C　②→①→③
D　①→②→③

‖ 2024年度 ‖ 愛媛県 ‖ 難易度 ■■■■■□

【15】次の英文を読んで，(1)〜(3)の問いに答えよ。

Keeping off weight during the holiday season can be tough. But there are many reasons to maintain a healthy weight all year round. A healthy weight lowers your risk for (　ア　) diseases, like diabetes, heart disease, and certain cancers. It can also help you stay more mobile as you age.

Excess weight comes from taking in more energy, or calories, than your body needs. Some extra energy may be stored as fat. ◻︎◻︎◻︎◻︎

"In the U.S., we all live in an obesity-promoting environment to some degree," says Dr. Susan Yanovski, an expert on obesity and eating disorders. "We are constantly tempted with low-cost, high-calorie foods. And, we're expending a lot less energy than we used to in everyday life. Many jobs are (　イ　), and even household activities like washing dishes take less energy to do now. You throw them in the dishwasher. We have to work hard to (　ウ　)."

(1)　本文中の(　ア　)，(　イ　)に入れるのに最も適切な語を次のA〜Dから一つずつ選び，その記号を書け。

　　ア　A　chronic　　　B　feasible　　　C　noble　　　D　oriental
　　イ　A　awkward　　　B　scarce　　　C　sedentary　　　D　tight

148

(2) 本文中の(ウ)に入れるのに最も適切なものを次のA～Dから一
つ選び，その記号を書け。

A incorporate activity into our everyday life

B strive for simplicity in our everyday life

C manage time effectively in our everyday life

D infuse creativity into our everyday life

(3) 本文中の_____に入る次の①～③の英文の順序として最も適切
なものを以下のA～Dから一つ選び，その記号を書け。

① Certain medications affect weight gain, too.

② These include poor diet, lack of sleep, and not getting enough physical
activity.

③ Many factors influence your risk for weight gain.

A ③→②→①   B ②→③→①   C ①→③→②

D ①→②→③

2024年度 ▌ 愛媛県 ▌ 難易度 ■■■■■□

【16】次の英文を読んで，以下の問い(1)，(2)に答えなさい。

It is so easy to overestimate the importance of one defining moment and
underestimate the value of making small improvements on a daily basis. Too
often, we convince ourselves that massive success requires massive action.
Whether it is losing weight, building a business, writing a book, winning a
championship, or achieving any other goal, we put pressure on ourselves to
make some earth-shattering improvement that everyone will talk about.

Meanwhile, improving by 1 percent isn't particularly notable—sometimes it
isn't even *noticeable*—but it can be far more meaningful, especially in the
long run. The difference a tiny improvement can make over time is
astounding.

Habits are the compound interest of self-improvement. The same way that
money multiplies through compound interest, the effects of your habits
multiply as you repeat them. They seem to make little difference on any given
day and yet the impact they deliver over the months and years can be
enormous. It is only when looking back two, five, or perhaps ten years later

149

that the value of good habits and the cost of bad ones becames strikingly apparent.

This can be a difficult concept to appreciate in daily life. We often dismiss small changes because they don't seem to matter very much in the moment.

Unfortunately, the slow pace of transformation also makes it easy to let a bad habit slide. If you eat an unhealthy meal today, the scale doesn't move much. If you work late tonight and ignore your family, they will forgive you. If you procrastinate and put your project off until tomorrow, there will usually be time to finish it later. A single decision is easy to dismiss.

But when we repeat 1 percent errors, day after day, by replicating poor decisions, duplicating tiny mistakes, and rationalizing little excuses, our small choices compound into toxic results. It's the accumulation of many missteps —a 1 percent decline here and there—that eventually leads to a problem.

The impact created by a change in your habits is similar to the effect of shifting the route of an airplane by just a few degrees. Imagine you are flying from Los Angeles to New York City. If a pilot leaving from LAX adjusts the heading just 3.5 degrees south, you will land in Washington, D.C., instead of New York. Such a small change is barely noticeable at takeoff—the nose of the airplane moves just a few feet—but when magnified across the entire United States, you end up hundreds of miles apart.

Similarly, _____ can guide your life to a very different destination. Making a choice that is 1 percent better or 1 percent worse seems insignificant in the moment, but over the span of moments that make up a lifetime these choices determine the difference between who you are and who you could be. Success is the product of daily habits—not once-in-a-lifetime transformations.

〔James Clear, *Atomic Habits* より一部抜粋〕

(1) 下線部を本文の流れに即して日本語にせよ。

(2) 英文の内容を踏まえて，_____ に入る適当な6語～10語の英語を書け。

▎2024年度 ▎群馬県 ▎難易度 ■■■■■

150

【17】 次の英文を読んで, 以下の(1)～(3)の問いに答えなさい。

What is different about teaching a foreign language to children, in contrast to teaching adults or adolescents? (ア)<u>Some differences are immediately obvious:</u> children are often more enthusiastic and lively as learners. They want to please the teacher rather than their peer group. They will have a go at an activity even when they don't quite understand why or how. However, they also lose interest more quickly and are less able to keep themselves motivated on tasks they find difficult. Children do not find it as easy to use language to talk about language; [イ], they do not have the same access as older learners to metalanguage that teachers can use to explain about grammar or discourse. Children often seem less embarrassed than adults at talking in a new language, and their lack of inhibition seems to help them get a more native-like accent. But these are generalisations which hide the detail of different children, and of the skills involved in teaching them. We need to unpack the generalisations to find out what lies underneath as characteristic of children as language learners. (ウ)<u>We will find that imoortant differences do arise from the linguistic, psychological and social develonment of the learners,</u> and that, as a result, we need to adjust the way we think about the language we teach and the classroom activities we use.

[LYNNE CAMERON, Teaching Languages to Young Learners より 一部抜粋]

(1) 下線部(ア)について, 外国語を学ぶ子どもの特徴は何か, 本文に書かれていることから2つ日本語で書きなさい。

(2) 文中の空欄[イ]に適する語句を, 次のa～dから1つ選んで記号を書きなさい。

a by the way   b in other words   c for example

d even though

(3) 下線部(ウ)を踏まえて, 外国語を教えることについて筆者が必要だと考えていることを日本語で書きなさい。

| 2024年度 | 群馬県 | 難易度 ■■■■■ |

【18】 Questions (1) and (2) are based on the following passage. Choose the most appropriate answer from ① to ⑤.

There are many adventures in the world, and not all of them involve climbing mountains. If you are young, mostly you just need to want to do something remarkable. You also need the courage to try something different.

Travel has always been one of the great adventures. This does not mean getting on a bus with a herd of other tourists and being led by someone waving a flag and shouting through a megaphone.

Instead, to have a real adventure, set out by yourself or with a friend to really explore. This way, you have to struggle to understand everything about a new place, including the language and customs. A real adventure is to hike or bike, following an old path. For example, you could trace the route of China's Grand Canal that once went from Beijing to Hangzhou. Or you could try to find the Fifty-three Stages of the Tokaido, the ancient coastal road connecting the Japanese cities of Kyoto and Edo (modern-day Tokyo).

One way to travel for a longer time and get more involved in another country is to volunteer. Volunteering, especially in poorer countries, can include building homes, helping with medical care and teaching. Other volunteer programs let you dig for dinosaur bones or lost tombs or even cities.

Not every adventure means you have to leave your home. It can be an adventure just to explore new ideas. Cambridge University professor Stephen Hawking is someone who will never climb mountains. He has a disease that affects his muscle control. He uses a wheelchair and speaks using a computer. Hawking's adventures are in what he thinks.

"My goal is simple," he says. "It is complete understanding of the universe, why it is as it is and why it exists at all." Now, that's an adventure!

[based on *Read and Think! A Reading Strategies Course*]

(1)　What is the theme of this passage?

①　A real adventure is climbing a mountain with your friends because you can have a great experience in the nature.

②　A tour by bus is not an adventure because you cannot have dangerous experience with a guide.

③　A real adventure can be exploring new places, cultures, or ideas.

④　Studying at a university is not an adventure because you do not use your muscles.

⑤　Dr. Hawking's goal is to completely understand the universe because he is a Cambridge University professor.

(2)　Which statement is true?

①　Trying what is different from your daily life needs some knowledge to accomplish.

②　Intellectual thinking is a kind of adventure.

③　Reading books requires readers to have enough knowledge.

④　Climbing mountains is the most difficult adventure.

⑤　Walking the Tokaido is completely different from a real adventure.

▮2024年度▮岐阜県▮難易度▮▭▭▭▭▭▭▭▭

【19】次の英文を読み，各問いに答えなさい。

Birds do not have propellers any more than human beings move around on wheels. Wings and ⬚ ア ⬚ are different but fulfill the same flight function; legs and wheels are different but fulfill the same movement function.

Interest in the behavior of computers as information-processing systems has aroused interest in the behavior of the brain itself as an information-processing system. It is probable that without the (　1　) interest there would be much less interest in the possibility of treating the (　2　) in this way. Many useful ideas have originated in the computer field and proved useful in understanding the function of the brain. But there may be very fundamental differences in behavior between computer systems and the brain system. (3) <u>In some ways the dominance of computer ideas may actually lead away from a better understanding of brain function.</u>

Laughter is a fundamental characteristic of the brain system but not of the computer system. And with laughter goes creativity. It will be a sinister day when computers start to laugh, because that will mean they are capable of a lot of other things as well.

It is perfectly possible that a computer could be deliberately programmed to

imitate the functions of the brain system, probably even to the extent of
[イ] and [ウ]. But this would not mean that the two systems were
functioning in a similar manner except on the final level, that is to say the
outcome level. It is quite easy to tell someone to draw a square, but much
more cumbersome to give him the mathematical definition of a square, though
(4) the outcome would be the same. A similarity of outcome does not imply a
similarity of [エ].

(旺文社　1999年度版　全国大学入試問題正解　を参照)

(1) 空欄[ア]～[ウ]に，それぞれ適切な英単語一語を本文中
　　より抜き出して書きなさい。

(2) 空欄(1)，(2)に，computerかbrainのいずれか適当なものを
　　選択して書きなさい。

(3) 下線部(3)を和訳しなさい。

(4) 下線部(4)とは具体的にはどういうことか，日本語で説明しなさい。

(5) 空欄[エ]に適切な英単語一語を書きなさい。

2024年度 ▎ 鳥取県 ▎ 難易度 ▊▊▊▊▊▊

【20】次の文章を読み，以下の設問の答えとして最も適切なものを，選択
肢の中からそれぞれ一つ選びなさい。

　The famous psychologist B.F.Skinner once wrote that all human behavior
can be viewed as being adaptive to either the individual, the gene pool, or to
society at large. However, these three forces are often at odds, causing
significant [A]. The rules made by society are a huge presence in our
lives, created by the government, religious groups, our employers, our
schools, our neighbors, and our families. Because these social groups craft the
explicit rules around us, we often find ourselves in situations where we are
driven to break them to satisfy our personal desires or the drives of our
species. These social rules and norms are designed to make the world around
us more organized and predictable, and to prevent us from hurting one
another.

　But when is a rule really just a suggestion? And when do suggestions
morph into rules? Every day, physical signs tell all of us what to do, written

instructions direct us how to behave, and social guidelines urge us to act within specific parameters. In fact, we also make lots of rules for ourselves, in large part encouraged by others. These rules become woven into our individual fabric as we go through life. We draw <u>imaginary lines</u> around what we think we can do — lines that often limit us much more than the rules imposed by society at large. We define ourselves by our professions, our income, where we live, the car we drive, our education, and even by our horoscope. Each definition locks us into specific | B | about who we are and what we can do. I'm reminded of a famous line from the movie *My Dinner with Andre*, that states that New Yorkers "are both guards and prisoners and as a result they no longer have...the capacity to leave the prison they have made, or even see it as a prison." We always make our own prisons, with rules that we each create for ourselves, locking us into specific roles and out of an endless array of possibilities. What if you challenge the underlying assumptions? What are the consequences — good and bad — of getting off the prescribed path? What happens to those who break the rules?

(出典：『*What I Wish I Knew When I Was 20: A Crash Course on Making Your Place in the World*』)

1　Choose the best word to put in | A | .
　① theories　② thrills　③ symbols　④ tension
　⑤ trails

2　Choose the best word to put in | B | .
　① archives　② cities　③ nationalities　④ horoscopes
　⑤ assumptions

3　Which of the following is the closest in meaning to the underlined part?
　① Unbounded lines that enhance people's potential.
　② Visible lines that limit people's potential.
　③ Unbounded lines to make society comfortable.
　④ Lines to make society better.
　⑤ Invisible lines that limit people's potential.

4　Which one of the following statements is true based on the passage?
　① The only rule is that we are limited by our energy and tradition.

② We make lots of rules for ourselves so we cannot predict what happens next.

③ Without social rules and norms we might hurt one another.

④ People describe themselves by their horoscopes, but not by their education.

⑤ Three elements -the individual, the gene pool and society at large- make education.

▌ 2024年度 ▌ 三重県 ▌ 難易度 ■■■■■

解答・解説

【1】① イ ② エ ③ イ ④ イ ⑤ ア ⑥ ウ ⑦ イ ⑧ イ ⑨ エ ⑩ ア

○**解説**○ ① 出生率を上げるために子育てを奨励する「助成金」を増やすということなのでgrantが適切。 ② 出生率の低下は社会の「基盤」を揺るがす事態なので foundationsが適切。 ③ 世界の先進諸国では出生率が「転落している」ということなのでtumblingが適切。

④ fearfully という副詞からCatholic News Agency はヨーロッパの人口減少に危機感を抱いていることが分かる。その危機感とは，コロナ感染症の流行により将来への不安から出産を控えてしまう気持ちが払拭されずに根深く残ってしまうことへの危機感に他ならない。その将来への不安を，これから何が起こるのか全く予見できないuncertainty「不確実性」という言葉で表現できる。 ⑤ a "jaw-dropping" fall という表現から，極端に人口が減るということを考える。halve「半分になる」。 ⑥「韓国の女性は，現在では，他のいかなる国の女性たちよりも子供の数が少なくなっている」という意味からcounterparts を選ぶ。 ⑦ ここで述べられているような，様々な国における出産と結婚の関係を研究対象とする学問は社会学の範疇と考えられるので，sociologist「社会学者」が適当。心理面や生物学的なことには触れていない。 ⑧ 空所の後で「日本の若者に現金を投げつけてやれば，魔法でもあ

るかのように若者たちは何百万人もの赤ん坊を作り出すなんて誰が信じるのであろうか」と述べているところから，政府の子育て支援助成金により出生率を上げる政策には懐疑的である。政府による推進策は出生率向上には効果がないということで inducements「誘因，誘導」を選択。　⑨　「出生率を上げることにばかり執着するのは見当違いになっていないか，深く検討するようになるかもしれない」。ponder「熟考する」。　⑩　空所前に「世界人口が80億人」いることを述べ，空所後に「ピークに達するまでにさらに30億人が追加される」と述べているので，By calculations「計算(推定)によると」が適切。

【2】1　②　　2　④　　3　③　　4　②　　5　①
〇解説〇　1　「しかし子どもたちが学校から帰ってきて，コンピューティングの世界の専門用語を使い始めると，親たちはしばしば驚く」。technical term「専門用語」。　2　「ICTは，わずか5歳の子ども向けのコーディング・レッスンを含む新しい『コンピューティング』カリキュラムに取って代わった」。be replaced by～「～に置き換わる」。3　「BCS(公認IT協会)の教育ディレクターであるBill Mitchellによると，英国は，5歳からすべての子どもたちにコンピューティングを必修科目とした世界初の国である」。compulsory school subject「必修科目」。4　「しかし『現在，自信を持って教えることができる学校はせいぜい40パーセントなので，そこにはまだやるべきことがたくさんある』と彼は付け加えている」。at best「最高でも，よくても」。　5　「貴族院デジタルスキル委員会の報告書は，もし英国がこの分野の教育を子どもたちに施さなければ，『繁栄と影響力が大幅に低下したブランチ・エコノミー』になる危険性があると警告している」。prosperous「繁栄している」。

【3】(1)　4　　(2)　3　　(3)　1　　(4)　5　　(5)　2
〇解説〇　(1)　空欄の直前の文に着目すると，The boy who won the long jump has also won the high jump,の文が手話だとboy＋win＋past time＋long jump＋also＋high jumpのように表現されると述べられており，語を省略してもよいことがわかる。これに続く文としては，「さらに，

語順も文法通りの語順にしなくてよい」という4が適切。 (2) 空欄の前後に着目すると，空欄の前にはイギリスの手話を知っている人が中国の手話を知っていると考えてはいけないと述べられており，空欄の後にはこれらの2つの手話は200年以上前に異なる方向に進んだと述べられている。従って，これらの間に入る文章としては，「イギリスの手話しか知らない人は，アメリカの手話さえ理解できない」という3が適切。(3) 空欄の後の3文に着目すると，手話で象を示す場合，特徴的な象の鼻を示すにしても，その示し方が1つだけではないと述べられている。従って，「少なくとも世界中の手話の間に共通するものがあるのではないかと考えるかもしれない」という1が適切。

(4) 空欄の直前に着目すると，言語における方言や訛りのようなものが手話にもあることが述べられている。従って，「ある国のある地域出身の聴覚障害者には，別の地域とは異なる手話がいくつかある」という5が適切。 (5) 空欄の直後に着目すると，手話は他の話し言葉や書き言葉と同じように複雑で，有用で，そして美しいと述べられている。従って，「手話を単なる原始的なジェスチャーのように考えてはいけない」という2が適切。

【4】(1) ① (2) ③ (3) ③ (4) ② (5) ④

○**解説**○ (1) 空欄の直前の文に着目すると，それらの言葉はまさにちんぷんかんぷんであると書かれており，具体的な単語の例も述べられている。従って，「意味が分からない」を意味する①が正解。 (2) 空欄の直前と直後の文に着目すると，幼い子どもの脳は見知らぬ人の声よりも母親の声により強く反応するが，十代の脳は母親の声よりも見知らぬ人の声により強く反応すると述べられており，前後で「正反対」のことが述べられていることが分かる。 (3) 本パラグラフでは，十代の子どもが母親より見知らぬ人の声に反応するようになる理由を述べている。よって，冒頭の文としては，「(前のパラグラフで，母親の声より見知らぬ人の声に注意を払うと述べたけれど，そうであっても) 十代の脳は，母親の声に対して反応することを『止めない』」となるのが適切。なお，空欄の文に続くIt's just that～の文は，相手が多分思っているであろうことを，「そうではなくて～である」と，理由を説

明するときに使う。　(4)　空欄を含んだ文の前にある1〜2文に着目すると，(成長過程にある十代の)子どもの脳は広い世界に注意を払う必要があり，他人の声に着目するようになっていくのはその現象を「反映」したものであるということである。　(5)　空欄の直前にある文に着目すると，脳は思春期の新たなニーズに適応していると述べられており，「母親からの支援」に依存しなくなっていくという意味になる④が正解。

【5】(1)　エ　　(2)　オ　　(3)　イ　　(4)　カ　　(5)　キ

○解説○ (1)　空欄の前後に着目する。空欄前では，与えられた課題について生徒がどのように，どのくらい時間をかけ，そしてできているかをAIは観察することができると述べられている。また，空欄後では，このようなリアルタイムなフィードバックは難しいと述べられていることから，「もし生徒が苦戦していればシステムが助けることができ，一方で，生徒がうまくいっていれば，システムがもっと難しい課題を課すことで，挑戦的な活動を続けさせることができる」を意味するエが正解。　(2)　空欄の前後に着目する。空欄前では，スタンフォード大学の研究者が，Inquireと名付けたいわゆるインテリジェント・テキストブック(学習者の質問に答える機能を備えたデジタル教科書)の原型を開発し，テストを行っていることが述べられている。また，空欄後では，その双方向的なテキストはタッチやクリックでキーワードの意味が表示され，生徒は読解の間にマーカーを引いたり注記を書いたりできると述べられている。従って，「それ(Inquire)は，生徒がどのように双方向的にやりとりしているかに注意することで，生徒の読解中の集中や注意を観察することができるiPad用のアプリである」を意味するオが正解である。　(3)　空欄の直後に着目すると，そのテストは一連の標準的な問題から開始されるが，生徒がどのように問題に解答したかに基づいて，生徒の正確な能力や弱みをすぐに特定し，より難しい問題や簡単な問題を選択すると述べられており，あるテストの具体的な内容について述べられている。従って，「例えば，Duolingoという言語学習の会社は，AIと機械学習を用いて，大学，企業そして政府機関向けの英語熟達度テストの作成と採点を行っている」を意味する

イが正解。　(4)　空欄の直前に着目すると，ゲームの中には，大人と子どもが現実のシナリオに基づいたキャラクターとしてロールプレイをするものもあると述べられており，このゲームについての説明として，「これらのゲームは，子どもたちが適切な学年のレベルで読解ができるかどうかを効率的に判断し，できていない場合は，親や教師がそれを改善させるのを支援する」を意味するカが正解である。

(5)　空欄の直前に着目すると，これらのチャットボットは科目の内容や構成に関する質問に答えることができると述べられており，このチャットボットについての説明が続くことが予想できる。従って，「このことは，学生たちがモチベーションや意欲を維持したまま，自身の学習状況を把握することに役立つ」を意味するキが正解である

【6】問1　③　　問2　④　　問3　②　　問4　②　　問5　①
○**解説**○　問1　第3段落では，従業員をコントロールしようとする場合のデメリットが述べられている。従業員を常に警戒していなければならないので，「それは一日を腐ったように過ごすことであり，あなたは『生産的な』ことができなくなる」。　問2　「彼らの仕事ぶりや関連する職場での行動を評価するとき，あなたの『ものの見方』を試してみてください」となる。　問3　空所の前で，「多くの上司が我流か常道かという基準で管理しすぎている」と述べているので，「彼らは異なるアプローチを自分の『権威』を脅かすものとみなす」とするのが適切。　問4　マネジャー，コーチの仕事のひとつとして従業員の個々のワークスタイルを学ぶことを挙げているので，「可能な限り彼らのやり方を『認める』」となる。allow O to～「Oが～するのを許す」。問5　参考にすべき3つのスローガンに共通する語を選択する。fix「直す」，call it「切り上げる」，support「支持する」，show「見せる，示す」。1つ目は「問題がないなら，『直す』な」。2つ目は「問題があるなら，『直さ』せなさい」。3つ目は「もし彼らが『直せ』ないなら，一緒に『直そ』う」となる。

【7】1　②　　2　④
○**解説**○　与えられた英文を論理的に並べる問題だが，まず選択肢に手掛

160

かりがある場合があるのでよく観察しておこう。 1 大学や研究機関での有期契約研究者の継続雇用について記述されている。選択肢を見ると，最初に来るのがBかD，最後の英文がAかC (Dの可能性もある)と念頭に入れておこう。空欄の前に雇用期間10年ルールについて言及しており，英文Bでは「雇用契約10年ルールは(国立大学だけでなく)研究機関でも同じように〜」と対比的に述べられているので，英文Bが1番目。英文Aと英文Cで，Not〜But…の対比表現に注目し，「失業という差し迫ったリスクに直面しているわけではないが，若手研究者を解雇すると日本の学術研究に計り知れない打撃を与える」となるので，Aの後にCが来ると考える。B→A→Cの順番を含むのは選択肢②。最後に英文Dの意味を確認する。「科学分野の研究者だけでなく社会科学や人文科学での研究者も同じ運命に直面している」とあり，ここの「同じ運命」で，10年ルールの雇用契約はどの分野の研究者にも当てはまり，現状差し迫った失業の危険はなくても10年経過後の契約期間満了時に解雇される危機感を示唆していると考えれば，選択肢②で論理的に問題ない。なお，Cのgive〜the bootは「〜を解雇する」。bootは「ブーツ→蹴り→解雇」というイメージ連想で覚えられるだろう。

2 同じように選択肢を観察し，1番目はBかCであると予測する。まず，冒頭でiPad製造の背景には様々な逸話がある(There are different stories 〜)と始まり，その逸話の中でもJobsがiPadの構想を思いついたのはMicrosoft の技術者と食事に行った時だったと言われている(Some people say〜)と続くのは，逸話を紹介する冒頭上で自然な文体である。CのitはiPadを指すと考え，1番目の英文とする。次に，その食事の時に何が起きたかというと，Jobsが自分で考えているタブレットについて熱く語ったのであり，ここまでが状況説明となりC→Aとなる。この後にさらに具体的な内容であるDとBに進み，JobsとMicrosoftとの構想上の違いが明らかになり，JobsはMicrosoftが採用しているスタイラスペンより指先タッチのほうがよいことを示すために，アップルタブレットの製造に踏み切った，という結論に至る。冒頭部の逸話の紹介，状況説明，そして具体的な内容という文体の流れを読み取り，選択肢④を選ぶ。

● 英文解釈

【8】問1 ③ 問2 ④

○**解説**○ 選択肢が限られているので，書き出しに続くものは何か等を考えるだけでも正解にたどり着くことができる。 問1「男女の身体的差異を否定する人はほとんどいない」という書き出しから，3「脳や行動には著しい差異がないと心理学者を含め多くの人が論じている」→1「男女間の心理学的な違いがあるという科学的な証拠があるにもかかわらず，それらを否定したり軽視したりすることがますます一般的になっているようだ」→4「女性はより利他的な行動をとる傾向があり，特定の共感性の尺度でより高い評価を得ている」→2「概して男性は対象物を頭で理解しながら動かす作業が得意で，女性は位置を記憶するのが得意である」→「男性と女性は様々な生殖や生存のプレッシャーに直面したので，性差が生じたと進化論者は仮定している」に続く。 問2「コウモリは，深い森の中でも，夜空中を飛んでいる虫を巧みにとるため高周波の音のシグナルを使うことで知られている」という書き出しから，2「しかし，食虫のコウモリ種の40パーセント以上が葉や他の表面で休んでいる獲物を仕留める」→4「コウモリが発する音波はあらゆる角度で草木に反射するので，エコーが交錯して，木の葉に覆われた昆虫を実際知覚できないはず，そこで科学者たちはコウモリは視覚，におい，獲物が発する音からの手がかりを使うと思っていた」→3「しかし今では生物学者たちが，コウモリがエコーロケーションだけを使って，いかに葉の上で静かに動かないでいる虫を見つけるのか示している」→1「特別な軌道で対象物に近づくことにより，一般的なオオミミコウモリ(*Micronycteris microtis*)は不要なエコーを反射して攻撃角度から遠ざけるため，葉を音響ミラーとする」→「これが虫のシグナルを際立たせる」に続く。

【9】イギリスの研究者は，仕事での精神的刺激と認知症の関連比を調査した。精神的に刺激のある仕事を，多くのことが要求され自由裁量が大きい仕事と定義付けた。そのような仕事をする人は，そうでない人より高齢期に認知症のリスクが低くなることを発見した。これは，成人としての精神的刺激が認知症の発症を遅らせ得ることを裏付けている。脳の健康には，すべての人にこのような仕事を見つけることが政

162

策的に重要かもしれない。(197字)

○**解説**○ 英文を180以上200字以内の日本文に要約する問題。公式の解答用紙には，文字数カウント入りのマス目が設けられている。例示や重複する内容を省きながら，イギリスの研究者の研究内容と結果を中心にまとめる。例えば，冒頭の文では，Researchers in the U.K.「英国の研究者」，the link between the mental stimulation at work and dementia「仕事での精神的刺激と認知症との関連」を残す。解答例では，第1段落の3文目 They defined a mentally stimulating job as one that includes demanding tasks and more decision-making freedom.，第2段落の3・4文目 People with mentally stimulating jobs have a lower risk of dementia in old age than people who have non-mentally stimulating work. This supports the idea that mental stimulation as an adult could delay the onset of dementia.，最終段落の This study's results might be important for policy…since they suggest that finding mentally stimulating work for everyone will be important for future brain health. を抜き出しまとめている。

【10】 1 （エ）　　2 （b）（エ）　（f）（イ）　　3 （エ）　　4 so that the newborn flies can spread their wings during the warm　　5 （ア）

○**解説**○ 1 (a) internal clock「体内時計」 (d) lay an egg「卵を産む」。laidは過去分詞。 2 (b) 下線部を含む文意は「約50年前，科学者たちは体内時計が体内の遺伝子，いわゆる時計遺伝子によって制御されていることを発見した」。governedはcontrolledと同意。 (f) 下線部を含む文意は「KonopkaとBenzerは，ハエが決まった朝の羽化時間を迎えるのに必要な遺伝子があるかどうかを調べるため，DNAを損傷する化学物質，すなわち変異原にハエを曝露し，個々の遺伝子の機能をランダムに撹乱した」。perturbingはdisruptingと同意。 3 Ron KonopkaとSeymour Benzerが投げかけた疑問を完成させる。「通常1日のうち特定の時間帯にのみ起こる特定の行動に，必要な遺伝子はあるのだろうか」。次の段落で，その実験について触れ，ハエの羽化が早朝にしか起こらないことが書かれている。 4 so that S can～「Sが～できるように」，the newborn flies「生まれたばかりのハエ」，spread their wings「羽を広げる」，during the warm day「暖かい日中に」。 5 遺伝子変異

が羽化のタイミングを変えるかどうかの実験について述べている部分。　(g)「すべてのハエが朝に羽化するのではなく，変異したハエは昼と夜の不規則な時間に羽化したのである」。　(h)「さらに研究者たちは，不規則な時間に羽化する代わりに，ハエの24時間の羽化サイクルをそれぞれ19時間に短縮または28時間に延長する2匹の変異体を発見した」。共通してinstead ofが入る。

【11】A　6　　B　5

○**解説**○　論理の展開が把握できているか問われているので，ディスコースマーカーやキーワードの出現順序を手掛かりにして考える。A　学校では教わらない科学上の疑問に対する回答を得るのに子ども向けポッドキャストの "Tumble" を紹介している。空欄①を含む第2段落では，空欄①の前にこの番組の司会者と進行方法が説明されており，空欄①の後にその具体例が述べられている。In additionは情報追加，For exampleは例示，In shortは要約を表すので，ここではFor exampleを選ぶ。空欄②を含む第3段落では，司会者のPatterson女史が科学に対する個人的な思いを述べている。「子どものころ科学には関心がなかった」→空欄②→「科学によって解明されるべきものはすべて知り尽くされていると思った」→「科学者と話してみて初めて自分の考えが間違っていることに気づいた」という流れでは，空欄②は理由を表すbecauseが正答。everything there was to be known by scienceは，後続するwas already knownの主語である。構造はeverything (関係代名詞that) there was / to(形容詞的用法) be known by scienceと考え，「科学によって知られるべきものはすべて」。everything (that) there is to see「見るべきものはすべて」という表現を覚えておくとよい。強調構文とonly afterの組合せで，It is only after～that S＋V…「～して初めて…」。他にIt is not until～that S＋V…, It is only when～that S＋V…なども確認しておこう。　B　樹木愛好家Randy氏は，古木や高木の伐採は望まずに保護したがっていることを念頭に置いて，問題を考える。第3段落では古木や高木を伐採してしまう業者の存在に触れ，それに対抗すべくRandy氏が考え実現したことは，「一般の人々が高木を見ることができるように森林歩道を作った」→ウ「(その理由として)そのような木の凄さ

に人々は畏怖の念を抱くだろう」→ア「(そうすれば人々が関心を持ち始め、結果として)その木の植わっている森林の保存を望む人々が増えた」→イ「そのような人々のおかげで現在ではその森林が公園化された」→「カナダで一番高い木がその公園で今でも保護されている」の順番となる。優しい語彙で述べられている分、行間の意味に注意して論旨を汲み取ること。

【12】(1) ① (エ) ② (ウ) (2) ③ タイトル…(イ) 訳…羊は約8割(5回中4回くらい)の割合で見覚えのある顔を認識することがわかった。 ④ タイトル…(ア) 訳…ハトたちは今週ロンドン上空を飛び回り、大気中の有害物質を記録し、その結果をツイッター上に送っている。 (3) 人間の仕事が人工知能技術(AI)に取って代わられる時代が来るということ。

○解説○ (1) 「戦前の数十年間は、日米両国民の友好関係が樹木の贈り合いで示されていた」。「日本からの贈り物は咲き誇り、ワシントンD.C.のタイダルベイスンで例年のハイライトとなった」。
(2) ③ 2文目および5文目より、タイトルは「羊は顔を認識するようになる」が適切。It turns out〜「〜と判明する」。four times out of five「5回中4回」。 ④ 1文目および4文目より、タイトルは「ハトが大気汚染を監視する」が適切。track the toxic air「有毒な大気を追跡する」。tweet back「ツイートを返す」。readings「読取り値」。 (3) that is what's to come.「それがこれから起きることである」。AIニュース・キャスターを例に、人間の仕事がAIに取って代わられることを指している。

【13】① waiting ② please ③ feeling ④ put
⑤ Tearing ⑥ cried ⑦ survived ⑧ invalidated
⑨ emerge ⑩ has
○解説○ ①「私は…いつも以上に期待してクリスマスを待ったことを覚えている」。remember〜ing「〜したことを覚えている」。 ②「父のために私がこっそり編んだマフラーは彼を喜ばせるだろうか…」。please〜「〜を喜ばせる」。 ③「私は当惑し、自分の内気さ、簡単に

冗談を言ってはしゃぎ笑うクラスメートたちとの絶望的な差をずっしりと感じながら無言でそれらを見つめた」。feeling〜「〜を感じながら」。
④ 「…それらを耳につけた」。put〜on「〜を身につける」。
⑤ 「それらを耳から取って…」。tear〜from…「〜を…からもぎ取る」。
⑥ 「私が泣き止むまで父は何も言わなかった」。cry oneself out「泣き止む」。　⑦ 「青春時代を生き抜いてこられたことに心から感謝している」。survive〜「〜を乗り越える」。　⑧ 「しかし、それは私の痛みを軽視し、私の経験、その瞬間の真実さえ無にすることになるだろう」。invalidate〜「〜を無効にする」。　⑨ 「物事の成り行きの中で自然に変化が現れるという彼の信念が全てを変えた」。emerge「姿を現す」。
⑩ 「レースが終わるまで、勝ち負けは分からない」。No one has won or lost until the race is over.「レースが終わるまでは、誰も勝ったとも負けたとも言えない」。

【14】(1)　ア　C　　イ　B　　ウ　C　　エ　D　　(2)　C
○**解説**○ (1)　ア　A　cabins「客室」, B　cavities「空洞」, C　cells「細胞」, D　curbs「縁石」より文意に合うのはCとなる。nerve cellsで「神経細胞」の意味。　イ　空所を含む文は「音は私たちの生活の中で重要で(　　)な力である」という意味である。選択肢でプラスの意味を持つ単語はBのprofound「奥深い」のみである。　ウ　主語がmusicで目的語がthe brainとなる文で適切な動詞はCのstimulatesしかなく、「音楽は脳を刺激する」という意味になる。　エ　involved in〜で「〜に関与している、関わる」の意味で、「感情、記憶、身体の動作に関わる脳の領域」となる。　(2)　それぞれの文の指示語に着目する。②のTheseを指す語は①や③にはなく空所直前のsound wavesしかないことがわかる。よって②が最初に来る。そして、②の文末のelectrical signalsを①の冒頭のThe electrical signalsで受けているため、①が続く。さらに、①の文末のbrain's auditory cortex(大脳聴覚野)を、③の冒頭のThis brain areaで受けいるため、最後に③が来る。よってCが正解となる。

【15】(1)　ア　A　　イ　C　　(2)　A　　(3)　A

○**解説**○　(1)　ア　chronic diseaseで「慢性的な疾患」の意味。　イ　空所前文we're expending a lot less energy than we used to in everyday life.よりsedentary「座って行う，デスクワークの」が適切。　(2)　(1)のイとも関連するが，毎日の生活でより少ないエネルギーしか使わなくなっていると空所を含む段落では述べられている。We have to work hard to incorporate activity into our everyday life.「運動を日常生活に組み込むために一生懸命取り組む必要がある」のみが当てはまる。それ以外の選択肢ではBのsimplicity，Cのmanage time effectively，Dのinfuse creativityなど本文の内容に当てはまらない語句があり不適切だと判断できる。　(3)　それぞれの文の指示語や副詞に着目する。②のTheseを指す語は③のMany factorsしかないため，まず，③→②の順になる。体重増加には様々な要因があることを③で述べ，その要因の具体例を次の②で挙げ，②の追加情報として，①ではそのほか薬剤による体重増加を挙げている。よって，③→②→①であることが確認できる。

【16】(1)　2年，5年，あるいは10年後に振り返ってはじめて，良い習慣による利益と悪い習慣による損失がはっきりと目に見えてくる。

(2)　a slight change in your daily habits

○**解説**○　(1)　「習慣は自己改善の複利である。お金が複利で増えていくのと同じように，習慣の影響も繰り返せば繰り返すほど増えていく。習慣はその日一日ではほとんど変わらないように見えるが，数カ月，数年と続けていくうちに莫大な影響を与えるようになる」に続く文。It～thatの強調構文になっている。　(2)　第6段落以降，最終段落までは「小さなミスの積み重ねがやがて大きなことを引き起こす」という内容が例を示しながら繰り返し述べられている。解答例は「日々の習慣を少し変えること」を空所に入れて「人生をまったく違う目的地へと導くことができる」の主語としている。最終段落は「成功とは日々の習慣の産物であり，一生に一度の変革ではない」で締めくくられている。

【17】(1)　・子どもたちの方が学習者として，熱心で活発であること　・友達よりも先生を喜ばせたがること　　・たとえ活動の意味ややり方をよく理解していなくても，活動に取り組むことができること　・すぐに興味ややる気を失うこと　　・教師が説明する文法や語法について大人と同じようには理解できないこと　　・恥ずかしがらずに言葉を使うことができること　から2つ　(2)　b　(3)　教師が教える言語や教室で使用する活動に関する考え方を調整すること

○**解説**○ (1)　下線部の文意は「いくつかの違いは一目瞭然である」。外国語を学ぶ子どもの特徴は，下線部以降に数文にわたり書かれているので，そのうちの2つを訳出する。　(2)　空所前の文意は「子どもたちは，言語について話すための言語を使うことをそれほど簡単だとは思わない」。「言語について話すための言語」のことを空所後に「メタ言語」と言い換えられる。よってin other words「つまり，言い換えると」が入る。　(3)　下線部の文意は「私たちは学習者の言語的，心理的，社会的発達から重要な違いが生じることがわかるだろう」。直後のas a result, 以降を訳出する。

【18】(1)　③　　(2)　②

○**解説**○ (1)　第1段落をはじめとしてadventureという語が繰り返し出てきており，この文章のキーワードだということがわかる。第3段落よりa real adventureの話になり，第3段落がnew placesについて述べられている。第4段落では，海外でのボランティア経験がnew culturesを示唆しており，第5段落ではnew ideasについて述べられている。これらを考慮すると③が正解となる。　(2)　第5段落で実際に家を出ずに頭の中で考えていることも冒険の一種だと述べられている。選択肢②のIntellectual thinkingはこのことを指すためこれが正解となる。

【19】(1)　ア　propellers　　イ　laughter　　ウ　creativity
(2)　1　computer　　2　brain　　(3)　いくつかの点では，コンピュータの概念ばかりに考えが縛られると，脳の機能をもっと理解することには実はかえって邪魔になることもあるかもしれない。　(4)　正方形ができること。　　(5)　process(procedure)

○**解説**○ (1)　ア　「翼とプロペラは異なるが同じ飛行機能を果たし…」となる。文の後半で脚と車輪を対比させていることから判断する。イ・ウ　第3段落の「笑いは脳システムの基本的な特徴であるが，コンピューターシステムにはない。そして笑いには創造性が伴う」を受けて，「コンピュータが脳システムの機能，おそらく笑いや創造性までを模倣するようプログラムされる…」となる。　(2)　第2段落の1文目「情報処理システムとしてのコンピュータの動作に興味を持ったことで，情報処理システムとしての脳そのものの動作に興味を持つようになった」を「コンピュータへの関心がなければ，このように脳を扱う可能性への関心はもっと低かっただろう」と言い換えている。よって，1はcomputer, 2はbrain。　(3)　dominance「優勢，優越」。lead away from～「～から遠ざかる」。　(4)　「誰かに正方形を描くように指示するのは簡単だが，正方形の数学的定義を与えるのは，結果は同じでもずっと面倒だ」。結果は「正方形ができること」を指す。
(5)　「結果が同じであることはプロセス，または手順が同じであることを意味しない」となる。

【20】1　④　　2　⑤　　3　⑤　　4　③
○**解説**○　人間の行動と規則，規範の関係についてのエッセイである。深い内容なので，重要なキーワードを拾いながら，点と点を結んで線を描くイメージで，それぞれのキーワードがどのようにつながっていくのかまとめながら読むこと。　1　3つの力が反目し合って発生するのは，対立状況が生み出す緊張関係なので，④が正解。trailは「痕跡」。
2　空欄Bの2文前にWe draw imaginary lines around what we think we can doとあるが，「自分たちはここまではできるが，ここから先はできないと考える境界線を頭の中で描いてしまう」のであり，職業，収入，居住地，所有する車，学歴，星占いなどを根拠に自分がどういう存在なのか，どのような能力を有しているのかを頭の中で決めつけてしまい，さらなる可能性を見失ってしまう存在だと述べている。自分自身を束縛するものは，自分の頭の中で考え決めつけてしまったことに起因するということから，与えられた選択肢からは⑤assumptions「決めてかかること，仮定」を選ぶ。　3　設問2の解説と重なるが，⑤「見

えない境界線が人々の可能性を制限する」を選ぶ。　①　enhance「高める」と述べているので不適切。　②　visible「目に見える」とあるので不適切。　③④「社会を快適にする」，「社会をより良くする」とあるが，本文では「社会全般が課した規範よりもはるかに」自分自身を束縛してしまうとあるので，どちらも不適切。　4　第1段落最終文の後半部分で，社会の規則や規範は人々がお互いに傷つけ合うのを防止するために設けられているとある。逆を言えば，それらが無ければ傷つけ合ってしまうことになるため③が正しい。　①　規則と人々の活力とか伝統との関連性については言及がない。　②　第1段落最終文の前半部分で「社会の規則や規範のおかげで，人々を取り巻く世界が秩序のある予測可能な環境となっている」とある。　④　第2段落7文目に「…所有する車や，学歴や，星占いによってさえ自分自身を定義してしまう」とある。　⑤　第1段落参照。これら3つの要素と教育については本文に言及がない。

英文解釈②

【1】次の文を読んで, (1)～(3)の質問に対する答えとして, 適切なもの
を選びなさい。

What Is Inquiry?

Having defined what *humility* means in this analysis of Humble Inquiry, we need next to ask what *inquiry* means. Inquiry is also a complex concept. Questioning is both a science and an art. Professional question askers such as pollsters have done decades of research on how to ask a question to get the kind of information they want. Effective therapists, counselors, and consultants have refined the art of questioning to a high degree. But most of us have not considered how questions should be asked in the context of daily life, ordinary conversations and, most importantly, task performance. When we add the issue of asking questions across cultural and status boundaries, things become very muddy indeed.

What we ask, how we ask it, where we ask it, and when we ask it all matter. But the essence of Humble Inquiry goes beyond just overt questioning. The kind of inquiry I am talking about derives from an *attitude of interest and curiosity*. It implies a desire to build a relationship that will lead to more open communication. It also implies that one makes oneself vulnerable and, thereby, arouses positive helping behavior in the other person. Such an attitude is reflected in a variety of behaviors other than just the specific questions we ask. Sometimes we display through body language and silence a curiosity and level of interest that gets the other person talking even when we have said nothing.

Feelings of Here-and-now Humility are, for the most part, the basis of curiosity and interest. If I feel I have something to learn from you or want to hear from you some of your experiences or feelings because I care for you, or need something from you to accomplish a task, this

---

makes me temporarily dependent and vulnerable. It is precisely my temporary subordination that creates psychological safety for you and, therefore, increases the chances that you will tell me what I need to know and help me get the job done. If you exploit the situation and lie to me or take advantage of me by selling me something I don't need or giving me bad advice, I will learn to avoid you in the future or punish you if I am your boss. If you tell me what I need to know and help me, we have begun to build a positive relationship.

Inquiry, in this context, does imply that you ask questions. But not any old question. The dilemma in U.S. culture is that we don't really distinguish what I am defining as Humble Inquiry carefully enough from *leading* questions, *rhetorical* questions, *embarrassing* questions, or statements in the form of questions — such as journalists seem to love — which are deliberately provocative and intended to put you down. If leaders, managers, and all kinds of professionals are to learn Humble Inquiry, they will have to learn to differentiate carefully among the possible questions to ask and make choices that build the relationship.

HUMBLE INQUIRY   Edgar H. Schein

(1) Referring to the text, what does "Humble inquiry" mean?

ア People ask questions to confuse others.

イ People ask only in the context of daily life or ordinary conversation.

ウ People ask with an attitude of interest and curiosity.

エ People ask under cultural and status boundaries.

(2) Referring to the text, what will people learn to do to build relationship?

ア They will learn to choose valid questions.

イ They will learn to express a curiosity through body language.

ウ They will learn to feel no psychological safety.

エ They will learn to give others bad advice or sell others something unneccesary.

(3) Referring to the text, which of the following is true?

ア　Any old questions lead to a positive relationship.

イ　Effective therapists have never refined the art of questioning.

ウ　Even if people are lied to, they never avoid you.

エ　When people ask humbly, others will be more open to them.

┃ 2024年度 ┃ 北海道・札幌市 ┃ 難易度 ■■■■□□

【2】次の文を読んで，以下の各問いに答えなさい。

Masayoshi Son May Die, But Justice Never

"I was born with a sense of conviction."

Masayoshi Son was born in Tosu City, Saga Prefecture on August 11, 1957, to his father Son Mitsunori and mother Lee Tamako, as the second oldest of four sons. The area where they lived was populated by ethnic Koreans, who had built barracks and started living there before the war. Son was a third-generation *zainichi kankokujin* (Korean permanent resident of Japan).

The Son family ①(said / moved / have / from / to / is) China to Korea. The family was a distinguished one that had produced generals, academics, and more, and even had a genealogical record.

The Son family moved from Daegu, Korea to the Kyushu area during Masayoshi's grandfather's generation.

(ア) Masayoshi's father Mitsunori started in the fish and pork industries, then moved onto selling shochu(Japanese liquor), and finally pachinko stores, restaurants, and real estate, establishing a financial foundation for the family.

The family was poor, however, when Masayoshi was born.

"Thanks for giving me a good name, dad. You really, really gave me a good name," said Son to his father, many times.

Once, when his father dealt with him in a rather lukewarm way, Masayoshi went in and criticized his father.

"What are you doing, dad? What is this? Masayoshi was always like that, even when he was little. From around the time when he was in elementary school, he was like that — scary. In times like this he was always right, and it was scary," said his father, looking back.

There was a time when he was little when he was discriminated against, made fun of for his origins.

"Hey, Korean!" They threw a rock that hit the back of his head, spattering bright red blood.

"I wanted to die, it felt so horrible. Even now, sometimes, on rainy days, I feel the pain of this moment."

The pain remains as a scar on his soul.

But Masayoshi didn't bear them a grudge.

②<u>"You shouldn't hold grudges against people," his grandmother had taught him.</u>

(イ) At the age of 19, Masayoshi wrote a clear and detailed life plan for himself— his "50-Year Life Plan."

In his 20s, he would make his name known.

In his 30s, he would save up capital.

In his 40s, he would throw everything he had at his goal.

In his 50s, he would "complete" his business.

In his 60s, he would pass his business down to the next generation.

"I have never once changed this plan."

"Masayoshi Son may die, but justice never."

(出典：「孫正義　事業家の精神」井上　篤夫)

(1)　下線部①について，文脈にそって(　　　)内の語を正しく並べかえ たときの，3番目と5番目の組合せとして適当なものを，以下の選択 肢から1つ選び記号で答えなさい。

The Son family ①(said / moved / have / from / to / is) China to Korea.

→The Son family (　　) (　　) (　③　) (　　) (　⑤　) (　　)

China to Korea.

ア　③　to　　⑤　from　　イ　③　to　　⑤　said

ウ　③　to　　⑤　have　　エ　③　to　　⑤　moved

(2)　下線部②に意味が最も近いものを，次の選択肢から1つ選び記号で答えなさい。

　ア　Masayoshi's grandmother thought that discrimination was against the law.

　イ　Masayoshi's grandmother had established the family business in 1957.

　ウ　Masayoshi's grandmother had taught him how to establish a large company.

　エ　Masayoshi's grandmother had told him not to bear malice against people.

(3)　本文の内容として最も適当なものを，次の選択肢から1つ選び記号で答えなさい。

　ア　Masayoshi's father started up an organization, such as a labor union.

　イ　Masayoshi didn't have a happy childhood, but he had a strong will.

　ウ　When Masayoshi was 50 years old, he made "50-Year Life Plan."

　エ　There is a history of discriminatory hiring in Japan.

(4)　本文中の(ア)，(イ)の段落の内容を表しているものとして適当なものを，次の選択肢からそれぞれ1つずつ選び記号で答えなさい。

　ア　Background　　　　　イ　Father's work experience

　ウ　A great ambition　　エ　Hardship

| 2024年度 | 宮崎県 | 難易度 ■■■□□ |

【3】次の英文を読んで，以下の(1)～(4)の問いに答えなさい。

　Scheduling is a state of mind that affects how you organize your day, how you run a meeting, how far you must plan in advance, and how flexible those plans are. Yet what is considered appallingly late in one culture may be acceptably on time in another.

　Consider the morning you wake up to that harmonica sound from your mobile phone reminding you about a meeting with a supplier on the other side of town at 9:15 a.m.... But your day has an unexpectedly chaotic start. Your

175

toddler breaks a jar of raspberry jam on the floor and your older son accidentally steps in it, leading to several stressful minutes of cleanup. You manage to drop the kids off at school just as the bells are ringing and the doors are closing. At that moment, your mobile phone chimes 9:00 a.m., which means (ア)you'll be about six or seven minutes late for the important meeting — provided the crosstown traffic is no worse than usual.

What to do?

You could of course call the supplier to apologize and explain that you will be arriving exactly at 9:21. Or possibly 9:22.

Or you consider that six or seven minutes late is basically on time. You decide not to call and simply pull your car out into traffic.

And then perhaps you just don't give the time any thought at all. Whether you arrive at 9:21 or 9:22 or even 9:45, you will still be within a range of what is considered acceptably on time, and neither you nor the supplier will think much of it.

If you live in a linear-time culture like Germany, Scandinavia, the United States, or the United Kingdom, you'll probably make the call. If you don't, you risk annoying your supplier as the seconds tick on and you still haven't shown up.

On the other hand, if you live in France or northern Italy, chances are you won't feel the need to make the call, since being six or seven minutes late is within the realm of "basically on time." (If you were running twelve or fifteen minutes late, however, that would be a different story.)

And if you are from a flexible-time culture such as the Middle East, Africa, India, or South America, time may have an altogether different level of elasticity in your mind. In these societies, as you fight traffic and react to the chaos that life inevitably throws your way, it is expected that delays will happen. In this context, 9:15 differs very little from 9:45, and everybody [イ] that.

When people describe those from another culture using words like *inflexible, chaotic, late, rigid, disorganized, inadaptable*, it's quite likely the scheduling dimension is the issue. And understanding the subtle, often unexpressed assumptions about time that control behaviors and expectations in various cultures can be quite _(ウ)challenging.

[ERIN MEYER, THE CULTURE MAP より一部抜粋　※問題作成において一部改訂]

(1) 下線部(ア)のような場合において，筆者が考える3つの行動を日本語で書きなさい。

(2) 空欄[　イ　]について，本文の流れに合うように，適する語を次のa～dから1つ選んで記号を書きなさい。

　　a　accepts　　b　discusses　　c　opposes　　d　rejects

(3) 下線部(ウ)について，筆者はどのようなことがchallengingであると考えているか。日本語で書きなさい。

(4) 次の①～⑤の英文について，本文の内容に合うものには○を，合わないものには×を書きなさい。

　① In a flexible-time culture, people must call and explain if they will be late for an important meeting.

　② In France, people think that six or seven minutes late is basically on time.

　③ In India, people may think that being delayed by heavy traffic jams happens.

　④ When we have a conflict with others, it is often caused by time management.

　⑤ Everybody is always punctual for appointments in any country.

┃ 2024年度 ┃ 群馬県 ┃ 難易度 ┃■■■■■□□┃

【4】Read the following essay and the answer each of the questions.

Do you check the weather forecast every day?

I acquired this habit when living in Japan, but since moving back to Singapore, I seldom do so. After all, Singapore's weather doesn't vary that much. As an equatorial country, high temperatures and humidity are pretty much a constant throughout the year. We are also relatively sheltered from natural disasters such as earthquakes and tropical cyclones.

What we aren't sheltered from are sudden showers and small-scale thunderstorms. On average, Singapore experiences about 170 thunderstorm days per year and we have one of the highest occurrences of lightning activity in the world. For people who work outdoors, forecasts of thunderstorms and real-time warnings of lightning risks are crucial to safeguarding their lives. For the rest of us, we simply make sure we have an umbrella with us.

Of course, we try to check the weather forecast before we plan certain activities, for instance a picnic at the beach or an excursion to the zoo. But many say the forecasts aren't always accurate. Those who've lived overseas tend to wonder: Why is it that Singapore's forecasts don't seem as accurate as those in foreign countries?

Contrary to common perception, weather forecasting in the tropics is actually relatively challenging. As a small island country surrounded by the sea, Singapore is subject to copious amounts of heat from the sun, moisture and atmospheric instability — all of which are key ingredients for the formation of rain showers and thunderstorms.

Moreover, our thunderstorms tend to be transient in nature. As a meteorologist explained to me recently, our rain clouds can be highly localised. It is common for one part of tiny Singapore to experience rain and another part to be sunny at the same time.

What complicates things further is that the winds over the tropics are often light. So even a slight shift in wind conditions may result in the difference between rain falling within or outside Singapore.

Countries located in the mid-latitudes have weather systems which are vastly different from ours. While the weather has higher variation, it is typically driven by larger-scale weather systems that span a few hundred kilometres to a thousand kilometres and can be tracked a few days ahead. In the tropics, rain clouds may be as small as a couple of kilometres wide. They may develop rapidly overhead before disappearing just as quickly.

Unfortunately, heavy rain and flooding have become more common in Singapore in recent years. With increasing awareness of climate change and extreme weather phenomena, I believe more Singaporeans may start, to check weather forecasts more regularly, too. Regardless of where we live, weather forecasts and data are likely to become increasingly important in our everyday lives.

(Tan Ying Zhen, "Rain or shine?" the japan times alpha Online 2022.1.28)

(1)　According to the passage, why is it said that Singapore's forecasts aren't always accurate? Write your answer using the characters from A to D.

A　Because Singapore's weather doesn't change so often.

B　Because people in Singapore don't care about the weather even when they plan to go out.

C　Because there are sudden showers and small-scale thunderstorms in Singapore.

D　Because the weather is typically driven by larger-scale weather systems.

(2)　According to the passage, what does the writer predict the future? Write your answer using the characters from A to D.

A　The importance of weather forecasts and data will increase in their daily lives.

B　Heavy rain and flooding will become more common in the world.

C　Singaporeans will be sheltered from sudden showers and small-scale thunderstorms.

D　Rain clouds will be as small as a couple of kilometres wide in Singapore.

(3)　Please write about a habit that you want to acquire and how you will acquire the habit. Use more than 30 words.

(4)　Write the suitable word from the passage in each blank. The first letters of the words are written in each blank.

　① The word "(c　　)" means "happening regularly or all the time." For example, "There was a (c　　) stream of visitors to the house."

　② The definition of (e　　) is "a short journey arranged so that a group of people can visit a place, especially while they are on holiday." Things like, "We went on an (e　　) to the Pyramids."

　③ The word "(c　　)" means "existing or being produced in large quantities." An example is "She listened to me and took (c　　) notes."

④　The meaning of "(m　　)" is "small amounts of water that are present in the air, in a substance, or on a surface." As in, "Plants use their roots to absorb (m　　) from the soil."

┃ 2024年度 ┃ 長野県 ┃ 難易度 ■■■■■ ┃

【5】 In passages (1) and (2), each paragraph has a ☐. Arrange the scrambled sentences A, B, C, and D to make sense when inserted. Then choose the most appropriate answer from ① to ⑤.

(1)　These days it is very common for young men to give flowers to young women when they are in love, but this hasn't always been the custom.

In the 1700s in Turkey, it was quite popular for people in love to secretly send each other baskets full of strange things. Usually, an old woman who sold flowers or fruit on the street left the basket beside the door of the person receiving it.

These gift baskets included a variety of objects, such as flowers, stones, feathers, wax, and even charcoal. Each thing in the basket had a special meaning and by figuring out the secret message contained in each item, the person who received the basket could determine the true feelings of the giver.

For example, the flowers from an orange tree meant, "You are beautiful and pure." Pink carnations meant, "My love for you is strong and great." Yellow roses, on the other hand, meant, " I saw you with someone else."

Many flower dictionaries were made to help young people in love understand the meaning of the flowers they received. Not all of the dictionaries agreed, however, on the meaning of each flower, so a person had to watch out what flowers they chose to send. For example, depending on which dictionary you used, and which color you gave, a young man's roses could mean, "I love you," "love is dangerous," or even, "my love has decreased."

By the 1880s, using flowers to send messages had fallen out of fashion, and the more direct way of sending love letters began. Today, flowers are still considered a lovely gift, but the meaning for each kind of flower has been lost.

[based on *Reading Advantage*]

A. A bunch of flowers told young ladies about the feelings in the hearts of young men.

B. However, over time, only sending flowers remained popular.

C. This idea of sending gifts of love with secret meanings quickly spread to Germany, France, and England.

D. Each different flower had a different meaning.

① B→A→C→D   ② C→B→A→D   ③ B→A→D→C

④ C→D→A→B   ⑤ B→C→A→D

(2) If the learners are going on to do academic study in English, then they need to learn the 570 word families in the Academic Word List. This list contains words that are very frequent across a wide range of academic texts and which are not in the first 2,000 words of English. A list of these words can be found in the Vocabulary Resource Booklet, and there is also a website focusing on these words. These words cover around 10% of the running words in academic text, but they cover only around 2% of the running words in novels. So, if your learners do not have academic purposes but simply wish to learn English to speak, to watch movies and television programs, and to read novels and magazines, then the next step is to go on to learn the mid-frequency words of English. The words from the Academic Word List cover around 4% of the running words in newspapers and thus are useful for such reading. Most of the words in the Academic Word List are in the mid-frequency words.

The mid-frequency words include the 3rd to 9th 1,000 words, a total of 7,000 word families.

[based on *What Should Every EFL Teacher Know?*]

A. This means that there would only be two unknown words in every hundred, or around six unknown words on a 300 word page of a book.

B. This is a small enough number for a learner to be able to read without having to keep looking up words in a dictionary.

C. It will take learners many years to learn these words, but they are important because when a learner has a vocabulary of around 9,000 words, they will know 98% of the running words in most texts except technical texts.

D. They cover around 10% of the running words in most texts.

   ① D→C→A→B   ② C→A→D→B   ③ D→C→B→A
   ④ C→B→A→D   ⑤ D→A→B→C

| 2024年度 | 岐阜県 | 難易度 ▮▮▮▯▯ |

【6】 Answer the following questions.

〔1〕 The following passage has an unnecessary sentence that is logically improper. Choose the unnecessary underlined sentence from among ① to ④. Answer from among 1 to 4.

The roles of comics are multiplying. They can simplify medical information, making arcane concepts more accessible to children. Examples include helping patients to grasp the notion of informed consent, understand how electronic health records work or negotiate handovers between carers. Government health agencies are harnessing the medium for public education. ①In 2020 Stark County, Ohio, commissioned Cara Bean, an artist, and the Centre for Cartoon Studies in Vermont to produce a comic to introduce pupils to mental health.

Behind this burst of activity is a group of enthusiastic medical professionals and artists. Some have been fans of the medium since childhood; others stumbled upon it as adults. ②In 2007 Ian Williams, a Welsh doctor-turned-artist, made a website to gather those interested in what he called "graphic medicine". The name stuck.

It is still a young field. ③Mr Williams — who in 2014 published "The Bad Doctor", a semi-autobiographical graphic novel about a doctor —

recalls being invited to speak at conferences as a practitioner rather than comic relief. But a growing body of evidence attests to the art form's uses, and new textbooks are codifying its applications. "The idea of graphic medicine is getting into the medical mainstream now in a way which would have been unimaginable ten years ago," says Michael Green, who teaches the subject at Penn State University and guest-edits the digital-comics section of *Annals of Internal Medicine*, a respected journal.

Comics are not for everyone, notes John Pollard, a researcher, and using them in therapy requires tact and expertise. ④But he can vouch for their potential from his personal experience. "If I hadn't had any kind of contact with comics," he reflects, "I have my doubts that I would have gone to university."

Adapted from Comic relief
(The Economist, May 21st, 2022)

1 ①　2 ②　3 ③　4 ④

〔2〕 Choose the most appropriate location from among 《 A 》 to 《 D 》 in which to put the following sentence. Answer from among 1 to 4 .

> So the team led by technical manager Günther Brennsteiner is taking out insurance.

Surrounded by rugged peaks so high they tear clouds apart, the tractor-size groomer backs over a 40-foot-tall mound of compacted snow, unrolling a bolt of white fabric. On top of the mound, six workers are stitching fabric panels together with a handheld, heavy-duty sewing machine. It's June at Kitzsteinhorn in Austria, one of the highest and coldest ski areas in the Alps, and meltwater is gushing into ravines on the flanks of the mountain. 《 A 》 But up on the glacier, the slope maintenance crew is preparing for the next season.

Even at 10,000 feet, counting on natural snow has become too risky. 《 B 》 They've spent a month plowing the last of this season's snow into eight multistory mounds, of which the largest are bigger than football fields. They're now spending another month covering the mounds with fabric to insulate them over the summer. When the new season begins, if it's too warm for fresh snow to fall ─ or even for artificial snow to be made ─ dump trucks and groomers will spread old snow on the slopes.

Figuring out how to stockpile snow at this scale hasn't been easy, says one of the workers, Hannes Posch. 《 C 》 Before the crew started stitching the panels together, wind gusts sometimes ripped them apart, uncovering the mounds. Other times, the fabric froze solid into the snow.

"Everything that could go wrong, has," Posch says, as he zip-ties a sandbag to the fabric. Once, at the nearby resort of Kitzbühel, lightning set a fabric-covered snow depot like this ablaze, and 30 firefighters battled the flames for hours. Snow is that precious these days.

"With the warming climate, everything has changed," Brennsteiner says. He started working here 31 years ago, during what now seem like the glory years of Alpine skiing. 《 D 》

Adapted from Denise Hruby, *Saving Winter*
(NATIONAL GEOGRAPHIC, March, 2022)

1 《 A 》 2 《 B 》 3 《 C 》 4 《 D 》

▌2024年度 ▌東京都 ▌難易度 ▭▭▭▭□□

【7】 Read the following passage and choose the most appropriate answer for each question.

"Global" is a very popular word in Japan ─ you can even find "global flavored" potato chips ─ but what exactly does "global" mean? On the most basic level it refers to the sharing of popular culture, products, brand names, and the like. In this sense, eating at KFC is "global." A more meaningful concept, (a), is "international," which emphasizes working together across cultures to meet mutual goals. This is what goes on in most international business offices. "Multicultural," a related word, indicates an even deeper understanding and acceptance of another culture, a "gift" that comes only after a long time of living or working in, or marrying into, another culture. Ⓐ

184

Especially in business, we must be able to communicate our needs and thoughts "on the spot." But communication is not only about good grammar and a large vocabulary; it also means being able to negotiate, being able to express thoughts clearly, and having "plan B" strategies when communication becomes difficult. <u>We cannot let our cultural differences interfere.</u>

You often hear it said that there is no "keigo" in English, but Business English can be very formal and polite. It in fact has many set expressions that might be considered "keigo." The words and phrases "please," "thank you," "excuse me," and "I'm sorry" are good examples. Men are addressed as "sir," and women as "ma'am." Absolute respect is shown to visitors and senior staff — both in words and actions. Ⓑ

What may make others assume that English has no "keigo" is native English speakers' more casual approach. This is especially true in Australia and North America. Whereas Japanese value group consensus and a harmonious atmosphere, Westerners value the individual and bold, direct opinions. Each person's ideas are listened to. People who don't "speak up" are seen as being dishonest — as hiding something. Ⓒ

Some foreigners may have trouble understanding Japanese people. You often hear that Japanese can't be trusted because their faces don't show their emotions. Japanese don't express their real feelings or give clear, complete answers. They often say "sorry" without meaning it, and so on. To hear complaints about or criticisms of one's culture is not easy. To be truly international, we have to be able to adjust to circumstances and work together. Ⓓ

When I got a job in Japan that required me to go to meetings regularly, it was at first hard for me to accept some of the cultural differences. Eventually, I learned that young committee members give their opinions only after more senior members have done so — in some cases, only when asked. One thing I still do not understand, though, is why some senior members cross their arms, close their eyes, and fall fast asleep during a meeting. Trying to change another culture doesn't work. It is up to us to adjust ourselves as best we can to it.

(Kitzman, A., Mihara, K., Tatemoto, S., & Kimura, H. (2017). Business communication style. *English Indicator 4 [Upper Intermediate]: Vital Business Rules*)

1. Where in the passage does the sentence below best fit?

It is difficult to get to this level, because many beliefs, values and prejudices get in the way.

① Ⓐ　　② Ⓑ　　③ Ⓒ　　④ Ⓓ

2. Fill in the blank(a) with the most appropriate word.

① accordingly　② supposedly　③ however　④ indeed

3. What does the underlined sentence "<u>We cannot let our cultural differences interfere.</u>" mean?

① Our cultural differences can prevent us from getting along with each other.

② We cannot make friends with people from foreign countries because of our cultural differences.

③ Interference by our cultural difference will lead us to trouble.

④ Our communication should not be disturbed by our cultural differences.

4. Which statement is mentioned about "keigo" in this passage?

① A lot of learners of Japanese struggle to master "keigo" because of its difficulty.

② Many people think that English has no "keigo" because most native English speakers are less formal than Japanese speakers when giving opinions.

③ The author assumes that "keigo" is unique to the Japanese language of all languages.

④ Business English is categorized as "keigo" in Australia and North America.

5. What is the author's claim in this passage?

① Better to ask the way than go astray.

② So many men, so many minds.

③ When in Rome, do as the Romans do.

④ It is no use crying over the spilt milk.

▌2024年度 ▌沖縄県 ▌難易度 ▬▬▬▬□□

【8】次の英文を読んで, (1)〜(3)の問いに対する答えとして最も適切な
ものを, それぞれ1〜5から1つずつ選べ。

An increasing number of nursing homes are introducing a Swedish therapeutic method that enables elderly people to play music.

Developed by Swedish music therapist Sten Bunne, 64, for elderly people, children and the disabled in 1980, the unique method overcomes physical difficulties and has proved to be an effective therapy even for dementia patients.

The Bunne method uses easy-to-play musical instruments such as a guitar that has lever that strikes chords when the player moves it right or left by following an instructor's hand movements. Special flutes are among other instruments of the method, which makes playing music possible for anyone.

A home for the aged operated by Maihama Club Co. in Urayasu, Chiba Prefecture, conducts two concert sessions per week based on the Bunne method. Participants are divided into several groups and play assigned instruments or sing while following a teacher's instructions. Each session lasts about 40 minutes.

"I can't wait" for the sessions, said Takeo Arakawa, an 80-year-old resident. "I feel elevated after participation."

The Bunne method creates a sense of unity among participants as they complete a concert together, said 44-year-old instructor Takanori Shimamura. "All participants play instruments and become confident because they have a sense of accomplishment by playing their roles."

In addition to two weekly sessions, Maihama Club holds a 20-minute session before meals almost every day for residents heavily in need of nursing care. Many of them have their appetite stimulated as a result and can eat without assistance, said staff members.

Since 2009, some 50 care facilities in Japan have introduced the Bunne method. In Sweden, about 1,500 facilities have already adopted the method.

The Bunne method helps many elderly people stay healthy physically and mentally and avoid increases in the level of required nursing care, according to Gustav Strandell, the president of Maihama Club.

The method is said to improve a parson's brain function, memory and voicing capacity.

In addition, it was found to enhance the breathing capacity of participants, according to a 2010 survey of people in their 50s to 90s who visit care centers for dementia patients in Tokyo.

(1) What aspect of the Bunne method allows it to be particularly useful for elderly people, children, and the disabled?

1 It focuses on teaching complex musical skills.

2 It uses simple musical instruments and accessible techniques.

3 It requires extensive prior musical knowledge.

4 It relies on traditional musical instruments and compositions.

5 It emphasizes individualism and self-expression.

(2) According to the passage, what effect does the Bunne method have on residents with higher nursing care needs at the home for the aged operated by Maihama Club Co.?

1 It helps them regain full mobility and independence.

2 It reduces their need for medication and therapy.

3 It increases their appetite, allowing them to eat without assistance.

4 It enables them to teach music to other residents.

5 It fosters a competitive environment for personal growth.

(3) Based on the passage, what is a key component of the Bunne method's success in helping participants feel confident?

1 The strict, structured nature of the sessions

2 The emphasis on individual performance and talent

3 The accomplishment experienced from fulfilling assigned roles in a performance

4 The competition among participants to excel at their instruments

5 The focus on mastering a wide variety of musical genres

2024年度 ┃ 奈良県 ┃ 難易度

【9】 次の英語の文章を読んで，(1)～(6)の各問いに答えなさい。

　　Parents, teachers, and anyone who regularly deals with teenagers knows how difficult the ①adolescent years can be. Adolescents have always been known to do wild － even dangerous － things. This was thought to be due to the foolishness of youth. Now, brain-imaging technology allows scientists to study the physical development of the brain in more detail than ever before. Their discoveries have led to a new theory of why teens act the way they do.

　　Recently, scientists discovered that though our brains are almost at their full size by the age of six, they are far from fully developed. Only during adolescence do our brains truly "grow up". During this time, they go through great changes, like a computer system being upgraded. This "upgrade" was once thought to be finished by about age 12. Now, scientists have concluded that our brains continue to change until age 25. Such changes make us better at balancing our impulses with the need to follow rules. However, a still-developing brain does this ②clumsily. The result, scientists claim, is the unpredictable behavior seen in teenagers.

　　The studies confirm that teens are more likely to take risks and behave in extreme ways. Fortunately, ⓐthe news isn't all negative. As brain scientist B. J. Casey points out, the teen brain inspires such behavior in order to help teenagers prepare for adult life.

　　One way the brain does this is by changing the way teens measure risk and reward. Researchers found that when teens think about (A) , their brains release more of the chemicals that create pleasure than an adult brain would. Researchers believe this makes the (B) seem more important than the (C) , and makes teens feel the excitement of new experiences more ③keenly than adults do.

　　Research into the structure of the teen brain also found that it makes social connections seem especially rewarding. As such, teens have an intense need to meet new people. Scientists suggest this is because as teens, we begin to realize that our peers may one day control the world we live in. Because it is still developing, a teen brain can change to deal with new situations. ⓑ<u>It</u> therefore connects social rewards with even more pleasure. In this way, the brain encourages teens to have a wide circle of friends, which is believed to make us more successful in life.

Unfortunately, this hunt for greater rewards can sometimes lead teens to make bad decisions. However, it also means that teens are more likely, and less afraid, to try new things or to be ⌐ (Ⅰ) ⌐. The scientists' findings suggest that in the long run, the impulses of the teen brain are what help teens leave their parents' care and live their own lives successfully.

READING EXPLORER Split 2B Third Edition, Paul MacIntyre and David Bohlke, 2020 Cengage Learning, Inc.

(1) 文中の下線部①～③の語と同じ意味を表しているものを次のア～エからそれぞれ1つずつ選び，記号で答えなさい。

① ア adult   イ child   ウ old

　　エ youth

② ア actively   イ awkwardly   ウ considerately

　　エ critically

③ ア politely   イ delicately   ウ enthusiastically

　　エ simultaneously

(2) 下線部ⓐthe news isn't all negative という理由は何ですか。脳科学者B. J. Caseyの主張を基に日本語で答えなさい。

(3) 文中の(A)～(C)に入る単語の組み合わせとして適切なものを次のア～オから1つ選び，記号で答えなさい。

ア (A) risks   (B) risks   (C) rewards

イ (A) risks   (B) rewards   (C) rewards

ウ (A) risks   (B) rewards   (C) risks

エ (A) rewards   (B) risks   (C) risks

オ (A) rewards   (B) rewards   (C) risks

(4) 下線部⑭が指す具体的な語句を本文中より抜き出しなさい。

(5) 文中の(Ⅰ)に入る適切な語を次のア～オから1つ選び，記号で答えなさい。

　ア　independent　　イ　selfish　　ウ　kind　　エ　competent

　オ　conservative

(6) 次のア～キの記述のうち，本文の内容に合っているものを2つ選び，記号で答えなさい。

　ア　Changes in our brains help us to be better at balancing our impulses with the need to follow rules.

　イ　Scientists discovered that though our brains are almost at their full size by the age of 25 they are far from fully developed.

　ウ　Studies show that teens are less likely to take risks and behave in extreme ways.

　エ　Like a computer system being upgraded, teens go through great changes that are thought to start at around age 12.

　オ　Research proves that adults have an intense need to meet new people.

　カ　Teens are usually on the hunt for greater rewards which sometimes causes them to make bad decisions.

　キ　Because a teen brain is still developing, a teen brain has difficulty changing with new situations.

▌2024年度 ▌名古屋市 ▌難易度 ■■■■□□

【10】 次の3つの英文を読んで，あとの(1)，(2)の問いに答えよ。

　　Cambridge (June 8) － The Science Museum of Cambridge has finally completed its long-awaited renovation after five years of closure. The museum's director, Dr. Elizabeth Hill, said, "We wanted to create a more interactive and informative experience for visitors, and we believe that the new museum will achieve just that." The renovation was made possible thanks to a grant from the government and donations from various scientific organizations, including the British Association for the Advancement of Science.

　　The museum will officially open its doors to the public on July 1st,

英文解釈

with a week-long series of special events. Visitors will be able to participate in interactive exhibitions and educational workshops featuring topics ranging from physics and chemistry to biology and astronomy. For more information about the museum and its opening events, please visit the museum's website at www.cambridgesciencemuseum.org.

www.cambridgesciencemuseum.org

Opening Events

Day 1 ～ Meet the Scientists ～
10:00 – 11:30 A.M., The Auditorium
Have you ever wondered what it's like to be a scientist? Join us for a panel discussion with several leading scientists in various fields, including physics, chemistry, and biology. You'll have the opportunity to ask questions and learn about their exciting research.

Day 2 ～ Science Experiments for Kids ～
11:00 A.M. – 1:30 P.M. (including a 45-minute break for lunch), Workshop Room 201
Bring your kids to our science experiment workshop, where they'll learn about the scientific method and conduct fun experiments with our expert instructors. Registration is limited to 20 children. Since the experiments will take a long time, there will be a lunch break during the workshop. During the lunch break, sandwiches and drinks will be provided for children without charge.

Day 3 ～ The Future of Space Exploration ～
1:00 – 3:00 P.M., Lecture Room 3
Join us for a fascinating discussion about the future of space exploration with a panel of experts from NASA, SpaceX, and the European Space Agency. Learn about the latest developments in space technology and what we can expect in the coming years.

Note:
•Attending the event on Day 2 costs $15 for materials. The other events are free of charge.
•Online reservations must be made beforehand to participate in the events.
Please e-mail events@cambridgesciencemuseum.org to let us know your contact details, the number of participants, and the event you would like to attend.

To	:	events@cambridgesciencemuseum.org
From	:	Sarah Patel <sarahp@abcmail.com>
Date	:	June 25
Subject	:	Event reservation

Dear Sir/ Madam,

I am writing to reserve a spot for my son for the science experiment workshop on Day 2. His name is Jack Patel and he is 10 years old. I would also like to know if I can accompany him during the workshop or if parents are not allowed. Please let me know if there are any requirements for parents.

Thank you for your time, and I look forward to hearing back from you.

Best regards,
Sarah Patel

(1) 次のア，イが本文の内容に合う英文になるように，(　　)に当て

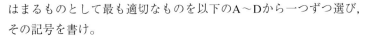

はまるものとして最も適切なものを以下のA～Dから一つずつ選び，その記号を書け。

ア　According to the article, The Science Museum of Cambridge (　　).

A　has been donated the land for renovation by the government and the organizations

B　receives regular government subsidies and is being renovated regularly for its visitors

C　has been the recipient of funds from the government and organizations for its renovation

D　is rebuilt every five years for the valuable experience of visitors by the government and the organizations

イ　According to the article and the website, (　　) at the opening events.

A　you can virtually experience weightlessness in space

B　children can get complimentary refreshments for lunch

C　all events are open to an unlimited number of participants

D　you are required to bring materials for the workshop

(2)　本文の内容を踏まえ，The Science Museum of Cambridge が行う，Sarah Patel からのメールへの返信の内容として最も適切なものを次のA～Dから一つ選び，その記号を書け。

A　Sarah can attend the panel discussion with some leading scientists during the workshop.

B　Children can learn about space technology with experts from NASA during the workshop.

C　Both Sarah and Jack can take part in the science experiment workshop without charge.

D　Sarah can stay with her son during the workshop but she need to bring her own lunch.

┃ 2024年度 ┃ 愛媛県 ┃ 難易度 ┃

【11】次の英文を読み，以下の(1)～(6)の問いに答えよ。

According to a U.S. survey, Japanese became the most common language used in blog posts in the fourth quarter of 2006. It turned out that Japanese

(①) for 37 percent of all blog posts, English for 36 percent, and Chinese for 8 percent. This figure is all the more remarkable when we think of the fact that Japanese is spoken by only 1.8 percent of the world's population.

Interestingly, Japan's blogging culture has evolved in a very different manner from ②that in other nations. According to a 2007 survey, 75 percent of Japanese blog content is about everyday events, which are mostly trivial matters. Writing a diary does not require any special skill, knowledge or experience, making it easier for many Japanese to start their own blogs. Another characteristic of Japanese blogs is the use of many photos, ③which may be an extension of the diary-like desire to document everyday life. What is more, Japanese bloggers often write anonymously. ☐ A ☐

By contrast, many U.S. and European blogs are journalistic or opinion-oriented. The authors, using their real names, present information and perspectives that are not usually available in the mainstream media. Actually, about 40 percent of English-language bloggers said that their primary goal was to raise their own visibility as an authority in their respective fields. They usually write less often than Japanese bloggers but their postings are longer. ☐ B ☐

But why is Japanese blogging culture so different from the rest of the world? Many experts believe that the answer is deeply embedded in traditions that date back hundreds of years. Japanese have long been using diaries as a medium for writing down things like changes of season and about nature. In the Heian period (794-1192), women expressed their personal feelings in kana characters and lifted the lid on court lifestyles and romances. ☐ C ☐

Just as the use of kana made it easier for women in the Heian period to write diaries, the increasing availability of personal computers, digital cameras and other blog tools has transformed Weblogs — long regarded as a program for engineers and researchers — into a common medium used by modern Japanese women. ☐ D ☐

Generally speaking, Japanese are good at adopting foreign cultures, blending them with their own traditions and then developing a distinctive mix of both. Since the term "Weblog", was first used in the United States a decade ago, the concept of blogging has become deeply rooted in Japanese society.

E

(1) 本文中の①の(　　)内にあてはまる最も適切な語を，次のア〜エ
から一つ選んで，その記号を書け。

　ア　fell　　イ　accounted　　ウ　stood　　エ　allowed

(2) 下線部②のthatが示す具体的な内容を，次のア〜エから一つ選ん
で，その記号を書け。

　ア　blog content　　イ　blogging culture　　ウ　a manner

　エ　the figure

(3) 下線部③について，その内容について最も適しているものを，次
のア〜エから一つ選んで，その記号を書け。

　ア　専門分野において権威を示したいという願望の表れのようなも
の。

　イ　社会的な出来事に対する批評のようなもの。

　ウ　日々の出来事を記録する日記の延長のようなもの。

　エ　社会問題について調査・分析した報告のようなもの。

(4) 本文の内容と一致するグラフとして最も適切なものを一つ選ん
で，その記号を書け。

　ア　blog which photos are used in Japan

　イ　Japanese blog content in 2007

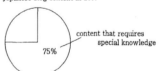

　ウ　U.S. and European blogger's purpose

　エ　language usage among the world population

(5) 次のア，イの文は，本文中の　A　〜　E　のいずれかに入る。
最も適切な箇所を一つ選んで，その記号をそれぞれ書け。

　ア　In the same way Heian people developed kana from kanji introduced
from China, Japan adopted the Internet, which developed in the United
States, to create its own blogging style.

195

イ　This may be linked to present-day blogging culture.

(6)　本文の内容と一致するものを，次のア〜オから二つ選んで，その記号を書け。

ア　More than one-third of blog posts until 2006 were shown to have been written in Japanese.

イ　Western bloggers make effective use of photographs to attract readers to the content.

ウ　More and more Japanese bloggers are using their real names in the blog posts.

エ　Japanese are said to have a remarkable ability to incorporate foreign cultures into their own traditions.

オ　Some English-language bloggers blog to make themselves renowned in their field.

┃ 2024年度 ┃ 香川県 ┃ 難易度■■■■□□

【12】Read the following passage and answer the questions below.

In our own childhoods, we were not taught how to deal with anger as a fact of life. We were made to feel guilty for experiencing anger and sinful for expressing it. We were led to believe that to be angry is to be bad. Anger was not merely a misdemeanor; it was a felony. With our own children, we try to be patient; in fact, so patient that sooner or later we must explode. We are afraid that our anger may be harmful to children, so we hold it in, as a skin diver holds his breath. In both instances, however, the capacity for holding in is rather limited.

Anger, ⬚ ① ⬚, is a recurrent problem. We may not like it, but we cannot ignore it. We may know it intimately, but we cannot prevent its appearance. Anger arises in predictable sequences and situations, yet it always seems sudden and unexpected. And, though, it may not last long, anger seems eternal for the moment.

When we lose our temper, we act as though we have lost our sanity. We say and do things to our children that we would hesitate to inflict on an enemy. We yell, insult, and attack. When the fanfare is over, we feel guilty and we

196

solemnly resolve never to render a repeat performance. But anger inevitably strikes again, undoing our good intentions. Once more we lash out at (あ)<u>those</u> to whose welfare we have dedicated our life and fortune.

Resolutions about not becoming angry are worse than futile. They only add fuel to fire. Anger, ② , is a fact of life to be acknowledged and prepared for. The peaceful home, ③ , does not depend on a sudden benevolent change in human nature. It does depend on deliberate procedures that methodically reduce tensions before they lead to explosions.

Emotionally healthy parents are not saints. They're aware of their anger and respect it. They use their anger as a source of information, an indication of their caring. Their words are congruent with their feelings. They do not hide their feelings. (い)<u>The following episode</u> illustrates how a mother encouraged cooperation by venting her anger without insulting or humiliating her daughter.

Jane, age eleven, came home screaming: "I can't play baseball. I don't have a shirt!" The mother could have given her daughter an acceptable solution: "Wear your blouse." Or, wanting to be helpful, she could have helped Jane look for the shirt. Instead, she decided to express her true feelings: "I'm angry, I'm mad. I've bought you six baseball shirts and they're either mislaid or lost. Your shirts belong in your dresser. Then, when you need them, you'll know where to find them."

Jane's mother expressed her anger without insulting her daughter, as she commented later: "Not once did I bring up past grievances or reopen old wounds. Nor did I call my daughter names. I did not tell her she's a scatterbrain and irresponsible. I just described how I felt and what needed to be done in the future to avoid unpleasantness."

Her mother's words helped Jane herself come up with a solution. She hurried off to search for the mislaid shirts at her friend's house and in the locker room in the gym.

There is a place for parental anger in child education. In fact, failure to get angry at certain moments would only convey to the child indifference, not goodness. Those who care cannot altogether shun anger. This does not mean that children can withstand floods of fury and violence; it means only that they can stand and understand anger that says, "There are limits to my tolerance."

For parents, anger is a costly emotion: To be worth its price, it should not be employed without profit. Anger should not be used so that it increases with expression. The medication must not be worse than the disease.

1　In paragraph 3, what does the underlined part (あ) refer to? Answer in English.

2　Which is the best phrase to fill in the each blank from ① to ③? Choose the correct order.

ア　like a hurricane
イ　like the common cold
ウ　like the hoped-for peaceful world

A　① ア　② ウ　③ イ
B　① イ　② ア　③ ウ
C　① ウ　② ア　③ イ
D　① イ　② ウ　③ ア

3　In paragraph 5, what does the underlined (い) refer to?
ア　Finally, Jane's mother helped Jane look for the shirt.
イ　Jane's mother instructed Jane to wear a blouse when Jane came home screaming.
ウ　Jane's mother didn't say anything when Jane said that she couldn't play baseball.
エ　Jane's mother expressed her anger without insulting Jane.

4　Choose the answer that best completes the sentence below.

According to the passage, if parents never get angry at their child, the child _____.

ア　will learn there are limits to their tolerance
イ　will not think that they are interested in him/her
ウ　will think that they are emotionally healthy
エ　will never get angry with other people

【13】 Read the following passage and answer the questions below.

Trunk Tricks

I　Elephants move their powerful trunks with precision and complexity, delicately picking up a single leaf as easily as they heft a log. But researchers have struggled to explain how, exactly, the trunks manage ①to do so. New research published in *Current Biology* reveals part of the answer, (②) motion-capture technology typically used to make movies.

II　"Elephants have evolved these amazing organs with an infinite number of degrees of freedom," says lead author and University of Geneva biologist Michel Milinkovitch. His team traveled to a South African elephant reserve to study how the animals *specifically use that freedom. The researchers taped *retroreflective markers to two bull elephants' trunks and put various items in front of them. As the elephants moved the objects around, the researchers filmed them with a semicircle of *infrared cameras, capturing (③) the markers moved in three-dimensional space— similar to the process used for mapping movie actors' movements to computer-generated characters.

III　An elephant's ④proboscis, like a human tongue, is a type of muscular hydrostat: it has no bones, so it can move in myriad ways. The new study shows that the bulls combine simple actions—such as curling, twisting and *elongating parts of their trunks—to achieve complex movements. The animals also form pseudo-joints, or rigid sections of trunk, that they can shift from point to point.

IV　"It's the first time that we've gotten a hint of (⑤) these more simplified commands might be in elephants," says William Kier, a biologist at the University of North Carolina at Chapel Hill, who studies trunk, tongue and *tentacle movement and was not a part of the study. "I think it is a pretty important advance."

V　This investigation into how an elephant's 40,000 trunk muscles work together will be invaluable for developing new, versatile robots, says Cecilia Laschi, a roboticist at the National University of Singapore, who

199

was not involved in the new study: "For roboticists, ⑥<u>this</u> is sort of a dream." A team of engineers in Pisa using the study data expects to have a trunklike robot prototype in 18 months. —Susan Cosier

Adapted from [*Scientific American, December 2021*]

注　*specifically＝具体的には　　　*retroreflective＝逆反射の
　　*infrared＝赤外線の　　　　　　*elongate～＝～を長くする
　　*tentacle＝触手，触覚

1　What does the underlined part① refer to? Answer in Japanese.

2　Which is the most appropriate phrase to fill in the blank②? Answer (A)～(D).

(A)　compared to　　(B)　thanks to　　(C)　up to

(D)　with regard to

3　Fill in the blank③ with the most appropriate word from paragraph Ⅱ, according to the context.

4　Replace the underlined part④ with the most appropriate word, choosing from this passage.

5　Which is the most appropriate word to fill in the blank⑤? Answer (A)～(D).

(A)　whether　　(B)　which　　(C)　what　　(D)　that

6　What does the underlined part⑥ refer to? Answer using within 50 characters in Japanese.

7　Which is the most appropriate subtitle for the title of this passage to fill in ⬜? Answer (A)～(D).

(A)　Elephants build simple actions into complex motions, intriguing roboticists.

(B)　Elephants combine complex movements with simple activities, inspiring roboticists.

(C)　Elephants do simple actions with 40,000 trunk muscles, confusing roboticists.

(D)　Elephants use complex actions to perform simple motions, fascinating roboticists.

【14】 次の英文を読んで, (1)〜(6)の問いに答えよ。

Long ago, the Greeks and Romans created stories to explain happenings around them. (　ア　), there were stories to explain why the world was created, why we die, why there are stars in the sky, and more. We call these myths because they are old explanations that we now know are not true. One of the more interesting myths explained why spring came each year. 〔　①　〕

Thousands of years ago, there was a goddess named Demeter. She was the goddess of the cornfields. All year round, the fields were full of crops. The sun shone, it rained, the weather was warm, and fruits and vegetables grew all the time. It was a rich, beautiful earth.

Demeter had a daughter named Core. She loved Core dearly. One day, however, while Core was out walking through a green field, the ground opened up. Hades, the god of the underworld, raced out in a chariot. He had been watching Core from far away and had dreamed of taking her to be his wife. He raced back into the hole, with Core (　イ　) at his side.

(　ウ　) For nine days and nights she walked the earth, looking for her daughter. She ate and drank nothing. She dressed in black. Finally, she met Helios, the god of the sun. He had seen everything. He told Demeter that Core had been taken away and that her name had been changed to Persephone. 〔　②　〕

Demeter (　エ　) crops and plants to grow. The earth became a wasteland. Finally, Zeus talked to Hades. He ordered Hades to release Persephone, provided that she had not eaten any food in the underworld. 〔　③　〕

She had not eaten any food, but a kind gardener had given her six fruit seeds. She had eaten them. Zeus thought long and hard, but he had to tell Persephone that (オ)she could stay in her mother's world just six months out of the year. She would then have to return to the underworld and stay six months, one for each seed she had eaten.

Therefore, when Persephone returns to the underworld, our good earth stops giving us plants and crops. We have to (カ)put up with six months of autumn and winter, with their cold and darkness. When Persephone returns to the earth, her mother lets the crops grow in plenty. 〔　④　〕

In many cultures, the coming of spring is a big event. In Germany, people light fires at the end of winter to burn away bad feelings caused by the cold months. In Scandinavia, young people _(キ)shoot off fireworks to welcome spring with a bang. Everything comes to life in the seasonal regions of the world. It is as if something bright and welcoming has returned. Someone or something like Persephone, perhaps?

(1) 本文中の(ア), (イ), (エ)に入れるのに最も適切な語 (句)を次のA～Dから一つずつ選び, その記号を書け。

ア　A　For example　　B　On the other hand　　C　Nevertheless
　　D　Unfortunately

イ　A　scream　　　　B　screams　　　　　　C　screamed
　　D　screaming

エ　A　compelled　　　B　forbade　　　　　　C　permitted
　　D　recommended

(2) 本文中の(ウ)に入れるのに最も適切なものを次のA～Dから一 つ選び, その記号を書け。

A　Demeter was crushed.　　　B　Demeter got married.
C　Demeter was kidnapped.　　D　Demeter got divorced.

(3) 下線部(オ)について, その理由として最も適切なものを次のA～D から一つ選び, その記号を書け。

A　Demeter was in despair and turned the earth into a wasteland.

B　Demeter gave up hope of finding her beloved daughter.

C　Persephone had a strained relationship with her mother after a quarrel.

D　Persephone ate six fruit seeds given by a kind gardener.

(4) 下線部(カ), (キ)に最も意味の近い語を次のA～Dから一つずつ選 び, その記号を書け。

(カ)　A　beckon　　B　oppress　　C　refute　　D　tolerate
(キ)　A　abandon　　B　appreciate　　C　launch　　D　suppress

(5) 次の英文を入れるのに最も適切な場所は本文中の〔　①　〕～ 〔　④　〕のどれか。以下のA～Dから一つ選び, その記号を書け。

This is why we have four seasons.

A　①　　B　②　　C　③　　D　④

(6) 本文の内容と一致するものを次のA～Dから一つ選び，その記号
を書け。

A　Demeter proposed that Core should stop growing fruits and vegetables.

B　Core had her name changed by Hades, the god of the underworld.

C　Helios didn't know what had happened to Core until he met Demeter.

D　People should learn that each region has its own myth about seasons.

┃2024年度┃愛媛県┃難易度 ▪▪▪▪▪▪

【15】Read the following passage and answer the questions below.

It's sometimes assumed that the main role of a teacher is direct instruction. There's an essential place for direct instruction in teaching. Sometimes it's with a whole class, sometimes with smaller groups, and sometimes one-on-one with individual students. But expert teachers have a repertory of skills and techniques. Direct instruction is only one of ①them, and knowing how and when to use the appropriate technique is what great teaching is all about. Like all genuine professions, it takes judgment and connoisseurship to know what works best here and now.

You expect your doctor to know a lot about medicine in general as well as having some specific area of expertise. But you also expect her to apply what she knows to you in particular and to treat you as an individual with specific needs. ②Teaching is the same. Expert teachers constantly adapt their strategies to the needs and opportunities of the moment. Effective teaching is a constant process of adjustment, judgment, and responding to the energy and engagement of the students.

In her book, *Artistry Unleashed*, Hilary Austen explores great performances in work and life. In one example, she looks at the work of Eric Thomas, a former philosophy student at Berkeley, who now teaches horsemanship. The essence for the rider, he says, is to become one with the horse, a living animal with its own energy and moods. Dr. Austen describes one class where things aren't going so well for the student, who reins the horse in while Eric offers some coaching.

He tells the student that she's putting a lot of effort into trying to get the horse to turn better, but that every third or fourth turn she drops the ball and doesn't do anything. What's that about? he asks. The student says, "I'm too early and then too late, and then he reacts and I can't tell what to do." Eric pauses and then says, "You're trying to do too much. Stop thinking, and pay attention to your horse. It's about trying to feel what is happening underneath you right now. ③*You can't ride yesterday's horse*. You can't ride what might happen. Everybody who rides has the same problem: we're hoping what we learned yesterday will always apply. You often ride the problem you had a minute ago, all for the goal you want to achieve. But this is not a recipe. It changes every second, and ④you've got to change with it."

Good teachers know that however much they have learned in the past, today is a different day and you cannot ride yesterday's horse.

(1) What does the underlined ① refer to? Search the text and extract the sequential words.

(2) Regarding the underlined ②, in what aspect is teaching identical to seeing a patient? Explain it with about 50 Japanese characters.

(3) What does the underlined ③ indicate? Explain in Japanese.

(4) Regarding the underlined ④, what change do you think is happening in high school English education and what do teachers need to do to adapt themselves to the change you mention? Express your own idea with concrete examples and reasons, using about 150 words in English

▌2024年度 ▌京都府 ▌難易度▌

【16】 Read the passage below and choose the most appropriate answer.

After six years in the United States, Heejung Kim was getting irritated with professors needling her to talk. She had been taught that silent contemplation, not half-baked chattering, paved the path to wisdom. As the great Confucian sage Lao Tzu wrote: "He who knows does not speak. He who speaks does not know."

Kim knew she felt comfortable listening without talking in a way that many of her European-American colleagues did not. And she knew that connecting what she heard with what she already knew was a lot of work. She definitely did not feel she was freeloading.

As a budding cultural psychologist, Kim was learning that irritation was often the bellwether of a good research idea. So she decided to explore why Americans worry so much about silence in the classroom. Hers was a rather revolutionary hypothesis: for European Americans, talking helps thinking, but for Koreans and many other East Asians, talking can actually hinder thinking.

She tested her hunch with Richard, a European-American graduate student from New York. Having logged many hours talking on his high school's debate team, Richard opined, "Talking really helps clarify what you're thinking. Sometimes it's hard to know what you think *without* talking."

Kim then consulted with other East-Asian students. Akiko, a graduate student from Japan, shared Kim's frustration with the American assumption that talking is thinking, and supplied her own set of proverbs: "The mouth is the source of misfortune," "Guard your mouth as though it were a vase," "You have two ears and one mouth, to be used in that proportion," and "The duck that quacks the loudest gets shot."

Armed with these insights, Kim set out to test her ideas. She first devised a survey with statements that reflected both Eastern beliefs about talking and thinking such as "Only in silence can you have clear thoughts and ideas," and Western beliefs such as "An articulate person is usually a good thinker." She then asked people in San Francisco and Seoul how much they agreed with the statements. She found that Americans of many different ages and professions thought that talking is good for thinking. Koreans, in contrast, more readily agreed that talking can impede thinking.

Just because Americans believe that talking helps them think, however, does not mean they are right. Likewise, East Asians may mistakenly believe that talking interferes with thinking. To find out exactly how talking affects thinking for European Americans and East Asians, Kim asked American students who had grown up speaking English to take a nonverbal intelligence test called the Raven Progressive Matrices. Half the students had European backgrounds, and half had East-Asian backgrounds (including Korean, Chinese, Vietnamese, and Japanese). All the students completed half the intelligence test items in silence, and the other half while "thinking out loud," that is, verbalizing their problem-solving process.

Kim found that the European Americans performed better when they were solving the problems while speaking. In contrast, the Asian Americans performed much worse when they solved the problems while thinking aloud. But when the Asian Americans were allowed to solve problems in silence, they performed better than the European Americans.

For Asian Americans, then, silence is not a sign of checking out. Instead, it produces their best thinking.

(Adapted from Markus, H. R. & Conner, A. *Clash!*∶ *How to Thrive in a Multicultural World*. Plume, 2013)

(1) According to the passage, "She definitely did not feel she was freeloading," would mean "(　　)"

①　She felt comfortable with her European-American colleagues who did not talk to her.

②　She felt uncomfortable with her way of listening.

③　She was certain that her silence in the classroom was not laziness.

④　She was uncertain whether her way of listening was right.

(2) The author uses the phrase "Guard your mouth as though it were a vase," to demonstrate "(　　)"

①　Thinking helps talking.

②　Thinking helps listening.

③　Talking helps thinking.

④　Silence helps thinking.

(3) According to the passage, "An articulate person is usually a good thinker," would mean "(　　)"

①　Talking impedes thinking.

②　Talking is thinking.

③　Thinking hinders talking.

④　Thinking clarifies talking.

(4) Which of the following statements is NOT true according to the passage?

① Americans are inclined to believe silence impairs deep thinking.

② Koreans were more likely to agree that talking would not help thinking than Americans.

③ The European Americans performed better on the intelligence test while speaking.

④ The Asian Americans performed worse on the intelligence test while speaking.

2024年度 ‖ 千葉県・千葉市 ‖ 難易度

【17】次の火星探査プロジェクトに関する英文を読んで，以下の各問いに答えよ。

Never before had space scientists tried anything like this. They were about to land a remote control robot, called Sojourner, on Mars.

If you had been standing on Mars that day, here is what you would have seen: Glowing like a *meteor, Pathfinder would have blazed across the *predawn Martian sky. The Earth would have been visible as a blue morning star in the background.

In the Mission Operations room, a tense crowd clustered around *Rob Manning*, chief flight engineer, who was monitoring Pathfinder's entry, descent and landing. They waited.

At the Laboratory in *Pasadena, hung with banners proclaiming "Mars or Bust," the Pathfinder team broke into applause. They ①yelled, shook hands and hugged each other. The project's leader, *Donna Shirley*, her dream realized, got tears in her eyes in the middle of an interview with a television reporter.

After their initial rush of excitement, flight controllers wondered what position Pathfinder had touched down in. If it had landed upside down, it would have to right itself by extending a *petal and tipping itself over. But the lander ②signaled a thumbs-up to Earth. Not only had the spacecraft's unconventional *belly-flop from the heavens succeeded, but Pathfinder had landed right side up.

③The flight team was delighted, but geologist *Matthew Golombek* was worried about the smooth landing. What if it was too smooth? What if Pathfinder had come down on flat ground? What if there were no rocks? The painstaking selection of a landing site, although it had involved 60 scientists from the United States and Europe back in 1994, had been based on educated guesses about the geology of *Ares Vallis, an ancient Martian flood plain. There were no guarantees. *Matthew* waited uneasily for Pathfinder to send down ④the first photos. It didn't take long.

Pathfinder pointed its antenna toward Earth, ready to transmit images and data. Now its camera could start taking pictures. The scientists and engineers could hardly wait. The first priority was to confirm that the air bags had retracted properly. The initial image, a black and white photo about the size of a bathroom tile, showed a section of the lander and a deflated air bag billowing like an untucked shirttail.

As Pathfinder beamed down 2 images per minute, more of the air bags came into view. The pictures revealed that one had bunched up over the petal that Sojourner would use to exit the lander. It was blocking Sojourner's path to the Martian surface. Fortunately, engineer *David Gruel* had foreseen ⑤such a problem and had a solution. Controllers told Pathfinder to lift one of its petals about 45 degrees and reel in the offending air bag.

More photos streamed down. Finally, the view of Mars beyond the lander took shape, giving the scientists what they had come for. "Rocks!" cried *Matthew Golombek*

※斜体の英語は人名

*meteor　流星　　predawn Martian sky　夜明け前の火星の空
　Pasadena　パサデナ(都市名)
　petal　ペタル(花びらの形状をした太陽光パネルの一種)
　belly-flop　腹ばい飛行　　Ares Vallis　アレス渓谷
　　　(Houghton Mifflin「Reading」から一部抜粋　※問題作成において
　　　て一部改訂)

1　下線部①と同様の意味を持つ英語一語を本文中から抜き出して書け。

2 下線部②と同じ内容を指す最も適当なものを次の(ア)～(エ)から一
つ選び，記号で答えよ。

(ア) showed something injured

(イ) showed something dangerous

(ウ) showed something unreliable

(エ) showed something unharmed

3 下線部③の理由を具体的に日本語で書け。

4 下線部④に写っていた全てのものを日本語で書け。

5 下線部⑤が指す部分を本文中から抜き出し，最初と最後の三語を
それぞれ書け。ただし，記号や符号は一語に含めない。

6 次の(1)～(4)について，本文の内容に合っているものに○を，合っ
ていないものに×を書け。

(1) People who were monitoring in the Mission Operations room waited
on Pathfinder's entry nervously.

(2) After the Pathfinder landed, flight controllers were so relieved and
nobody worried about future development.

(3) The landing site was decided based on educated guesses of scientists
and they had no doubt it was the best decision they could make.

(4) The Pathfinder team overcame difficulties, but they couldn't find what
they had looked for.

┃ 2024年度 ┃ 岡山市 ┃ 難易度 ■■□□□

【18】次の英文を読み，各問いに答えなさい。

There is one episode from the history of medicine that illustrates
particularly well how (ア)an evidence-based approach forces the medical
establishment to accept the conclusions that emerge when medicine is put to
the test. Florence Nightingale, today a well-known figure, was a woman with
very little reputation, (1) she still managed to win a bitter argument
against the male-dominated medical establishment by arming herself with
solid, unquestionable data. (2), she can be seen as one of the earliest
advocates of evidence-based medicine, and she successfully used it to
transform Victorian healthcare.

Florence and her sister were born during an extended and very productive two-year-long Italian honeymoon taken by their parents William and Frances Nightingale. Florence's older sister was born in 1819 and named Parthenope after the city of her birth — Parthenope being the Greek name for Naples. Then Florence was born in the spring of 1820, and she too was named after the city of her birth. It was expected that Florence Nightingale would grow up to live the life of a privileged English Victorian lady, but as a teenager she regularly claimed to hear God's voice guiding her. Hence, it seems that her desire to become a nurse was the result of a "divine calling." ₍₃₎This distressed her parents, because nurses were generally viewed as being poorly educated, indecent and often drunk, but these were exactly (4).

The prospect of Florence nursing in Britain was already shocking enough, so her parents would have been doubly terrified by her subsequent decision to work in the hospitals of *the Crimean War. Florence had read scandalous reports in newspapers such as *The Times, which highlighted the large number of soldiers who were dying of cholera and malaria. She volunteered her services, and by November 1854 Florence was running the Scutari Hospital in Turkey, which was notorious for its filthy wards, dirty beds, blocked sewers and rotten food. It soon became clear to her that the main cause of death was not the wounds suffered by the soldiers, but rather the (5) that were widespread under such filthy conditions. As one official report admitted, "The wind blew sewer air up the pipes of numerous outdoor toilets into the corridors and wards where the sick were lying."

Nightingale set about transforming the hospital by providing decent food, clean linen, clearing out the drains and opening the windows to let in fresh air. In just one week she removed 215 handcarts of filth, flushed the sewers nineteen times and buried the carcasses of two horses, a cow and four dogs which had been found in the hospital grounds. The officers and doctors who had previously run the institution felt that these changes were an insult to their professionalism and fought her every step of the way, but she pushed ahead regardless. The results seemed to validate her methods: in February 1855 the death rate for all admitted soldiers was 43 per cent, but after her reforms it fell dramatically to just 2 per cent in June 1855. When she returned to Britain in the summer of 1856, Nightingale was greeted as a (h 6).

(旺文社　2016年度版　全国大学入試問題正解　を参照)

注

*the Crimean War：クリミア戦争(1853 － 56年；ロシアがトルコ・フランス・英国・サルディニアを相手に主にクリミア半島で戦った)

*The Times：『タイムズ』(1785年創刊の英国の新聞)

(1)　空欄(　1　)と(　2　)に入る英語として適切な組み合わせを次の(A)～(D)から一つ選び，記号で答えなさい。

	(A)	(B)	(C)	(D)
1	so	so	but	but
2	Nonetheless	Indeed	Nonetheless	Indeed

(2)　下線部(3)の内容を日本語で説明しなさい。

(3)　空欄(　4　)に入る適切な英語を次の(ア)～(エ)から一つ選び，記号で答えなさい。

(ア)　the prejudices that Florence was determined to crush

(イ)　the conclusions that Florence was determined to object to

(ウ)　the opinions that Florence was determined to agree to

(エ)　the biases that Florence was determined to accept

(4)　空欄(　5　)に入る適切な英単語一語で書きなさい。

(5)　下線部(ア)について，ナイチンゲールにおける例を示しながら日本語で説明しなさい。

(6)　本文の内容から判断して，空欄(　6　)にあてはまる英語を，与えられたアルファベットで始まる英単語一語で書きなさい。

▋ 2024年度 ▋ 鳥取県 ▋ 難易度 ▋▬▬▬▬▬

【19】次の文章を読み，以下の設問の答えとして最も適切なものを，選択肢の中からそれぞれ一つ選びなさい。

A passage from a book can stay in your mind for a long time and support your life. It is vital to carefully protect places and environments in which people can pick up a book so that opportunities to encounter a good book are not lost.

The 14-day Book Week kicked off on Oct.27, which is Characters and Print Culture Day. This year, "autumn reading promotion month," a 28-day campaign widely participated in by publishers, bookstores and others, also started on the day. The campaign includes events about reading books and stamp rallies at bookstores.

Behind these efforts is a publishing slump and a decline in the number of bookstores in towns. The spread of the internet has led to more and more people turning away from magazines, and paperback sales continue to be sluggish. The estimated combined sales of print and electronic publications in 2021 were about ¥1.67 trillion, less than two-thirds of the 1996 peak for the sales of print publications. The number of bookstores nationwide also fell below 12,000. It is hoped that the monthly campaign for reading books will be an opportunity for many people to become familiar with books.

Bookstores have the function of disseminating information as well. Many bookstores have set up a section of books related to news such as Russia's invasion of Ukraine. These days, hotels and coffee shops where people can read books as much as they like are also gaining popularity.

The novel coronavirus pandemic has made the online world part of our lives, but it is all the more important at a time like this to reaffirm the advantages of the "real" world in which people can actually hold a book in their hands. The power of word of mouth also cannot be underestimated. According to a Yomiuri Shimbun survey, 60% of respondents have received a book recommendation from someone close to them. Some who recommended a book said that it caused them to talk to the other person more often. Books that were introduced on the video-sharing app TikTok have also become popular among young people. The power to connect people is one of the unique attractions of books.

As children get older, they tend to spend more time on their smartphones and less time reading books. It is hoped that schools will work on "morning reading" before the start of classes and improving their libraries to help students develop reading habits. The central government allocates funds to local governments for the purchase of books at schools, but because the usage of these grants is unspecified, they are often used for other purposes. The average number of books purchased with the funds is also decreasing.

The experience of diving into the world of books and sharing joy, anger, sorrow and pleasure with the characters enriches the mind. Hopefully, those related to local governments will understand that creating an environment in which children can access books is an investment in the future.

(出典：『The Japan News』 (2022年10月28日)を一部改変)

1　Which of the following statements is true of "autumn reading promotion month"?

① It was intended to decrease the number of young people who read books.

② It was a campaign supported by funds from the central government.

③ It started on the day The 14-day Book Week began.

④ It aimed to revitalize the fishing industry and libraries.

⑤ Events like reading books and stamp rallies were held only during this campaign.

2　According to the passage, which of the following statements best describes the effect of books?

① Video-sharing apps can be powerful tools to connect people in place of books.

② People who are recommended a book by someone are likely to do the same to others.

③ More and more coffee shops and hospitals are now providing places to read books freely.

④ Their power to connect people has been diminishing due to the coronavirus pandemic.

⑤ People who recommend a book to others tend to have more communication with them.

3　What does the writer hope those related to local governments to do for children?

① To set up laws or rules in order to prevent the overuse of smartphones by children.

● 英文解釈

②　To not specify the purpose of funds to local governments from the central government.

③　To ask for more funds to purchase books from the central government.

④　To spend government grants on creating an environment in which children can access books.

⑤　To encourage children to read more books on investment to prepare for the future.

2024年度 ┃ 三重県 ┃ 難易度

【20】次の英文は，『リスニングとスピーキングの理論と実践』というタイトルの本からの要約である。英文を読み，各問いに答えなさい。

Section 1

"What is English Speaking?"

It is essential to obtain a clearer understanding of ①the characteristics of speaking skills and the mechanism of speech production. The L2 speaking skill should be developed in a language classroom with a deep understanding about the characteristics of speaking; otherwise speaking could be regarded as too difficult by learners, though it is the skill many of them would like to learn most.

Section 2

"Influential Factors for Speaking"

This section focuses on major factors that influence speaking processes and outcomes. First, we provide basic information concerning the effects of the cognitive complexity of tasks on speaking, showing various kinds of speaking tasks. Second, we discuss ②factors that make speaking difficult from the viewpoint of learner factors (e.g., motivation, proficiency), code complexity (e.g., topic familiarity, task familiarity), cognitive complexity (e.g., the amount and clarity of information), and communicative stress(e.g., time pressure, speaking speed). Finally, the section illustrates major characteristics of facilitating factors for successful speaking, demonstrating the effects of borrowing and repetition by referring to numerous previous studies.

Section 3

"Teaching English Speaking"

This section deals with a variety of activities to develop speaking skills. Oral communication ability is closely related to listening, reading and writing. Proper and sufficient input is indispensable for meaningful oral output. Creating an encouraging atmosphere is essential in the classroom setting. Therefore, this section begins with "Classroom English". Tourism dialogues that provide practical situations for English use are introduced next. Advanced activities, such as public speaking and (3)debate, are also discussed with teaching tips. Lastly, creating dramas and drama techniques are exemplified as a promising method to develop oral communication skills with group dynamics.

(大修館書店　リスニングとスピーキングの理論と実践　より抜粋)

(1)　下線部①について，次の図を見て，図の中央部にある左右方向の矢印が意味していることはどういうことか，日本語で説明しなさい。

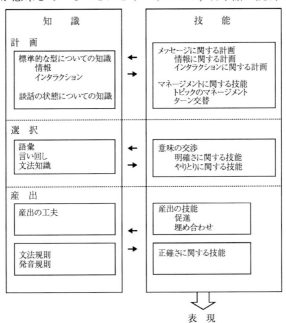

図：Bygate(1987)によるスピーキング技能の概観

(2) 下線部②について，その要因の一つに様々なスピーキング活動の
タスクの複雑性と条件を理解していないことが考えられる。次の表
を見て，それぞれのスピーキング活動の特徴を考え，空欄(1)～
(4)に当てはまるものを，以下の①～④から一つずつ選び，番号
で答えなさい。

表：スピーキングの種類例

タスクの条件		タスクの複雑さ	
方向性	タイプ	プランあり・先行知識あり	プランなし・先行知識なし
一方向	オープン	(1)	即興のスピーチ
	クローズド	自宅までの道順を説明	(2)
双方向	オープン	ディベートの一部	(3)
	クローズド	問題解決タスク	(4)

① インフォメーション・ギャップゲーム

② 即興スキット

③ 絵の描写

④ Show & Tell

(3) "Classroom English"の意義について，Section 3に書いてあることか
ら判断し，日本語で説明しなさい。

(4) 下線部③について，授業の帯活動として，授業の最初に毎時間異
なる論題でミニディベートをする場合，どのような論題が適するか，
あなたが考える論題を一つ英語で書きなさい。

▎2024年度 ▎鳥取県 ▎難易度▮▮▮▮▮▮

解答・解説

【1】(1) ウ (2) ア (3) エ

○**解説**○ (1) 第2パラグラフの2～3文目に着目する。Humble Inquiryとは，
ただ表面的な質問というわけではなく，興味や関心に由来したもので
あると述べられている。 (2) 第4パラグラフの最後の文に着目する。

Humble Inquiryを学ぶためには，質問する可能性のあることを注意深く区別して，関係性を構築するような選択をする必要があると述べられている。よって，妥当な質問を選択するというアが正解。　(3)　第2パラグラフ3〜4文目に，Humble Inquiryは，関係性の構築を強く望む質問であり，よりオープンなコミュニケーションにつながることが述べられている。よって，謙虚に問いかけることによって，相手がよりオープンになるというエが正解。

【2】(1)　エ　　(2)　エ　　(3)　イ　　(4)　(ア)　イ　　(イ)　ウ
○解説○ (1)　The Son family is said to have moved from China to Korea.となる。be said to have p.p.「〜したと言われている」は，to不定詞に完了形が使われているので，述語動詞be saidの時点よりも以前に起きたことを表している。　(2)　「他人を恨む心を抱くべきでない」ということなのでエが正解。malice「悪意，恨み」。　(3)　孫正義氏の生い立ちと信条が述べられている英文で，貧しい家に生まれた彼は幼少期の頃に在日韓国人ということで差別され，自分の生まれを嘲られたと述べられている。また，本文冒頭で「自分は生まれながらにして信念を貫く性格であった」と述べたり，19歳の時に書いた人生設計に対し「自分の人生設計を一度たりとも変えることはなかった」と述べたりしている。以上よりイが最も適当といえる。　(4)　段落(ア)では，父親の職歴に触れているのでイを選ぶ。段落(イ)では，19歳の時に考えた自分の人生設計に触れており，いわば「将来の夢」を語っているのでウが適当といえる。

【3】(1)　・取引先に電話して謝罪し，9時21分か9時22分には確実に到着すると伝える。　　・6，7分の遅刻ならば，基本的には時間通りと考え，電話をせず，車で渋滞へと向かう。　　・45分の遅刻さえも，許容範囲の時間としてあまり気にしない。　(2)　a　(3)　さまざまな文化における，(相手の)行動や(相手への)期待を管理する時間についての，曖昧で言語化されない思い込みを理解すること
(4)　①　×　②　○　③　○　④　×　⑤　×
○解説○ (1)　下線部は「あなたは重要な会議に6，7分くらい遅刻するこ

とになる」。このような場合，筆者がどう行動すべきと考えるかについては，第4〜6段落を訳出すればよい。 (2) 該当段落では，時間に柔軟な文化圏に言及している。よって「このような状況では，9時15分は9時45分とほとんど変わらず，誰もがそれ(遅刻すること)を受け入れる」となる。accept「認める，受け入れる」。 (3) can be quite challenging「かなり難しいことである」の主語にあたる部分を訳出する。understanding the subtle, often unexpressed assumptions about time「時間に関する微妙で，しばしば言外の前提を理解すること」，control behaviors and expectations in various cultures「様々な文化における行動や期待をコントロールする」。 (4) ②「フランスでは，6, 7分の遅刻は基本的に時間通りと考える」。第8段落参照。正しい。
③「インドでは，大渋滞で遅れることはよくあることだと思われている」。第9段落参照。正しい。 ①「時間に柔軟な文化では，重要な会議に遅れる場合は必ず電話で説明しなければならない」，④「他人と対立する時，それはしばしば時間管理によって引き起こされる」，⑤「どんな国においても，誰もがいつでも約束に遅れない」は誤り。

【4】(1) C (2) A (3) A habit that I want to acquire is exercise. I want to get some exercise for my health. I will start with a short walk in the early morning and keep doing that. (33 words) (4) ① constant
② excursion ③ copious ④ moisture
○**解説**○ (1) シンガポールの天気予報が正確ではない理由としては，第5パラグラフに着目する。シンガポールは大量の太陽熱，湿気そして不安定な大気の影響を受けるため，にわか雨や雷雨が発生すると述べられている。 (2) 英文の著者が将来的な予想として考えていることについては，第9パラグラフに着目する。シンガポール人も天気予報をもっと定期的に確認するようになり，どこに住んでいても天気予報や天気の情報が日々の生活においてますます重要になるだろうと述べられている。 (3) 本文に関連して，自身が身につけたい習慣を30語以上の英語で書く問題である。解答例にあるように，その習慣を身につけたい理由や，具体的にどういうことから始めたいかを書くとよいだろう。 (4) 与えられた語義から対応する語を本文から抜き出す問

題である。まず①は，「定期的にまたはいつも生じる」を意味する constantであり，第2パラグラフの3文目にある。次に②は，「特に休日に，何人かのグループである場所を訪れるように手配された短い旅行」を意味するexcursionであり，第4パラグラフの1文目にある。また③は，「大量に存在するまたは作られている」を意味するcopiousであり，第5パラグラフの2文目にある。最後に④は「大気中，物質中または表面上に存在する少量の水」を意味するmoistureであり，第5パラグラフの2文目にある。

【5】(1) ②　(2) ①

○**解説**○ (1)　空所の前の段落では贈り手のどんな贈り物にも特別な意味があり，受け取る側が秘密のメッセージを見つけ出すことでその意味を理解することができたということが述べられている。それに続くのはThis idea of sending gifts of love with secretで始まるCが適切であり，②か④に絞られる。Cの文の後にD「それぞれ異なる花は異なる意味を持っていた」はつながらないため④は不適切で②が正解となる。

(2)　空所の前後から選択肢を検討するのは難しいため，空所の文同士の関係を検討する。AとCに着目すると，Cは「約9,000語の語彙を習得すれば，技術的な文章を除くほとんどの文章で登場する語の98％を知っていることになる」という内容で，Aは「100語ごとの中で知らないのは2語のみで，1冊の本の300語あるページでは約6語となる」という内容である。ここからAはCをわかりやすく例示したことがわかり，AのThisはCの内容を指すと読み取れる。よってC→Aとなり①か②に絞られる。次にDを検討すると，「Theyはほとんどの文章に出てくる語の10％を占める」の意で，このTheyがAのtwo unknown wordsやsix unknown wordsを指すことはありえずA→Dとはならない。ここから②は不適切で①が正解となる。

【6】〔1〕3　〔2〕2

○**解説**○ 〔1〕　医療現場での漫画の活用についての文章である。③の"The Bad Doctor"についての事例の話が文脈的に不自然である。この部分を飛ばすと，医療分野での漫画の使用はまだ新しい分野だが，芸

術様式(＝漫画)の使用実例が増えており，教科書で整理されつつある，という文になる。　〔2〕オーストリアのスキー場の整備についての話である。挿入文の訳は「なので，テクニカルマネージャーのギュンター・ブレンシュタイナーが率いるチームは保険をかけている」である。「なので」で始まるため，文章の前に保険をかけなければいけない理由が示されるはずである。Bの前では，ゲレンデのメンテナンスチームが，次シーズンのために準備をしていることが書かれており，「標高1万フィートでも，自然の雪をあてにするのはリスクが高すぎる」とある。それゆえ，B「保険をかける」のである。具体的には，すでに今ある雪を次シーズンまで溶けないようにする工夫がB以降で述べられている。

【7】1　①　　2　③　　3　④　　4　②　　5　③
○**解説**○　1　挿入文は「多くの信念や価値観，偏見が邪魔をするので，このレベルに到達するのは難しい」。Multicultural「多文化」の説明後の④に入り，異文化をさらに深く理解し受け入れることを「このレベル」と表現している。　2　冒頭で「グローバル」の基本的な定義を述べているが，それではうまく表現できないという流れに続く文であるので，空所にはhoweverが入り，「しかし，より意味のあるコンセプトは『インターナショナル』であり，相互の目標を達成するため文化を超えて協力し合うことを強調するものである」となる。　3　第2段落では，ビジネスにおいてコミュニケーション力が大切だと述べている。下線部は「私たち(のコミュニケーション)は文化の違いに邪魔されてはならない」という意味。　4　敬語について述べられているのは第3，4段落。「英語に『敬語』がないと思わせるのは英語を母国語とする人たちのカジュアルなアプローチである」から，②「英語を母国語とする人の多くは，日本語を母国語とする人に比べて，意見を言うときに堅苦しくない」が適切。　5　第5段落最終文の「真に国際的であるためには，状況に適応し協力し合うことができなければならない」や，第6段落最後の2文で述べている「他の文化を変えようとしてもうまくいかない。自分たちができる限り適応していくしかない」等から，③「郷に入っては郷に従え」が適切。他のことわざは，①「聞くは一

時の恥，聞かぬは一生の恥」，②「十人十色」，④「覆水盆に返らず」。

【8】(1)　2　　(2)　3　　(3)　3

○**解説**○　英文の内容は，スウェーデンの音楽セラピストSten Bunne氏の考案したBunne Methodの説明である。Bunne Methodの特徴は第3段落で，その実例は第4段落と第7段落で，その効果は第6段落，第7段落，第9段落，第10段落，第11段落でそれぞれ言及されている。

(1)　Bunne Methodの特徴に言及している第3段落に，誰にでも簡単に操作できる特別な楽器を使用することが述べられており，2と一致する。　(2)　舞浜倶楽部が運営する介護施設で実践されているBunne Methodの効果として，第7段落最終文に「入居者の多くは食欲が刺激され，介助なしに自分で食事をとれるようになっている」とあるので3が正解。　(3)　Bunne Methodにより参加者が自信を持てるようになった主な要因について，第6段落に「Bunne Methodを実践してみると，参加者が皆で演奏をやり遂げることで一体感が生まれる。自分の役割を果たすことで達成感が得られるので，参加者全員が楽器を演奏し，自信を持てるようになる」とある。したがって，3が正解。

【9】(1)　①　エ　　②　イ　　③　ウ　　(2)　10代の脳がリスクを冒したり，極端な方法でのふるまいを誘発したりすることは，大人の生活に備えることを助けるものであるから。　　(3)　オ　　(4)　(a／the) teen brain　　(5)　ア　　(6)　ア，カ

○**解説**○　(1)　①　下線部を含んだ文の直後の文に着目すると，下線部の単語はいつも暴力的，さらには危険なことをすると知られている年齢，つまり思春期や青年期のことである。従って，エが正解。　②　下線部を含んだ文の直後の文に着目すると，脳が発達途中である結果，10代の若者は予想できない行動を起こすと述べられている。そのため，「ぎこちない」を意味するイが正解。　③　下線部を含んだ節に着目する。この節の主語となっているthisは，10代の脳は快楽を生み出す物質を大人の脳よりも多く放出するということを指しており，10代は新しい経験に対して大人よりも強く興奮を感じるという意味になる。そのため，ウが正解。　(2)　脳科学者のCaseyの名前があることから，

下線部を含んだ文の直後の文に着目すればよい。その際，その文にあるsuch behaviorが，下線部を含んだ文の直前の文にあるtake risks and behave in extreme waysを指していることに留意しながら説明するとよい。　(3)　(1)の③の解説で述べた，10代の脳は大人よりも快楽を生みだす物質を放出することから，新しい経験に対して大人よりも強く興奮を感じるということを踏まえればよい。空欄Bと空欄Cの箇所は，「報酬の方がリスクよりも重要に思える」という意味に，そして，空欄Aの箇所は，快楽物質を放出するのは「10代が報酬を考えた時」という意味になるオが正解。　(4)　下線部を含んだ文の直前の文に着目する。Becauseで始まる従属節にあるitは，主節のa teen brainを指し，下線部もそのまま同じものを指す。　(5)　空欄部を含んだ文の次の文に着目すると，10代の衝動は親元から離れてうまく自分の人生を生きていくための手助けとなると述べられており，このことを踏まえると「自立している」を意味するアが正解。　(6)　まず，第2パラグラフの6文目にアと対応した記述がある。次に，第5パラグラフの1文目にカと対応した記述がある。

【10】(1)　ア　C　　イ　B　　(2)　D
○**解説**○ (1)　ア　第1段落1文目The Science Museum of Cambridge has finally completed its long-awaited renovation after five years of closure.及び第3文The renovation was made possible thanks to a grant from the government and donations from various scientific organizations, including the British Association for the Advancement of Science.よりCが一致する内容となる。　イ　Opening EventsのDay 2の最終文During the lunch break, sandwiches and drinks will be provided for children without charge.よりBが一致する内容となる。complimentary refreshmentsは「無料の軽食」という意味。　(2)　Sarahは息子をDay 2に参加させたいとメールで言っているのでDay 2のイベントに該当しないAとBは不適切である。またCもNote: *Attending the event on Day 2 costs $15 for materials.の内容と一致しないので不適切である。よって残ったDが適切だと判断できる。保護者であるSarahにも無料の軽食が提供されるという情報はないため矛盾することはない。

【11】(1) イ　　(2) イ　　(3) ウ　　(4) エ　　(5) ア　Ｅ
イ　Ｃ　　(6) エ，オ

○解説○ (1)　空所を含む文は「日本語はすべてのブログの投稿の37パーセントを占める」といった内容になることがわかる。選択肢でそのような意味を表すのはイでaccount for〜で「〜を占める」の意。

(2)　このthatは前に出てきた語句の繰り返しを避ける代名詞であり，blogging cultureの繰り返しを避けるためにここでは用いられている。

(3)　extension「延長」，diary-like desire to document「日記のように文章を書きたいという願望」といった語句から，ウが適切だと判断できる。

(4)　エの内容が第1段落最終文と一致する。　(5)　ア　挿入文は，アメリカで発展したインターネットを後から日本が取り入れて，日本独自のスタイルを確立したという内容であり，ほぼ同じ内容の空所Eの直前の文にスムーズにつながる。　イ　挿入文は「これは現在のブログ文化につながるかもしれない」という意味であるため，直前に昔の時代の内容が来ると判断できる。空所直前で昔の時代の内容が述べられているのは，平安時代の文化を述べている空所Cの直前のみである。

(6)　エの内容が最終段落1文目，オの内容は第3段落3文目と一致する。

【12】1　our children　　2　Ｂ　　3　エ　　4　イ

○解説○ 1　下線部を含んだ文は「私たちは再び，私たちが人生と財産を捧げてきた人たちを激しく批判する」の意である。この文を含んだ第3パラグラフの2文目にあるように，怒りをぶつける対象は子どもたちである。　2　まず，空欄①は，その空欄前後に着目すると，「怒りは再発する問題である。私たちはそれを好まないかもしれないが，それを無視することはできない」とある。従って，「普通の風邪のような」を意味するイが適切である。次に，空欄②は，その前後に着目すると，「怒りは人生の事実であって，それを認めて備えておくべきである」とある。従って，「台風のような」を意味するアが正解である。この時点で正答選択肢は選べるが，最後に，空欄③は，その前後に着目すると，「平和な家庭は，人間の本性が突然慈悲深く変化することに依拠しているわけではない」とある。従って，「望まれる平和な世界のように」を意味するウが正解である。　3　下線部は，「下記のエ

ピソード」の意味であり，下線部の直後に着目すればよい。「どのように母がジェーンを侮辱したり辱めたりすることをせずに怒りをぶつけつつ，協力を促したか」の意であり，この内容をまとめているのはエである。　4　与えられた文の空欄の前までは「文章によると，親が子どもに対して全く怒らないと，子どもは」の意である。第9パラグラフの2文目に対応する記述がある。

【13】1　丸太を持ち上げるのと同じくらい簡単に，一枚の葉を繊細に拾い上げること。　2　(B)　3　how　4　trunk　5　(C)　6　象の4万個の鼻の筋肉がどのように連携して働くかを利用して，新しい多用途のロボットを開発すること。(48字)　7　(A)

○**解説**○　1　設問の下線部to do soは，「そうすること」という指示語であり，前文のdelicately picking up以下の具体的動作を日本語で表せばよい。　2　空所の直前で「答えの一部が明らかにある」とあり，空所の直後に「モーションキャプチャーの技術」が来ていることから，thanks to「～のおかげで」が適切。　3　capturingの目的語が空所を含む語句に来るのと，空所の後にS＋Vの構造があることから，段落Ⅱにある語の中ではhow「～する方法」を用いるのが適切。　4　下線部の後で，象のproboscis(口吻)を「骨がなく，無数の方法で動かすことができるmuscular hydrostat(筋肉包骨格)で，人間の舌のようである」と説明している。これに該当する象の体の部位は，2文目にあるtrunk(鼻)である。　5　前の段落を見ると，象が鼻の単純な動きを組み合わせることによって，複雑な動きを実現していることが述べられている。さらに，後の段落では，象の鼻の動きの研究は，ロボット工学に有用であることが述べられている。従って，空所には疑問詞whatが入り，「象のより単純化されたコマンドがどんなものであるか，ヒントを初めて得た」の意となる。　6　thisは直前の内容を指すのでCecilia Laschiの発言である1文目のsaysの前までの内容をまとめればよい。　7　段落Ⅲの2文目にあるように，象は単純な動作を組み合わせて複雑な動作をするため，この内容に合致するのは(A)だと判断できる。

【14】 (1) ア A　イ D　エ B　(2) A　(3) D
(4) (カ) D　(キ) C　(5) D　(6) B

○**解説**○ (1)　ア　空所前のGreeks and Romans created stories to explain happenings around them.の後にstoriesの具体例が述べられているためAのFor exampleが適切。　イ　with＋S＋Vingで「Sが～しながら」という付帯状況を表す構文となりDのscreamingが適切。　エ　空所の次の文The earth became a wasteland.「地球は荒れ地となった」より空所にはBのforbade「禁じた」(原形はforbid)が入る。　(2)　空所の前の段落で愛する娘のCoreを失い，空所の次の文で9日間も飲まず食わず娘を探していたと述べられている。よってAのDemeter was crushed.「デーメーテール(ギリシャ神話の豊穣の女神)は打ちひしがれた」が適切。(3)　解答参照。　(4)　(カ)　put up with～は「～を我慢する」の意でDのtolerateが同じ意味となる。　(キ)　shoot off～は「～を発射する」の意でCのlaunchが同じ意味となる。　(5)　季節の話が述べられているのは後ろから2段落目であるため④が適切となる。　(6)　第4段落最終文の内容がBと一致する。

【15】 (1)　skills and techniques　(2)　知っていることを個人個人に合わせて当てはめ，その一人一人を特別な手助けの必要な個々人として扱うという点。(52字)　(3)　過去に学んだことは，必ずしも全てに当てはめることができるわけではないということ。　(4)　Based on the current Course of Study, high school teachers are required to develop students' four skills of English in a balanced way. Teachers should not focus too much on just one of the skills or grammar alone. In order to accomplish the goal, teachers have to introduce integrated language activities into class. One integrated language activity, for example, is to have students read a text and understand the abstract and main point, and then ask them to speak to each other or in a group about what they think about the main point. To have them write what they have learned from the text is another example. In other words, through these activities, students have to use two skills in an integrated way to achieve the goal. Such integrated activities make it possible for teachers to implement what the Course of Study mentions and increase the four English language skills comprehensively. (152 words)

○**解説**○ (1)　直前の複数形の語句であるskills and techniquesを指す。

(2)　下線部の前文の，医者に期待していることの内容をそのまま記述すればよい。医者に期待することと教師に期待することは同じだというのがここで述べたいことである。　(3)　下線部の後ろから最終文までの内容を検討すると，「過去の馬に乗る」というのは「過去に学んだこと」の比喩である。今日は過去とは別の日であるから，過去に学んだことは全てのことに当てはまるわけではない，ということを記述すればよい。　(4)　(3)とも関連するが，下線部を含む文では，過去に学んだことがいつでも通用するわけではないため，自分自身も変化する必要がある旨が述べられている。それを踏まえて，現在の高校英語教育に起こっている変化と，その変化にどのように生徒を適応させるか150語程度で書く。従来の英語教育では「読むこと」，「書くこと」，「聞くこと」，「話すこと」などを個別に指導していた。一方，現行の高等学校学習指導要領(平成30年3月告示)外国語科では，学んだことを実際に活用・運用できる能力を身に付け，コミュニケーション能力を高めることを目的に，複数の領域を結び付けた統合的な言語活動を通して，5つの領域を総合的に扱うことと明示されている。さらに，従来一つの分野であった「話すこと」が，「話すこと[やり取り]」と「話すこと[発表]」という2つの領域に分離されたため，英語の技能は「聞くこと」，「書くこと」，「読むこと」と合わせて「5領域」(英訳版：five skill areas)に分類されることとなった。解答例では，こうした高等学校学習指導要領の改訂点を踏まえ，統合的な学習の利点とその具体的な活動例を挙げている。なお，解答例中にはfour skills of English，four English language skillsの記述があるが，高等学校学習指導要領外国語科・英語科においては，「5領域」という表現に統一されていることから，学習指導要領の表記に準じることが望ましいと思われる。

【16】(1)　③　　(2)　④　　(3)　②　　(4)　①

○**解説**○ (1)　第2パラグラフの1〜2文に着目する。Kimは自分から話をするよりは聞くことを好んでいて，知っていることと聞いたことを結びつけることが大変な作業であると知っていたとあることを踏まえる

と、「彼女は教室で沈黙していることは怠けていることにはならないと確認していた」を意味する③が正解。　(2)　該当する節を含んだ第5パラグラフの2文目に着目する。Kimと同じようにAkikoも話すことよりも聞くことの重要性を支持していることを踏まえればよい。

(3)　該当する節を含んだ第6パラグラフの2文目に着目する。該当する記述がWestern beliefsであることに着目すれば，話すことによって考えが整理されるという内容を選べばよく，「話すことは考えることである」を意味する②が正解。　(4)　アメリカ人は話すことが思考を促すと考えてはいるが，沈黙によって深い思考が損なわれるとまでは書かれていない。

【17】1　cried　　2　(エ)　　3　着陸機が腹ばい飛行に成功し，無事正しい向きで着陸することができたから。　　4　着陸機の一部としぼんだエアバッグ。　　5　最初…one had bunched　　最後…the Martian surface　　6　(1)　○　　(2)　×　　(3)　×　　(4)　×

○解説○　1　yelled「叫んだ」。最終段落のcriedと同意。　　2　signaled a thumbs-up「親指を立てて合図した」。thumbs-upはgoodを意味するしぐさ。着陸が成功したことを知らせた場面なので，(エ)の「無傷だったことを示した」を指す。　　3　飛行チームが大喜びした理由を書く。第5段落最終文を訳出する。　　4　最初の写真についての描写は第7段落後半にThe initial image, a black and white photo about the size of a bathroom tile, showed a section of the lander and a deflated air bag billowing like an untucked shirttail.とある。　　5　エンジニアのデビッド・グルーエルが予見していた問題を英文中から抜き出す。one had bunched up over the petal that Sojourner would use to exit the lander. It was blocking Sojourner's path to the Martian surface「ソジャーナーが着陸船から脱出する際に使用するエアバッグが，太陽光パネルの上で束になっていて，それがソジャーナーの火星表面への進路をふさいでいた」。

6　(1)　「ミッションオペレーションルームで監視していた人々は，緊張しながらパスファインダーの突入を待った」。第3段落の内容と一致する。　　(2)　「パスファインダーが着陸した後，管制官たちはほっと胸をなでおろし，誰もその後の展開に不安を抱かなかった」。第5段落に，

227

着陸後，管制官たちはパスファインダーがどのような姿勢で着陸したのかを気にしたと書かれているので誤り。　(3)「着陸地点は科学者たちの経験に基づく推測に基づいて決定され，彼らはそれが最善の決定であると信じて疑わなかった」。第6段落に，着陸地点の選定には何の保証もなかったとあるので誤り。　(4)「パスファインダー・チームは困難を乗り越えたが，探していたものを見つけることはできなかった」。最終段落参照。科学者たちは求めていたものを手に入れたとあるので誤り。

【18】(1)　(D)　　(2)　看護師になりたいというナイチンゲールの願望　(3)　(ア)　　(4)　diseases(illnesses, sicknesses)　　(5)　食事内容を改良し，清潔な寝具を提供するなど病院を改革することで(環境衛生の徹底，下水の清掃など病院を改革することで)全兵士の死亡率を43パーセントから2パーセントに減少させたデータに基づく取り組み。

(6)　hero(heroine)

○**解説**○ (1)「今日ではよく知られた人物であるナイチンゲールは，ほとんど名声のない女性であった」と「彼女は…男性優位の医学界に対抗して辛辣な論争を勝ち抜くことに成功した」は逆説の関係。「実際，彼女はエビデンスに基づく医療の最も初期の提唱者の一人と見ることができ，ヴィクトリア朝の医療を一変させることに成功した」と続く。(2)　ナイチンゲールの両親を悩ませた内容を答える。her desire to become a nurse「看護師になりたいという願望」。　(3)　空所前は「看護婦は一般的に教養が低く，不品行で，しばしば酒に溺れるものと見られていた」という内容。しかし，これらはまさに「フローレンスが打ち砕こうと決意した偏見」だったと続ける。　(4)　the main cause of death was not～but rather…「死因の主なものは～ではなく，むしろ…だった」。…にあてはまる英単語として，「(このような不潔な環境下で蔓延していた)病気」が適切。　(5)　下線部の意味は「エビデンスに基づくアプローチ」。最終段落から，彼女がすすめた病院の改革とその結果のデータに触れてまとめる。　(6)「ナイチンゲールは英雄として迎えられた」等が考えられる。

【19】1 ③　　2 ⑤　　3 ④

○**解説**○ 比較的長めの読解問題だが，7段落構成なので，段落ごとに何が述べられているかキーワードを拾いながら整理し読み進めること。1 「秋の読書推進月間」については第2段落で言及。「14日間の読書週間」が10月27日に始まり，「秋の読書推進月間」もまたその日に始まったとある。　2　本の持つ効用については第5段落に集約されている。
①　5文目に「動画共有アプリTikTokで紹介された本は若い人々の間で人気になる」と言及しているだけなので，選択肢のように「本にとって代わり人々を結びつける強力なツール」とは書いていない。
②　4文目に「本を人に紹介すると，その人とはより頻繁に話すようになった」とあるだけで，さらに他の人にその本を薦めることまでは書かれていない。　③　第4段落にカフェへの言及はあるが，病院への言及は文章全体のどこにもない。　④　コロナの影響については1文目「コロナの影響でオンラインが生活の一部なったが，そのためにかえって(オンライン空間にはない)実際に本を手に取ることができる『現実』世界の良さを再確認する」とあるので，「人々を結びつける力が減少」とは述べていない。　⑤　正解である。上記②の説明を参照。
3　地方自治体と児童については，第6段落，第7段落を参照する。
①　スマホ使用については第6段落1文目で触れているが，過度な使用防止や規則を作るなどとは述べていない。　②　第6段落3文目，4文目で，学校での図書購入に際し政府から地方自治体へ支給される地方交付税交付金は，使途が特定されていないため，他の目的に使われることがあり，交付金による購入図書数が減少しているとある。
③　交付金増額への言及はない。　④「子どもたちが本を読める環境を整備することために政府補助金を使うこと」は，第6段落3文目及び第7段落最終文の内容と合致するので正解。　⑤「子どもたちに投資の本を読むように勧める」とあるが，本文には言及なし。

【20】(1)　・スピーキングを行うためには知識があるだけでは行えないこと。　　・実際にスピーキングを行うことで，必要な知識を高めていくこと。　から1つ　　(2)　1 ④　　2 ③　　3 ②　　4 ①
(3)　スピーキングの力を身に付けさせるには，授業の中で教師ができ

るだけ英語で話し，生徒もできるだけ英語で話すという雰囲気をつく
ることが大切だから。　　　(4)　We should wear school uniforms.

○**解説**○ (1)　インプット(知識の習得)とアウトプット(実践練習)の両方
が必要だという観点からまとめる。　(2)　①　異なる情報を持つ者が，
コミュニケーションを通してお互いの情報の差を埋めていく活動。
「双方向」で特定の答えを見つけ出す活動なので「クローズド」。
②　即興スキットは「双方向」で「オープン」。　③　絵の描写は
「一方向」で「クローズド」。　④　自分の持ち物等について示しなが
ら，それについて話す活動。「一方向」で「オープン」。

(3)　Section3には「意味のある口頭でのアウトプットのためには，適
切で十分なインプットが不可欠」，「教室では，励まし合える雰囲気づ
くりが不可欠」とある。これらと関連付け，まとめる。　(4)　ミニディ
ベートの論題として高校生のアルバイト，レジ袋の有償化など生徒
に身近な問題から，消費税率や週休3日制導入の是非など社会問題に
も発展させられる。

【1】次の恵美子さんの書いたエッセイを読んで，以下の各問いに答えなさい。

How can we make our presentations more appealing? When somebody speaks, we normally do not remember everything that is said in detail. According to research into *"the audience memory curve," attention remains high during the beginning of a speech, drops off in the middle and rises again at the end of a speech. This suggests that the opening and closing of a speech are critical moments.

While readers can decide for themselves when to start reading, listeners may be distracted or have other things on their mind when a speaker starts to talk. Therefore, it is important to grab the attention of listeners as soon as possible.

For example, recounting a personal experience, asking a question, showing an eye-catching chart or image are useful means of attracting the attention of listeners. Telling a joke can also be effective but as it is not always easy to make everybody laugh, caution is advised.

Giving an outline of what you will be covering in your presentation is a good way of helping your audience understand the message you want to convey. For example, in a formal setting, an overview of a presentation may sound like this: "Over the next fifteen minutes, I will discuss sales in each of three regions: Europe, America and Asia." On a slightly less formal occasion, one might say: "I'd like to go over the sales figures in three regions."

Another point to bear in mind is the need to limit the number of main points. As listeners cannot process as much information as readers, when you have a lot of information to give, try to group it into a maximum of five sections. Also, when moving to a new topic, try to use an explicit phrase of transition such as: "My second recommendation is" or "Let's move on to the second point."

Furthermore, a summary to conclude each major section of your presentation can also be quite useful as follows: "Now that we have looked at the three main elements of the marketing plan, let's turn to the financial implications of this plan."

Finally, be sure to repeat what you would like to emphasize at the end of the presentation. Never detract from an otherwise good presentation with concluding remarks such as: "Well, that's all I have to say" or "I guess that's about it." Such closing remarks will spoil any presentation. Restating your main point, referring to your opening remark or stating your recommended course of action are some of the most effective ways of concluding.

It is certainly true to say that "(④)"

(出典：「NHK ラジオビジネス英会話 土曜サロン・ベスト・セレクション-プレミアム-」)

*Figure 1　Typical attention the audience pays to an average presentation

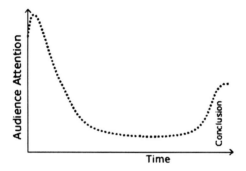

※出典："How to give successful oral and poster presentations" J.W.Niemantsverdriet

(1)　恵美子さんが*"the audience memory curve," について述べている内容として，最も適当なものを，次の選択肢から1つ選び記号で答えなさい。

ア　Presentations need to be most memorable for their content.

イ　The introduction of the presentation should be designed to attract attention.

ウ　The audience remembers the beginning and the end of the content the most.

エ　Audience memory in presentation is higher at the beginning and highest at the end.

(2)　ひろきさんは，恵美子さんのエッセイを読んで英語の授業で発表するプレゼンテーションを作成しました。それぞれの場面に入る最も適当なものを，以下の選択肢からそれぞれ1つずつ選び記号で答えなさい。

Making Effective
Presentations.

-Introduction-
・Provide concrete examples
・Ask the audience questions
・Talk about personal experience
・(　①　)

-body-
・Tell the outline
・(　②　)
・Provide a summary
・Use the explicit phrase of transition

-Conclusion-
・(　③　)
・Suggest specific actions
・Back to what you said at the beginning

ア　Repeat the point you want to emphasize
イ　Use gestures to talk
ウ　Use visual aids
エ　Focus the point within five sections

(3)　文中の(　④　)に入る最も適当なものを，次の選択肢から1つ選び

記号で答えなさい。

ア　failure teaches success.

イ　Different strokes for different folks.

ウ　all's well that ends well.

エ　Make haste slowly.

| 2024年度 | 宮崎県 | 難易度 ■■■■■□□

【2】次の英文を読み，問1～問4に答えなさい。

　　Life in Japan has taught me—among many other things—to believe in good fortune and bad and to see the wisdom in age-old beliefs that some call superstitions. I take Lady Luck seriously now and treat her with respect. When I first came to Tokyo in 1962, however, I was a ①cynical young thing in charge of my own destiny, thank you. So it was disconcerting to find myself in a world where traditional ways and beliefs were still largely intact.

　　In those days, I often (　A　) the image of a chubby lady in the entrances of houses, in corners of rooms, on packages, and on fortune papers at Shinto shrines. I was told that her name was Otafuku or Okame. Other than laughing at her silly face and noticing that she came in a host of shapes and attitudes — charming, coquettish, vulgar, cutesy, and downright ugly — I paid her little attention.

　　But as my years in Japan sped past, I began to see that there was more to the ancient rituals than meets the eye. Japan's native system of belief, with its devotion to gods and spirits and ancient ritual, gave order to the course of daily life. Forces of evil were quelled by regular ministrations to the forces of good. And these forces, always present but needing assuagement, were charged with bringing good fortune and happiness.

　　Otaftiku has been part of this scene for a long time. She is not so much invoked as always there, overseeing the ups and downs of our everyday lives. Her smiling face takes away worry and brings joy. Her chubby cheeks and tiny red mouth suggest robust health and earthy simplicity. She makes us smile when we see her, even as she assures us that she has been watching over us and that everything is all right.

During my early years in Japan, I noted her presence. Now, I can feel her even before I see her. It happened when a friend introduced me to a new restaurant. I liked everything about the place — the design, the food, the presentation. Then, on the way out, a trip to the bathroom...and hanging over a small window in the door, there she was, harbinger of good, a quirky little Otafuku mask. She has become a real friend.

This book has been brewing in my soul for a long time. Years ago, as an innocent — and ignorant — young college graduate, I came to Japan unaware of how radically my (　B　) would be changed. I have lived here now for longer than in my own country and have been the beneficiary of uncountable kindnesses as well as profound lessons in living. Like Alice, I entered a wonderland where people opened their lives and hearts and let me come in and feel at home. When I think of this, I suspect that certain forces have been steering me in the right direction, keeping me from harm's way. And that the lady in charge of it all has been Otafuku.

She's not much to look at. She tends to be plump and frumpy, but something about Otafuku makes her the one you want to come home to. She's always there, waiting, with a smile and warmth in her heart. She brings ②jollity to any occasion and greets each new situation with laughter and bright-heartedness. She's fun and playful and open.

I love her. I have been drawn to her for 25 years! (　C　) she has been beckoning, inviting me into Japan. Come explore the home and the hearth and the everyday life of the heart, she has been telling me. Come inside and play with me. Drink, eat with me, if you will. Let's chat and gossip. Open up and have a good time. Let's enjoy our lives.

I have always been drawn by interesting people. Hair out of place, maybe, hat askew, button forgotten, a twinkle of eye, a flashing smile. Someone different and warm and content with one's self and ready to laugh at the world and, most of all, flow with it.

My creed of imperfection, of enjoying human foibles and originality seems to be best embodied in Otafuku. She is my passport to the side of Japan that is not formal or ordered. She is different things to different people, but to me she is warm, cozy, loving, accepting. Her joyful attitude toward life is one we could all espouse and one that I aspire to myself. She is a universal goddess who bids us all know what is amusing in life and in other people. She is a ③fount of generosity, of sharing her own abundance.

Adapted from AMY KATOH, *Otafuku Joy of Japan* (Tuttle Publishing)

問1　本文の内容から考えて，（　A　）～（　C　）に入る語として，最も適当なものをそれぞれ選びなさい。

A　ア　damaged　　イ　encountered　　ウ　referred
　　エ　drew

B　ア　friend　　　イ　country　　　ウ　life
　　エ　college

C　ア　Somehow　　イ　However　　　ウ　Therefore
　　エ　Literally

問2　下線部①～③と意味が近い語として，最も適当なものをそれぞれ選びなさい。

①　ア　hasty　　　イ　superior　　　ウ　affordable
　　エ　twisted

②　ア　confession　イ　liveliness　　ウ　commerce
　　エ　lapse

③　ア　sage　　　　イ　fad　　　　　ウ　source
　　エ　disgrace

問3　本文の内容から考えて，次の英文の（　　）に入る英語として，最も適当なものを選びなさい。

As the author has lived in Japan over time, (　　).

ア　she became more and more accustomed to Japan where only traditional ways prevailed

イ　she has come to believe in ancient rituals and the discipline they provide for daily life

ウ　she realized that Otafuku's smile sometimes makes us uneasy and makes us feel that something needs to be improved

エ　she has been granted numerous kindnesses from Otafuku, but not to the point where she feels like Japan is a wonderland

オ　she has grown to love Otafuku, but feels that it is precisely in Western-style restaurants that she was encouraged to feel Otafuku

問4　本文の内容にあっている英文の組合せとして，正しいものを選びなさい。

1　The author has lived in Japan and learned, among other things, that one should gain insight from the ancient beliefs that exist in Japan.

2　Since coming to Japan, the author has been conscious of Otafuku whenever and wherever she is at home or out and about.

3　In Japan, there are many restaurants that are designed around Otafuku, and the author liked it.

4　When the author was still a clueless college student, she met Otafuku in her home country, and since then it has guided her in the right direction to come to Japan.

5　Different people have different perceptions of Otafuku, but the author believes that the attitude that Otafuku has is one that all can embrace, and that she is a goddess existing everywhere and involving everyone.

ア　1, 3　　イ　1, 5　　ウ　2, 4　　エ　2, 5　　オ　3, 4

▌2024年度 ▌ 北海道・札幌市 ▌ 難易度 ▰▰▰▱▱

【3】次の英文を読んで，以下の各問いに答えなさい。

A 90-year-old Kenyan woman who goes to class with six of her great-great-grandchildren is believed to be the oldest primary school pupil in the world. Sitting at the front of class four in her school uniform, ①Priscilla Sitienei listens intently while she writes the English names of animals in her notebook.

She joined Leaders Vision Preparatory School five years ago and has also served her village of Ndalat in the Rift Valley as ②a midwife for the last 65 years. In fact, she has helped deliver some of her own classmates, who are aged between 10 and 14.

Affectionately known as "Gogo", which means grandmother in the local Kalenjin language, she says at 90 she is finally learning to read and write－an opportunity she never had as a child.

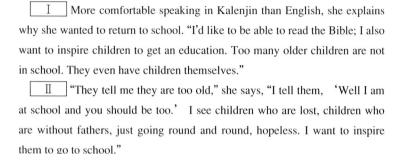 More comfortable speaking in Kalenjin than English, she explains why she wanted to return to school. "I'd like to be able to read the Bible; I also want to inspire children to get an education. Too many older children are not in school. They even have children themselves."

Ⅱ "They tell me they are too old," she says, "I tell them, 'Well I am at school and you should be too.' I see children who are lost, children who are without fathers, just going round and round, hopeless. I want to inspire them to go to school."

At first the school turned her away but they soon understood how committed she was to learning. Headmaster David Kinyanjui believes Gogo, who boards at the village school, is an example to the rest of her class. Ⅲ "I'm very proud of her," he says, "Gogo has been a blessing to this school. She has been a motivator to all the pupils. She is loved by every pupil. They all want to learn and play with her. She is doing well... considering her age I can say I have seen a big difference in this school since she came."

Ms Sitienei grew up in a Kenya occupied by the British and she lived through her country's struggle for independence. Ⅳ Now a prefect, she takes part in all of the classes－Maths, English, PE, dance, drama and singing. In her blue school uniform and green jumper, she also tells stories to her classmates under trees near the playing fields to make sure her knowledge of local customs is passed on.

The children sit and listen to every word she says. An 11-year-old girl says she is Gogo's best friend, "because she tells us stories and we go to PE together". A 10-year-old schoolboy says the grandmother also likes to keep them in order. "We love Gogo because when we make noise she tells us to keep quiet," he says.

The current record for oldest primary school pupil in the Guinness Book of World Records is held by another Kenyan, the late Kimani Maruge. He went to school at the age of 84 in 2004 and died five years later. The primary school in Ndalat says it will write to the record keepers to inform them about their 90-year-old student.

Gogo says she also wanted to learn how to read and write so she could help pass on her midwifery skills and write down her knowledge of herbal medicines. Expectant mothers still come to see her－usually on Saturdays－and she has been known to assist in births in her dormitory, which she shares with one of her great-great-grandchildren.

"I want to say to the children of the world, especially girls, that education will be your wealth, don't look back and run to your father," she says. "With education you can be whatever you want, a doctor, lawyer or a pilot."

Gogo's own lesson is that [a].

「Kenyan grandmother at school with her great-great-grandchildren」

※問題の作成上，原文を一部変えて出題しています。

問1　下線部①の人物を表す表現として適切でないものを，次の1~4のうちから1つ選びなさい。

1　an example to the rest of the class

2　a blessing to the school

3　a motivator to all the pupils

4　the headmaster of the school

問2　下線部②の単語の説明として最も適切なものを，次の1~4のうちから1つ選びなさい。

1　a woman who stays at home to cook, clean, and take care of the children

2　a member of a tribe who is important and respected because they are old

3　a person, especially a woman, who is trained to help women give birth to babies

4　a teacher of the highest rank in a university department

問3　次の英文が入るのに最も適切な場所が，本文中の $\boxed{\text{I}}$ ~ $\boxed{\text{IV}}$ の中に1つあります。以下の1~4のうちから1つ選びなさい。

Gogo says she confronts children who are not in school and asks them why.

1　$\boxed{\text{I}}$　　2　$\boxed{\text{II}}$　　3　$\boxed{\text{III}}$　　4　$\boxed{\text{IV}}$

問4　[a]に入る最も適切なものを，次の1~4のうちから1つ選びなさい。

1 it is never too late

2 easy come, easy go

3 where there's smoke, there's fire

4 who knows most, speaks least

問5 本文の内容に合うものを、次の1〜4のうちから1つ選びなさい。

1 "Gogo" is a grandmother who helps six of her great-grandchildren attend the same primary school where she learned as a child.

2 Leaders Vision Preparatory School accepted "Gogo" because she was believed to be the oldest pupil in the world.

3 "Gogo" not only learns to read and write but also shares her knowledge of local customs with other children at school.

4 According to the Guinness Book of World Records, "Gogo" has the current record for the oldest primary school pupil at the age of 84 in 2004.

▎2024年度 ▎宮城県・仙台市 ▎難易度 ▮▮▮▮▢▢

【4】次の英文を読んで、以下の各問いに答えなさい。なお、文章の左にある I 〜 VII は段落の番号を表しています。

I It has been learned that starting in the 2024 academic year, all textbooks for elementary schools in Japan will carry QR codes for audio and video content in order to enhance active learning promoted by the National Government Curriculum Guidelines.

II On March 28th the Ministry of Education, Culture, Sports, Science and Technology released screening results for textbooks that can be used at elementary schools from April 2024, marking the first inspection since the distribution of digital devices to each elementary and middle school student. A total of 149 textbooks to be used at elementary schools from the 2024 academic year will come with QR codes irrespective of subject and grade or year level.

III The move is aimed at enhancing proactive and interactive learning, as highlighted in the Education Ministry's Guidelines for the Course of Study.

IV For elementary school textbooks, the latest screening was the second of its kind since the Educational Guidelines were updated in 2017. Under the government's "GIGA School Program," most elementary and middle school students across the country were issued digital devices by the end of the 2021 academic year. Based on the premise that all students have digital gadgets at hand, publishers applied for the textbook screenings, after upgrading their current editions.

Ⅴ According to the Education Ministry, applications for the latest screening were filed for 149 textbooks covering all 11 elementary school subjects, with all of them being approved. [a] 155 out of 164 textbooks in the previous screening conducted in the 2018 fiscal year contained QR codes, many of the textbooks that passed the latest screening significantly boosted their number of QR codes present in each title.

Ⅵ The screening criteria this time requires for textbooks to have QR codes that are closely associated with the textbook content, with the websites linked from QR codes managed by the publishers. However, the digital content referenced by the textbooks is not subject to the screenings, as they are regarded as supplemental educational materials only. Publishers have significantly expanded included learning material such as videos and worksheets linked from the QR codes, with one textbook boosting its total content by more than tenfold from its previous edition. Online discussions and research studies using the Internet have become common within "active learning", prompting publishers to respond to this digital transformation when creating their textbooks. As digital textbooks are ①slated to be introduced in English classes for fifth and sixth graders from the 2024 academic year, many textbooks have included pronunciation, as well as animation and video-based conversation examples.

Ⅶ The average number of textbook pages for each subject totaled 14,813 when converted into A5 size paper, up 2% from the previous screening. In Health and Physical Education textbooks, the corresponding figure rose by 21% due to descriptions regarding the coronavirus having been added. Some textbooks, however, managed to reduce their number of pages by simplifying the content and/or using QR codes to reference end-note appendices. These efforts indicate that publishers have taken into account the concerns of school educators for "weighty textbooks" and "*cramming education."

    *cramming education : to study intensively in order to absorb large volumes of information in a short period of time

「Mainichi Japan March 29, 2023」

※問題の作成上，原文を一部変えて出題しています。

問1　第Ⅰ段落及び第Ⅱ段落について，本文の内容に合うものを，次の1〜4のうちから1つ選びなさい。

1　The Curriculum Guidelines require textbooks have QR codes only for visual contents.

2　In Japan, all textbooks used for elementary school students will have QR codes.

3　Textbooks with QR codes will be limited to only some subjects and grades.

4　The government distributed digital devices to publishers in order to update the Educational Guidelines.

問2　第Ⅲ段落及び第Ⅳ段落について，次の英文の（　　）に入る最も適切なものを，以下の1〜4のうちから1つ選びなさい。

Textbook publishers probably made new textbooks with QR codes included because (　　).

1　most students have been equipped with some kind of digital device

2　they thought that textbooks with QR codes would be enjoyable for elementary students

3　the educational guidelines forced publishers to produce textbooks with QR codes

4　the government said textbooks should include QR codes under the GIGA School Program

問3　　a　に入る最も適切なものを，次の1〜4のうちから1つ選びなさい。

1　Even if　　2　Unless　　3　When　　4　While

問4　下線部①と同じ意味の語を，次の1〜4のうちから1つ選びなさい。

1 welcomed 　　2 scheduled 　　3 encouraged 　　4 accustomed

問5 本文の内容について述べたものとして，意見ではなく事実を表しているものを，次の1～4のうちから1つ選びなさい。

1 It is a good move for elementary students to have access to digital devices for their studies.

2 With QR codes, textbooks can include much more content and be even more useful than ever.

3 Textbooks with QR codes should be approved for proactive and interactive learning.

4 Some textbooks have reduced their number of pages thanks to QR codes.

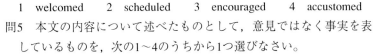

┃ 2024年度 ┃ 宮城県・仙台市 ┃ 難易度 ■■■■□□

【5】次の英文を読み，(1)～(6)の問いに答えなさい。

Related to a language teacher's relationships with individual learners is the subsequent effect this has on the atmosphere of the whole class. Essentially, everyone benefits when the group is happy and working harmoniously together. First and foremost, when teachers are positive, happy, rested, and motivated, there is a strong chance the group will be, too. Our emotions are 　　①　　, and we have already considered how teacher and learner wellbeing are 'two sides of the same coin' (Roffey, 2012). When you are feeling positive, you are likely to convey that to your learners. They, in turn, are more likely to be positive themselves, and you can gain positivity from their enthusiasm and engagement; so begins the positive upward spiral. Our hope is that working through this book and placing your own wellbeing centre stage will ensure that you are in the best frame of mind to teach, and that your learners feel the benefits, too, thereby generating a positive, reinforcing cycle of uplift.

Even though working in groups is valuable in almost every subject, the linguistic and emotional benefits of positive ②group dynamics are especially advantageous for teachers and learners of languages (Verner, 2018). First and foremost, working together gets students talking and interacting in the target language, and minimizes the self-consciousness that is often felt by language learners as they speak aloud.

Positive group work in international, multilingual language classes also offers the opportunity for people from across the globe to interact, meaning that learners are exposed to individuals with different values, expectations, and beliefs. ③This can, in turn, promote sociocultural competence—a core feature of overall linguistic communicative competence.

There are benefits of positive group dynamics for language teachers, too. ④Every teacher knows that it is much easier and more comfortable to work [any / a group / that / well together / with / without / works] friction. Better group dynamics tend to make task work more effective and enhance the willingness of learners to engage with the learning opportunities offered by the teacher. We also know that teachers draw a lot of positivity from their work with learners, and when a class goes well and the classroom climate is positive, teachers tend to experience a boost to their mood.

So, how can we promote positive group dynamics in our language classes? There are various steps teachers can take, such as setting up learning contracts, creating recognizable routines, defining student roles, and reflecting on the effects of environmental factors, on classroom relations and climate (Dörnyei & Murphey, 2003). Among the practical strategies outlined by Dörnyei & Malderez (1999) are:

· spending time on group processes
· using ice breakers to put learners at ease
· promoting peer relationships via opportunities to work together
· personalizing language tasks
· encouraging group cohesiveness through game-like competitions, extracurricular activities, and the creation of group legends and rituals
· formulating explicit group norms and goals that are accepted by all
· preparing learners for the inevitable communication breakdowns and heartaches
· encouraging learner autonomy.

As we mentioned earlier, particularly in the language classroom, learners can benefit from working together on collaborative and cooperative activities. These strategies promote effective language use and at the same time ⑤ . Remember that just because learners are working in a group does not mean they are cooperating and collaborating—that requires a different level of commitment and investment from the learners, which we, as teachers, can foster.

(Teacher Wellbeingより引用)

(1) ① に入る語を次のA～Dの中から1つ選び，その記号を答え なさい。

A competent   B constant   C contagious   D component

(2) 下線部②の意味に最も近いものを次のA～Dの中から1つ選び，そ の記号を答えなさい。

A attraction to do something or act together in a language class

B conditions where people work together and interact with each other

C outcomes derived from emotional feedback

D qualities associated with being physically strong

(3) 下線部③の内容に合うように，次の文の(A)と(B)に入る 適当な語をそれぞれ本文より1語ずつ抜き出して書きなさい。

   By learning languages positively in groups in international, multilingual settings, learners from around the world have the opportunity to (A) and are exposed to (B) cultural backgrounds.

(4) 下線部④の[   ]内の語句を意味が通るように並べ替え，書きな さい。

(5) 本文中の ⑤ に入る最も適当なものを次のA～Dの中から1つ 選び，その記号を書きなさい。

A strengthen group ties and class atmosphere

B enable learners to have a good grade in their learning

C prevent learners from sleeping in class

D disrupt group ties and the classroom climate

(6) 本文の内容に合うものを次のA～Fの中から2つ選び，その記号を 書きなさい。

A The authors hope that you will notice your learners' happiness is the centre of your own wellbeing as a teacher.

B　If learners have a good mood in class, they will begin to learn willingly.

C　A good mood in class is not always brought up even though teachers figure out a good way to teach.

D　Whether learners will work positively together depends on them having common goals.

E　To individualize language tasks and show a strict group rule will never do good to learners.

F　Learners always commit themselves to class and invest their energy when they are in a group.

2024年度 ┃ 福島県 ┃ 難易度

【6】次の英文を読み，(1)〜(6)の問いに答えなさい。
(説明書き)

County Science Fair Application Instructions

In order to participate in this year's County Science Fair, students must submit the following: (1) the Application Form*, and (2) the Project Results Summary Form.

If your project is approved, then you will be invited to participate in the County Science Fair. You will also be assigned to a group based on your area of research:

・Group A:Biology, microbiology, and zoology

・Group B:Physics, astronomy, and chemistry

・Group C:Environmental science and alternative energy

・Group D:Engineering, electronics, and mathematics

All forms and deadlines for each step in the application process can be found on the official County Science Fair Web site: *www. trdsciencefair. org*

*You will be required to submit: (A) your research topic, (B) your hypothesis, and (C) your testing and research plans.

(スケジュール)

County Science Fair Schedule		
7:00 A.M. － 9:00 A.M.	Project Display Set-Up
9:00 A.M.	Science Fair Opens
10:00 A.M. － 10:45 A.M.	Group A Presentations
11:00 A.M. － 11:45 A.M.	Group B Presentations
12:00 P.M. － 12:45 P.M.	Group C Presentations
1:00 P.M. － 1:45 P.M.	Group D Presentations
4:00 P.M.	Winners Announced

(Eメール)

To: Melanie Albright <melanie@trdsciencefair.org>
From: Samir Raju <samir.raju@bixcommz.net>
Date: April 10
Subject: Re:Science fair schedule

Dear Ms. Albright,

I would like to thank you for accepting my application to participate in this year's County Science Fair.

I just received the official schedule and I wanted to ask a question. On the day of the fair, I will be arriving by airplane, and I just learned that my departure time was changed. As a result, I will not be able to reach the Science Fair until 12:50 P.M. at the latest. I will still be on time for my presentation, but I will not be able to set up my project display in the morning. Is it all right if I have some friends set up my display for me?

I understand if this is not acceptable, but I hope that you will make an exception.

I am sorry for the trouble,

Samir Raju

(1) 説明書きに書かれていない情報はどれか。最も適切なものを，次のa～eの中から一つ選びなさい。

a Where the students can download the forms.

b How the students will be grouped.

c What the students have to write in the forms.

d When the forms must be submitted.

e How the students apply for the fair.

(2) 説明書きから読み取れることはどれか。最も適切なものを，次のa～eの中から一つ選びなさい。

a All necessary forms to join the fair are attached to the instructions.

b Adult researchers can take part in the fair to give a presentation.

c Not all applicants can be qualified to participate in the fair.

d Some students are exempt from submitting forms.

e Applicants can receive some forms in print form.

(3) フェアのスケジュールについて述べたものとして，最も適切なものを，次のa～eの中から一つ選びなさい。

a Winner will be announced right after the presentations.

b All presentations will be completed in the morning.

c The project display needs to be ready before the fair starts.

d One group has 45 minutes to make a single presentation.

e Some groups have longer presentation times than others.

(4) Melanie Albrightは誰か。最も適切なものを，次のa～eの中から一つ選びなさい。

a The sender of the schedule to participants.

b One of the presenters at the fair.

c The authoritative researcher.

d One of the sponsors of the fair.

e The mentor of Samir Raju.

(5) なぜSamir RajuはEメールを送ったのか。最も適切なものを，次の
a～eの中から一つ選びなさい。

a To inform of a scheduling error.

b To obtain approval for a request.

c To report irregularities of other participants.

d To send back the appropriate forms.

e To ask for a change in a presentation time.

(6) Samir Rajuが興味のある研究分野はなにか。最も適切なものを，
次のa～eの中から一つ選びなさい。

a Biology, microbiology, or zoology.

b Physics, astronomy, or chemistry.

c Environmental science or alternative energy.

d Engineering, electronics, or mathematics.

e Humanities or social science.

| 2024年度 | 茨城県 | 難易度 |

【7】 Read the following passage and choose the most appropriate answer for each question.

It was a floating toothbrush and a bottle top that changed everything for Emily Penn.

Penn, the founder of the ocean research nonprofit eXXpedition was at the time sailing from England to Australia to start a new job as an architect. She dipped into the water for a bath. "When I came up to the surface, I saw a toothbrush floating by. And then a bottle top," Penn said.

The now 35-year-old was 800 miles away from land and realized "that actually there was this plastic soup all around us in one of the most remote parts of our whole planet. I'd say that for me was the moment when everything started to change," Penn said.

Ⓐ Her firsthand experience with the ocean's plastic problem led Penn to change her plans. Ⓑ She never started that job. Ⓒ In 2014, she founded eXXpedition, a nonprofit that takes all-female crews on sea voyages to understand the oceans' plastic pollution problem and find solutions. Ⓓ

Since then, the organization has taken 19 voyages with women from around the world. Penn focused on involving women after learning that harmful chemicals from plastic pollution that end up in our food have particularly negative consequences for those who are pregnant and their fetus, or unborn child.

The women who make up the crew come from different backgrounds: "everyone from scientists to artists, journalists, designers, teachers, industry leaders, policymakers," Penn said.

(　a　) scientists might seem like an obvious choice for a voyage studying ocean pollution, women from creative professional backgrounds are also tapped because of their storytelling skills.

"What we're looking for is people who have the biggest opportunity to create change when they get back home and what that opportunity is. Because the solutions are so varied, that opportunity is varied," Penn said.

One voyage included a woman who was a packaging designer. Plastic packaging is a major cause of pollution. "Someone who literally for a living designs and decorates plastic: ... That type of person has a really powerful experience at sea when they start seeing products [in the ocean] that they've actually put on the shelves," Penn said. The woman quit her job after the voyage and now works as an independent design consultant for mission-based companies.

There is a lot to observe and study on these voyages. By 2050, plastic will probably outweigh all the fish in the sea, according to the United Nations' Intergovernmental Oceanographic Commission. Between 8.8 million and 11 million tons of plastic make it to the ocean every year.

Plastic doesn't decompose as other materials might. Water and wind cause plastic to disintegrate into much smaller pieces, known as microplastics. Microplastics are harder to clean up and easier for ocean species to ingest.

On the eXXpedition voyages, the women take samples from sea and land for data collection, and they also have workshops to think about and talk through potential solutions.

"The last part of the voyage — we really focus on what happens next and start putting together an action plan," Penn said. She added that the team identifies "what I like to call your superpower, you know, the thing that makes you unique and brilliant that you can contribute to this wider issue."

The data eXXpedition collects is shared with research universities. The nonprofit group's "round the world" voyage in 2019 — which ended early because of the pandemic — resulted in a research paper being published about pollution in the southern Caribbean. The paper found that a holistic approach was necessary to finding solutions. A holistic approach means understanding that there are many parts of a whole instead of focusing on one thing.

It was this holistic mind-set that led to eXXpedition launching its Shift platform. It's a website filled with ideas about how one person, a small group or even a large company can reduce plastic in the ocean. Visitors to the site can scroll through rows of cards and click on one or more to explain the idea, reveal its benefits, challenges and links to additional information. At first the number of ideas can seem overwhelming, but visitors don't need to see them all at once.

"So, the idea behind the Shift platform was to provide filters ... — including one on kids — to help filter down these hundreds of solutions to just a handful, and that you can find a place to start and get started," Penn said.

The nonprofit group emphasizes that there are many ways to (b) plastic pollution. "It's really looking at how we solve this problem from the source and the realization that actually there's not a silver bullet, there's not one solution," Penn said. "And the good news is that there are hundreds."

(Haben, K. (2022). Science and sisterhood: Creating a network to tackle ocean plastic problem. *Newsela*)

1．Where in the passage does the sentence below best fit?

Instead, she began organizing beach cleanups and going on more sea trips.

① Ⓐ　② Ⓑ　③ Ⓒ　④ Ⓓ

2．Fill in the blank (a) with the most appropriate word.

① When　② Since　③ While　④ Unless

3．Fill in the blank (b) with the most appropriate word.

① emit ② generate ③ monitor ④ combat

4．According to the passage, which statement is NOT true about eXXpedition?

① It focuses on preventing not only water pollution but also air pollution.

② Its members consist of people from various professions.

③ It is a non-profit organization, established by Penn.

④ It launched a website about plastic in the ocean.

5．According to the passage, why is eXXpedition composed entirely of women?

① Women are said to be good at storytelling according to a study.

② It believes that plastic pollution is likely to adversely affect women.

③ It would like to provide a place where women can play an active role.

④ Its members need to do work that only women can do.

6．According to the passage, which statement is true?

① Microplastics are so small that they can be easily removed from the ocean.

② A study suggests that we have to focus on a particular solution to prevent plastic pollution.

③ One of the members quit a plastic-related job in order to join the eXXpedition voyage.

④ The eXXpediton voyages have contributed to research on ocean pollution.

▌2024年度 ▌沖縄県 ▌難易度 ▊▊▊▊▢▢

【8】次の英文を読んで，各問いに答えよ。

During the war, the weaknesses of all of the above approaches˙ became obvious, as the American military found itself short of people who were conversationally fluent in foreign languages. It needed a means to quickly train its soldiers in oral/aural skills. American structural linguists stepped into the gap and developed a program which borrowed from the Direct Method, especially its emphasis on listening and speaking. It drew its rationale from Behaviorism, which essentially said that language learning was a result of habit formation. Thus, the method included activities which were believed to reinforce "good" language habits, such as close attention to pronunciation, intensive oral drilling, a focus on sentence patterns, memorization. (A), students were expected to learn through drills rather than through an analysis of the target language. The students who went through this "Army Method" were mostly mature and highly motivated, and their success was dramatic.

This success meant that the method naturally continued on after the war, and it came to be known as *Audiolingualism*. Because the emphasis in Audiolingualism was on teaching structual patterns, the vocabulary needed to be relatively easy, and so was selected according to its simplicity and familiarity (Zimmerman, 1997). New vocabulary was rationed and only added when necessary to keep the drills viable. "It was assumed that good language habits, and exposure to the language itself, would eventually lead to an increased vocabulary" (Coady, 1993. p. 4), so no clear method of extending vocabulary later on was spelled out. A similar approach was current in Britain during the 1940s to 1960s. It was called the *Situational Approach*, from its grouping of lexical and grammatical items according to what would be required in various situations (e.g., at the post office, at the store, at the dinner table)(Celce-Murcia, 2014). Consequently, the Situational Approach treated vocabulary in a more principled way than Audiolingualism.

Noam Chomsky's attack on the behaviorist underpinnings of Audiolingualism in the late 1950s proved decisive, and it began to fall out of favor. Supplanting the Behaviorist idea of habit formation, language was now seen as governed by cognitive factors, particularly a set of abstract rules which were assumed to be innate. In 1972, Hymes added the concept of *communicative competence*, which emphasized sociolinguistic and pragmatic factors. This helped to swing the focus from language "correctness" (accuracy) to how suitable language was for a particular context (appropriateness). The approach which developed from these notions emphasized using language for meaningful communication － *Communicative Language Teaching* (CLT). The focus was on the message and fluency rather than grammatical accuracy. Language was taught through

253

problem-solving activities which required students to transact information, such as information-gap exercises. In these, one student is given information the other does not have, with the two having to negotiate the exchange of that information. In the 2000s, CLT evolved into *Task-Based Language Teaching*(TBLT), where learners carry out a series of tasks devised to emphasize various linguistic features, and to provide meaningful practice in using those features (e.g., Ellis, 2003). For example, a task based on discussing last week's activities could be designed to focus on past-tense verbs.

all of the above approaches*＝Grammar-Translation and the Direct Method

(1) 英文中の(A)に入る英語として最も適切なものを，次の1〜6から1つ選べ。

1　On the other hand

2　Instead

3　In addition

4　On the contrary

5　However

6　In short

(2) 英文に関して，次の①〜⑤の問いに対する答えとして最も適切なものを，それぞれ1〜6から1つずつ選べ。

① What was the primary influence on the development of the "Army Method" during the war?

1　The success of the Direct Method in teaching reading and writing

2　The demand for soldiers with advanced problem-solving skills

3　The necessity to quickly train soldiers in oral/aural language skills

4　The popularity of behaviorism in the field of psychology

5　The emphasis on cognitive factors in language learning

6　The need for soldiers to be proficient in multiple languages

② According to the passage, what was the rationale behind the emphasis on drills in Audiolingualism?

1　The belief that language learning is inherently innate

2　The assumption that language learning is a result of habit formation

3 The idea that vocabulary is best acquired through repetition

4 The necessity to focus on grammatical accuracy in communication

5 The desire to encourage self-expression in the target language

6 The preference for teaching language through problem-solving activities

③ In what way did the Situational Approach improve upon Audiolingualism's treatment of vocabulary?

1 It provided a more systematic way to introduce new vocabulary.

2 It relied solely on the simplicity and familiarity of vocabulary items.

3 It prioritized the teaching of grammatical structures over vocabulary.

4 It emphasized the importance of habit formation in vocabulary acquisition.

5 It used problem-solving activities as the primary means of teaching vocabulary.

6 It focused on the innate capacity of learners to acquire new vocabulary.

④ What does underlined "Supplanting" mean?

1 Representig

2 Following

3 Approving

4 Replacing

5 Maintaining

6 Generating

⑤ How does Task-Based Language Teaching (TBLT) reflect the principles of Communicative Language Teaching (CLT)?

1 It encourages learners to memorize large sets of vocabulary items.

2 It emphasizes the use of language for meaningful communication.

3 It requires students to learn grammar through intensive drilling.

4 It focuses on the innate nature of language learning and cognitive factors.

5 It groups lexical and grammatical items according to various situations.

6 It strives for grammatical accuracy in every communicative context.

┃ 2024年度 ┃ 奈良県 ┃ 難易度 ▰▰▰▰▱

【9】次の英文を読んで，1〜5の問いに対する答えとして最も適切なものをア〜エの中から一つずつ選び，その記号を書きなさい。

In 2009, Lady Gaga sang about being caught in a bad romance, and people the world over were, almost instantly, able to sing along. Even now, seven years later, the odds are pretty good that her love woes are already playing on loop in your mind, based solely on the fact that you just read something about it. "Rah-rah ah-ah-ah." Just in case you weren't there yet.

"Bad Romance" and many songs like it are well-known to musical experts as "earworms," due to their ability to stick inside your brain, on repeat, long after you've heard them. But a new study, published in the journal Psychology of Aesthetics, Creativity and the Arts, now has some insight into why this happens. "We were interested because it's such a common phenomenon. People say certain songs are more catchy than others, but there wasn't a lot of scientific evidence on this topic," said Kelly Jakubowski, a music psychologist at Durham University in the UK who herself gets earworms all the time.

It's estimated that 90% of us experience an earworm at least once a week, with some having them even more frequently than others. Jakubowski's team identified three main reasons why they occur, and it comes down to pace, the shape of the melody and a few unique intervals that make a song stand out. "These three factors stood out above the rest ... the songs need to be not too simple and not too complex," Jakubowski said. "None of these have been revealed in previous research."

As for pace, the earworms highlighted in the study were faster and more upbeat in tempo and generally had a rhythm that people could move to. "We have a propensity to move to earworms," Jakubowski said, citing songs that people may use to pace themselves during a run.

Next on the list was musical shape or contour, with earworms generally being simple in structure, but with a rhythmic pattern. Sounds may rise in pitch, go back down low and then rise again as a pattern, such as "Twinkle, Twinkle, Little Star." Many nursery rhymes fit this pattern to help children remember them — so their creators knew what they were doing. "The quite simple melodic contour might help the brain to recall these things," said Jakubowski.

Last was the need for some unusual intervals within the song, just enough to add some catchy surprises while maintaining a simple, uniform pattern overall. "Although the overall melody has a simple shape, you'll find some unique intervals," Jakubowski said. "So it's simple but different."

To find out what makes certain song catchier than others, the researchers used an online survey to ask 3,000 people, mostly from the UK, between 2010 and 2013 to name their most frequent earworms. The songs most commonly listed as earworms were compared against other songs by the same artists that had ranked similarly on the UK music chart to look for differences in their musical structure. Lady Gaga's "Bad Romance" was at the very top with Jakubowski saying she hears it in her head every time she looks at the ranking.

The team believes that in addition to simply understanding how and why this common phenomenon happens, understanding how earworms affect our brains could add insight into how we process memories and moods, as earworms are also known to be linked to memories and to perk people up. Memories can trigger an earworm, even if you haven't heard it recently, if you are with a person or in a place that you associate with a certain song. "It's memory association," Jakubowski said.

According to the researchers, two-thirds of earworm episodes are considered to be either neutral or positive by the people experiencing them. "Some people find them helpful ... for various reasons, such as getting things done," she said. "There are so many cues in our environment," she said.

Though (A) of us may not find earworms offensive, the reality is that at some point, a song may become annoying, and you'll want it to wiggle out of your head. To enable this, the study has three options: Engage fully with the song by listening to it through to the end, distract yourself with a different song — though this could just leave you with another to get rid of — or simply let it run its course and don't think about it, which is easier said than done. "A lot of the time, people get the song stuck because they don't remember how it ends," Jakubowski said, explaining why it could work to listen to a song through to the end.

Once a tune becomes stuck in our heads, how can you get rid of it? In a separate study, Dr Jakubowski and her colleagues discovered that the most common method is the "let it be" strategy, which involves trying to ignore it until it fades away on its own. However, others preferred to engage with the earworm song. "Those who chose to engage with the earworm song itself often found that doing something like listening to the whole song all the way through to break the loop or identify some unknown element, such as lyrics or song title, helped to get rid of the earworm." Other research efforts have noted that chewing gum can decrease the occurrence of earworms. This is likely to be because chewing gum interferes with the articulatory muscles that are need to mentally 'sing' a piece of music.

Yet another strategy is filling your mind with a different song. Jakubowski asked the trial participants to name other songs they use to get rid of an earworm. The most common answer was "God Save the Queen," the national anthem of the UK. Before you reach for the medication, perhaps try the other options first and, if you can remember how it goes, try praising the Queen of England in musical form.

1 The phenomenon in the passage is called "earworms" because

　ア　it has the ability to repeat itself in the brain long after it has been heard.

　イ　it has the power to make songs catchy for many people.

　ウ　it is a common symptom among music experts.

　エ　it is caused by insects entering the brain through the ears.

2 Choose the correct feature of a song that is most likely to cause earworms.

　ア　Songs made with simple and featureless melodies.

　イ　Songs with a slow tempo that are just right for exercise.

　ウ　Songs with a specific pattern of rising and falling pitch.

エ　Songs you wrote by yourself when you were a child.

3　Choose the correct one about the 2010-2013 survey in this passage.

ア　It was the survey asking what features made a song catchy.

イ　Jakubowski and her colleagues asked 3,000 people living in the UK.

ウ　The songs listed were compared to other songs by the same artists.

エ　The survey was carried out for a decade.

4　Which is the most suitable to put into (　A　)?

ア　few　　イ　half　　ウ　one-third　　エ　two-thirds

5　Which of the following is NOT mentioned as an effective means of getting rid of earworms?

ア　Chewing gum white singing the song.

イ　Filling your mind with another song.

ウ　Listening to the entire earworm song.

エ　Waiting until it disappears with time.

┃ 2024年度 ┃ 岩手県 ┃ 難易度 ┃▮▮▮▮▮▮┃　┃

【10】次の英文の内容について，問1～問4に対する答えとして最も適切なものを，以下のそれぞれ①～④のうちから選びなさい。

The art of accurate thinking is not difficult to acquire, although certain definite rules must be followed. To think accurately one must follow at least two basic principles, as follows:

1．Accurate thinking calls for the separation of facts from mere information.

2．Facts, when ascertained, must be separated into two classes: important and unimportant, or irrelevant.

The question naturally arises, 'What is an important fact?' and the answer is, 'An important fact is any fact that is essential for the attainment of one's Definite Chief Aim or purpose, or which may be useful or necessary in connection with one's daily occupation. All other facts, while they may be useful and interesting, are comparatively unimportant as far as the individual is concerned.'

No one has the right to have an opinion on any subject, unless they have arrived at that opinion by a process of reasoning based upon all the available facts connected with the subject. Despite this fact, however, nearly everyone has opinions on nearly every subject, whether or not they are familiar with those subjects or have any facts connected with them.

Snap judgements and opinions that are not opinions at all, but mere wild conjectures or guesses, are valueless. There's not an idea in a carload of them. Anyone may become an accurate thinker by making it a point to get the facts — all that are available with reasonable effort — before reaching decisions or creating opinions on any subject.

When you hear someone begin a discourse with such generalities as 'I hear that so and so is the case,' or, 'I see by the papers that so and so did so and so,' you may put that person down as one who is not an accurate thinker, and their opinions, guesses, statements and conjectures should be accepted, if at all, with a very hefty grain of salt. Be careful, also, that you do not indulge in wild, speculative language that is not based upon known facts. It often requires considerable effort to learn the facts on any subject, which is perhaps the main reason why so few people take the time or go to the trouble to gather facts as the basis of their opinions.

You are presumably studying this philosophy for the purpose of learning how you may become more successful. If that is true then you must break away from the common practices of the masses who do not think and take the time to gather facts as the basis of thought. That this requires effort is freely admitted, but it must be kept in mind that success is not something that one may come along and pluck from a tree, where it has grown of its own accord. Success is something that represents perseverance, self-sacrifice, determination and strong character.

Everything has its price, and nothing may be obtained without paying this price; or, if something of value is thus obtained, it cannot be retained for long. The price of accurate thought is the effort required to gather and organize the facts on which to base the thought.

'How many cars pass this petrol station each day?' the manager of a chain of such stations asked a new employee. 'And on what days is traffic the heaviest?'

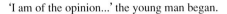

'I am of the opinion...' the young man began.

'Never mind your opinion,' the manager interrupted. 'What I asked you calls for an answer based upon facts. Opinions are worth nothing when the actual facts are obtainable.'

With the aid of a pocket calculator, this young man began to count the cars that passed his station each day. He went a step further, and recorded the number that actually stopped and purchased petrol or oil, giving the figures day by day for two weeks, including Sundays.

Nor was this all! He estimated the number of cars that should have stopped at his station, day by day, for two weeks. Going still further, he created a plan that cost only the price of one-page flyers and that actually increased the number of cars that stopped at his station for the following two weeks. This was not a part of his required duties, but the question he had been asked by his manager had got him thinking, and he made up his mind to profit by the incident.

The young man in question is now a half-owner in a chain of petrol stations, and a moderately wealthy man, thanks to his ability to become an accurate thinker.

本文はNapoleon Hill : Success : The Best of Napoleon Hill (2008, 11.
ACCURATE THINKING 129-132)から。一部表記を改めたところ
がある。

問1　According to the passage, which of the following four sentences is TRUE?

① Perseverance, self-sacrifice, determination and strong character are not always necessary when people achieve success.

② Either perseverance and self-sacrifice or determination and strong character are indispensable when people achieve success.

③ Not all of perseverance, self-sacrifice, determination and strong character are important when people achieve success.

④ It goes without saying that perseverance, self-sacrifice, determination and strong character are essential when people achieve success.

問2　According to the passage, which of the following four sentences best describes accurate thinking?

①　In order to get accurate thought, we have to make an effort to gather the facts especially on which to base the thought.

②　In order to get accurate thought, we have to make an effort to gather and organize the facts on which to base the thought.

③　In order to get accurate thought, it might be better for us to gather and organize the facts on which to base the thought.

④　In order to get accurate thought, we have to either gather or organize the facts on which to base the thought.

問3　According to the passage, why is the young man successful now?

①　He had the ability to consider the matter very accurately.

②　He had outstanding human characteristics such as tenderness and kindness.

③　He had a lot of money to get an excellent pocket calculator.

④　He had a talented manager to assist him at the petrol station.

問4　Which is the most proper title for this passage?

①　The only two principles of mastering the art of accurate thinking.

②　The difference between accurate thinking and inaccurate thinking.

③　The importance of accurate thinking and the evidence of it.

④　The secrets of becoming an accurate thinker without thinking accurately.

| 2024年度 | 神奈川県・横浜市・川崎市・相模原市 | 難易度 ■■■■□□

【11】次の英文を読み，問1〜問3に答えなさい。

Philosophical ethics had for some decades held back (at least in the Anglo-Saxon world) from reflection on practical issues, focusing instead on the analysis and the meaning of concepts. But from the 1960s new issues in medicine (such as experimentation on human subjects and the requirements of informed consent) brought a new lease of life to the ancient sub-discipline of medical ethics, and the spread of nuclear weapons rekindled reflection on the ethics of war.

[A]. Up to the start of the 20th century, philosophy had always been understood as applicable to practical issues (think of the political philosophy of Plato, Aristotle, Spinoza, Locke, and Kant). The various branches of applied philosophy now set about rescuing this longstanding tradition and bringing it back to life and vigour.

At a World Congress of Philosophy held in Bulgaria in 1973, Richard Routley (later Sylvan), an Australian philosopher, gave an address entitled 'Is There a Need for a New, an Environmental Ethic?' [B]. He took the traditional Western view to be that only human interests matter, and that we humans may treat nature as we please. He rejected this view on the basis of thought-experiments. For example, if 'the Last Man', a survivor of a nuclear holocaust, lays about him, eliminating, as far as he can, every remaining living being, animal or vegetable, what he does would be permissible for the traditional view, but in most people's ①intuitive judgment his action is to be condemned as wrong. Such thought-experiments (several were presented) disclose, Routley argued, that there is a growing environmental ethic at odds with the traditional view, and one which better responds to the assaults of human beings on the natural world. We should thus reject the human-interests-only stance (soon to be called 'anthropocentrism'), and adopt a stance for which other living creatures matter as well.

One widespread response to Routley's thought-experiments is that they concern such extreme and exceptional circumstances that people's intuitive judgements about them cease to be reliable, let alone indicative of the principles that we need. Critics suggested that, when judging the deeds of the Last Man, we inadvertently smuggle back into the scenario assumptions that fit more normal cases. We assume (they say) that other people or future people will somehow suffer from his behaviour, even though Routley's scenario was devised specifically to exclude all this.

Yet Routley could reply that he needs to supply a scenario of this kind to allow us to make judgements about a case where there are no remaining human interests (the Last Man, we may imagine, is shortly going to die himself), and where the only interests at stake are those of non-human animals and plants. Besides, he could insist that even in cases where it is clear that no human interests remain at stake, most people still consider it wrong to destroy other living beings.

So Routley's argument against anthropocentrism and in support of a new environmental ethic was widely found to be persuasive. At the very least it seemed to show that non-human animals should be taken into consideration in human decision-making. And if his thought-experiment were adjusted to exclude the remaining presence of animal interests (if, say, all animals in the vicinity had been killed by the same nuclear holocaust), the widespread judgement that the Last Man would be acting wrongly in destroying, as far as he could, the surviving plants could be held to suggest that the good of plants should be regarded as mattering, from an ethical perspective, alongside that of non-human animals and human beings.

But was Routley right in his characterization of Western traditions? [C   ]. Passmore held that the majority view was human-centred and involved no ethical restrictions on the treatment of nature.

Yet he also recognized two minority traditions. In one of these, human beings are stewards or trustees of the world of nature, and responsible for its care (hence the title of his book, *Man's Responsibility for Nature*)—and, in religious versions of this tradition, answerable for their stewardship to God. In the second tradition, the role of human beings is to enhance or perfect the world of nature by cooperating with and bringing out its potential. Both these 'minority' traditions were held to have ancient roots and a long history in Western culture, and thus Passmore's suggestion was that the development of an environmental ethic need not involve a complete rejection of these traditions, which are richer than is often recognized, but can rather involve moving towards these other traditional stances.

[D   ]. But these claims can be contested; for there is evidence that both of Passmore's 'minority' traditions were widely held and advocated in the early centuries of Christianity, and are thus hardly minority traditions at all. Equally, they can be interpreted (and have long been interpreted) in ways that recognize the ethical importance of non-human interests as well as the

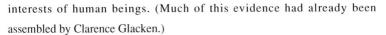

interests of human beings. (Much of this evidence had already been assembled by Clarence Glacken.)

Routley's contribution, then, was an important one with regard to the kind of ethic required, but his narrow view of Western traditions and their resources needs to be taken with a considerable pinch of salt. Many of the saints, for example, were prominent in treating animals, both wild and ②domesticated, with concern and kindness; so a broader view of Western traditions could well be preferable.

Adapted from Robin Attfield, *Environmental Ethics : A Very Short Introduction* (Oxford University Press)

問1　下線部①，②と意味が近い語として，最も適当なものをそれぞれ選びなさい。

① 　ア　inductive　　イ　clinical　　ウ　instinctive
　　エ　physical

② 　ア　tamed　　イ　natural　　ウ　carnivorous
　　エ　national

問2　[　A　]～[　D　]に入るものを1～4から選ぶとき，最も適当な組合せを選びなさい。

1　He was responding to a depiction of the Western tradition by John Passmore, whose book *Man's Responsibility for Nature* was published the following year (1974)

2　For his part, Routley maintained that Passmore's 'minority' views were fundamentally human-centred themselves, and, because they supposedly fail to take into account non-human interests, need to be rejected and superseded

3　His answer to this question was emphatically affirmative

4　The stage was thus set for the emergence in the early 1970s of environmental philosophy and ethics, and related attempts to apply philosophy to environmental concepts and problems

	A	B	C	D
ア	1	4	2	3
イ	2	1	3	4
ウ	2	3	1	4
エ	4	1	3	2
オ	4	3	1	2

問3　本文の内容にあっている英文を選びなさい。

ア　In the Anglo-Saxon world, philosophical ethics had been focusing on reflection on practical issues for some decades until the 1960s.

イ　We should not adopt anthropocentrism but adopt a stance for which other living creatures matter as well as human beings.

ウ　Routley claimed that many people think it's right for humans who don't have any interests in other living things to destroy them.

エ　Passmore suggested that 'minority' traditions should be rejected for the development of an environmental ethic.

オ　In the early centuries of Christianity, both of Routley's 'minority' traditions were held and advocated to some extent.

▌2024年度 ▌北海道・札幌市 ▌難易度 ￭￭￭￭￭

【12】 *Read the following passage and answer each question.*

FUKUOKA — The idea came to him after his grandmother lost her eyesight. Instead of a sidewalk of asphalt, could one be made with something else that is safer for the visually impaired? The answer was wood, which also made it eco-friendly. Kyushu University Associate Prof. Akihiko Higuchi is now leading a team that is refining a sidewalk it created using wood from cedar trees, with the aim of preventing the visually impaired from accidentally entering a road by (a) make a different sound from asphalt when hit with a cane. The project also incorporates the United Nations Sustainable Development Goals (SDGs) by using wood, as well as by (b) from recycled plastic bottle caps. By (c) on top of the beams, it creates a cavern under the walkway, enhancing sound that travels through it — such as the tapping of a cane. As cedar has a certain softness, it also provides a different feeling than (d).

266

Higuchi, who teaches landscape design, started his research in 2007 after his grandmother lost her eyesight due to an illness. At first, the team made a sidewalk with a rough surface, but found it was not much different than a conventional sidewalk. Then, the team tried a sidewalk like a wooden deck and found it (①). They chose cedar as a material as it is relatively easy to procure. The team carried out an experiment in which 101 visually impaired people were asked to tap on three different sidewalk-like structures with their canes. One was made of concrete, another asphalt, and the third cedar. Ninety-eight of them could distinguish the difference in sound. ☐ A ☐

Chizuko Hashiguchi, 71, a participant in the study from Fukuoka, said she had an incident on a sidewalk a year ago. When she tried to go around a car parked on the sidewalk, she lost her sense of direction and didn't notice when she walked out into the road. A passerby called "Watch out!" and pulled her back. "It's easy to recognize because of the sound as I tapped," Hashiguchi said about walking on the cedar walkway. "It's also a different feeling while walking, and I would notice if I stepped off it. I hope it will be built on streets that are on public transportation routes," she added. ☐ B ☐

One problem was with the durability of the wood, as cedar is easily damaged by insects and rot. For that reason, the team used technology developed by Kyushu University to solidify cell walls by injecting resin. Studies show this can prevent decay for more than 20 years. ☐ C ☐ ②The technology was put into practical use with the cooperation of the Fukuoka prefectural government and Kyushu Mokuzai Kougyou Co., a company based in Chikugo, Fukuoka Prefecture, that specializes in timber preservation and insect-proofing. The technology was used in renovation work at Itsukushima Shrine, a World Heritage site in Hiroshima Prefecture. A Kyushu Mokuzai official proudly claims that wood processed with the technology "loses nothing to stone or concrete." ☐ D ☐

Higuchi points out that while production costs are twice that of asphalt, there is also the advantage that sections that are damaged can be easily replaced. The prefectural government has begun studies into (③) the wooden sidewalks, and checked out the prototype at Kyushu University at the end of last year. "We will do research on durability in places where cars will constantly cross over it, and issues related to maintenance," an official said. "We hope to use it if we can find appropriate places."

From the (④) of SDGs, the sidewalks offer a benefit because they have captured carbon dioxide in the atmosphere and stored it in the wood. According to calculations made by Higuchi's team, a sidewalk four meters wide and 100 meters long made of cedar wood would weigh as much as 5.6 tons. Of that amount, 2.8 tons is carbon that originated from carbon dioxide in the atmosphere that was captured as the tree grew. "It can be said that wood sidewalks are storing carbon dioxide captured from the air. Unlike asphalt and concrete, which use large amounts of energy and emit carbon dioxide during the manufacturing process, the more these are put in place, the more they can help (⑤) global warming," Higuchi said.

【Modified from the article of The JAPAN NEWS (January 16, 2022)】

1 *Choose the best phrases from the six choices to fill* (a) ー (d).
Write the letter on your answer sheet.

　ア　walking on the cedar sidewalk

　イ　placing the planks of cedar

　ウ　walking on asphalt

　エ　placing recycled plastic bottle caps

　オ　having the sidewalk

　カ　making the underlying beams

2 *Choose the best word or phrase from the four choices to fill* (①),
(③) ー (⑤). *Write the letter on your answer sheet.*

　①：ア　impossible　　　イ　did the evaluation　　ウ　inefficient

　　　エ　did the trick

　③：ア　implementing　　イ　interpreting　　　　ウ　interrupting

　　　エ　implying

　④：ア　appreciation　　　イ　perspective　　　　ウ　objectivity

　　　エ　prospect

　⑤：ア　provoke　　　　　イ　accelerate　　　　　ウ　combat

　　　エ　fuel

3 *What does the "The technology" in the underlined part ② refer to? Write the answer in Japanese within 15 letters on your answer sheet.*

4 *Where does the following sentence correctly fit? Choose one from* ⎡ A ⎤ − ⎡ D ⎤ .

> In another test on prototype sidewalks, none went out into the road from the cedar sidewalk.

5 *Choose one statement that agrees with the article from the four choices. Write the letter on your answer sheet.*

ア All of the visually impaired who participated in the experiment could distinguish the difference in three kinds of sound.

イ Higuchi and his team found a sidewalk with a rough surface was almost the same as a conventional sidewalk.

ウ Kyushu University Associate Prof. Higuchi indicated that the durability of the wood is twice that of asphalt.

エ It can be said that wood sidewalks use large amounts of energy and emit carbon dioxide during the manufacturing process.

6 *Choose the best title for the article from the four choices. Write the letter on your answer sheet.*

ア Japan's Kyushu Univ. proves that wood sidewalk offers a benefit from the viewpoint of economics

イ Wood sidewalk can help store carbon dioxide

ウ Japan's Kyushu Univ. creates wooden sidewalk that helps the blind and environment

エ Wood sidewalk is safer for the visually impaired

▌2024年度 ▌兵庫県 ▌難易度 ▰▰▰▱▱

【13】 Read the passage below and answer the questions that follow.

①Arthritis has plagued humanity for millennia. More than 2,000 years ago, Hippocrates, "the father of Western medicine," weighed in on a possible cause. He recognized a connection between oral infection and joint issues. He suggested pulling teeth could cure arthritis. He was on the right track, sort of.

Infected gums release bacteria into the bloodstream where they are targeted as invaders by the immune system. And chronic gum infection sparks an ongoing war; immune cells course through the body, causing collateral damage by destroying tissue, even far from the mouth, including the joints.

"We discovered that the immune response to oral bacteria in the blood was associated with joint flare-ups," says Camille Brewer, a Stanford University graduate student. She was lead author on a recent study that provides insights into how oral disease and arthritis may be connected. With regularly scheduled blood tests for people with and without rheumatoid arthritis(RA), her team discovered the first real-time ②correlation between oral pathogen levels in the blood and joint pain.

As the immune system attacks its own tissues, joints grow painful and swell; hands, wrists, and knees may become misshapen. "Within 10 years of onset, 50 percent of people with RA are disabled and unable to work," says William Robinson, a Stanford professor of medicine.

Hundreds of studies over the past few decades have explored how severe oral disease may cause or worsen other serious diseases, and scientists are still teasing out the mechanisms behind this relationship.

Everybody has plaque in their mouths, but some people have a more robust inflammatory response. "There's clearly a susceptibility factor; probably a genetic factor," says Thomas Van Dyke, vice president of clinical and translational research at the Massachusetts-based Forsyth Institute and professor at the Harvard School of Dental Medicine.

While still early, convincing data is emerging that people with periodontitis (oral disease) are at greater risk of developing rheumatoid arthritis and other inflammatory illnesses. Van Dyke adds that those with both systemic disease and oral disease are potentially in the crosshairs for other health "events," such as worsening diabetes, heart attack, or joint flare-ups.

To find out if a healthier mouth could help RA patients, Purnima Kumar, who chairs the Department of Periodontics and Oral Medicine at the University of Michigan School of Dentistry, and her team treated RA patients' oral disease, scaling and root-planing their teeth, a type of deep dental cleaning. They compared inflammation markers in the mouth and systemic markers in the blood measured before and after. The markers that were specific for rheumatoid arthritis dropped.

That shows that "along with treating your arthritis, you should also be treating your gum disease to break the cycle," Kumar says. Bleeding, red, swollen gums are not normal. "If you are spitting blood into the sink when you brush, seek professional care," she advises. Simple cleaning, deep cleaning, or surgery can help build back lost tissue.

It's clear that consistent brushing, flossing, and rinsing are critical for everyone, Kumar says. "If you care about your body, ③<u>you need to protect the doors to your house.</u>"

> (出典：Sharon Guynup, "Can gum infections trigger arthritis symptoms? There's growing evidence of a link." , National Geographic, 19 April 2023 改変)

(1)　Which of the following statements best explains the underlined part ① in the passage?

　ア　a disease that causes a lot of pain in the joints of your body

　イ　a medical condition of the eye in which the lens of your eye becomes white

　ウ　a serious disease in which there is too much sugar in your blood

　エ　a serious condition of not being able to sleep

(2)　Which of the following statements best explains the underlined part ② in the passage?

　ア　a change made in something in order to correct it

　イ　a connection between two ideas, facts, etc., especially when one may be the cause of the other

　ウ　the fact that two things are happening at the same time by chance

　エ　the way in which people or groups of people behave towards each other

(3)　Complete the following sentence with the most appropriate option below.

　　"The doors" in the underlined part ③ is a metaphor for＿＿＿.

● 英文解釈

　ア　your blood
　イ　your body
　ウ　your immune system
　エ　your mouth

(4)　Choose the best statement that explains the main point of this article.

　ア　The treatment Hippocrates suggested for arthritis was partially correct even though he did not indicate any scientific connection between them.

　イ　Now that we have discovered that oral diseases are the direct cause of every heart attack and diabetes, we should invent ways to treat them before they get worse.

　ウ　A healthier mouth could be one of the options to maintain one's health, so people should not ignore any small oral changes.

　エ　We should always keep it in mind that a genetic factor is a potential cause of a more robust inflammatory response.

(5)　Choose the TWO statements which are NOT true about this passage.

　ア　When the immune system recognizes the bacteria released by infected gums as invaders, it starts to attack, resulting in havoc.

　イ　There is no one who never has plaque in their mouths and some of them have a stronger inflammatory response.

　ウ　People with periodontitis have a greater possibility of developing inflammatory illnesses including rheumatoid arthritis.

　エ　Kumar and her team figured out a healthier mouth would not do RA patients any good after giving them oral treatment.

　オ　Spitting blood into the sink when they brush is no longer a big sign for someone to book a dental appointment.

| 2024年度 | 宮崎県 | 難易度 |

【14】Read the following passage and answer the questions below.

When developing a rubric, you must first define the ability or construct that the test is measuring. The components of the ability are the criteria that each response must contain. For example, you can define content, organization, and grammar as the criteria in a rubric and, based on those descriptions, assess

272

the construct of writing and whether a learner's performance is above, meets, or is below the desired ability level.

At this stage, it is also important to decide whether you will use your rubric to score a response holistically or analytically, because the criteria must be combined for the former and separated for the latter for each level in the rubric. In holistic scoring, a learner's response is judged in terms of the overall quality displayed, and a single score is given to the performance. In analytical scoring, the response is judged in terms of specific features of the ability or construct. Thus, each feature has its own subscale and receives its own rating. Primary trait scoring uses a holistic rubric but includes aspects that are specific to the task (e.g., in a writing assignment, a test-taker will be asked to include ideas from a text they have read). The decision to use a holistic or analytic scoring approach depends, of course, on the purpose of the test, how the results will be used, and so on.

Holistic rubrics are useful when, for administrative purposes, it is impractical to break down student performance into separate categories, each with its own separate score. Instead, a holistic or overall evaluation suffices to accomplish the purpose of an assessment. Placement tests, for example, must be scored quickly enough to (　①　) students to ability-based classes, sometimes as early as the next day.

Analytic rubrics, on the other hand, offer more information to the teacher and student in terms of several subcategories of performance. A writing test broken down into the separate criteria of content, organization, vocabulary, grammar, and mechanics offers more (　②　) information, which in turn may serve to individualize a student's objectives.

The next part of the process is to decide on the levels or bands in which to place a learner's response. How many levels to include in a rubric also depends on the purpose of the rubric and what the score conveys. Just two rating levels can be used to show the presence or absence of a criterion, or whether a standard was met. Four or five rating levels can be used to provide more details, for example, *beginning, developing, competent, accomplished.* Although more rating levels can provide greater detail, more than five levels become difficult to use, particularly differentiating descriptions among so many levels. With too many levels to assess, multiple raters—or even the same rater at different moments in time—may not score the same performance consistently (Bachman & Palmer, 1996).

Writing the descriptors for each level is the final part of the process. Successful descriptors should describe observable and measurable behavior. For example, rating a writing test may have in its guide the following description: *the essay effectively addresses the writing task; has a clear thesis that is supported by details; is well organized; and demonstrates a variety of syntax and appropriate word choice.* Descriptors should be kept as brief as possible and should include sufficient details to describe what a learner *can* do and not what they *cannot* do. Descriptors should also contain parallel language at each level—only the degree to which the criterion is met should (③). For example, a speaking test may have the following descriptors at different levels: *communication almost always effective; communication generally effective; communication somewhat effective; communication generally not effective; communication not effective.*

Once the rubric is developed, it is important to pilot it by scoring sample learner responses. In addition to using the rubric yourself, you should also ask a colleague to rate the same samples and provide feedback on the usefulness of the criteria, levels, and descriptors in the rubric. Next, make any changes to the rubric based on the trials and score another set of learner responses with the revised rubric.

When the rubric is ready to be used, it is essential to train any other users. Even if the rubric is clear, another teacher/rater may not apply the descriptors in the same way, and rater training will increase scoring reliability, especially with novice teachers and untrained raters, who are less (④) in scoring (Bonk & Ockey, 2003; Lovorn & Rezaei, 2011; Weigle, 1994,1998).

Even experienced and fully trained teachers/raters can

benefit from reviewing a rating scale before they begin grading. The act of practice rating is referred to as norming—a way to standardize scoring among raters and thus further ensure reliability of test scores.

Adapted from [Brown, H. Douglas. (2019). *Language Assessment: Principles and Classroom Practices (3rd Edition)*. Hoboken, NJ: Pearson Education.]

Questions

1　Fill in the blanks (　①　), (　②　), (　③　) and (　④　), choosing the most appropriate word from those given below.

[　assign　consistent　diagnostic　pass　tentative　vary　]

2　Answer the following questions on the basis of what is stated in the passage, choosing the best answer from the four choices (A), (B), (C) and (D) beneath each question unless otherwise instructed.

(1)　Which option is true?

(A)　In holistic scoring, the learner is judged with the combined criteria, so each learner receives several ratings at a time.

(B)　In holistic scoring, the learner is judged with the separated criteria, so the teacher combines the ratings in the end.

(C)　Holistic rubrics are useful when the teacher needs more information about specific features of the learner's ability.

(D)　Holistic rubrics are useful when it is not suitable to break the learner's performance down into several subcategories.

(2)　Which is discussed about determining levels?

(A)　The rubric with two levels can make it difficult to check whether the criteria have been achieved.

(B)　The rubric with four or five levels can help to provide more information than one with two levels.

(C)　The rubric with two levels shows the degree to which a learner is above the standard set by raters.

(D)　The rubric with six or more levels helps raters score consistently when there are multiple raters.

(3)　Rearrange the following sentences in the right order so they best match ☐ in the passage.

(A)   Rater training begins with the teachers or raters reviewing the rubric or rating scale and discussing each level and the descriptors.

(B)   The next stage is to have raters score another set of sample student responses with the scoring rubrics, then discuss why they assigned certain scores and describe what features of the student samples matched the descriptions in each level.

(C)   Then raters should be given samples of student responses that are clear examples of each level; after reviewing these samples, they should discuss why each of the samples is an example of that level of ability.

(4)   Which is not discussed in the passage?

(A)   How to define the ability or construct measured.

(B)   How to increase reliability among raters.

(C)   How to pilot the rubric before raters use it.

(D)   How to write descriptors for the rubric.

┃ 2024年度 ┃ 栃木県 ┃ 難易度 ████████

【15】 Read the following passage and answer the questions below.

Our lives are dominated by ①two great rhythms, one much slower than the other. The fast one is the daily alternation between dark and light, which repeats every 24 hours, and the slow one is the yearly alternation between winter and summer, which has a repeat time of a little over 365 days. Not surprisingly, both rhythms have spawned myths. The day-night cycle especially is rich in myth because of the dramatic way the sun seems to move from [②] to [③]. Several peoples even saw the sun as a golden chariot, driven by a god across the sky.

The aboriginal peoples of Australia were isolated on their island continent for at least 40,000 years, and they have some of the oldest myths in the world. These are mostly set in a mysterious age called the Dreamtime, when the world began and was peopled by animals and a race of giant ancestors. Different tribes of aborigines have different myths of the Dreamtime. This first one comes from a tribe who live in the Flinders Ranges of southern Australia.

During the Dreamtime, two lizards were friends. One was a goanna (the Australian name for a large monitor lizard) and the other a gecko (a delightful little lizard with suction pads on its feet, with which it climbs up vertical surfaces). The friends discovered that some other friends of theirs had been massacred by the 'sun-woman' and her pack of yellow dingo dogs.

Furious with the sun-woman, the big goanna hurled his boomerang at her and knocked her out of the sky. The sun vanished over the western horizon and the world was plunged into [④]. The two lizards panicked and tried desperately to knock the sun back into the sky, to restore the light. The goanna took another boomerang and hurled it westwards, to where the sun had disappeared. As you may know, boomerangs are remarkable weapons that come back to the thrower, so the lizards hoped that the boomerang would hook the sun back up into the sky. [⑤] They then tried throwing boomerangs in all directions, in a vague hope of retrieving the sun. Finally, the goanna lizard had only one boomerang left, and in desperation he threw it to the [⑥], the opposite direction from where the sun had disappeared. This time, when it returned, it brought the sun with it. Ever since then, the sun has repeated the same pattern of disappearing in the west and reappearing in the east.

Many myths and legends from all around the world have the same odd feature: a particular incident happens once, and then, for reasons never explained, the same thing goes on happening again and again for ever.

Here's another aboriginal myth, this time from southeastern Australia. Someone threw the egg of an emu (a sort of Australian ostrich) up into the sky. The sun hatched out of the egg and set fire to a pile of kindling wood which happened (for some reason) to be up there. The sky god noticed that the light was useful to men, and he told his servants to go out every night from then on, to put enough firewood in the sky to light up the next day.

The longer cycle of the seasons is also the subject of myths all around the world. Native North American myths, like many others, often have animal characters. In this one, from the Tahltan people of western Canada, there was a quarrel between Porcupine and Beaver over how long the seasons ought to be. Porcupine wanted winter to last five months, so he held up his five fingers. But Beaver wanted winter to last for more months than that — the number of grooves in his tail. Porcupine was angry and insisted on an even shorter winter. He dramatically bit off his thumb and held up the remaining four fingers. And ever since then winter has lasted four months.

I find this a rather disappointing myth, because it already assumes that there will be a winter and summer, and explains only how many months each will last. The Greek myth of Persephone is better in ⑦<u>this respect</u> at least.

Persephone was the daughter of the chief god Zeus. Her mother was Demeter, fertility goddess of the Earth and the harvest. Persephone was greatly loved by Demeter, whom she helped in looking after the crops. But Hades, god of the underworld, home of the dead, loved Persephone too. One day, when she was playing in a flowery meadow, a great chasm opened up and Hades appeared from below in his chariot; seizing Persephone, he carried her down and made her the queen of his dark, underground kingdom. Demeter was so grief-stricken at the loss of her beloved daughter that she stopped the plants growing, and people began to starve. Eventually Zeus sent Hermes, the gods' messenger, down to the underworld to [⑧] the land of the living and the light. Unfortunately, it turned out that Persephone had eaten six pomegranate seeds while in the underworld, and this meant (by the kind of logic we have become used to where myths are concerned) that she had to go back to the underworld for six months (one for each pomegranate seed) in every year. So Persephone lives above ground for part of the year, beginning in the spring and continuing through summer. During this time, plants flourish and all is merry. But during the winter, when she has to return to Hades because she ate those pesky pomegranate seeds, the ground is cold and [⑨] and nothing grows.

(1) What are the two great rhythms mentioned in the underlined ①? Answer both of the rhythms in Japanese respectively.

(2) Choose the best combination of words for [②], [③], and

[⑥] from the four choices below.

A. ② east ③ west ⑥ east
B. ② east ③ west ⑥ west
C. ② west ③ east ⑥ east
D. ② west ③ east ⑥ west

(3) Choose the most appropriate word to put into [④] and [⑨] from the four choices below respectively.

④ A. brightness B. colorlessness C. darkness
D. silence

⑨ A. aesthetic B. barren C. fertile
D. immortal

(4) Choose the best sentence for [⑤] from the four choices below.

A. It did. B. It didn't. C. It was. D. It wasn't.

(5) What does the underlined ⑦ indicate? Explain in Japanese.

(6) Choose the best expression for [⑧] from the four choices below.

A. exile Demeter from B. expel Persephone from
C. take Demeter back up to D. fetch Persephone back up to

(7) Filling in the blanks with the designated number of words, complete the following summary of the myth from the Tahltan people of western Canada.

> There was a quarrel between two ___A(1-2)___, Porcupine and Beaver. Beaver wasn't satisfied with Porcupine's first suggestion that winter ___B(3-5)___. Beaver demanded a longer winter, but Porcupine didn't agree and made another suggestion. Since this quarrel, winter ended up ___C(3-4)___.

2024年度 京都府 難易度

【16】次の英文を読み，以下の問1〜問7に答えなさい。

On 13 March 1964, a young woman named Kitty Genovese was returning to her apartment in New York City's borough of Queens when she was the victim of a random and vicious attack. Although she parked her car less than 100 feet from her door, she was overpowered by a total stranger during the short walk to her apartment, and repeatedly stabbed. Despite the ordeal, Genovese managed to scream for help and stagger towards her apartment block. Unfortunately, her attacker caught up with her and inflicted a second set of injuries that proved fatal.

On 27 March, the *New York Times* ran a front-page article about the attack, describing how a large number of 'respectable, law-abiding citizens' had either witnessed or heard the attack, but had not telephoned the police during the assault. The detective in charge of the case was reported as being unable to understand why so many witnesses had done so little. The story was quickly picked up by other media, and most journalists concluded that Genovese's neighbours simply didn't care enough to get involved. ①They saw the incident as damning evidence of how modern-day American society had lost its way. The tragic story caught the public imagination and has since inspired several books, films, and songs, and even formed the basis for a sensitively entitled musical drama *The Screams of Kitty Genovese.*

The witnesses' lack of involvement also puzzled two social psychologists working in New York at the time*. Bibb Latané and John Darley were (②) that the apparent widespread apathy was due to a lack of empathy, and set about investigating some of the other factors that may have caused the witnesses to turn their backs rather than pick up the telephone. The two researchers reasoned that the large number of witnesses may have played a pivotal role, and carried out a series of ingenious experiments that have since been described in almost every social psychology textbook published in the last thirty years.

In their first study, Latané and Darley arranged for a student to fake an epileptic seizure* on the streets of New York, and observed whether passers-by would take the time to help. As they were interested in ③(have / of / that / might / witnesses / the number / the effect) on the likelihood of any one of them helping, the researchers restaged the fake seizure again and again in front of different numbers of people. The results were as clear as they were counter-intuitive. As the number of witnesses increased, the chances of any one of them helping decreased. The effect was far from trivial, with the student receiving assistance 85 per cent of the time when there was one other person present, but only around 30 per cent of the time when there were five others there.

　④In another study, the researchers moved off the streets and turned their attention to groups of people sitting in a waiting room. Rather than faking an epileptic seizure, they created another apparent emergency by arranging for smoke to seep under the waiting room door, suggesting that a fire had broken out in the building. Once again, the larger the group, the smaller the chance of anyone raising the alarm. Seventy-five per cent of people sitting on their own reported the leak, versus a 38 per cent reporting rate when there were three people in the room.

　From helping a stranded motorist to donating blood to reporting a shoplifter or making an emergency telephone call, exactly the same pattern has emerged time and again. It seems that the witnesses to the Kitty Genovese attack were not especially uncaring or selfish — there were just too many of them.

　Why should the urge to help others decrease, the more people there are in the room? When faced with a relatively uncommon event, such as a man falling down in the street, we have to decide what's going on. Often, there are several options. Maybe it really is a genuine emergency and the man is having an epileptic fit, or maybe he has just tripped over, or perhaps he is faking it as part of a social psychology experiment, or maybe he is part of a hidden-camera stunt show, or perhaps he is a mime just about to start his street act. Despite the various possibilities, we have to make a quick decision. But how do we do that? One way is to look at the behaviour of those around us. Are they rushing to help, or continuing to go about their daily business? Are they telephoning for an ambulance, or still chatting with their friends? Unfortunately, ⑤because most people are reluctant to stand out from the crowd, everyone looks to everyone else for pointers, and the group can end up deciding on a 'nothing to see here, move along' option. Second, even if there exists a clear and present need for help, there is still the issue of (　⑥　). In most everyday situations, there is no clear chain of command. Is it your job to help, or should you leave it to the guy over there (not him, the guy behind him)? Everyone in the group thinks in the same way, which can result in no one helping out at all.

The situation is very different when you are on your own. Suddenly, you are carrying all the weigh on your shoulders. What if the guy who has just fallen over really is in need of help? What if the building really is on fire? Are you prepared to be the person who turned the other cheek and walked away? Under these circumstances, most people are far more likely to find out if there is a problem and, if necessary, provide a helping hand.

Latané and Darley's ground-breaking studies into what has become known as the bystander effect were initiated by the behaviour of thirty-eight witnesses who saw the tragic murder of Kitty Genovese but didn't lend a helping hand. Interestingly, recent work suggests that the original media reports of the murder may have exaggerated the alleged apathy, with one of the attorneys involved saying that they could only find about half a dozen good witnesses, that none of them actually reported seeing Genovese being stabbed, and at least one claimed that the incident was reported to the police while it was happening. However, regardless of the reactions that took place on that particular night, the experiments that followed from the media reports of the murder provided a compelling insight into why being surrounded by strangers in a moment of need provides no guarantee of receiving help.

an epileptic seizure*　てんかん発作

(出典) Richard Wiseman, "Why Too Many Cooks Leads to No Cooking at All, and What Can Be Done About It", 59 Seconds　より一部変更

問1　下線部①について，なぜ彼らはジェノベーゼの事件をそのようにみなしたのか。その理由を50字～70字の日本語で説明せよ。

問2　(　②　)に入る文脈上最も適当な語を，次のア～エの中から1つ選び，記号で答えよ。

ア　impressed　　イ　satisfied　　ウ　unconscious

エ　unconvinced

問3　下線部③を，文脈上意味が通るように並べかえよ。

問4　下線部④の研究では，どのような状況を設定したか。日本語で

説明せよ。

問5　下線部⑤を日本語に直せ。

問6　(　⑥　)に入る文脈上最も適当な語を，次のア～エの中から1つ選び，記号で答えよ。

ア　capability　　イ　responsibility　　ウ　serendipity

エ　availability

問7　本文の内容に合うものを，次のア～エの中から1つ選び，記号で答えよ。

ア　People's behaviour is strongly affected by what issue they are trying to address.

イ　Kitty Genovese's case was so horrific that it was considered taboo to discuss in various media.

ウ　A study carried out recently has again emphasized the validity of media coverage at the time of the incident.

エ　The results of experiments by two researchers remain prominent in the field of social psychology today.

2024年度　佐賀県　難易度

【17】次の英文を読み，以下の(1)～(5)の問いに対し最も適する答えをア～エからそれぞれ1つ選び，その記号を書きなさい。

YONEZAWA, Yamagata Prefecture — A multiple-institute effort using computer graphics and DNA technology reproduced the assumed features of a woman who was likely a person of noble birth 1,600 years ago.

An image and a video of the re-created model released on Nov. 4 show that "Himiko of Okitama" had droopy eyes, a flat nose and black straight hair when she was alive, features that indicate she was a direct ancestor of modern people, researchers said. Her skin color and hair type were determined based on genetic data from her skeletal remains, which were uncovered in 1982 from the Totsukayama burial mound group in Yonezawa's Asagawa district. Seven research institutes, including Tohoku University, worked with Yonezawa city's education board to reproduce her whole body through such methods as DNA analysis and forensic facial reconstruction.

About 200 graves are located around the foot of Mount Totsukayama in Yonezawa, which is part of the Okitama area. Himiko's bones were found in a box-shaped stone coffin in the No. 137 Totsukayama grave, built from the latter half of the fifth century, along with a long-tooth comb and a small knife. A Dokkyo Medical University study found that she was 143 to 145 centimeters tall. She is estimated to have died at around 40 years old.

The reproduction project started after Tohoku Gakuin University excavated the Haizukayama burial mound site in Kitakata, in neighboring Fukushima Prefecture, in fiscal 2017. The bones of a man aged 50 or older were unearthed there. Nuclear DNA was sampled from the ancient woman's teeth for comparison with the man's remains. The study found that 96 to 97 percent of her genetic information was well preserved. "We obtained nearly the entire data of nuclear DNA, or humankind's design drawing," said Hideto Tsuji, a professor of Japanese archaeology at Tohoku Gakuin University, who headed the reproduction project. "Such affluent information rarely remains in old human bones."

In fiscal 2021, Yuka Hatano, an assistant professor of forensic medicine at Tohoku University's Graduate School of Dentistry, and Toshihiko Suzuki, an associate professor of forensic medicine at the school, started re-examining the woman's remains and rebuilding her facial features. The National Museum of Nature and Science in Tokyo was commissioned to analyze her nuclear DNA.

The right side of the woman's skull had been lost and the nasal bone was not found. But the study could show how she likely clenched her teeth, providing a better understanding of her dietary habits and lifestyle. "Her teeth were found worn down with apparent signs of temporomandibular joint dysfunction," Hatano said. "The conditions seemingly resulted from her chewing style and other habits, and her jaw was distorted slightly leftward." The "drooping eyes" conclusion was based on her skin's thickness.

The National Museum of Nature and Science's analysis showed that her hair was straight and black, her skin was brown or blackish brown, and her eyes were a color between black and brown. She was a descendant of the people who moved from the Chinese continent during the Yayoi Pottery Culture Period (1000 B.C.-A.D. 250).

But some characteristics typical of people from the earlier Jomon Pottery Culture Period (c. 14500 B.C.-1000 B.C.) were also identified in the woman's remains. "The Jomon people are said to have had craggier faces and prominent noses, but her nose was flat" Hatano said. "Relatively large eyes and single-fold eyelids were added to her reproduction."

Tohoku Gakuin University professor Tsuji said there is a possibility that Himiko and the man in what is now Fukushima Prefecture may have known each other. "With the advanced radiocarbon (C14) dating technology, an analysis of the human remains from Haizukayama and Totsukayama revealed the two belonged to the same period," Tsuji said. "She resembles us, suggesting she is a direct ancestor of us," he continued. "The research outcome is extremely important, and we wanted to share it with local people through imaging in an easier-to-understand way."

From：The Asahi Shimbun ：Researchers use latest technology to reproduce ancient woman

By TATSURO SAKATA/ Staff Writer　November 29. 2022

(1) According to the article, what did several research institutes work to do?

　ア　To prove Himiko was a direct decent of modern people.

　イ　To excavate graves in Yonezawa.

　ウ　To create videos and images of people from 1,600 years ago.

　エ　To create Himiko's whole body by using latetst technology.

(2) According to the article, how was Himiko's DNA found?

　ア　Within her teeth.

　イ　To be affluent.

　ウ　Poorly preserved due to dietary habits.

　エ　DNA was unable to be found.

(3) According to the article, what caused temporomandibular joint dysfunction?

　ア　She was born with it.

　イ　Her poor dietary habits.

285

ウ　Her jaw distortion to the right.

エ　Her clenched teeth, and jaw distortion.

(4)　According to the article, which is true about Himiko's feature?

　ア　Her hair was black and curly.

　イ　She had almond-shaped eyes.

　ウ　Her jaw was not straight and a little crooked to the left.

　エ　She had an outstanding nose.

(5)　According to the article, which statement is true?

　ア　Himiko was found at a burial site in Kitakata.

　イ　Himiko was living in the Jomon Pottery Culture Period.

　ウ　Himiko and the man found in Fukushima belonged to the same period.

　エ　All of Himiko's skeletal remains were found.

‖ 2024年度 ‖ 青森県 ‖ 難易度 ▪▪▪▪▪▪

【18】 Read the passage below and answer the questions that follow.

　It would be difficult to imagine life without the beauty and richness of forests. If humankind does not act quickly, however, planet Earth and all living creatures are in danger of losing forests forever. Deforestation has already resulted in the loss of over 80 percent of the natural forests of the world. Currently, the disappearance of forests worldwide constitutes a global problem affecting the temperate forests of the Pacific Northwest area of the US and British Columbia, and more urgently, the tropical forests of Central and South America, Africa, Southeast Asia, and Australia.

　Deforestation occurs for many reasons. In the temperate forests of the US and Canada, wood is harvested mainly for construction and paper products. In tropical rainforests, one of the most common reasons for deforestation is agriculture. Because the soil in many tropical regions is often nutrient-poor and since 90 percent of nutrients in tropical forests are found in the vegetation (and not the soil), many farmers practice an agricultural method known as "slash and burn." This method consists of cutting down the trees of an area in the rainforest and burning them to release their rich nutrients into the soil.

　The method is sustainable only if the population density does not exceed

286

four people per square kilometer of land. When this is the case, each farm has enough land to let sections of it ①lie fallow for ten years or more, which is enough time for the land to renew itself. In recent years, however, the population density has often reached ②three times the optimum load. This results in land being used more intensively with no chance to recover. Under these conditions, slash-and-burn farming becomes only a temporary solution. Within two or three years, the soil becomes depleted, and the farmer must repeat the slash-and-burn process elsewhere, leaving the used land severely damaged.

Deforestation causes changes in the Earth's atmosphere. For example, deforestation in tropical areas disrupts the cycle of rain and evaporation by removing the moist canopy of foliage that trees provide. Undisturbed, this canopy helps create about one half of the rainfall in a tropical forest. When this water evaporates, it causes clouds to form and promotes future ③precipitation. When trees are cleared away, the canopy is lost, and the cycle is disturbed. With less evaporation, the Earth's surface receives more energy from the sun. This can lead to the creation of deserts, ultimately causing atmospheric temperatures to rise. Moreover, when an area has been stripped of trees, rainfall and sunlight damage the topsoil, making it difficult for the forest to grow back.

Deforestation is also (A) responsible for rising atmospheric levels of carbon dioxide. Forests release large amounts of carbon dioxide into the atmosphere when trees are cut, especially when they are burned. The current yearly rate of carbon dioxide that enters the atmosphere from deforestation is about 1.6 billion metric tons. When we consider that the burning of fossil fuels releases approximately 6 billion metric tons of carbon dioxide per year, it is clear the burning of trees and vegetation contributes significantly to carbon dioxide levels in the atmosphere. These rising levels are a cause for concern because they will be responsible for 15 percent of the increase in global temperatures between 1990 and 2025.

(B), deforestation causes the extinction of thousands of species of wildlife annually. It is estimated that worldwide, 5 to 80 million kinds of

287

animals and plants make up the biodiversity of the Earth, but only about 1.5 million have been studied and named by scientists. Tropical rainforests, which cover about 7 percent of the Earth's land, are home to over half of these plant and animal species. If the rainforests disappear, many of these species will become extinct. This means many species will vanish before we ever discover them.

Is it possible to reverse the (　C　) effects of deforestation? Many experts think so, but it will require international laws to protect the remaining forests. It will also require a campaign to increase awareness of the problem, and a willingness to practice "green" consumerism.

(出典：Barbara Graber, Peggy Babcock and Kayang Gagiano, "Deforestation", Reading for the Real World 3 Second Edition, 2009 改変)

(1)　Which is the most appropriate combination of the words for (　A　), (　B　) and (　C　)?

ア　A　largely　　B　In addition　　C　alternative
イ　A　partially　　B　In addition　　C　devastating
ウ　A　totally　　B　In addition　　C　temporary
エ　A　largely　　B　In contrast　　C　temporary
オ　A　partially　　B　In contrast　　C　alternative
カ　A　totally　　B　In contrast　　C　devastating

(2)　Accoring to passage, which statement best describes the reason for the underlined part "slash and burn"?

ア　To gain more sunlight to penetrate to interior foliage.
イ　To get rid of pests which possibly deplete forests.
ウ　To intake essential substances from plants into soil.
エ　To make space for residence or settlement.

(3)　Which of the following phrases best explains the underlined part ① and ③?

①　lie fallow
　　ア　be covered with plastic sheets
　　イ　become depressed
　　ウ　be left unused

エ　lie hidden in the bushes

③　precipitation

　　ア　a prolonged period of abnormally low rainfall

　　イ　rain, snow, etc. that falls on the ground

　　ウ　the process of turning from liquid into vapor

　　エ　the rise of temperature

(4)　Choose the most appropriate number to represent the underlined part ②.

　　ア　4　　イ　9　　ウ　12　　エ　18

(5)　Which one is NOT suggested in the passage to slow or stop deforestation?

　　ア　To advocate sustainable consumption and purchases.

　　イ　To create cross-border legal frameworks and regulations against deforestation.

　　ウ　To undermine environmental consumerism and its practice.

　　エ　To urge people to become more conscious of the problem through movements.

(6)　Which one is NOT mentioned in this passage?

　　ア　Only one-fifth of the natural forests in the world remains due to large-scale deforestation.

　　イ　The soil in tropical rainforests is originally a little fertile, requiring land betterment for more productive agriculture.

　　ウ　The removal of rainforest foliage has caused the rain cycle in tropical areas to slide, resulting in desertification of the area.

　　エ　Approximately a quarter of the total carbon dioxide yearly released into the air comes from deforestation.

　　オ　The disappearance of rainforests has a significant impact on the ecological diversity since they cover more than half of species existing.

┃2024年度┃宮崎県┃難易度┃

【19】Read the following passage and the answer each of the questions.

Spelling

Of all the areas of dispute over correct English, spelling is the most contentious although not the most sensitive (that prize goes to the question of correct pronunciation). The spelling issue is a high-profile one for straightforward reasons. Mistakes tend to stand out since, almost invariably, only one way of spelling a word is regarded as correct. There have been different approaches to the teaching of spelling over the years but, underlying any approach is the belief that it can (and should) be taught in schools. Another, and not so minor, point is that spelling is a favourite media topic, particularly in newspapers, whenever the question of the 'decline of standards' emerges.

English is notorious for being a language that employs illogical, even perverse, forms of spelling. Those arguing for simplification point to inconsistencies. For example, why should the British English spelling of the noun *humour* (*humor*, in the US) become humorous as an adjective? There is not even consistency in the inconsistency: *colour* has an identical suffix and sound to *humour* yet its adjectival form is *colourful* in British English.

A more powerful weapon in the simplifiers' armoury is the gap between the way a word looks and the way it is sounded. The long 'ee' sound can be represented not only by the obvious doubled 'e' , as in *seem* or *teem*, but by (①) that contain quite different vowels, as in *quay, ski, debris, people*. A phonetic system, one which spells according to sound, would adjust the last four to 'kee' , 'skee' , 'debree' and 'peepul'. This would be more rational, so the argument goes, and it would also make it easier for those mastering the language not just as students but also as native speakers. English-speaking adults come near the bottom of the table in international studies of literacy and this is often ascribed to the vagaries of the way in which words are spelled (or spelt).

This is not a new campaign. Agitation to straighten out spelling goes back many decades. What gives it current force is the support of some academics and experts who, either out of despair at the scripts they have to read or impatience with the illogicalities of English, believe we should waste less time on teaching spelling. The rise of texting, with (②) like TLK2UL8R, and the increasing influence of Americanized spellings (*program, thru*, *center*) have also had a minor effect.

But ③the campaign will not succeed. A few small changes may occur but there can be no root-and-branch revolution in English spelling. There are several highly practical reasons for this. People who already know how to spell the words they use every day (give or take the occasional error) are not going to sit down and learn how to spell their language all over again. This would be the case even if spelling could be organized along simpler lines as the result of some diktat from an imagined Ministry of English.

The most substantial flaw in the phonetic argument is that, although spelling is regularized, pronunciation is not. To take a couple of examples; *think* is spelled in only one way but it is pronounced as 'fink' by plenty of English speakers and as 'tink' by Irish ones. The same th-f-t variation applies to *three*. In these cases, instead of one uniform spelling, we would end up with three regional ones. The point was made forcefully by Jonathan Swift 300 years ago:

(中略)

Finally, the attempt to simplify spelling would actually make things much more complicated. Any half-way experienced user of English recognizes the difference between *quay* and *key* when he or she sees it on the page; similarly with *bow / bough, caught / court, towed / toad / toed*, and countless other groups of (④). Adopting a simplified single form would make the language much the poorer as well as causing confusion. We recognize words not syllable by syllable but as a 'whole'. Under a simplified system we might have difficulty distinguishing at a glance between *whole* and *hole*. The latter is the more logical spelling for both concepts but it does not convey the idea of 'wholeness' straightaway.

(Philip Gooden (2009) The Story of English Quercus)

Write your answer using the characters from A to D.

(1) Choose the best answer from the four alternatives below for the blanks

(①), (②) and (④) in the passage.

① A systems   B combinations   C sounds

D connections

②   A   emoticons   B   colloquialisms   C   euphemisms

      D   abbreviations

④   A   homographs   B   synonyms   C   homophones

      D   syntactics

(2)   According to the passage, what is the underlying ideas about approaches to the teaching of spelling?

A   Spelling should be found in popular media topics.

B   Spelling should be taught in all the areas.

C   Spelling should be found in newspapers.

D   Spelling should be taught in schools.

(3)   See the ③, the campaign is that

A   increasing influence of Americanized spellings.

B   agitation to straighten out spelling.

C   wasting less time on teaching spelling.

D   root-and-branch revolution in English spelling.

(4)   Read the first part of the sentence below and choose the best answer from the four choices to complete the sentence.

①   According to the passage, those who argue that spelling should be simplified point to

A   a lack of irrationality.

B   a lack of consistency.

C   a lack of universality.

D   a lack of inconsistency.

②   According to the passage, English-speaking adults come near the bottom of the table in international studies of literacy because

A   there are phonetic systems which spells according to sound.

B   there are several highly practical reasons.

C   there are different ways of spelling words.

D   there are vagaries of the way in which words are spoken.

③   According to the passage, the most substantial flaw in the phonetic argument is that

A   pronunciation is not regularized.

B pronunciation is regularized.

C spelling is not regularized.

D spelling is regularized.

2024年度 ┃ 長野県 ┃ 難易度

【20】次の英文を読んで，以下の問に答えよ。

Children are heartily encouraged to read in their early years of school. However, once students have mastered this skill and they move from learning to read, to reading to learn, the role of pleasure in the activity can be forgotten.

If reading is just seen as a tool for learning, the will to read may not be fostered in young people. Recreational book reading involves (　A　) reading for pleasure, and research suggests that students in Australia and internationally are reading less over time.

Regular recreational book reading is one of the easiest ways for a student to (　B　) developing their literacy skills. The ability to read fluently is by no means the end of development of literacy skills.

Reading for pleasure has been associated with a range of benefits, including achievement across a range of literacy outcomes, with literacy levels linked to advantages for academic and vocational prospects. Regular recreational reading also offers benefits for cognitive stamina and resistance to cognitive decline, the development of empathy and even achievement in other subjects, including mathematics.

While much of the discussion around reading is concerned with skill acquisition, which usually (but not always) occurs during the early years of schooling, there is little focus on ①will acquisition, where students who have developed the skill to read continue to choose to do so.

Students with the skill to read, but without this will, are considered to be aliterate. They exclude themselves from ②the range of benefits conferred by regular reading, perhaps without ever understanding the consequences of their recreational choices.

The West Australian Study in Adolescent Book Reading (WASABR) examined adolescent attitudes to reading and how often they do it, as well as how teachers, schools and parents can contribute to supporting it. The WASABR found that the most common reason for (C) reading was related to (D) for other recreational activities; the more time spent playing video games and watching TV, the less time spent reading for pleasure.

③Teachers and parents may cool off in encouragement once students have demonstrated that they can read. Research suggests that adolescent aliteracy may be inadvertently perpetuated by withdrawn encouragement from both parents and teachers.

Parents may assume that once the skill of reading has been acquired, their job is complete. They may assume the role of encouraging further literacy development lies with the school.

Teachers may struggle to find time to encourage reading within the demands of a crowded curriculum, which focuses on reading skill, without recognizing the role that reading for pleasure plays in fostering reading skills. The WASABR study sought to provide insight into how teachers and parents can successfully continue to encourage recreational book reading into the teen years.

問1　本文中の(A)に入る最も適切な語を次のア～エの中から一つ選び, 記号で答えよ。

　　ア　necessary　　イ　compulsory　　ウ　voluntary　　エ　intensive

問2　本文中の(B)には英語1語が入る。その語を本文中から抜き出して書け。

問3　下線部①の内容を本文に即して30字程度の日本語で書け。

問4　下線部②について, その例として本文で挙げられているものを次のア～エの中から一つ選び, 記号で答えよ。

　　ア　To understand other people's feelings

　　イ　To prevent the cognitive decline in other people

　　ウ　To develop physical strength

　　エ　To focus on and succeed in one specific subject

問5　本文中の(C), (D)に入る語の組み合わせとして最も適切

なものを次のア～エの中から一つ選び，記号で答えよ。

ア　C：fluent　　　　D：dislike

イ　C：fluent　　　　D：preference

ウ　C：infrequent　　D：preference

エ　C：infrequent　　D：dislike

問6　下線部③の理由を本文に即して85字程度の日本語で書け。

問7　次の問に対するあなたの考えを，(例)に示されている内容のほか
　　に三つ英語で書け。

　　As a teacher, what can you do to encourage students' regular recreational reading in school?

　　(例)・Show my interest in reading

　　　　・Teach strategies for choosing books

┃ 2024年度 ┃ 鹿児島県 ┃ 難易度 ▊▊▊▊▊

【21】次の英文を読んで，以下の各問に答えなさい。

While you can positively interact with social media, it can also negatively create a fear of missing out (FoMO) and increase comparison.

Researchers and practitioners continue to try and understand how social media impacts us, including the pros and cons, while guiding us towards a positive use of this communication tool.

Social Media is designed to keep us coming back for more. The positive reinforcement, or a surge of the feel-good hormone dopamine, can come with certain "minor hits of pleasure" in the form of likes, comments or followers, Adam Stern, an assistant professor of psychiatry at Harvard Medical School, explains. This can lead people to communicate more about their lives to experience this surge.

Social media makes it easier to feel like you're in someone's life, but Stern emphasizes this convenience can come at a cost. People can become less motivated to make the extra effort to maintain real world connections. A survey of almost 17,000 people from 18 countries revealed one-third of people communicate with parents, friends and partners less in the real world because they connect on social media. It might not be a surprise that we are becoming [a] distracted, enjoying in-person interactions [b] and having [c] quality social interactions when phones are present.

Researchers are also finding depressed individuals use social media excessively to cope with anxiety and other problems, since online social networking can be a less threatening way to communicate with others. ①This maladaptive coping strategy can lead to less offline interactions, which could affect one's ability to cope with real world issues and lead to more problems with isolation, loneliness and worsened depression.

According to Charmaraman, director of the Youth, Media and Wellbeing Research Lab at Wellesley College, social media can provide a positive experience if you actively use it to engage with others, meet new people with similar interests, raise awareness about issues you care about, learn something new from reputable sources or create meaningful content.

However, if you just passively scroll, social media can create FoMO and increase comparison, Charmaraman says. A 2017 study published in *SPSSI* shows that passive users had lower levels of well-being. That being said, passive use might have some positive impacts on interpersonal communication. A 2020 study published in *Frontiers in Psychology* found participants who passively used social media scored better at decoding nonverbal cues, versus active users, or those who posted more.

Another benefit to social media is that more people are meeting online. A 2017 survey from Stanford University revealed that around 65 percent of same-sex couples, as well as 39 percent of heterosexual couples met online. The findings were compared to before 2013, when people met more frequently through one's [d]. While you can meet new people online, social media can impact the quality of relationships by what we communicate—or don't communicate—to our online audience. For example, having, or not having, a profile picture with a partner or making the relationship "Facebook Official" can cause disagreements and influence how satisfied someone is with their relationship.

Before social media, you didn't have these factors to think about because they simply didn't exist. Similarly, if you weren't invited somewhere, you might not ever find out.

"The online world makes it easier for you to know what you are missing out on," Charmaraman says. Simply put, FoMO is more intense. A 2020 study published in the *International Journal of Environmental Research and Public Health* revealed that when a small sample size of 61 people abstained from social media use for seven days, their smartphone use and FoMO decreased.

More research is needed to understand the long-term impacts of social media. To create a healthy relationship with the tool, it's essential to think about what your goal－or your kids' goal－is for using social media, Charmaraman says. Providing proper guidance for youth can lead to resilient use of these technologies.

「DISCOVER "Social Media May Be Changing The Way You Communicate"」

※問題の作成上，原文を一部変えて出題しています。

問1 ａ， ｂ， ｃ に入る語の組合せとして正しいものを，次の1〜4のうちから1つ選びなさい。

1 a less b less c less
2 a less b less c more
3 a more b less c less
4 a more b more c more

問2 下線部①の内容について，次の英文の(　　)に入る最も適切なものを，以下の1〜4のうちから1つ選びなさい。

"This maladaptive coping strategy" is a way that people with depression (　　).

1 overuse online social networking in order to deal with their difficulties
2 make offline interactions in order to cope with real world issues
3 try to maintain real world connections in order to get well
4 actively meet new people with the same interests in order to heal their isolation or loneliness

問3 本文の内容について，次の英文の(　　)に入る最も適切なものを，以下の1〜4のうちから1つ選びなさい。

Compared with active users of social media, passive users (　　).

1　are more contented than active users

2　might get a good experience no matter what he or she uses it for

3　might gain interpersonal communication skills

4　are able to create meaningful content better than active users

問4　　d　に入る語として適切でないものを，次の1～4のうちから1つ選びなさい。

1　school life

2　online lessons

3　part-time jobs

4　community events

問5　本文の内容に合うものを，次の1～4のうちから1つ選びなさい。

1　Researchers found that people are communicating less in the real world because of social media, so they are against its use.

2　Social Media is created to get us addicted to them, with some people becoming more communicative about their lives on these apps.

3　In the online world, our FoMO will decrease because we can see what we are missing out on.

4　Although the impact of social media on us is yet to be clarified, we should actively use it regardless of what our goals may be.

┃ 2024年度 ┃ 宮城県・仙台市 ┃ 難易度 ■■■□□

【22】 Read the following passage and answer the question below.

Earth's atmosphere can safely absorb only a limited amount of carbon dioxide. This is called the "carbon budget." Wealthy countries had already used up most of the planet's carbon budget before most poorer ones had a chance to industrialize. The reasons for this are complex, but they have to do with the legacies of colonialism and slavery. Now these lower-income countries are trying to catch up. Their people want many of ①[in / the things / granted / that / take / wealthier countries / for / people]: electricity, sanitation, and convenient transportation networks. And they have a right to them. But the trouble is ②this: if everyone in the world copies the wasteful, fossil-fuel-burning lifestyles that are common in rich nations, the planet's temperature will soar.

The idea of climate debt is a way of finding a fair solution to this dilemma. [③] in 2006, the relatively poor South American nation of Ecuador tried to show the world how this solution could work ― but few were willing to listen at the time.

Yasuní National Park in Ecuador is an extraordinary stretch of rain forest. Several Indigenous tribes that live in the park have rejected all contact with the outside world in order to protect their way of life. This means that they have little immunity to common diseases such as influenza and could be at great risk if forced into contact with outsiders. 【 A 】

The park is also home to a vast diversity of plants and animals. As many tree species grow in just 2.5 acres (1 hectare) of the park, for example, as are native to all of North America. It is also home to many threatened animal species, like the giant otter, the white-bellied spider monkey, and the jaguar. Yasuní is the kind of place that David Attenborough makes those amazing documentaries about!

But underneath that riot of life sits oil ― up to 850 million barrels of it. The oil is worth billions, and oil companies want to get at it. 【 B 】 That money could be used to fight poverty. On the down side, burning all that oil, and logging the rain forest to get it, would add 547 million tons of carbon dioxide to the atmosphere. This is a problem for everyone on Earth, [④] the people of Ecuador.

In 2006, an idea was [⑤] forth by an Ecuadorian environmental group called Acción Ecológica (Ecological Action). The government of Ecuador would agree not to allow drilling in Yasuní. In return, the other countries of the world would support that decision by paying Ecuador part of the money it would lose by leaving the oil in the ground.

₆This arrangement would be good for everyone. It would keep planet-warming gases out of our atmosphere. It would also protect the rich biological diversity of Yasuní. 【 C 】 And it would raise money for Ecuador to invest in health, education, and clean, renewable energy.

The point of this plan was that Ecuador should not carry the whole burden of leaving its oil in the ground. The burden should be shared by the highly industrialized countries that have already put most of the excess carbon dioxide into the atmosphere ― and have [⑦] wealthy doing it (with the help of slavery and colonialism, as you'll see in the next chapter). Under the plan, the money Ecuador received could be used to help the country [⑧] to a new era of green development, leapfrogging over the dirtier model that has prevailed for centuries. The Yasuní plan would be a model for paying the climate or ecological debt in other countries.

The government of Ecuador championed the Yasuní plan to the world. The people of Ecuador strongly supported it. A poll in 2011 showed that 83 percent of them wanted to leave Yasuní's oil in the ground. This was up from 41 percent just three years earlier, showing that a plan for positive change can capture people's imaginations quickly.

A goal of $3.6 billion for Ecuador was set to protect Yasuní from drilling. But contributions from developed countries were slow to arrive ― or never did. After six years, only $13 million had been raised.

So, because the plan had failed to raise the hoped-for payments, in 2013 the president of Ecuador said that he was going to allow drilling. Ecuadorian supporters of the climate debt plan did not give up. 【 D 】 Citizens' groups and nonprofit organizations campaigned against drilling. Protesters [⑨] up to arrests and rubber bullets. Yet in spite of their efforts, drilling began in Yasuní in 2016. Three years later the government allowed drilling in a third oil field inside the park, this time in the area where tribes had lived without contact with the outside world.

Ecuador's government says that the oil extraction ⑩[care / with / is / to / being / protect / done / great] the environment. But even if this is so, drilling in Yasuní means more use of fossil fuels, more greenhouse gas emitted into the atmosphere, and more climate change.

Latin America, Africa, and Asia are filled with opportunities for the richer parts of the world to step up and pay their climate debts. For that to happen, the wealthy peoples, and nations of the world must acknowledge what they owe to the countries that find themselves in a crisis they did little to create.

What are the responsibilities of the rich? What are the rights of the poor, no matter where they live in the world? Until we face these questions, we will not have a worldwide approach to climate change that is big enough to solve the problem. And we will keep having more heartbreaking lost opportunities like in Yasuní.

(1) Put the words from each of the underlined ① and ⑩ in the correct order respectively.

(2) What does the underlined ② indicate? Explain in Japanese.

(3) Choose the most appropriate word for each blank of [③], [④], [⑤], [⑦], [⑧] and [⑨] from the choices below. If necessary, make each one of them inflect appropriately and/or capitalize it. You can use each word only once.

> grow   include   move   put   stand   start

(4) Choose the most appropriate place from 【 A 】 — 【 D 】 in the text, to put the sentence below.

> If they did, it would bring a lot of investment to Ecuador's economy.

(5) What does the underlined ⑥ indicate? Explain in Japanese.

(6) Filling in the blanks with the designated number of words, complete the following summary of the story about Yasuní National Park.

> Yasuní National Park is home to a vast diversity of plants and animals, and it is also where several Indigenous tribes lead a life without ___A(5-6)___.
>
> Under Yasuní, there is oil that is worth billions. At first, the government of Ecuador didn't allow drilling. A poll in 2011 showed that many of the people in Ecuador were in ___B(2)___ the decision. However, Ecuador got so few payments that it couldn't help ___C(2-3)___ the Yasuní plan and allowed drilling.

(7) According to the text, which of the following is true?

  A. Each country is allowed to emit a certain amount of carbon dioxide, and the total amount of carbon dioxide each country is allowed to emit is called the "carbon budget."

B. As soon as Ecuador tried to show the world the idea of climate debt in 2006, many people welcomed the idea and took notice.

C. Contributions to Ecuador from other countries were not enough, and it received only about one third of the money it was expected to raise.

D. In order to prevent more heartbreaking lost opportunities like in Yasuní, we should think about the duties of rich people and the rights of poor people.

2024年度 ┃ 京都府 ┃ 難易度

【23】 Read the following passage and answer the question below.

By listing different senses for a word, dictionaries encourage us to think that each word has several different meanings that we need to learn and store. For example, the entry for 'guilt' many have at least three senses:

1 the fact that you have done something wrong

2 the responsibility for doing something wrong

3 the feeling you have done something wrong.

It is good for dictionaries to provide detail about the different senses of words, and this information can be very helpful when encountering a word in context. However, we should not see these senses as necessarily having psychological reality; they are distinctions created by the dictionary-makers. It is no accident that the three senses are all signalled by the same word form 'guilt' , since they all share the same core meaning: 'having done wrong' . When native speakers use the language either receptively or productively, they simply [①]. To put it another way, dealing with different word senses is usually an issue not of semantics but of pragmatics. Ruhl (1989) calls this the monosemic bias － that is, the assumption that a word has one inherent meaning (semantic), with the different senses in which it is used being determined by context (pragmatic). So if two words have the same or similar forms, we should assume they have the same meaning.

There are clearly exceptions to this, namely homonyms, homographs, and homophones, which are words that have the same spoken or written form (or both) but are unrelated in meaning. 【　A　】A commonly cited example is 'bank' (for money/by the river), but there are many other examples. Kevin Parent (2012) found that the 2,000 word families in the General Service List (1953) include 75 homonyms (words with the same spoken and written forms but unrelated meaning, for example 'bowl', 'rest' , 'yard', 'miss') and ten homographs (words with the same written forms but different pronunciation and meanings, for example 'bow', 'wind', and 'lead'). 【　B　】Wang and Nation (2004) found that around 10% of the 570 words in the Academic Word List (Coxhead, 2000) are homonyms and homographs. There are also exceptions, where a sense of a word has deviated so far from the core meaning that it is on its way to becoming a homonym. Although most homonyms are not etymologically related, a few are; for example, 'second' (after 'first'/part of a minute). The connection between these previously related meanings became [②] to users of the language, and they effectively became different words which need to be learned separately.

The *L1 also encourages learners to see the various senses of the same word form as different words if those senses are represented by two or more different word forms in the L1. For example, in Thai and French, 'to know a person' and 'to know some facts' are expressed by two different words. 【　C　】Similarly, the fork you eat with and a fork in the road are two different words in Indonesian and many other languages. In contrast, when an *L2 word form has a single meaning in the L1, then learners may be less likely to recognize different senses as different words.

The learning burden of word senses can be greatly reduced if both teachers and learners focus on the core meaning of words and deal with different senses largely as a matter of strategy and process rather than as a matter of learning additional meanings. 【　D　】First, and most importantly, the guessing from context strategy needs to be applied when a word is encountered which is used in an unfamiliar sense. Look at the following sentence from a reading text:

A couple were smoking pipes, shoving the black tobacco down into the cups with wrinkled fingers.

The use of the word 'cups' is unusual here (we would normally expect 'bowls'), but the reader should have no trouble understanding it, because it is clearly consistent with the core meaning of 'cup', which refers to a particular shape. Similarly, the use of 'cup' as a verb in 'he cupped her face in his hands' is comprehensible from the core meaning.

A second useful method of reducing the learning burden of word senses is to look at all the senses of a word given in a dictionary entry to work out the core meaning. It would be extremely helpful if dictionaries provided core meanings as well as senses, but at present this happens more by accident than by design. There is also value in learners being made consciously aware of the idea of core meanings and how a word which expresses a single core meaning in one language may express two separate meanings in another language. The goal should be to learn the core meaning of words in the L2 so that when a word is used in a strikingly new sense, it can be dealt with not as an unfamiliar word but as representing something related to what is already known about that word. Besides, seeing how different languages classify the word is part of the educational value of learning another language.

*L1 = first language   *L2 = second language

(1) Choose the most appropriate one for [①] from the four alternatives below.

A．adapt the understanding or use of this word to the current communicative context

B．check the way of using this word in the dictionary to understand it more

C．put a lot of emphasis on the senses of words from the dictionary

D．try to find the new sense of this word by asking native speakers about it

(2) Choose the most appropriate word for [②] from the four choices below.

A．close　　B．deep　　C．difference　　D．lost

(3) Choose the most appropriate place, from 【 A 】 ～ 【 D 】 in the text, to put the sentence below.

　　There are very practical ways of doing this.

(4) According to the text, which of the following is true?

　A．When you look up a word in a dictionary, you will find only a single sense of the word.

　B．You can suppose that two words will have the same sense if they come from the same or similar forms.

　C．It is unnecessary to think about the context when there is a word that is used in an unfamiliar sense.

　D．Dictionaries provides the core meaning and sense of words intentionally.

(5) Considering what is written in the passage, write your own thoughts on how teachers should teach vocabulary to students in approximately 100 words in English.

▌2024年度 ▌ 京都府 ▌ 難易度 ▌■■■■■■■

【24】 Read the passage below and choose the most appropriate answer.

HOW CAN YOU USE A TEXTBOOK AS A COURSE TOOL?

　To understand how a textbook is an instrument or a tool, we can compare it to a musical instrument, a piano, for example. The piano provides you with the means for producing music, but it cannot produce music on its own. The music is produced only when you play it. Playing well requires practice and familiarity with the piece. The more skilled you are, the more beautiful the music. Just as a piano does not play music, a textbook does not teach language. The textbook is a stimulus or instrument for teaching and learning. Clearly, the quality of the instrument also affects the quality of the music. However, if it is in tune, even the most humble piano can produce beautiful music in the hands of a skilled musician. The musical instrument analogy falls short because it involves only one performer, while success in teaching with a textbook depends also on (A). Perhaps as teachers, we are called on to be not only musicians, but also piano tuners, composers, and conductors.

In working with teachers, I frequently come across the attitude that a textbook is sacred and not to be tampered with. In a previous chapter I said that we often give too much power to written documents such as our syllabuses or lesson plans, which in turn may prevent us from paying attention to *how* the students are using them. This is multiplied a hundredfold when it comes to a textbook. Such an attitude is detrimental both to the students and to the teacher because it assumes that the way teachers teach is ⬚ ア ⬚ , and the way learners learn is ⬚ イ ⬚ ; that there is a certain way to teach a textbook, and that the results will be the same each time. Teachers' experiences disprove such assumptions repeatedly. The mental landscape of teaching is dotted with cries of "But it worked so well the last time I taught it."

A more disturbing aspect of such assumptions is the underlying notion that teaching doesn't involve decision making or skill based on our understandings, beliefs, and experience, which Michael Apple (1986) has called the "deskilling" of teachers. This deskilling is evident in the attitude that it is the textbook that teaches the students, rather than the teacher or the students themselves. One study of commercially prepared reading materials for elementary school students found that reading instruction was understood as students absorbing what was in the book rather than as a collaboration among author, teacher, and student (Shannon 1987). To reiterate the analogy with the musical instrument, just as the piano doesn't play the music, the textbook doesn't teach the language. A good textbook — one that meets students' needs, is at the right level, has interesting material, and so on — can be a boon to a teacher because it can free him or her to focus on what the students do with it. However, no textbook was written for your actual group of students, and so it will need to be adapted in some way.

There are two facets to understanding how to use a textbook. The first is the textbook itself: "getting inside it" so you can understand how it is constructed and why. The second is everything other than the textbook: the context, the students, and you, the teacher. The second facet is important, because when you evaluate a textbook, you generally use the lenses of your experience and context to evaluate it, and I think it is important to be aware of those lenses. The first facet, getting inside the textbook, is important so that you know *what* you are adapting or supplementing. The second facet helps you to be clear about *what* you are adapting it to.

The first step in using a textbook as a tool — getting inside it and understanding how it is put together and why — is actually a series of steps that includes three of the elements of designing a course: conceptualizing content, formulating goals and objectives, and organizing the course. In a sense, you retrace with the authors how they conceptualized content, what the organizing principle(s) is, how the text content is sequenced, what the objectives of each unit are, and how the units are organized. A good place to start is with (B), since it lays out both what is in the book, how the units are sequenced, and, depending on the text, the content and organization of individual units.

(Adapted from Graves, Kathleen. *Designing-Language Courses: A Guide for Teachers*. Heinle, Cengage Learning, 2000)

(1) Choose the best one for blank (A).
　① the familiarity with the contents
　② the students who use it
　③ the teachers who evaluate the students
　④ the quality of the textbook

(2) Choose one set to fill blanks [ア] and [イ].
　① ア uniform　　イ predictable
　② ア uniform　　イ unpredictable
　③ ア varied　　イ predictable
　④ ア varied　　イ unpredictable

(3) Choose the best one for the blank in the following sentence.
　According to the author, it is important for teachers to realize that they evaluate textbooks using the ( ) of their experience and context.
　① collaborations　　② rubrics　　③ sequences
　④ viewpoints

(4) Choose the best one for blank (　B　).

① the list of references　② the plan for each lesson

③ the rubric for evaluation　④ the table of contents

(5) Which of the following statements is true according to the passage?

① The quality of a textbook does not affect the quality of learning because a textbook does not teach language.

② For teachers, it is necessary to choose a textbook which students can use to study by themselves.

③ Even if teachers find the best textbook for their class, there is room for adaptation for their students.

④ When using a textbook, understanding the organization of the contents is not so essential for teachers.

┃ 2024年度 ┃ 千葉県・千葉市 ┃ 難易度 ┃

【25】 Read the following blog post and answer the questions below by marking the correct answer on the answer sheet.

1   Transforming our food systems is critical if the planet is to [A] meet our ambitious and necessary goals for climate, nature, and people. How we produce and consume food will determine the future of humanity. Science clearly states that agricultural production contributes over a quarter of greenhouse gas emissions and is the major driver of biodiversity loss and the degradation of soil and water globally. We neglect these impacts at our own peril because food production for future generations depends on what we do now to ensure healthy ecosystems and a stable climate. While the dual crises of climate and biodiversity loss are inseparable, so too are the solutions and it is here where agriculture has a critical role to play.

2   We know what to do and we need leaders to take urgent action. We must advance an ambitious agenda for food systems transformation, which includes production, consumption, and reducing our waste at every stage in between. Agriculture is the only sector that has the potential to be part of the solution for climate and nature, but there is no silver bullet. We must take a holistic food systems approach and work together to end agriculture-

commodity-driven deforestation and conversion of natural habitats; shift to more regenerative and resilient production systems; promote healthier, agrobiodiverse, and [B] sustainable diets; and drive more circular food systems that eliminate food loss and waste across global and local supply chains. We must also ensure a just and equitable transition by supporting producers on the frontlines of climate change's impacts and who are the most vulnerable to its impacts, especially. Indigenous Peoples and local communities, smallholders, women, and youth. It's imperative to strengthen their capacity for resilience, adaptation, and risk, and ensure that resources flow directly to support their needs and constraints on the ground.

3 The exciting news is that we don't have to develop any new technologies to harness the power of Nature. The solutions we need are already available. But we must uphold the truth that ecosystems and production systems are more valuable when they are conserved and sustainably managed than when they are destroyed. It is that simple.

4 Opportunities for urgent action on food systems cannot continue to pass us by. The United Nations COP27 just concluded yet momentum stalled on the Koronivia Joint Work Group on Agriculture, which is essential to keeping food and agriculture included in the climate agenda of member states. As CBD COP15 begins in Montreal, we must elevate food systems transformation in the Global Biodiversity Framework. A successful framework would include a plan to halve the footprint of production and consumption by 2030, with targets for all sectors driving nature loss, especially around food and agriculture. That plan should have a strong and effective implementation mechanism, including a method to ratchet up action over time. Kicking the can down the road towards future global policy conferences threatens to close our window of opportunity to limit global warming to 1.5 degrees Celsius and the accelerating loss of biodiversity. We can feed the world with food that is healthy and nutritious and celebrate the culture and diversity of the planet, but we must do so in ways that still conserve and protect our planet. This is the only way that we

can continue to feed and sustain future generations. (　C　).

(出典：worldwildlife.)

(1)　Choose the best meaning of [A] meet in this context from below.

①　to be in the same place as somebody by chance and talk to them

②　to come together formally in order to discuss something

③　to see and know somebody for the first time

④　to do or satisfy what is needed or what somebody asks for

⑤　to experience something, often something unpleasant

(2)　Concerning [B] sustainable, choose the best description of "sustainability."

①　the existence of a large number of different kinds of animals and plants which make a balanced environment

②　all the plants and living creatures in a particular area considered in relation to their physical environment

③　the ability of people or things to recover quickly after something unpleasant, such as shock, injury, etc.

④　a measure of the amount of the earth's resources used by a person or a population that lives in a particular way

⑤　the use of natural products and energy in a way that does not harm the environment or the ability to continue

(3)　Based on the second paragraph, what does the author believe we should do?

①　Change the method of transporting supplies to an environmentally friendly one

②　Focus on fishing as the silver bullet that is the solution to nature

③　Change the food system to one that is more reproducible and resilient

④　Take no action as food waste is decreasing

⑤　Support those least affected by climate change

(4)　Choose the most appropriate sentence which can be said from the third paragraph.

①　Ecosystems and production systems should be considered so that they are protected.

② Maintaining the complexity of species on Earth is easier said than done.

③ New technologies need to be developed to integrate the power of nature with the latest science.

④ Many ways of dealing with environmental problems are not yet ready for human implementation.

⑤ Methods of electricity generation using the power of nature should be unified into a simple one.

(5) Based on the article, which is the best to fill in the blank (C)?

① Depending on our mindset, we can live without electricity

② There is no Planet B

③ We should discuss the two crises, climate change and biodiversity loss, separately

④ Developing new technologies could be a silver bullet

⑤ There are only a few living creatures on earth

2024年度 神戸市 難易度

【26】次の英文を読み，(1)〜(5)に答えよ。

I do not like the Japanese word "content" loaned from English.

I first heard the word nearly 20 years ago while I was covering the communications industry as a reporter. It was used in the world of online business as a generic term referring to movies, music, dramas and so on.

Movies are movies, and music is music. They're not something you can lump together, I said to myself. The word "content" gained currency sooner than I thought it would, however. The word was probably a handy way to put together whatever makes money. Today, even literature and news articles are no (①).

I wonder if it is too obstinate of me to feel resentful about ②that. Perhaps many would remind me that movies and music have always been commercial products since olden times.

But I cannot help but worry that creators' stances could be affected by the emphasis placed on their products' commercial nature with the use of the word "content." I need not refer to the traditional Japanese belief in the mystical power of language when I say that words and phrases hold a major sway over our minds all on their own.

The Tokyo metropolitan government decided to adopt a new nickname for "ikuji kyuka" (child care leave). The old one was "iku kyu" which is short for "ikuji kyuka." This update was done probably because part of the phrase may give an unintended impression. The word "kyuka" also means the "vacation," but ③(＿＿) for a newborn baby is far from vacationing. The word "iku-gyo," the new term, can be translated as "child care work."

A colleague of mine who took child care leave upon becoming a father said it was really hard for him to hear his superior say, "Go take a good rest."

④The neologism iku-gyo could be effective to a certain extent if someone like his superior, who probably meant no harm in what he said, realizes that the phrase contains the kanji for "work."

Of course, the main goal should be developing a system or an environment that would (　⑤　) the hurdles for taking whatever the absence is called.

Whether mystical powers dwell in language or not, the way our society works is ingrained in words and phrases. Calling into question the way language is used provides us with the opportunity to question society's workings.

[出典：「天声人語」 一部改訂]

(1) ①，⑤にあてはまる最も適当な語を次のア〜エからそれぞれ一つ選び，記号で記せ。

① ア alternatives　イ exceptions　ウ deficits
エ artifacts

⑤ ア indicate　イ heighten　ウ constitute
エ lower

(2) 下線部②が示す内容を具体的に日本語で記せ。

(3) 下線部③にあてはまる最も適当な一語の英語を記せ。

(4) 下線部④を日本語に直せ。

(5) 本文の内容にあっているものを，次のア〜オから二つ選び，記号で記せ。

ア　About twenty years ago, while doing a report on the communications industry, the author was fascinated by the convenience of the word "content."

イ　The term "content," perhaps because it's generic and easy to use, has spread far more quickly than the author thought.

ウ　The author is concerned that using the word "content" may emphasize the marketability of, among other things, movies and music and affect the attitude of creators.

エ　A colleague of the author's was very upset because his superior told him to take as short child care leave as possible.

オ　The author strongly believes that language has mystical powers and that by using those powers, we have the opportunity to transform society.

| 2024年度 | 山梨県 | 難易度 |

【27】Read the following passage and answer the questions.

The Central African country of Gabon is home to the most forest elephants, about 95,000-two-thirds of the entire population.

On a sunny, humid morning, I joined Edmond Dimoto, a field researcher with Gabon's national park agency, on a hike through a lush forest on the slopes of a mountain called Le Chameau, since it's shaped like a double-humped camel.

Nearly every month for the past 25 years, Dimoto has hiked through patches of forest at Lopé National Park to monitor its trees, which bear a spectacular variety of fruits ranging from avocado-to watermelon-size. In his very first week on the job, a gorilla charged him. The experience was so terrifying that Dimoto told his colleagues, "I'm done." They had to coax him not to quit. Another time, he tripped and fell while running from a rampaging elephant. "I was certain I was going to die," he told me. Seeing him lying still, the elephant turned away.

Dimoto's observations are the continuation of a study that a primatologist named Caroline Tutin began in 1984, when she and her colleagues established a research station that's still operating inside the park. They wanted to understand how seasonal variations in the amount of fruit affected gorillas and chimpanzees. Tutin's research ended in the early 2000s, but the monthly monitoring of hundreds of trees marked with metal tags bearing unique numbers went on, making it the longest continuous study of its kind in Africa.

Starting in 2016, Emma Bush, a colleague of Robin Whytock's at the University of Stirling, began analyzing these data. She found a dramatic decline in the amount of fruit. On average, the probability of encountering ripe fruit for 73 tree species that were monitored had decreased by 81 percent from 1987 to 2018. If elephants had to search 10 trees in 1987 to find one with ripe fruit, they now had to search more than 50 trees.

Bush had a clue about why this could be happening. In the 1990s Tutin had observed a decline in the flowering and fruiting of certain tree species during years that were hotter than usual. She hypothesized that the nighttime temperature had to drop below about 66 degrees Fahrenheit for these trees to flower.

Examining Lopé's weather data for the previous three decades, Bush and her colleagues found that the average nighttime temperature had gone up by about 1.5 degrees. The amount of rainfall also had decreased significantly. Climate change was making Lopé hotter and drier.

"We think this is the most credible theory as to why fruit has been declining," Bush says.

After Bush shared her results with Whytock, the two discussed how to figure out whether this was affecting the park's wildlife. Whytock had just started a project to assess biodiversity in Lopé using hundreds of camera traps. He also had seen recent images of elephants from camera traps that Anabelle Cardoso of Oxford University had set up for her research.

Many of those elephants looked alarmingly emaciated. In some images, their ribs were clearly visible. Whytock recalled photos from the early 1990s, in which the elephants had plump bellies and ample behinds. The contrast was shocking.

Looking for old images of elephants, Whytock turned to Lee White, a biologist who is Gabon's minister of water, forests, the sea, and the environment. In the late 1990s, while doing research at Lopé, White had recorded hundreds of videos of elephants on his camcorder. "And he had kept all the tapes—literally hundreds of tapes," Whytock says. "I was handed this enormous case of tiny digital camera tapes. I had no way to play them."

Whytock's mother found a camcorder in her attic. From White's tapes and other sources, Whytock was able to compile a database of thousands of elephant photos. He found that, on average, the body condition of forest elephants-scored by such criteria as how bony the animals looked-had declined by a pronounced 11 percent from 2008 to 2018. The scarcity of fruit in Lopé was the likeliest explanation. "Fruits and seeds are the highest calorie food in the elephant diet," Bush says.

One way Lopé's elephants try to make up for the fruit shortage is by raiding people's gardens in the middle of the night. Jean-Charles Adigou, whose house was on the edge of the park in a settlement of a few dozen homes, told me he often was woken up by elephants visiting his backyard, where bananas and plantains grew. To scare them away, Adigou and his neighbors would make as much noise as they could. But frequently it was too late, he said. A herd of six elephants can destroy a backyard plantation in minutes. "When I was young, this didn't happen," he said. "Elephants stayed far away from the village."

Another resident in the settlement, a fisherman named Vincent Bossissi, was expecting the worst. I talked to him as he sat on a plastic chair under a mango tree in his backyard, where he also grows corn. When I asked him about elephants, he turned grim and looked away. (①) He fully expected them to visit one of these nights and strip his mango tree of all its fruit. This explained the row of ripe mangoes on a table beside him. As the conversation went on, I watched him eat one after another, apparently to preempt any losses from a nighttime raid.

Though Bossissi wasn't enthused about elephants, Brigitte Moussavou, one of his neighbors, told me that many in the community were aware that elephants enable the regeneration of certain tree species, including the greatly valued moabi tree, whose seeds are used for cooking oil.

"We want to protect our crops," she said, "but we are not against elephants."

At Lopé National Park, scientists now are investigating whether climate change is altering the elephant's diet. One morning, I accompanied two field researchers in search of elephant dung. We didn't have to drive far before coming upon a fresh brownish-green, bucketsize pile beside the road. After slipping on rubber gloves, one of the researchers counted the number of lumps and then determined the circumference of each with a tape measure.

The reason behind collecting such detail, he explained somewhat abashedly, was to document how much dung the elephants were producing-over time, these data would reveal how much they were eating.

After collecting the dung in a plastic bag, we drove to a stream. The researchers emptied the contents onto a rectangular wire mesh and lowered it into the water, letting the finer poo wash away while leaving behind seeds, stems, and branches. From the seeds, Whytock explains, scientists hope to discover which fruits-and how much of them-the elephants are eating and then compare that with the dung studies White and others did three decades earlier. "This is a more direct way to measure if the forest elephant's diet has been affected," he says.

On the drive out of Lopé early one morning, not far from where I'd seen the elephants, we saw a buffalo in the road, blocking our path. We stared at it, and it stared at us, standing its ground. A mist hung over the shrubs and trees. In the hushed silence, I found myself wondering about a world being reshaped by warming temperatures. The buffalo finally sauntered away, and we drove on. As the hills and forests receded, I was left with a troubling thought: Could the fraying of the ancient bond between trees and elephants in a place as pristine as Lopé be a forewarning? Was it the case that other seemingly untouched forests, with no Edmond Dimoto to observe their trees, already were being harmed in as yet unnoticed ways?

Adapted from Yudhijit Bhattacharjee, *A FRAGILE REFUGE FOR FOREST ELEPHANTS*

(NATIONAL GEOGRAPHIC, May, 2022)

〔1〕 Choose the most appropriate sentence from among 1 to 4 in order to fill in the blank (①).

1 I want to examine elephant dung, he thought.

2 Mangoes were especially attractive to the animals, he said.

3 He has decided to grow bananas and plantains in his backyard.

4 He tried to make them eat mangoes because mangoes are bad for their health.

〔2〕 Choose the statement from among 1 to 4 that is the most consistent in meaning with the passage.

1 Lopé's elephants are now overweight in comparison with the early 1990s because they are eating more fruit from people's gardens in the middle of the night.

2 The reason scientists now are collecting the dung of elephants at Lopé National Park is that they want to know what kinds and how much fruit Lopé's elephants are eating.

3 Dimoto's monitoring of trees in Lopé in the Central African country of Gabon for more than fifty years was not dangerous at all.

4 From Lopé's weather data for the past thirty years, Emma Bush had discovered that the scarcity of fruit in Lopé was not related to warmer temperatures.

▌ 2024年度 ▌ 東京都 ▌ 難易度 ■■■■□

【28】次の英文を読んで，以下の(1)〜(7)の各問いに答えよ。なお，文章の左端にある番号①〜③は，段落番号を表している。

[(1)(7)各2点，その他各3点]

① The ①genesis of the Word Knowledge Approach is usually traced back to an article in 1976 by Jack Richards in *TESOL Quarterly*, where he listed eight kinds of knowledge that one must have about a word in order to use it well. ア This list was refined and popularized by Nation (1990). He presented a revised and expanded version in 2013, which is the best specification to date of the range of word-knowledge aspects (Table 3.1).

317

英文解釈

TABLE 3.1 WHAT IS INVOLVED IN KNOWING A WORD (TYPES OF WORD KNOWLEDGE)

Form	spoken	R	What does the word sound like?
		P	How is the word pronounced?
	written	R	What does the word look like?
		P	How is the word written and spelled?
	word parts	R	What parts are recognizable in this word?
		P	What word parts are needed to express this meaning?
Meaning	form and meaning	R	What meaning does this word form signal?
		P	What word form can be used to express this meaning?
	concept and referents	R	What is included in the concept?
		P	What items can the concept refer to?
	associations	R	What other words does this make us think of?
		P	What other words could we use instead of this one?
Use	grammatical functions	R	In what patterns does the word occur?
		P	In what patterns must we use this word?
	collocations	R	What words or types of words occur with this one?
		P	What words or types of words must we use with this one?
	constraints on use	R	Where, when, and how often would we expect to meet this word?
	(register, frequency...)	P	Where, when, and how often can we use this word?

R = receptive element; P = productive element.
(Nation, 2013, p.49)

2 Nation's word-knowledge ②taxonomy is a good analytical specification of what complete mastery of a word entails. But it must be seen as an *ideal* range of knowledge, as even *¹L1 speakers will not necessarily have mastered all word-knowledge aspects for every word they "know." In fact, partial mastery of many of the aspects is probably the normal state for many words, even for very proficient language users. 　イ　 For example, a person may know most of the meaning senses for a word (*circle*= a round shape) but not know less frequent senses (= group of people with similar interests, e.g., a literary circle). Just as we often come across new words we don't know when reading or listening, the same is true for new meaning senses for words we are already familiar with. (A), we are constantly building up and refining intuitions of words and their collocates as we ③are exposed to more and more language. 　ウ　

3 The word-knowledge framework has been useful for both pedagogy and research. In pedagogy, its main influence has probably been in helping practitioners to think beyond just meaning and spelling/pronunciation. The framework shows that knowledge of many components is necessary to use a word well, and that these components somehow need to be addressed in instruction and teaching materials. The framework also suggests that vocabulary knowledge is complex and cannot be addressed with a single approach to instruction or learning. Some word-knowledge components are

318

relatively ④<u>amenable to</u> intentional learning, such as meaning and written form, while the more contextualized aspects, such as collocation and register, are much more difficult to teach explicitly. They have to be acquired instead through massive exposure to the *²L2. ┃ エ ┃ In research, the framework has encouraged scholars to think creatively about how to measure vocabulary knowledge, and to move beyond tests of the form-meaning link (e.g., Webb, 2005, 2007a, 2007b). With more multi-component studies now beginning to appear, the framework offers a way to conceptualize the acquisition of a more comprehensive version of knowledge than has been considered before.

(Adapted from Schmitt, N. & Schmitt, D. (2020). "The nature and size of vocabulary" in *Vocabulary in Language Teaching* [2nd ed.]. Cambridge University Press.)

(注)

*¹ L1：第一言語・母語(first language)　　*² L2：第二言語(second language)

(1)　本文中の下線①～④とほぼ同じ意味を表すものを，次の1～4からそれぞれ選び，記号で答えよ。

①　1　literacy　　2　origin　　3　fame　　4　scheme

②　1　consequence　　2　credence　　3　commodity　　4　classification

③　1　envision　　2　ensure　　3　encounter　　4　entangle

④　1　indispensable to　　2　tractable in　　3　inevitable in　　4　comparable to

(2)　次の英文が入る最も適切な箇所を，本文中の┃ ア ┃～┃ エ ┃から選び，記号で答えよ。

But at the beginning stages when we meet new words, we gain only some limited impression of a few of the word-knowledge aspects.

(3)　本文中の(A)に入る最も適切なものを，次の1～4から選び，記号で答えよ。

1　Likewise　　2　Nevertheless　　3　Overall　　4　Specifically

(4)　次のア，イの各英文について，本文の内容に合っている場合はT，合っていない場合はFと答えよ。

ア　The framework by Nation demonstrates that successful use of words requires knowledge of many word components.

イ　The author believes that the most important vocabulary knowledge is the relationship between meaning and spelling/pronunciation.

(5)　本文中のTABLE 3.1から読み取れる内容として適切なものを，次の1〜8から3つ選び，記号で答えよ。

1　Productive vocabulary learning is more demanding than receptive vocabulary learning for L2 learners.

2　Associations, which are listed as a type of word-knowledge, are related to synonym knowledge.

3　Nation has categorized vocabulary knowledge in terms of both receptive or productive aspects.

4　Having knowledge of the meaning and form of a word is more essential than knowing how to use it.

5　The receptive aspect is irrelevant because speaking is an activity that involves the production of words.

6　Knowing the appropriateness of the use of a word is also part of knowing a word.

7　Having knowledge related to grammar does not depend on knowing vocabulary.

8　Affixes such as prefixes and suffixes are not relevant to vocabulary knowledge.

(6)　本文の内容に関する次の質問に英語で答えよ。

Why do we have to think of Nation's word-knowledge framework as an ideal range of knowledge?

(7)　次の文章は，Nationが示した単語知識に関する枠組みが，「教育面」「研究面」に与えた影響を，本文に即してまとめたものである。文章中の(　①　)〜(　④　)に適切な日本語をそれぞれ入れよ。

教育面では，単語をうまく使うためには，単語の意味やつづり・発音だけではなく，多くの要素を知る必要があることが示されており，これらの要素は(　①　)という指針を示している。また，単語知識は複雑であるため，(　②　)ことも示唆している。研究面では，単語知識を測定するために，(　③　)ように促した。その結果，現在，(　④　)が現れ始めている。

2024年度　山口県　難易度

【29】 *Read the following passage and answer each question.*

Instructionism leads to shallow knowledge in a subject. And shallow knowledge does not support creativity. Fortunately, research now shows us the kind of knowledge that does: it's creative knowledge, and it's different from shallow knowledge in just about every way.

With creative knowledge, you understand the material you're learning, and you know *how* to think with it. With shallow knowledge, you memorize events that happened; with creative knowledge, you can explain why these events took place. Shallow knowledge includes a lot of facts that you've memorized; with creative knowledge, you understand where these facts came from and how we know that they're true.

Shallow knowledge is a collection of facts about the world, such as the following:

- The correct spellings of words
- The (　①　) of the letters on the standard QWERTY keyboard
- The multiplication tables
- The chemical structure of water (H_2O)

Personally, I think that students need to learn all of these things. I'm sure that you can add your own very long list. If teaching for creativity means that we have to stop teaching for subject-area knowledge, then creativity is going to lose out every time. It's ②a common criticism of progressive education that it's not rigorous enough, and that students don't learn important facts and skills.

|A| Students don't become less creative when they memorize facts. And students don't become more creative when you stop teaching them facts. To be creative in a subject, you need to memorize a lot of shallow knowledge. Students need to learn vocabulary to be (③), and many creative writers use a larger vocabulary than the rest of us. Students need to memorize a lot to do math calculations, including the multiplication tables, or the procedures for how to add fractions. I use ④this kind of knowledge when I'm out in the garage, measuring parts for my craft projects.

Creative knowledge includes shallow knowledge—the same facts, skills, and procedures that are taught in instructionism. |B| They form patterns that give them depth and meaning.

From studies of scientific expertise, we know that scientific creativity is grounded in *bundles* of knowledge, not small pieces of shallow knowledge. Cognitive psychologists call the small pieces of shallow knowledge *chunks* (Gobet et al., 2001), and disconnected chunks of knowledge don't support creativity. Chunks are the elemental "(⑤)" of knowledge, the smallest thing that can be learned. In shallow knowledge, each chunk is very small. In science, such chunks include naming the kinds of clouds or the three kinds of rocks, or knowing how to spell *cirrus* (clouds) and *metamorphic* (rocks).

In instructionism, students learn small pieces of knowledge, one by one, one after another. In guided improvisation, students learn the same chunks of shallow knowledge that they would learn from instructionism, but they learn those chunks bundled together in a broader understanding of the subject. |C| Instructionism teaches students to memorize the names of each of the 50 states in the United States—their shapes, the names of their capitals, and what year they joined the union. But with creative knowledge, students will understand how to think about the social and political dynamics that resulted in the (⑥) of that state, and why the state has the shape it does. I still remember winning a prize in elementary school, when I memorized the 50 state capitals. But I didn't understand much about the history of the states until a few years ago, when I started watching the wonderful TV show *How the States Got Their Shapes*.

Creative knowledge includes a lot of shallow knowledge. But those chunks of knowledge are connected into rich conceptual structures where students can see why they're learning it, and how it makes sense in a deeper conceptual structure.

【Modified from "THE CREATIVE CLASSROOM Innovative Teaching for 21ˢᵗ- Century Learners" (2019)】

1　*Choose the best word from the four choices to fill (　①　), (　③　), (　⑤　) and (　⑥　). Write the letter on your answer sheet.*

　　①：　ア　domiciles　　　イ　templates　　　ウ　textures
　　　　　エ　locations
　　③：　ア　reticent　　　　イ　literate　　　　ウ　sinewy
　　　　　エ　verbal
　　⑤：　ア　atoms　　　　　イ　conflicts　　　　ウ　means
　　　　　エ　aggregations
　　⑥：　ア　isolation　　　　イ　federation　　　ウ　creation
　　　　　エ　demise

2　*Choose the best sentence from the three choices to fill* 　A　 − 　C　. *Write the letter on your answer sheet.*

　　ア　My good news is that there's no conflict between teaching for creativity and teaching facts.

　　イ　Creative knowledge brings together chunks of shallow knowledge in bundles that form complex wholes.

　　ウ　But unlike in instructionism, these pieces of knowledge aren't isolated chunks; they're linked together in rich conceptual networks.

3　*Explain the underlined part ② in Japanese adjusting to match the Japanese given in your answer sheet.*

　　　　進歩的な教育は(　　　), (　　　)という批判

4　*What does the underlined part ④ refer to? Pick out 11 English words from the article (not including commas) and write them on your answer sheet.*

5　*Choose the best answer from the three choices to complete each sentence. Write the letter on your answer sheet.*

(1)　In instructionism, _____.

　ア　students are made to cram a lot of minute facts continuously

　イ　students learn how to develop their understanding of subject

　ウ　students can explain why events they've learned happened

(2)　When the author got a prize in his elementary school, he learned ____

_____.

　ア　the political dynamics over the history of the states

　イ　nothing but the names of 50 state capitals

　ウ　the wonderful TV show *How the States Got Their Shapes*

6　*What is specific to the chunks of shallow knowledge learned in guided improvisation compared to those learned in instructionism? Write the answer in Japanese within 40 letters on your answer sheet.*

7　*Choose two statements that agree with the passage from the four choices. Write the letters on your answer sheet.*

　ア　Shallow knowledge is an unrelated groups of data about the world.

　イ　Teaching for creativity means that we have to stop teaching for subject-area knowledge.

　ウ　Studies of scientific expertise show that innovation is founded upon fragments of knowledge.

　エ　Creative knowledge enables students to grasp the reason for learning shallow knowledge.

‖ 2024年度 ‖ 兵庫県 ‖ 難易度 ‖■■■■■■

【30】次の英文を読んで，以下の(1)〜(7)に答えなさい。

　Metacognition has two parts, according to experts. First, there's the planning aspect: How will I know what I know? [　①　] Do I need more background knowledge? Second, there's the monitoring part: Could I learn this idea in a different way? [　②　] Why am I doing what I am doing?

　This sort of metacognition often comes easily to experts. When a specialist works through an issue, they'll think a lot about how the problem is framed. They'll have a sense of whether or not their answer seems reasonable. They'll reflect on how they got to an answer.

The key is not to leave this thinking about thinking to the experts. The research suggests, in fact, that beginners often need this sort of metacognitive thinking just as much as the experts. [③], the faster that we ask metacognitive questions, the quicker we can master new skills.

When it comes to learning, one of the biggest issues is that people don't engage in metacognition nearly enough. We don't do enough to understand the things that we don't know. At the same time, people feel too confident [④]. The issue, then, is not that something goes in one ear and out the other. The issue is that individuals don't dwell on the dwelling. They don't push themselves to understand.

In this regard, metacognition often comes down to a set of questions that we ask ourselves: How will I know what I know? What do I find confusing? Do I have a way to measure my understanding? These sorts of queries are powerful, and metacognition is often more important than raw smarts when it comes to learning.

According to researcher Marcel Veenman, for instance, students who have a rich ability to manage their thinking can outscore students who have sky-high levels of IQ. "We've found that metacognition often accounts for about 40 percent of learning outcomes," Veenman told me, while "IQ only accounts for 25 percent."

The act of writing is a good example of metacognition because when we think about composing sentences and paragraphs, we're often asking ourselves crucial metacognitive questions: Who will be reading this? Will they understand me? What things do I need to explain? ⑤This is why writing is often such an effective way to organize one's thoughts. It forces us to evaluate our arguments and think about our ideas.

Some like psychologist Doug Hacker describe writing as a form of "applied metacognition," and it happens to me all the time. Before I start writing, for instance, I'll have some sort of idea—a flicker of a connection, a sparkle of reasoning—and the notion or argument will seem irrefutable. Maybe, for instance, I'll want to email my wife to ask if she could watch the kids on Saturday night because an old college buddy is in town.

But then I'll start writing the email, and my logic simply falls apart. I realize that my argument is actually pretty weak since I saw my buddy last month. My intended audience will never buy it—and the email gets trashed. To use Hacker's words, I applied a type of metacognition and found my logic to be lacking.

We can do this ourselves. Imagine, for a moment, that you want to become a better travel photographer. Then ask yourself metacognitive questions while you're starting to learn to shoot images: How would an expert think about taking this picture? What sort of assumptions am I making about light and composition?

For another example, imagine you want to improve your understanding of the notion of a leap year. So you ask yourself. What do I know about leap years? How would someone know about leap years? Why is it even called a leap year?

For their part, researchers recommend that people ask these sorts of questions well before they start learning something. By probing ourselves before we gain a bit of expertise, we're priming our metacognitive pump—and making our learning more durable. Indeed, psychologist Lindsey Richland and a colleague have shown that ⑥people who try to answer metacognitive questions before they read some text learn a lot more, even if they can't answer the metacognitive questions correctly.

(Ulrich Boser, "Learn Better")

(1) [①], [②]に入る英文の組合せとして最も適切なものを次のア～エから一つ選び，その記号を書きなさい。

ア ① Who am I? ② Am I making progress?
イ ① What are my goals? ② Who am I?
ウ ① Who am I? ② What are my goals?
エ ① What are my goals? ② Am I making progress?

(2) [③]に入る語句として最も適切なものを次のア～エから一つ選び，その記号を書きなさい。

ア On the other hand イ In addition ウ In other words
エ On the contrary

326

(3) 文中の[④]に当てはまるように，次の語を並べ替えて正しい英文を完成しなさい。

[they / know / in / what / do]

(4) 下線部分⑤が表す内容を日本語で書きなさい。

(5) 下線部分⑥を日本語に直しなさい。

(6) 本文の内容に最も当てはまるものを次のア～エから一つ選び，その記号を書きなさい。

　ア　As for metacognition, it is better to depend on experts because they have a sense of thinking deeply.

　イ　As we ask metacognitive questions faster, we can master new skills more quickly.

　ウ　Students who have very high levels of IQ are superior to those who have metacognitive thinking.

　エ　A professional travel photographer would hardly ask himself metacognitive questions.

(7) メタ認知を活用したあなたの経験を一つ取り上げ，5行程度の英語で具体的に書きなさい。

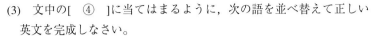

【31】次の英文を読んで，以下の[問1]～[問7]に答えよ。

1) Assessment and Learning

　Given the importance of assessment for student learning, it is important to consider how to best measure the learning that you want your students to achieve. Assessment should integrate grading, learning, and motivation for your students. Well-designed assessment methods provide <u>valuable information about student learning</u>. They tell us what students learned, how well they learned it, and where they struggled. Assessment then becomes a lens for understanding student learning, identifying invisible barriers, and helping us to improve our teaching approaches.

2) Formative and Summative Assessments

　Assessment can serve many different purposes. Most instructors are familiar with the traditional way of assessing students, such as by mid-term and final exams (usually using multiple-choice questions). There is a reason that this type of assessment is so popular — it is cost efficient (as in the example of multiple choice exams), takes a relatively short amount of time to create and grade, and provides a numerical summary (grade) of how much a student has learned.

The (1) of this method is that it does not provide the learner or instructor any feedback on the learning process that has taken place, only a summative result. This lack of opportunity to apply new learning and receive formative feedback hinders student ability to learn.

Another type of assessment, known as formative assessment, has a different purpose from summative assessment. Formative assessments capture learning-in-process in order to identify gaps, misunderstanding, and evolving understanding before summative assessments. Formative assessment may take a variety of forms, such as informal questions, practice quizzes, one-minute papers, and clearest/muddiest point exercises. Paul Black (1998) described the difference between these terms using the analogy of cooking. As a cook is making her soup, she occasionally tastes it to decide if it needs a bit more spices or ingredients. With each taste she is assessing her soup, and using that feedback to change or improve it — (2), the cook is engaging in formative assessment. Once the soup is served to the customer, the customer tastes it and makes a final judgment about the quality of the soup — otherwise known as [A] assessment.

3) Diagnostic Assessment

Another type of assessment, which is given at the beginning of the course or the beginning of the unit/topic, is known as diagnostic assessment. This assessment is used to collect data on what students already know about the topic. Diagnostic assessments are sets of written questions (multiple choice or short answer) that assess a learner's current knowledge base or current views on a topic/issue to be studied in the course. The goal is to get a snapshot of (3) students currently stand - intellectually, emotionally or ideologically - allowing the instructor to make sound instructional choices as to (4) to teach the new course content and (5) teaching approach to use.

4) ☐ B ☐

Formative assessment is a valuable tool that enables instructors to provide immediate and ongoing feedback to improve student learning. Formative assessment can involve providing feedback following an assessment, but more importantly, this feedback is delivered during instruction, allowing instructors to identify student misunderstandings and help them correct their errors. This formative feedback is crucial for improving knowledge, skills, and understanding, and is also a significant factor in motivating student learning. Students must use this feedback provided by the instructor to engage in the appropriate actions required to close the gap between the actual and desired level of performance. Therefore, for successful student learning, formative feedback must not be one-sided; instead it involves both the instructor and the students.

〔Adapted from QUEEN'S UNIVERSITY Teaching and Learning in Higher Education...一部省略等がある〕

[問1] 本文中の下線部<u>valuable information about student learning</u>について，その具体的内容を50字程度の日本語で書け。

[問2] 本文中の(1)に入る最も適切なものを，次の①～④の中から1つ選び，その番号を書け。

 ① upside ② downside ③ uptrend ④ downtrend

[問3] 本文中の(2)に入る最も適切なものを，次の①～④の中から1つ選び，その番号を書け。

 ① in addition ② in any case ③ in the end

 ④ in other words

[問4] 本文中の ☐ A ☐ に入る適切な1語を書け。

[問5] 本文中の(3)～(5)に入る最も適切なものを，次の①～③の中からそれぞれ選び，その番号を書け。ただし，同じものを繰り返し選んではいけない。

 ① how ② what ③ where

[問6] 本文中4)のパラグラフの見出しとして ☐ B ☐ に入る最も適切なものを，次の①～④の中から1つ選び，その番号を書け。

 ① How Assessment Improves Formative Feedback?

② How Feedback Improves Three Types of Assessment?

③ Why Feedback is Important to Learning?

④ Why Assessment is Important to Feedback?

[問7] 本文の内容と一致するものを，次の①～⑤の中から2つ選び，その番号を書け。

① Students' motivation for learning should not be considered when instructors make assessment of them.

② Summative assessment is popular among instructors because it can take a variety of forms, such as informal questions and presentations.

③ Formative assessment provides feedback during the instructional process, which improves student learning.

④ Diagnostic assessment can help instructors identify students' current knowledge of an issue to be studied.

⑤ Successful summative assessment should be both-sided, involving both the instructor and the students.

| 2024年度 | 和歌山県 | 難易度 ▰▰▰▱▱

【32】次の英文を読んで，以下の1～3に答えなさい。

Successful collaboration requires a particular attitude. One has to be willing to offer one's insights to others; to share one's perspective; to impart one's wisdom. It is only by giving that we gain the opportunity, in turn, to receive. In fact, perhaps the most powerful evidence for the growing importance of diversity is that people with a giving attitude are becoming ever more successful.

Consider a study of more than six hundred medical students, which found that the individualists — those focused on their own progress, and who cared little for others — performed very well in their first year. These 'takers' were good at extracting information from those around them, and by offering little in return they were able to focus on their own progress. Those who were more generous with their time and were willing to offer insights to their fellow students, the 'givers', got left behind.

(①) By the second year, the more collaborative cohort had caught up, and by the third year had overtaken their peers. By the final year, the givers had gained significantly higher grades. Indeed, the collaborative mindset was a more powerful predictor of school grades than the effect of smoking on lung cancer rates.

What was going on? The givers hadn't changed, but the structure of the program had shifted. Adam Grant writes in his book *Give and Take*:

> As students' progress through medical school, they move from independent classes into clinical rotations, internships and patient care. The further they advance, the more their success depends on teamwork and service. Whereas takers sometimes win in independent roles where performance is only about individual results, givers thrive in interdependent roles where collaboration matters. As the structure of class work shifts in medical school, the givers benefit from their tendencies to collaborate more effectively...

This is a finding that keeps re-emerging across the social sciences : people with a giving approach are flourishing. This is not a hard-and-fast rule: we can all think of people who have a taking attitude, who hate sharing credit, but who have nevertheless achieved marvelous things. (②) But the evidence suggests a broad pattern in favor of a giving approach. It also shows that the most successful givers are strategic, seeking out meaningful diversity, and cutting off collaborations if they are being exploited. This enables them to benefit from the upside of successful teamwork, while reducing the downside of partners who free-ride. As one researcher put it: 'the giver attitude is a powerful asset when allied to social intelligence'.

This willingness to give, to collaborate, has longer-term effects, too. You can see this in an experiment led by Professor Daniel Levin of Rutgers Business School when he asked more than two hundred executives to reactivate contacts that had been dormant for at least three years. The subjects asked two of these contacts for advice on an ongoing project at work. They were then asked to rate the value of this advice when compared with reaching out to two people on the same project.

Which contacts provided fresher insights, better ideas, stronger solutions? The answer was clear. The dormant ties offered advice that was significantly higher in value. Why? Precisely because they were dormant, these contacts were not operating in the same circles, or hearing the same stories, or having the same experiences. The dormant ties were effectively offering a diversity bonus — and it counted for a lot.

People who give are able to construct more diverse networks. They have a wider variety of dormant ties. They have access to a greater number of rebel ideas. By giving in the past, givers enjoy greater scope to reach out for ideas when it matters. As one executive put it: 'before contacting them, I thought that they would not have too much to provide beyond what I had already thought, but I was proved wrong. I was very surprised by the fresh ideas'.

The willingness to share, to offer knowledge and creative ideas, pays huge dividends in a world of complexity. It is the glue of effective collaboration, not just in the moment, but over time. (　③　) As Grant writes: 'according to conventional wisdom, highly successful people have three things in common: motivation, ability and opportunity... [but] there is a fourth ingredient: success depends heavily on how we approach our interactions with other people. Do we try to claim as much value [for ourselves] as we can, or do we contribute value...? It turns out that these choices have staggering consequences for success'.

(Matthew Syed.　2019.　*REBEL IDEAS: THE POWER OF DIVERSE THINKING.*　John Murray.)

1　本文中の(　①　)〜(　③　)には，次のア〜ウのいずれかの英文が入ります。それぞれどれが入りますか。その記号を書きなさい。

ア　The benefits compound.

イ　But here is the curious thing.

ウ　The world rarely fits into neat categories.

2　本文の内容について，次の質問に対する答えを英語で書きなさい。

　　According to the experiment led by Professor Daniel Levin, why was the advice offered by the dormant ties significantly higher in value?

3 次の質問に対するあなたの考えを，本文の内容を踏まえて，110〜140語程度の英語で書きなさい。なお，符号(,.?!など)は語数に含めないこととします。

What do you think are the key elements to facilitate student collaboration when you work as a teacher?

2024年度 ┃ 広島県・広島市 ┃ 難易度

【33】次の問に答えよ。

問1 次の英文を読んで，以下の(1)，(2)に答えよ。解答はア〜エの中から一つずつ選び，記号で答えよ。

Having a lot of money is a sign of social status and power. However, most average people in developed countries have less money now than they had a few decades ago. On the other hand, a small group of people have become extraordinarily wealthy.

In modern society, many Americans believe that everyone has an equal chance for financial success. They think that the reason people get rich is because they work hard, while poor people are lazy. But is this true? Researchers at the University of California at Berkeley did a study about the psychology of wealth in order to find out the differences between the rich and the poor.

In the study, researchers conducted several different experiments with different groups of volunteers. Participants were randomly divided into two groups: "wealthy" and "average." In one of the experiments, two people played a board game using play money. The "wealthy" player began the game with more money than the "average" player. The rules of the game were also unequal in that the "wealthy" player got extra chances to win. In this way, of course the "wealthy" player had a big advantage and always beat the "average" player. What surprised the researchers was what happened after each game was over. In every game, the "wealthy" player actually felt that he had won because he was a more skillful player, not just because he had been given an advantage over the "average" player from the start.

333

In a further experiment, the scientists left bowls of candy in an empty interview room. The participants were told that the candy was for some children taking part in the next experiment. While alone in the room (being recorded with a hidden camera), the people who had been in the "wealthy" group were more likely to take some of the candy for themselves, while the "average" people left it for the children. What do you think the researchers concluded based on this combination of test results?

(1)　Why do Americans tend to think people become rich?

　ア　They were born under a lucky star.

　イ　They were born with wealthy parents.

　ウ　They work much harder than poor people.

　エ　They regard money as a sign of social status.

(2)　Which of the following is an appropriate title for this passage?

　ア　The psychology of wealth and its effect

　イ　Playing board games with an advantage

　ウ　Kindness to children versus adults in advantage people

　エ　People in developed countries who have become poorer

問2　次の英文を読んで，以下の(1)，(2)に答えよ。解答はア～エの中から一つずつ選び，記号で答えよ。

In a recent issue of the Journal *Nature*, Dr Batchelor and colleagues detail their study of a swathe of seafloor off the central Norwegian coast, which reveals insights into ice sheet behavior in the process of retreats. The research focuses on over 7,600 ladder-like ridges found in the seafloor's muddy sediments. These ridges are thought to be remnants of a massive Northern European ice sheet that existed 20,000 years ago. The scientists interpreted these ridges to be features that are created at an ice grounding zone, where glacier ice flowing off the land becomes buoyant and begins to float as it enters the ocean. The ice moves up and down with the tides every day, and this movement makes it press against the ground over and over again. This creates the wavy patterns called corrugations.

For these patterns to be preserved, the ice must be in a retreat, and the tidal "clock" thus provides a rate for this reversal. The researchers found that the ancient European ice sheet retreated rapidly at speeds between 55 and 610 meters per day, with the fastest rates observed in areas where the seafloor was relatively flat. In these locations, ice above are more uniform in thickness, and less melting is needed for the ice to float and facilitate its retreat.

Similar corrugations have been detected on the Antarctic seafloor, but their extent is more limited. The Norwegian study area provides a clearer understanding of how quickly ice can retreat in a warming climate.

Today, scientists use satellites to monitor the grounding zones in Antarctica's ocean terminating glaciers. The spacecraft can trace where the ice is being lifted and lowered on the tides.

The fastest retreat has been observed at Pope Glacier in the west of the continent, with an average rate of 33 meters per day measured over 3.5 months in 2017.

Scientists are worried about large glaciers in Antarctica because these glaciers could potentially cause environmental catastrophe. One of them is Thwaites, which is the size of Britain and could raise global sea levels half a meter if it were to completely melt. Dr Frazer Christie, a co-author of the study, notes that a conduit-like channel located four kilometers inland of Thwaites' current grounding line is the perfect setting for a rapid, buoyancy-driven retreat. Even a short-lived retreat could significantly impact the glacier's future dynamics.

While Drs Batchelor and Christie assert that their findings will help refine the computer models used to predict Antarctica's fate in a warming world, Prof Julian Dowdeswell, another co-author, emphasizes the importance of studying the geological past to foresee what's possible in the future, as satellite records are very short-only 40 years or so.

(1) According to this passage, which of the following is a correct statement?

ア An ancient glacier in Norway has generated corrugations by repeatedly patting the sediments.

イ The ice retreats rapidly in places where the seafloor is uneven.

  ウ Thwaites Glacier concerns scientists as the fastest retreat has been seen there.

  エ Monitoring glacier movement can be utilized to predict future weather.

 (2) Which of the following is an appropriate title for this passage?

  ア Melting glacier leads to Norwegian sea level rising

  イ Movement of glacier directly affects global warming

  ウ Observing Antarctic glacier helps understand what happened in Norweigian seafloor

  エ Norweigian seafloor holds clue to Antarctic melting

【34】 次の英文を読んで，以下の問い(1)〜(5)に答えなさい。

Like any tests, satisfactory tests of listening and speaking have to fulfil three criteria—reliability, validity, and practicality. Usually some compromise has to be made between the criteria because what is most reliable might not be the most valid, and what is the most valid might not be practical.

Reliability

A reliable test is one whose results are not greatly affected by a change in the conditions under which it is given and marked. For example, if a test is given on different days by different people it should still give the same results. If the same answer paper is marked by different people, the score should be the same.

There are ways of checking statistically to see if a test is reliable. They all share similar features, but they look at different aspects of reliability. One way of checking is called test/retest. In this procedure the same test is given to the same people twice, usually with a gap of a week or so between the first test and the retest. A reliable test should give very similar results on the two occasions. Another way of checking is called <u>split halves</u>. In this procedure the test is given to a group of learners and then when the test is being marked the items in the test are split into two groups. For example, if the test had 50 items, all the odd numbered items would be put into one group, and all the even numbered items would be in the other. The scores for the two groups of items are compared. For a reliable test the scores for the two groups of items would be similar. A third way of checking is to make two equivalent forms of the same test. The two forms should be as similar to each other as possible without being exactly the same. When the same learners are tested with the two forms of the test, the scores for the two forms should be similar. What is common about all of these ways of checking reliability is that they are trying to see if the test does the same job on all occasions that it is used. If performance on the test keeps changing when the same learners sit it again, it cannot be measuring what it is supposed to be measuring. A reliable test is not necessarily a valid test, but an unreliable test cannot be valid.

Validity

A test is valid if it measures what it is supposed to measure and when it is used for the purpose for which it is designed. This last part of the definition of validity is important because a test may be valid when it is used for a particular purpose but not valid when it is used for another purpose. For example, a pronunciation test may be valid as a test of pronunciation but not valid as a test of spoken communicative ability. For a very clear discussion of authenticity and validity, see Leung and Lewkowicz (2006).

There are several kinds of validity, but because we are concerned with measuring progress and diagnosis, the two kinds that most concern us are face validity and content validity (Davies, 1990:24).

Face validity is a very informal judgement. It simply means that the people sitting the test, the people giving the tests, and others affected by it such as parents, employers, and government officials see the test as fair and reliable. A reliable test which may have good content and predictive validity may be so different from what the public expect or consider relevant that its poor face validity is enough to stop it being used. Good face validity is not a guarantee of reliability or other kinds of validity.

Content validity involves considering whether the content of the test reflects the content of the skill, language, or course being tested. For example, in order to decide if a test of academic listening skill has content validity, we would need to decide what are the components of the academic listening skill and how is this skill used. We might decide that academic listening involves note-taking, dealing with academic vocabulary, and seeing the organisation of the formal spoken discourse. Typically the listener has had some opportunity to read on the topic or it is one of a series of related lectures. Lectures are typically delivered at a certain speed. (data on speech rates can be found in Tauroza and Allison(1990)) . The next step is to see how well the test includes these components and to see if it includes components that are not part of normal academic listening. If the content of the test matches well with the content of the skill, the test has high content validity. If the test does not cover the components of the skill well, or includes other components that are not part of the skill, or requires the learner to process the components in an unusual way, then it has low content validity.

Practicality

Tests have to be used in the real world where there are limitations of time, money, facilities, and equipment, and willing helpers. There is no point in designing a one hundred item listening test that is too long to fit into the 40 minutes which are available for testing. Similarly, a speaking test which requires two or more testers to spend 20 minutes with every learner individually will be very expensive to run and will not be practicable if there is not money available.

Practicality can be looked at from several aspects: [(   ); (   ) ;and (   )]. Practicality can only be accurately determined in relation to a given situation, but generally a practical test is short (notice that this may conflict with reliability), does not require lots of paper and equipment, does not require many people to administer it, is easy to understand, is easy to mark, has scores or results which are easy to interpret, and can be used over and over again without upsetting its validity. It is not easy to meet all these requirements and still have a reliable and valid test. Most tests are a compromise between the various criteria. When making the compromise it is important that validity is not lost.

〔Paul Nation, Jonathan Newton, *Teaching ESL/EFL Listening and Speaking* より一部抜粋〕

(1) Explain "split halves" in detail in JAPANESE.

(2) What is the difference between "high content validity" and "low content validity"? Explain in ENGLISH.

(3) Which of the following is NOT appropriate for the three blanks in [　]?

　ア　ease of interpretation

　イ　similarity of the content of a test

　ウ　ease of administration and scoring

　エ　economy of time, money, and labour

(4) Which of the following is true about the passage?

　ア　When making a test, some compromise has to be made and it is good that validity is lost.

　イ　Even though face validity of one test is poor, you should not stop using it until it is finished.

　ウ　There are many real world limitations, but you must make a test to meet all of the requirements.

　エ　If you want to evaluate students' pronunciation, a test of spoken communicative ability should be used.

　オ　A reliable test means that the score of it would be almost the same on a different day in a different situation.

(5) What would you be careful about if you evaluate a student's perfomance test based on three criteria (reliability, validity, and practicality)? Explain your ideas and reasons in ENGLISH while describing at least two of the three criteria.

▊ 2024年度 ▊ 群馬県 ▊ 難易度 ▅▅▅▅▅▅

【35】 Read the passage below and choose the most appropriate answer.

The US scientists who created the first living robots say the life forms, known as xenobots, can now reproduce ― and in a way not seen in plants and animals. Formed from the stem cells of the African clawed frog (Xenopus laevis) from which it takes its name, xenobots are less than a millimeter (0.04 inches) wide. The tiny blobs were first unveiled in 2020 after experiments showed that they could move, work together in groups and self-heal.

Now the scientists that developed them at the University of Vermont, Tufts University and Harvard University's Wyss Institute for Biologically Inspired Engineering said they have discovered an entirely new form of biological reproduction different from any animal or plant known to science. "I was astounded by it," said Michael Levin, a professor of biology and director of the Allen Discovery Center at Tufts University who was co-lead author of the new research. "Frogs have a way of reproducing that they normally use but when you liberate (the cells) from the rest of the embryo and you give them a chance to figure out how to be in a new environment, not only do they figure out a new way to move, but they also figure out apparently a new way to reproduce."

Stem cells are unspecialized cells that have the ability to develop into different cell types. To make the xenobots, the researchers scraped living stem cells from frog embryos and left them to incubate. There's no manipulation of genes involved. "Most people think of robots as made of metals and ceramics but it's not so much what a robot is made from but what it does, which is act on its own on behalf of people," said Josh Bongard, a computer science professor and robotics expert at the University of Vermont and lead author of the study. "In that way it's a robot but it's also clearly an organism made from genetically unmodified frog cell." Bongard said they found that the xenobots, which were initially sphere-shaped and made from around 3,000 cells, could replicate.

But it happened rarely and only in specific circumstances. The xenobots used "kinetic replication" — a process that is known to occur at the molecular level but has never been observed before at the scale of whole cells or organisms, Bongard said. With the help of artificial intelligence, the researchers then tested billions of body shapes to make the xenobots more effective at this type of replication. The supercomputer came up with a C-shape that resembled a doughnut cut in half (Figure 1). They found it was able to find tiny stem cells in a petri dish, gather hundreds of them inside its mouth (Figure 2), and a few days later the bundle of cells became new xenobots. "The AI didn't program these machines in the way we usually think about writing code. It shaped and sculpted and came up with this C-shape," Bongard said. "The shape is, in essence, the program. The shape influences how the xenobots behave to amplify this incredibly surprising process."

The xenobots are very early technology — think of a 1940s computer — and don't yet have any practical applications. However, this combination of molecular biology and artificial intelligence could potentially be used in a host of tasks in the body and the environment, according to the researchers. This may include things like collecting microplastics in the oceans, inspecting root systems and regenerative medicine. While the prospect of self-replicating biotechnology could spark concern, the researchers said that the living machines were entirely contained in a lab and easily extinguished, as they are biodegradable and regulated by ethics experts. The research was partially funded by the Defense Advanced Research Projects Agency, a federal agency that oversees the development of technology for military use. "There are many things that are possible if we take advantage of this kind of plasticity and ability of cells to solve problems," Bongard said.

(Adapted from *https://edition.cnn.com/2021/11/29/americas/xenobots-self-replicating-robots-scn/index.html*)

Figure 1

Figure 2

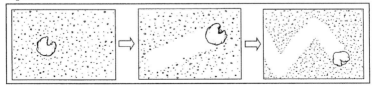

(1)　Which of the following statements does NOT describe xenobots?

　①　They are the first living robots that reproduce.

② They are programmable organisms created using stem cells.

③ They are biological machines that can heal themselves.

④ They are constructed around a little mechanical component.

(2) Why was Michael Levin surprised when he saw the liberated cells?

① Because the cells could replicate frogs' reproduction accurately.

② Because the cells' reproduction process didn't change at all.

③ Because the cells found a new method of reproduction.

④ Because the cells could free themselves from the embryo.

(3) What did Josh Bongard state?

① The xenobots were round and created from around 2,000 cells.

② Genetic manipulation was needed to make the xenobots incubate smoothly.

③ What a robot is made of is, of course, essential to define what is called a robot.

④ Robots carry out tasks independently for the benefit of people.

(4) Why did the supercomputer choose a C-shape as the best for effective replication?

① Because the xenobots were able to multiply without corralling and collecting loose stem cells.

② Because the xenobots could collect loose stem cells in their mouths efficiently.

③ Because the xenobots allowed the bundle of cells to be released as needed from their cells.

④ Because the xenobots themselves were capable of naturally transforming into new xenobots.

(5) Which of the following uses of xenobots is NOT mentioned in the passage?

① Bacteriological weapons　　② Tissue engineering

③ Botanical research　　④ Reducing pollution

2024年度 千葉県・千葉市 難易度

解答・解説

【1】(1) ウ　(2) ① ウ　② エ　③ ア　(3) ウ

○**解説**○ 本文は8段落構成で，効果的なプレゼンテーションの方法を書いたものである。　(1)　下線部について説明している箇所は後続するところである。観客の注意力はプレゼンテーションの進行に沿って冒頭，中頃，最終部で変化し，その度合いはFigure 1に図示されている。そこから，ウ「聴衆はプレゼンテーションの最初と最後を覚えている」を選ぶ。　(2)　①　Introductionの説明は第2段落，第3段落を参照。特に第3段落で，…showing an eye-catching chart or image are usefulとありvisual aidsに言及しているのでウを選ぶ。　②　Bodyの説明は第4段落，第5段落，第6段落を参照。特に第5段落でthe need to limit the number of main pointsと述べ，さらにtry to group it into a maximum of five sectionsと説明しているところからエを選択。　③　Conclusion の説明は第7段落を参照。repeat what you would like to emphasize at the end of the presentationとあるので，アを選ぶ。　(3)　ことわざを確認しておこう。ア「失敗は成功のもと」，イ「十人十色」，ウ「終わりよければ全てよし」，エ「急がば回れ」。第7段落にSuch closing remarks will spoil any presentation.とあり，要点を繰り返し述べて最後を締めくくることが大切と言っているのでウを選ぶ。

【2】問1 A イ　B ウ　C ア　問2 ① エ　② イ　③ ウ　問3 イ　問4 イ

○**解説**○ 問1　まずAの空欄を含んだ文は「私はよく家の玄関，部屋の隅，荷物の包み，そして神社のおみくじなどに，ぽっちゃりした女性を目にした」の意である。この直後の文からこれらの女性がおたふくやおかめと呼ばれるものであることがわかる。外国人である著者が東京に来たばかりの頃，おたふくなどを目にしたということである。次にBの空欄を含んだ節は「私の人生がどれだけ急激に変化するかなど知らずに日本に来た」の意である。著者はそれまで外国におり，変化するのは「人生」や「生活」を意味するウが正解である。最後にCの

空欄を含んだ文は「どういうわけか，彼女は私に対して手招きし続けており，日本に招き入れている」の意である。この直前の文から著者は25年間おたふくに惹きつけられていることがわかる。

問2　①　cynicalは「ひねくれた」や「皮肉な」の意であり，同じく「ひねくれた」を意味するエが正解。　②　jollityは「陽気(さ)」の意であり，同じく「陽気」や「快活」などを意味するイが正解。

③　fountは「源泉」の意であり，同じく「源泉」や「源」を意味するウが正解。　問3　空欄の前の節は「著者が日本で生活するにつれて」の意であり，第1パラグラフの1文目に対応する記述がある。著者は日本の生活を通して，昔ながらの迷信と呼ばれるようなものも信じるようになったと述べられている。　問4　まず1は，問3と同じことが述べられており正しい。次に5は最終パラグラフの3文目以降に対応する記述がある。著者にとっておたふくはどこにでも存在し，すべての人を巻き込む存在であると述べられている。

【3】問1　4　　問2　3　　問3　2　　問4　1　　問5　3

○**解説**○　問1　「Gogo」という愛称のPriscilla Sitieneiは，校長ではないので，4が不適切。　問2　midwifeは「助産師」。…she has helped deliver some of her own classmates「彼女のクラスメートのうち何人かは，出産のとき彼女が取り上げた」から，3「女性が赤ちゃんを産むのを手伝うよう訓練されている人，特に女性」。　問3　挿入文の文意は「Gogoは不登校の子どもと向き合い，理由をたずねていると言う」。これに続いて，「彼ら(不登校の子どもたち)は，もう学校に行くような年齢ではない，と言うのです」と不登校の理由を述べるのが自然な流れとなる。よって，空所Ⅱに挿入するのが最も適切。　問4　Gogo自身の教訓は1「遅すぎることはない」。　問5　1　「『Gogo』は6人のひ孫が，自分が子どもの頃に通った小学校に通うのを手伝っているおばあちゃんである」は誤り。玄孫6人と一緒に授業を受けている世界最高齢の小学生と言われている。彼女は子どもの頃学校に通ったことはない。

2　「『Gogo』は世界最高齢の小学生と信じられていたので，Leaders Vision Preparatory Schoolは彼女を受け入れた」は，理由が誤り。

3　「『Gogo』は読み書きを学ぶだけでなく，地元の習慣についての知

識を学校の他の子どもたちに教えている」は，第7段落の内容と一致する。　4「ギネス世界記録によると，『Gogo』は2004年に84歳で，現在の最高齢小学生記録を保持している」は，第9段落より誤り。現在，ギネスブックに登録されている最高齢の小学生記録はKimani Marugeのもの。

【4】問1　2　　問2　1　　問3　4　　問4　2　　問5　4
○解説○　問1　第1段落より，2024年度から日本の小学校で使用される教科書は，教科や学年・年次に関係なくQRコード付きになるので，2が内容に一致する。　　問2　教科書出版社がQRコード入りの新しい教科書を作った理由となる文を選ぶ。第4段落最終文の「すべての児童・生徒がデジタル機器を手にしていることを前提に…」という記述から，1が適切。　問3　前回と今回の審査を比較している文。「2018年度に実施された前回審査では164点中155点にQRコードが掲載されていたが，…」。while～「～だけれども」。　　問4　be slated to～「～する予定である」なので，be scheduled to～と同意。　問5　最終段落のSome textbooks, however, managed to reduce their number of pages by simplifying the content and/or using QR codes to reference end-note appendices. 「しかし内容を簡略化したり，巻末の付録をQRコードで参照したりすることでページ数を減らすことに成功した教科書もあった」から，4が正しい。

【5】(1)　C　　(2)　B　　(3)　A　interact　　B　different / various
(4)　with a group that works well together without any　　(5)　A
(6)　B，D
○解説○　(1)　空欄の前の文に着目すると，教師が前向きで，幸せで，休養が取れており，そして意欲があれば，そのグループも同じようになると述べられている。従って，「うつりやすい，伝染性の」を意味するCが正解。　(2)　下線部の次の文に着目すると，positive group dynamicsの有効性として，一緒に取り組むことで生徒たちに対象言語でやり取りをさせることができ，学習者が声を出して話すときに感じられることが多い自意識を最小限にすることができると述べられてい

る。このことから下線部は，人々が一緒に取り組んだりお互いにやり取りしたりする状況のことである。　(3)　下線部はその直前にある文の内容を指していることに着目すればよい。すると，国際的または多文化的な学習環境におけるグループワークは，世界中の人がやり取りをする機会を提供し，学習者は異なる価値観，期待そして信念を持つ人々と接することになると述べられている。この中で使用されている語をそのまま使うことができる。　(4)　完成した英文はEvery teacher knows that it is much easier and more comfortable to work with a group that works well together without any friction.であり，「軋轢なく協力し合える集団で仕事をする方がずっと容易で快適であることを，どの教師もみな知っている」の意である。関係代名詞のthatに着目し，worksの主語がa groupであることに気づくとよい。　(5)　空欄部はpositive group dynamicsで言語学習を行うことのメリットとして，効率的な言語使用に加えて何があるかを考えればよい。設問(2)の下線部の箇所で述べたように，positive group dynamicsは言語面だけでなく感情面にも好ましい影響がある。従って，「グループの絆とクラスの雰囲気を強化する」を意味するAが正解。　(6)　まず，Bについては全体として繰り返し述べられているが，第4パラグラフの3文目に対応する記述がある。次に，Dについては第5パラグラフで箇条書きされている項目の6つ目に対応する記述がある。

【6】(1)　d　　(2)　c　　(3)　c　　(4)　a　　(5)　b　　(6)　d

○**解説**○　(1)　All forms and deadlines for each step in the application process can be found on the official County Science Fair Web site〜の文に，提出書類の用紙と提出期限は公式ウェブサイトにあると述べられている。(2)「説明書き」のIf your project is approved, then you will be invited to participate in the County Science Fairより，裏を返せばプロジェクトが承認されなければ参加できないということが読み取れ，開催前にdisplayの準備が必要であると述べているのでcが適切な内容となる。(3)「スケジュール」の7:00 A.M. －9:00 A.M.　Project Display Set-Upよりcが適切だと読み取れる。　(4)「Eメール」の内容より，参加者のSamir Rajuがスケジュールについて相談をしている相手であり，主催

者側の人間であることが読み取れるためaが適切。　(5)「Eメール」中ほどで，displayのセットアップに間に合わないので，友人に代理でやってもらってよいか問い合わせていることから，許可を求めているbが適切。　(6)　I will not be able to reach the Science Fair until 12:50 P.M. at the latest. I will still be on time for my presentationより，12:50には間に合わないが，その後の自分のプレゼンには間に合うとSamir Rajuは「Eメール」で述べている。「スケジュール」を見ると，これに当てはまるのはGroup Dのみであり，dが正解だと判断できる。

【7】1　③　　2　③　　3　④　　4　①　　5　②　　6　④
○解説○　1　挿入文は「代わりに彼女は海岸清掃を企画し，さらに海に出かけるようになった」なので，「彼女はその仕事(建築家としての仕事)を始めることはなかった」の後のⒶに入るのが適切。　2　空所に入る接続詞を選択する問題。前半は「科学者が海洋汚染を研究する航海に参加するのは当然の選択と思われるかもしれない」。後半は「クリエイティブな職業に携わる女性もまた，語り部としての能力を買われて選ばれている」。while〜「〜だけれど」でつなぐ。　3　空所を含む文意は「非営利団体は，プラスチック汚染と(　　)する方法はたくさんあると強調する」。combat〜「〜と戦う」が適切。emit「放出する，口にする」，generate「生み出す，もたらす」，monitor「監視する」。4　eXXpeditionは，海のプラスチック汚染問題解決のための組織とあるので，①「それは水の汚染だけでなく大気汚染を防止することにも重点を置いている」は誤り。第6段落より，②「メンバーは様々な職業の人から成る」は正しい。第4段落より，③「Pennによって設立された非営利団体である」は正しい。第15段落より，④「海洋プラスチックについてのウェブサイトを立ち上げた」は正しい。　5　第5段落参照。「Pennは，プラスチック汚染に起因し，結果として食品に混入する有害な化学物質が，特に妊娠中の女性やその胎児に悪影響を及ぼすことを知り，女性の参加に焦点を当てた」とある。eXXpeditionが女性で構成されている理由は，②「女性に悪影響を与える可能性が高いと信じているから」。　6　第11段落より，①「マイクロプラスチックはとても小さいので，海から容易に取り除かれる」は誤り。第14段落

より，②「研究はプラスチック汚染を防止するため，特定の解決策に焦点を当てなければならないと提案している」は誤り。第9段落より，③「メンバーの一人はeXXpeditionの航海に参加するためプラスチック関連の仕事を辞めた」は誤り。

【8】(1) 6 (2) ① 3 ② 2 ③ 1 ④ 4 ⑤ 2

○**解説**○ 戦時中から2000年代に至る間の外国語教授法の推移について，概略的に説明した英文である。Grammar-Translation Method, Direct Method, Audiolingualism, Situational Approach, Communicative Language Teaching, Task-Based Language Teachingなどの用語が出てくるが，それぞれの概念がどのような過程を経て生み出されてきたかをまとめながら読むとよい。 (1) 空所Aの前後を読み比べると，空所Aの前で「言語学習は習慣形成の結果であるので，良い言語習慣を強化する練習が取り入れられた」と述べ，空所Aの後で「学習者は，目標言語を分析するのではなく演習を繰り返して言語を身に付けることが期待された」と述べており，言語習慣を強化する学習方法に触れていることから，空所Aには「言い換え」表現が必要となる。6の in short「要するに，つまり」が正解。on the other hand「一方では」，instead「そうではなくて」，on the contrary「逆に」，however「しかし」は，いずれも逆接的な表現。in addition「加えて」は情報追加の表現。(2) ①「戦時中，Army Methodの開発に影響を与えた第1の要因は何だったか」という問いに対して，第1段落冒頭で述べられている「米軍は外国語で流暢に会話ができる人材が不足していることに気づいた」ということと「米軍には兵士たちの話す力，聞く力を短期間で訓練する手段が必要であった」という内容から，3が適切。6では「複数の言語に堪能な兵士」と言っているが，「流暢に会話できる」点に絞り込んだ3の方がより適切。 ②「Audiolingualismで反復練習を重要視する根拠は何だったか」の問いに対し，第1段落4文目に「行動主義の考えに基づき，本質的に言語学習は習慣形成の結果である」という記述があり，5文目の「良い言語習慣を強化すると想定された練習」を行うことにより，必要な言語スキルを習得できるという文脈から2を選択。3は語彙のことにしか触れていないので不十分。

③ 「Situational ApproachではAudiolingualismでの語彙の扱い方をどのように改善したか」という問いに対し，第2段落4文目と最終文から「言語習慣化が進み，その言語に接し続ける限りいずれ語彙が増強されてくるという，根拠があいまいなAudiolingualismよりも，Situational Approachでは原理に基づいた方法論により語彙を扱う」と説明しているので，1のa more systematic way に通じる。　④　Supplantは「取って代わる」の意なので4が正解。　⑤　「TBLTはCLTの原理をどのように反映しているか」の問いに対し，第3段落の最後から2文目で「TBLTはCLTの進化形である」と述べ，TBLTは，「文法のような言語の形式的な面ではなく多様な言語学的特徴に目を向け，その特徴を実際に使って意味のある練習が行えるように設計された一連の作業を学習者に行わせる」教授法であると説明しているところから，2が適切。

【9】1　ア　　2　ウ　　3　ウ　　4　エ　　5　ア
○解説○　1　対応する記述は第2パラグラフの1文目にある。ある曲が頭の中で繰り返し再生されるような現象がearwormと呼ばれる理由を求められているので，due to以下に着目すればよい。　2　対応する記述は第5パラグラフの2文目にある。earwormを引き起こすような曲の特徴として正しいものを選ぶことが求められている。直接的な記述はないが，第3パラグラフの2文目にもearwormが生じる要因が述べられている。　3　第7パラグラフの2文目に対応する記述がある。　4　第9パラグラフの1文目に着目すると，earwormを経験した3分の2の人はearwormを中立的または肯定的に捉えていると述べられている。空欄の前後はこの部分の言い換えになっており，「私たちの3分の2はearwormを不快に思っていないかもしれないが」という意味になる。　5　第11パラグラフの最後から1〜2文目に着目すると，アはwhile singing the songが不適切であることがわかる。なお，イは第12パラグラフの1文目，ウは第11パラグラフの3〜4文目に，そしてエは同パラグラフ2文目に対応する記述がある。

【10】問1　④　　　問2　②　　　問3　①　　　問4　③
○解説○　問1　冒頭の2つの原則から5つ目の段落参照。4文目のSuccess is

something〜が，選択肢④「人が成功を収める時，忍耐，自己犠牲，決意，そして強い個性が必須であることは言うまでもない」と一致する。

問2　正確な思考を最もよく表す記述を選ぶ問題。冒頭の2つの原則から6つ目の段落参照。2文目のThe price of accurate thought is〜で「正確な思考の代価は，思考の基礎となる事実を集め，整理するために必要な努力である」と述べられている。よって，「集める」と「整理する」の2つが書かれている②が正解。　問3　質問は「その若者がなぜ今成功しているのか」。最終段落参照。thanks to his ability to become an accurate thinker「正確な思考者になる能力のおかげで」から，①が正しい。　問4　本文のタイトルとして適切なものを選ぶ。①「正確な思考の技術を身に着けるためのたった2つの原則」，②「正確な思考と不正確な思考の違い」，④「正確に考えることなしに正確な思考者になるための秘訣」などは明らかに誤り。主題は「正確な思考のために，基礎となる事実を集め整理することが必要」ということ。よって，③「正確な思考の重要性とその根拠」が適切。

【11】問1　①　ウ　　②　ア　　問2　オ　　問3　イ

○**解説**○　問1　①　「直観的な」の意であり，同じく「直観的な」や「本能的な」を意味するウが正解。　②　「飼い慣らされた」の意であり，アが正解。　問2　まずAは空欄直後に着目すると，20世紀初頭までは哲学がずっと現実的な問題に適用可能なものとして理解されてきたと述べられている。それを踏まえると，1970年代前半に環境哲学や環境倫理学が登場したという4が適切。次にBは空欄直前に着目すると，1973年にブルガリアで開催された哲学の世界会議で，Richard Routleyが「新しい環境倫理は必要か」と題する講演を行ったと述べられている。すると，この質問に対する彼の答えは断固として肯定的であったという3が適切。「新しい環境倫理は必要か」というのが質問と対応している。さらに，Cは空欄直後でPassmoreという哲学者の立場が述べられていることに着目すると，彼は，翌年(1974年)に出版されたJohn Passmoreの著書である『自然に対する人間の責任』における西洋の伝統の描写に反応していたという1が適切。この時点で空欄Dは2が適切であることがわかるが，Dは空欄直後にある「these claims」が，

Passmoreのminorityに対するRoutleyの考えであることに着目すればよ
い。　問3　第3パラグラフの最後の文に対応する記述がある。人間中
心主義を否定し，他の生物も重要という立場をとるべきだと述べられ
ている。

【12】1　a　オ　　b　カ　　c　イ　　d　ウ　　2　①　エ　　③　ア
④　イ　　⑤　ウ　　3　樹脂を注入して細胞壁を固める(技術) (14字)
4　A　　5　イ　　6　ウ

○解説○　視覚障害者にとってより安全な歩道を作ろうと考えた，大学の
准教授の取り組みについて書かれている。　1　a　「杖で歩道を叩く時
に，アスファルトとは異なる音を鳴らせることで」。〈have＋O＋原形
不定詞〉「O に～させる」。　b　「ペットボトルのキャップを再利用し
て土台となる梁を作るだけでなく，木材を使用することで」。A as well
as B は「BだけでなくAも」。　c　「梁の上に杉の板を置くことで」。
d　「アスファルトの上を歩くのとはまた違った感覚」。　2　①　「そこ
で，ウッドデッキのような歩道を作ってみたところ，これがうまくい
くことが分かった」。do the trick「目的を達する」。　③　「県庁は木製
歩道の導入に向けた検討を始めて」。implement「実行する」。
④　「SDGsの観点から見ると」。perspective「視点」。　⑤　「これが整
備されればされるほど，地球温暖化対策に貢献できる」。combat「戦
う」。　3　第4段落2文目参照。technology developed by Kyushu
University to solidify cell walls by injecting resin「(九州大学によって開発
された技術により)樹脂を注入して細胞壁を固める技術」。　4　挿入文
は「試作の歩道を使った別のテストでは，杉製の歩道から道路に出た
人はいなかった」。視覚障害者の協力のもと様々な構造物を杖で叩い
てもらう実験について述べているAに入る。　5　ア　「実験に参加し
た視覚障害者は全員，3種類の音の違いを聞き分けることができた」。
第2段落5文目以降に，101人中98人が聞き分けたとあるので，「全員」
は間違い。　イ　「ヒグチらの研究チームは，表面が粗い歩道が従来の
歩道とほとんど変わらないことを発見した」。第2段落2文目の内容よ
り正しい。　ウ　「九州大学のヒグチ准教授は，木材の耐久性はアスフ
ァルトの2倍であると指摘した」。第5段落1文目参照。製造コストがア

スファルトの2倍で，木材は耐久性に問題があると述べられている。エ「木製の歩道は製造過程で大量のエネルギーを使い，二酸化炭素を排出すると言える」。最終段落1文目参照。木製の歩道は，大気中の二酸化炭素を吸収して取り込む。　6　ア　木製歩道の経済的効果については述べられていない。　イ　木製歩道は二酸化炭素を取り込むと指摘しているが，タイトルにはなりえない。エの「木製歩道は視覚障害者にとってより安全である」は実験で検証されている事柄ではあるが，九州大学の取り組みが中心なので，タイトルとしては，ウの「日本の九州大学が視覚障害者と環境に配慮した木製歩道を開発」が適切。

【13】(1)　ア　　(2)　イ　　(3)　エ　　(4)　ウ　　(5)　エ，オ
○**解説**○　(1)　arthritisは関節炎の意。　(2)　correlationは相関関係の意。
(3)　第2段落で口腔感染と関節炎の関係を述べ，第5段落で口腔疾患が他の病気の原因や悪化要因になる可能性があることを述べている。さらに第10段落で定期的な歯の手入れが重要だと言っている。これらから，健康維持には口腔疾患の予防が大切であることが分かる。人間の口が家の出入り口に例えられているのでエが正解。　(4)　この英文全体の趣旨として正しい選択肢を選ぶ設問。　ア　第1段落の導入部にしか言及していないので不適切。　イ　第7段落の例示部分で，口腔疾患と全身疾患があると心臓発作や糖尿病を悪化させる潜在的な危険因子になると述べているが，直接的な原因とは言っていない。
エ　遺伝的要因がより激しい炎症反応の潜在的な原因である点に触れているが，第5段落，第6段落を見る限りまだ推論の域を出ておらず，そのメカニズムを研究している段階であるので，本文全体の趣旨とはならない。口腔ケアは健康維持の方法の一つであり，口腔内の異変を放置してはいけないと述べているウが正解。　(5)　本文の趣旨からは異なる英文を選ぶ問題。　ア　「体内の免疫システムが歯肉感染の細菌を察知すると攻撃しはじめ戦争状態になる」は第2段落に一致する。イ　「誰でも口内にはプラークがあり，中にはさらに強い炎症反応を引き起こしていることがある」は第6段落冒頭で述べている。　ウ　「歯周炎のある人は関節リウマチを含む炎症性疾患を発症させてしまう危険性が高い」は第7段落冒頭に一致する。　エ　「クマール女史と彼女

の研究チームは，たとえ口腔治療を行って口腔内を健康にしても関節リウマチ患者の症状に影響を与えることはないと解明した」。第8段落で，歯のクリーニングの前後で測定した口腔内炎症マーカーと血液中の全身性炎症マーカーの数値を比較した結果，関節リウマチのマーカー数値が低下した事実を突き止めたと述べていることから影響があると判断できるので，本文に一致しない。　オ　「歯磨きの際に歯茎から血が出たときが歯医者に予約を入れるべきタイミングであるとは，もはや言うことができない」。第9段落では，そのような時にはseek professional careと述べているので，歯医者での治療の必要性を説いているところから，本文に一致しない。

【14】 1　① assign　② diagnostic　③ vary　④ consistent
　　2　(1) (D)　　(2) (B)　　(3) (A)→(C)→(B)　　(4) (A)
○**解説**○ 1　①　enough toの直後なので動詞が来ることと，動詞 A to B という形をとっていることからassign「割り当てる」が適切。assign A to Bで「AをBに割り当てる」となる。　②　空所の後のwhich以下で「生徒の目的を個別に扱うのに今度は役立つかもしれない」とあり，個々の生徒に対応できるという意味でのdiagnostic「診断に用いる」が適切。空所が名詞informationの直前にあるため形容詞が来ることも手がかりになる。　③　shouldの直後に空所があることや空所の後はピリオドのため，空所には自動詞が入ることがわかりvary「異なる」のみが入る。空所を含むonly以下は「その判断基準が満たされる度合いのみが異なるべきである」となる。　④　空所の前のnovice teachers and untrained raters「新人の教師や訓練されていない評価者」と，空所の直前に否定的な語のlessがあることから空所はconsistent「一貫性のある」が適切。　2　(1)　(D)が第3段落1文目の内容と一致する。
(2)　(B)が第5段落4文目の内容と一致する。　(3)　(B)のanother set of sample student responsesに着目。anotherが来るということは，直前に同じような話題があることを示す。よって，(C)にも同様の語句があることから，(C)→(B)となることがまずわかる。また，空所の前の段落でrater trainingについて言及していることから，空所の冒頭はrater training を説明している(A)が適切だと判断でき，(A)→(C)→(B)となる。

(4)　(B)は第8段落及び空所を含む最終段落，(C)は第1〜5段落，(D)は第6段落でそれぞれ述べられているが，(A)のみは本文中に記述がなくこれが正答となる。

【15】(1)　昼と夜，夏と冬　　(2)　A　　(3)　④　C　　⑨　B
(4)　B　　(5)　そもそもなぜ夏と冬があるのかに言及しているという点。　　(6)　D　　(7)　A　animal　　B　should last five months
C　being four months

○**解説**○ (1)　下線部の後で「昼と夜」，「夏と冬」の対比が述べられておりこれらが解答となる。　(2)　太陽は東から昇り西に沈むため②にはeast, ③にはwestが入る。⑥は空所の後でthe opposite direction from where the sun had disappeared「太陽が消えたのと反対の方向」に着目する。同段落4文目で太陽は西に消えたことが述べられており，その反対の方向であるeastが⑥に入る。よって正しい組み合わせはAとなる。
(3)　④　空所の前で「太陽が西の地平線に消える」とあるのでその後に残るのはdarkness「漆黒」となる。　⑨　空所の前後は冬で地面が冷たくなり何も育たなくなるという内容なので空所にはBのbarren「不毛の」が入る。　(4)　空所はその前のthe boomerang would hook the sun back up into the skyを受けての文で，itがthe boomerangを指し，didn'tがdidn't hook the sun back up into the skyの省略を表すことができるBが適切。　(5)　Greek myth of Persephoneは下線部の次の段落で述べられているようになぜ夏と冬ができたのかについての神話である。一方，下線部の前の段落で述べられている神話は夏と冬があるのが前提であり，夏と冬がそれぞれ何カ月続くかについての神話である。両者の差は「なぜ夏と冬ができたのかについて言及している点」であり，Greek myth of Persephoneの優れている点である。よってthis respectはこの点を記述すればよい。　(6)　Persephoneが連れ去られたことで母のDemeterが悲しみ植物が成長しなくなり人々が飢えてきたという問題を解決すべく，Persephoneを連れ戻すという内容のDが入ると読み取れる。　(7)　第7段落の内容より空所に適語を補充する。　A　解答例ではanimalとなっているが，1・2文目よりanimalsが適切と思われる。B　3文目よりshould last five monthsとする。　C　最後の2文よりfour

monthsとなるが，end upの後なので動名詞が続く必要がありbeing four monthsとする。

【16】問1　多くの人がジェノベーゼの事件を目撃したり，その音を耳にしたりしたにもかかわらず，その事件との関わりを避けようとし，何もしなかったから。(67字)　　問2　エ　　問3　the effect that the number of witnesses might have　　問4　待合室のドアの下から煙が漏れてくるように仕組み，建物内で火災が発生したかのように思わせるような状況。　　問5　ほとんどの人は群衆の中から目立つことを嫌がるので，誰もが他の人が指示を出すことを当てにして，居合わせた人々は「そこでは何も見なかったことにして，その場を去る」という選択肢をとることがある。　　問6　イ　　問7　エ

○**解説**○　問1　下線部の文意は「彼ら(ジャーナリスト)はこの事件を，現代のアメリカ社会がいかに道を踏み外しているかを示す忌まわしい証拠だとみなした」。新聞記事の「いかに多くの『立派な，法律を守る市民』が襲撃を目撃，あるいは聞いたにもかかわらず襲撃の最中に警察に電話しなかったか」等を中心にまとめる。　問2　空所後に「Bibb LatanéとJohn Darleyは，目撃者が通報せずに背を向けたと思われる他の要因の調査に着手した」とあることから，unconvincedが入り「無関心が蔓延しているように見えるのは共感の欠如によるものだと『確信できなかった』」となる。　問3　Bibb LatanéとJohn Darleyは，目撃者の数を変化させて何度も実験を行っている。As they were interested in the effect that the number of witnesses might have on the likelihood of any one of them helping，「研究者たちは，目撃者の数が，そのうちの誰かが助けてくれる可能性に与える影響について興味を持っていたので」とする。　問4　実験の説明は，下線部を含む文の次の文の後半に記述がある。… by arranging for smoke to seep under the waiting room door, suggesting that a fire had broken out in the building「待合室のドアの下から煙が入ってくるように仕組んで，建物内で火災が発生したように見せかけることで…」をまとめる。　問5　be reluctant to～「～したがらない」，stand out「目立つ」，look to someone for～「人の～に期待する」，end up～ing「結局～することになる」。

問6 「第二に，助けを求める明確なニーズが存在するとしても，『責任』の問題がある」となり「たいていの日常的な状況では明確な指揮系統は存在しない。助けるのが自分の仕事なのか，それともあそこの人(彼ではなく，その後ろにいる人)に任せるべきなのか」と続く。他の選択肢は，capability「能力」，serendipity「思わぬものを偶然に発見する才能」，availability「利用できること」。 問7 ア 「人の行動は，どのような問題に取り組もうとしているかに強く影響される」は誤り。どのような問題に取り組もうとしているかではなく，周りの状況に影響される。 イ 「Kitty Genoveseの事件はあまりに凄惨で，さまざまなメディアで論じることはタブーとされていた」は誤り。様々なメディアに取り上げられた。 ウ 「最近行われた研究では事件当時のメディア報道の妥当性が改めて強調されている」は誤り。最終段落に，事件当時の報道は人々の無関心さを誇張している可能性があると述べられている。 エ 「2人の研究者による実験結果は，今日でも社会心理学の分野で際立っている」は正しい。第3段落参照。2人については，「過去30年間に出版された社会心理学の教科書のほとんどに記載されている一連の独創的な実験を行った」とある。

【17】 (1) エ (2) ア (3) エ (4) ウ (5) ウ

○解説○ 9段落構成の英文であるが，内容が日本の歴史に関するものなので読みやすいと思われる。ただし設問を考える際にヒントとなるキーワードをつかむために前後しながら読むことになるので，最初から段落ごとにポイントを押さえながら速読で対応したい。 (1) 第2段落最終文に，東北大学を含む7つの研究機関がHimikoの全身像を復元したと述べられている。 (2) Himiko's DNAが採取された場所は第4段落3文目で言及されている。 (3) 顎関節の機能不全の原因については，第6段落2文目と4文目に，歯を食いしばる等の習慣と顎の変形であると述べられている。 (4) 第6段落4文目に，顎が左側に歪曲していたとある。 ア・イ・エ 第2段落に，髪は直毛で鼻が低く垂れ目であったと述べられている。 (5) 第9段落にthe two belonged to the same period とあるので，ウが適切。 ア 第4段落1・2文目より，Kitakataで発見されたのは男性の方である。 イ 第7段落2文目に，弥

生時代に中国大陸から渡来した人々の子孫とある。　エ　第6段落1文目に頭蓋骨右側頭部が欠落し，鼻骨がなかったと述べられている。

【18】(1)　イ　　(2)　ウ　　(3)　①　ウ　　③　イ　　(4)　ウ
(5)　ウ　　(6)　エ

○**解説**○　森林伐採の影響について述べられた，7段落構成の英文である。第1段落で森林伐採の現状について触れ，第2段落から第6段落までは森林伐採の原因とその及ぼす結果について説明し，第7段落で解決策について言及している。　(1)　A　第5段落でCO_2の大気中濃度の上昇について森林伐採と化石燃料を比較しており，前者が1.6 billion metric tons，後者が6 billion metric tonsとCO_2年間放出量を試算している。この結果から読む限り，大気中へのCO_2放出に関して森林伐採の影響力は部分的とみられるのでpartiallyが適切。　B　第5段落で森林伐採とCO_2による気温変動について，第6段落で森林伐採と種の絶滅危惧について述べており，負の側面として並列的に議論しているので，BにはIn additionが適切。　C　空所を含む英文は，第5段落や第6段落で述べられたように，森林伐採による否定的な影響をひっくり返すことができないだろうか，という問いかけになっている。否定的な意味合いからdevastating「壊滅的な」が適切。　(2)　「焼畑農業」の良い点として，下線部に後続する英文でto release their rich nutrients into the soilと地力回復を述べているのでウを選ぶ。　(3)　①　lie fallow「休耕中である」の意でウが正解。　③　precipitation「降水(量)」の意でイが正解。(4)　第3段落で，焼畑農業による地力回復を持続可能にするには1平方キロ当たりの人口密度4人までが条件であるとしながら，近年になると人口密度が適正負荷の3倍に達するようになり，地力回復の手だてが困難になってきていると述べている。この文脈からウが正解。
(5)　主に第7段落を参照して解答を得る。ア「持続可能な発展を意識した消費活動と購買行動を提唱すること」，イ「森林伐採に対し国境を越えた法的枠組みと規制を作成すること」，ウ「環境に配慮した消費行動を徐々に弱まらせること」，エ「活動を通じて森林伐採に対する問題意識を高めていくこと」。本文の文脈からenvironmental consumerismはgreen consumerismと同義と捉えられるので，ウを選ぶ。

アに関して，第2段落で森林伐採の原因の一つに建設と紙製品を挙げているところから，人の消費活動や購買行動の影響も示唆されている。現代社会においてサステナビリティを実現するという観点からは，これらの活動や行動も環境保全を意識して行うことの大切さにつながってくるので，本文の趣旨に合致すると考える。　(6)　ア「大規模な森林伐採により世界の自然林は5分の1しか残っていない」は第1段落3文目と合致する。　イ「元来，熱帯雨林の土壌肥沃度は低いので，農産物の生産性を向上させるためには土地改良が必要である」は第2段落，第3段落の説明と合致する。熱帯雨林地帯では焼畑農業による地力回復が限界点に達しており，このままでは地力がなくなっていくと危惧されている。　ウ「熱帯雨林の群葉が取り除かれると熱帯地域での降雨サイクルが崩れ始め，その地域で砂漠化が起こり始める」は第4段落の趣旨と合致する。　エ「大気へのCO_2年間放出総量の約4分の1は森林伐採に起因するものだ」について，第5段落では，CO_2年間放出量に関し森林伐採による放出量と化石燃料の燃焼による放出量はそれぞれ言及されているが，CO_2年間放出総量には触れていないため不一致。オ「生存する動植物の半分以上が熱帯雨林に生息しているので，熱帯雨林の消失は生態学的多様性に多大な影響をもたらす」は第6段落と合致する。

【19】(1)　①　B　　②　D　　④　C　　(2)　D　　(3)　B
(4)　①　B　　②　C　　③　A

○**解説**○ (1)　空欄に当てはまる語を選ぶ問題である。まず空欄①を含んだ文は「長い "ee" の音は，"seem" や "teem" のように明らかな "e" を二重にしたものだけでなく，"quay"，"ski"，"debris" そして "people" のように全く異なる母音の『組み合わせ』で表すことができる」の意である。次に空欄②を含んだ文は「TLK2UL8Rのような『略語』を用いたテキストメッセージの台頭や，アメリカ化された綴りの影響もあるようだ」の意である。なお，TLK2UL8Rとは「Talk to you later.」を意味する略語である。最後に空欄④を含んだ文は「英語を学習途中のどんな人でも紙面上で見れば "quay" と "key"，同様に "bow" と "bough"，"caught" と "court" そして "towed" と "toad" と "toed" などの無数にある

『同音異義語』の違いを認識する」の意である。　(2)　綴りの教育法に共通する考えは，第1パラグラフの4文目に述べられている。

(3)　下線部③は第5パラグラフにあるが，第4パラグラフの1文目にThis is not a new campaign.とあることに着目したい。その直後の文にcampaignの説明がなされている。　(4)　まず①は綴りについて議論している人が指摘していることに関する問題であり，第2パラグラフの2文目に対応する記述がある。次に②は読み書き能力に関する国際的な研究において英語母語話者が最下位に近い理由に関する問題であり，第3パラグラフの5文目に対応する記述がある。最後に③は音韻の議論における最も本質的な欠陥に関する問題であり，第6パラグラフの1文目に対応する記述がある。

【20】問1　ウ　　問2　continue / encourage　　問3　読む技能を身に付けた生徒が読み続けようとする意志を持つこと。(30字)　　問4　ア
問5　ウ　　問6　読む技能の習得後，親は自分たちの役割は終わり，それ以上は学校の役割だと考えるが，教師は読む技能に焦点を置いた過密なカリキュラムの中で，読むことを勧める時間を持てないから。(85字)　　問7　・Talk about books in class　　・Find out what books students are interested in　　・Take students to the library

○解説○　問1　recreational book reading「娯楽の読書」についての説明となるようにする。「自発的な楽しみのための読書が含まれる」。
問2　日常的な娯楽の読書は，生徒が読み書きの能力発達を(　　)する最も簡単な方法のひとつである」。第5段落と第10段落からcontinue「継続する」，第10段落からencourage「奨励する」を抜き出す。
問3　where以下を訳出する。下線部を含む文意は「読書をめぐる議論の多くは，通常(必ずしもそうとは限らないが)学校教育の初期に起こる技能の習得に関するものであるが，読む技能を身につけた生徒がそれを選択し続けるという意志の取得(will acquisition)にはあまり焦点が当てられていない」。　問4　下線部は「日常的な読書によってもたらされるさまざまな恩恵」。第4段落2文目参照。the development of empathy「感情移入の発達，人の気持ちを思いやれること」からア「他人の感情を理解する」が正しい。　問5　WASABR(West Australian

Study in Adolescent Book Reading)の調査結果が述べられている部分。第7段落最終文「ビデオゲームやテレビ視聴に費やす時間が長いほど，楽しみのための読書に費やす時間は少なくなる」から，「WASABRによると，読書頻度が低い最も一般的な理由は，他の娯楽活動への嗜好と関連していたことがわかった」となる。infrequent「めったに起こらない，めずらしい」，preference「好み，優先傾向」。　問6　下線部の文意は「教師や親は(生徒が読めることを示すと)励ましの手を緩めることがある」。親については第9段落「親は読書の技能が身につけば，自分の仕事は終わったと思い込んでいるかもしれない」，教師については第10段落「教師は，多忙なカリキュラムの中で読書を奨励する時間を確保するのに苦労しているかもしれない」参照。　問7　設問は「教師として学校での日常的な娯楽の読書を奨励するために何ができるか」。解答例では「授業で本について話す，生徒が興味のある本を探す，生徒を図書室に連れていく」ことを挙げている。

【21】問1　3　　問2　1　　問3　3　　問4　2　　問5　2
○**解説**○　問1　ソーシャルメディアのもたらす影響として，「私たちがより注意散漫になり，対面での交流を楽しめなくなり，質の低い社会的交流をするようになっている」。more distracted「より気が散った」，enjoy～less「～を楽しまない」，less quality「低品質」。　問2　下線部の文意は「この不適応な対処戦略」。具体的には直前の「うつ病患者が不安やその他の問題に対処するためにソーシャルメディアを過度に利用している」ことを指す。　問3　第7段落参照。3「ソーシャルメディアの能動的な利用者に比べ，受動的な利用者は対人スキルを身につけることができるかもしれない」が正解。　問4　空所までの文意は「ソーシャルメディアのもう一つの利点は，オンラインで会う人が増えていることだ。スタンフォード大学の2017年の調査では，同性カップルの約65％，異性カップルの39％がオンラインで出会っていることが明らかになった。この調査結果は，2013年以前と比較されたもので…」。空所には，その当時の出会いの場所や手段として不適切なものを選ぶ。「学校生活，アルバイト，地域のイベント」は適切。online lessonsが不適切と言える。　問5　1　「研究者たちは，人々がソーシャ

ルメディアのために現実世界でのコミュニケーションを減らしている
ことを発見し，ソーシャルメディアの使用に反対している」。研究者
たちは，このコミュニケーションツールをポジティブに活用するよう
言っている。　2「ソーシャルメディアは，私たちを夢中にさせるた
めに作られたもので，これらのアプリで自分の生活についてより多く
の人とコミュニケーションをとるようになる人もいる」。第3段落参照。
正しい。　3「オンラインの世界では，私たちが見逃しているものが
わかるので，私たちのFoMOは減っていくだろう」。FoMOが減るとは
書かれていない。　4「ソーシャルメディアが私たちに与える影響は
まだ解明されていないが，目的が何であれ私たちは積極的に活用すべ
きである」。ソーシャルメディア利用の目的が何であるかを考えるこ
とが重要だと言っている。

【22】(1)　①　the things that people in wealthier countries take for granted
⑩　is being done with great care to protect　　(2)　もし世界の全員が，
豊かな国々でよく見られるような，無駄の多い，化石燃料の生活スタ
イルを真似すると，地球の気温が上昇してしまうということ。
(3)　③　Starting　　④　including　　⑤　put　　⑦　grown
⑧　move　　⑨　stood　　(4)　B　　(5)　石油を採掘することで得ら
れるであろうお金の一部を，世界の他の国々が支払うという取り決め。
(6)　A　contact with the outside world　　B　favor of　　C　giving up
on　　(7)　D

○**解説**○ (1)　①　関係代名詞thatの先行詞であるthe thingsは，take O for
granted「Oを当然のことと思う」のO(目的語)である。　⑩　is being
doneは受動態の現在進行形で「～されているところだ」の意味。この
後にwith great care「とても注意を払って」という語句が入り，目的の
to不定詞を用いてto protect the environmentと続く。　(2)　このthisは後
ろの内容を表し，the trouble is thisは「問題は以下の通りである，こう
である」という意味である。よって解答としてはif以下の文を日本語
にまとめればよい。　(3)　③　Startingが入る。カンマの後にS＋Vが
続くことから分詞構文を用い，目的語がないため自動詞が入ることが
わかる。空所の後のin 2006につながるのはstartしかないと読み取れる。

361

④　including「〜を含む」が入る。空所の前にeveryoneがあることから「エクアドルの国民を含む全ての人」となる。　⑤　put forth〜「(考え・アイデア)を出す」の受動態が入る。putは過去形・過去分詞形も語形変化せずputが適切となる。　⑦　grow wealthyで「裕福になる」。haveの後なので過去分詞grownが適切となる。　⑧　move to a new era of green development「緑化に配慮した開発の新時代へ移行する」となりmoveが適切となる。　⑨　stand up to〜「〜に抵抗する」を用い，時制は過去形のためstoodが入る。　(4)　主語Theyや動詞didが示しそうな単語があるのはBとDに絞られる。BとDを比較すると，多くの投資をもたらすという挿入文の内容にDはそぐわないことがわかりBが適切と判断できる。　(5)　This arrangementの内容は前文のby paying以下となる。part of the money it would lose by leaving the oil in the ground「地中に石油を残しておくことで失うであろうお金の一部」を「石油を採掘することで得られるであろうお金の一部」とわかりやすく解答例では言い換えている。　(6)　A　第3段落2文目のhave rejected all contact with the outside worldが該当し，語数指定を考慮してcontact with the outside worldとする。　B　第9段落3文目の内容から，国民の8割以上が石油の不採掘を望んだことがわかるので，in favor of〜「〜に賛成する」が適切。　C　第11段落の内容が該当する。「最初は石油の採掘を許さなかったが最終的には要求に屈した」という内容が入るため「〜に屈する」の意味を持ち，helpの後であることを考えて動名詞にしたgiving up onを入れる。　(7)　豊かな者の義務と貧しい者の権利について疑問を投げかけた最終段落の内容がDと一致する。

【23】(1)　A　　(2)　D　　(3)　D　　(4)　B　　(5)　In order to develop the five areas of English, teachers should try to increase students' vocabulary. When teaching vocabulary to students, it is necessary to teach the meaning, phoneme, and form of the vocabulary to help student retain the information. It is important to have students read or listen to the vocabulary many times in communication tasks so that students will gradually become more familiar with speaking and writing the vocabulary. That will also help students understand the appropriate context or scene to use each word. (86 words)

○**解説**○ (1) 空所の後でsemanticsとpragmaticsのそれぞれの意味が述べられており，異なる語の意味を扱う辞書では文脈の中で意味が決定されるpragmaticsが用いられると説明されている。これらに該当するAが空所に入ると判断できる。　(2) 空所の後で「実質的に異なる語となり別に学ぶ必要がある」とあることから，The connectionを主語とした文の空所はlost「失われた」が適切。　(3) There are very practical ways of doing this.「これをする大変実践的な方法がある」より，その後にその実践的な方法が述べられると推測できる。この点を考慮に入れて空所A〜Dを見ていくと，空所Dの後のみに具体的な方法が述べられていることよりDが正解と判断できる。　(4) Bの内容が第2段落最終文の内容と一致する。　(5) 本文では語のcore meaningを学ぶことで単語の学習の負担が減ることが述べられている。この内容を踏まえて，解答例では英語の5領域の上達においてまず意味，音，形式といったcore meaningにあたる情報を生徒に学ばせ，リーディングやリスニングで何度もその語に触れさせることでスピーキングやライティングに役立てるだけでなくその語が用いられている文脈を理解する助けとする，という教授法が述べられている。なお，解答例では「5領域」をfive areasとしているが，現行の中学校学習指導要領(平成29年3月告示)英訳版においてはfive skill areasと訳されているので，英訳版の表記に準じることが望ましいと思われる。

【24】(1)　②　　(2)　①　　(3)　④　　(4)　④　　(5)　③

○**解説**○ (1) 空欄を含んだ文と直前の文に着目する。調律が整っていれば，粗末なピアノでも熟練した音楽家は優れた音楽を奏でられるということ，そしてこの音楽家が1人しかいない点は教育の例としては不十分であるということが述べられている。教育においては音楽家つまり教師だけでなく，学習者がいることを踏まえると②が正解。

(2) 空欄直後の節に着目すると，教科書を教える一定の方法があり，その結果は毎回同じであると述べられている。ここの言い換えになっていることを踏まえると①が正解。　(3) 第4パラグラフ4目に，「教科書を評価するときは，一般に，自分の経験やコンテクストのlenses(視点)を使い，こうしたlenses(視点)を意識することが大切だ」と

いう著者の見解が述べられている。このlensesを言い換えたのが
viewpointsであると判断できる。　(4)　空欄直後の節に着目すると，
空欄Bのものが，教科書の中に何があって，どのように各単元が並ん
でいて，ものによっては，個々の単元の構成や内容まで示しているも
のであることが分かる。そのため「目次」を意味する④が正解。

(5)　教科書の使い方を決めるためには，教科書それ自体の分析も重要
であるが，同時に，教科書が使用されるコンテクストを考慮する必要
がある。よって，③が正解。

【25】(1)　④　　(2)　⑤　　(3)　③　　(4)　①　　(5)　②

○**解説**○　長文読解では段落構成と各段落の趣旨を確認しながら読むこ
と。また，引用が多い場合には，誰が何を指摘しているのかを簡単に
整理しながら読み進めること。本設問については，語彙，第2段落，
第3段落，結論部の概要把握ができれば解答できる。　(1)　meetには
「期待や要求などを満たす」の意があり，選択肢④の文中のsatisfy what
is neededがヒントとなる。なお，meet a goal「目標を達成する」という
表現を覚えておこう。　(2)　sustainability「持続可能性」とは，環境，
社会，経済などの分野で，現在の好ましい環境，価値観，経済状況が
損なわれることなくいかに持続させていくか，そのための取り組みを
意味している語である。　(3)　第2段落では，食料システムの変革を
推し進めるためにWe must～や It's imperative～という表現を使って私
たちが取り組まなくてはならない点を列挙している。4文目の中ほど
にshift to more regenerative and resilient production systems「再生的で回
復力のある生産システムへ移行しなければならない」とあることから，
③を選択。　(4)　第3段落では，そのため(＝サステナビリティを意識し
た食料システムの変革)に必要な解決策はすでにあり，自然界の力を利
用する新しい技術を開発する必要性はないと言っている。ただし，we
must uphold the truth that ecosystems and production systems are more
valuable when they are conserved and sustainably managed than when they
are destroyed. 「生態系と生産システムは，破壊される場合よりも，大
切に扱われ持続可能な形で管理される場合のほうが，より価値が高い
という真実を，私たちは支持しなければならない」とあることから，

①を選択。 (5) 英文全体の結論に関わる問題である。最終段落でwe must do so in ways that still conserve and protect our planet. This is the only way that we can continue to feed and sustain future generations.「我々の惑星をまだ保存し保護する方法で、そうしなければならない。これこそが食料を供給し続け、未来の世代を残せる唯一の方法である」と言っていることから、人類が他の惑星(Planet B)に移住して存続していくような選択肢は考えていないことになる。よって、Planet Bはないとする②が適切。① electricity には言及なし。③ 第1段落最終文でthe dual crises of climate and biodiversity loss are inseparable「気候と生物多様性喪失という二重苦は切り離せない」とあるので不適切。④ 第3段落1文目及び2文目にwe don't have to develop any new technologies to harness the power of Nature. The solutions we need are already available.とあるので不適切。 ⑤ 「地球にはほんのわずかな生物しか住んでいない」とは言っていない。

【26】(1) ① イ ⑤ エ (2) お金を生み出す商品性という観点から、映画や音楽などを「コンテンツ」という言葉で、ひとかたまりにしていること。 (3) caring (4) もし、自分の発言に決して悪気がなかった彼の上司のような人が、育業に「業」の働くという意味の漢字が含まれていることに気付いたなら、育業という新語は、ある程度効果があるだろう。 (5) イ、ウ

○解説○ (1) ① 「コンテンツという言葉は、お金になるものなら何でもまとめてしまう便利な表現だったのだろう」に続く文。「今日、文学やニュース記事でさえ例外ではない」。exception「例外」。 ⑤ 育休にかわる新語の「育業」を決めた背景について述べている文。「主な目的は、その休みが何であれそれを取得するハードルを下げる制度や環境を整えることであるべきだ」。lower「下げる」。 (2) 下線部を含む文意は「そのことに憤りを感じるのは、私があまりに頑なであるからなのだろうか」。筆者が憤っていることを前段落の内容を中心にまとめる。 (3) care for〜「〜の世話をする」。…caring for a newborn baby is far from vacationing「新生児の世話は休暇とはほど遠い」。 (4) The neologism iku-gyo could be effective to a certain extent

「育業という新造語はある程度有効だろう」。if someone like his superior realizes that the phrase contains the kanji for "work"「彼の上司のような人が，このフレーズに『仕事』(＝業)という漢字が含まれていることに気付けば」。who probably meant no harm in what he saidは，superiorを修飾して「(上司の)言葉におそらく悪気はないのだろうが」。　(5)　ア「20年前，通信業界に関するレポートを書いていた時，筆者は『コンテンツ』という言葉の便利さに魅了された」。第1段落参照。誤り。イ「『コンテンツ』という言葉は，一般的で使いやすいためか，著者の想像をはるかに超えて急速に広まった」。第3段落3文目及び4文目参照。正しい。　ウ「著者は『コンテンツ』という言葉を使うことで，特に映画や音楽の市場性が強調され，クリエイターの姿勢に影響を与えることを懸念している」。第5段落1文目参照。正しい。　エ「筆者の同僚が，上司から『育児休暇をできるだけ短く取れ』と言われ非常に憤慨していた」。第7段落参照。同僚は，上司から『ゆっくり休んでこい』と言われるのが辛かった。　オ「著者は，言葉には神秘的な力があり，その力を使うことで社会を変えることができると強く信じている」。最終段落参照。言葉の神秘的な力を著者が信じているとは述べられていない。筆者は「言葉の使われ方に疑問を投げかけることは，私たちに社会の仕組みを問い直す機会を与える」と考えている。

【27】〔1〕2　　〔2〕2
○**解説**○　アフリカ，ガボンの研究者の体験をエッセイ調に書いた文章。〔1〕空欄①の2段落前から，食糧不足に陥った象が，民家の庭を襲い，畑などを荒らすことが説明されている。①の直前は，その一例であるヴィンセント・ボシッシ氏について書かれている。①の前後を確認すると，「筆者が象について質問すると，目を逸らした→①→ボシッシ氏は，いつか象がやってきてマンゴーを持っていってしまうだろうと予測し，その前に収穫してしまった」という流れである。したがって，「マンゴーは動物にとってとりわけ魅力的だ」という2が文脈的に正しい。1と3はマンゴーと関係なく，4は「マンゴーは象の体に悪いので食べさせようとした」は，前後の文脈と論理的につながらない。〔2〕最後から4段目に，研究者が気候変動の影響で象の食事がどの

ように変化しているのかについて分析するとあり，続く段落では糞の調査についての記述がある。さらに，糞を洗い中にある種を調査することで，どの種類の果実をどれだけ食べているかを調査できるとある。よって，適切な選択肢は「科学者たちが国立公園で象の糞を集めているのは，どんな種類の果物をどれだけ食べているかを知りたいからだ」の2である。

【28】(1) ① 2 ② 4 ③ 3 ④ 2 (2) ウ (3) 1
(4) ア T イ F (5) 2，3，6 (6) Because even L1 speakers will not necessarily have mastered all word-knowledge aspects for every word they "know." (7) ① 教育や教材で対応する必要がある
② 指導や学習に対する単一のアプローチだけでは対処できない
③ 形と意味の関係を測定するだけでなく，創造的な方法を考える
④ 語彙知識を多面的に見た研究

○**解説**○ (1) ① genesisは「起源」でoriginとほぼ同じ意味となる。
② taxonomyは「分類(学)」でclassificationとほぼ同じ意味となる。
③ be exposed to～は「～にさらされている」の意味で最も近いのはencounter「出くわす」となる。 ④ amenable to～は「～に従順である」の意味で最も近いのはtractable「扱いやすい」となる。 (2) 新しい語に出会った時の状況が書かれているのは第2段落のためイとウのいずれかになると推測できる。設問の英文は「しかし，新しい語に出会った初期の段階では，語の知識の側面のいくつかの限られた印象しか会得できない」であり，冒頭のButと結びつくのは，「ますます多くの言葉にさらされていると，語の知識やコロケーションを私たちは常に作り上げ洗練させている」というウの前の文だと判断できる。
(3) 空所の後の文の意味は(2)で記載した通りである。空所の前の文は「読んだり聴いたりしている時に知らない新しい語に遭遇するのとまったく同じように，同じことがすでに見慣れている語の新しい意味にも当てはまる」である。いずれの文も新しい語あるいは意味に出会った時の私たちの反応を示しているため，Likewise「同様に」が適切だと判断できる。 (4) ア 第2段落第1・2文より，Nationが提唱する語の知識の分類は理想上の完璧なもので，第一言語の話者でさえ語の全

ての意味をマスターしているわけではないということが述べられている。ここから設問文の「Nationが提唱するフレームワークでは，うまくいっている語の使用は多くの語の構成要素の知識を必要とすることを示している」は正しいと判断できる。　イ　設問文の趣旨は，「著者は，最も重要な語彙の知識とは，意味と綴りの関係にあると考えている」と思われる。第3段落1文目および2文目で，著者はフレームワークが教育と研究の両方で役に立ってきたことを述べ，その効果の一つとして設問文とは逆の意味の「学習者が，単なる意味や綴りを超えて考えるようになった」ことを挙げているため，不適切と判断できる。

(5)　2　synonymは「同義語」の意味。TABLE3.1のassociations「関連語」に当てはまり，正しいと判断できる。　3　TABLE3.1のいずれの項目にもreceptive elementとproductive elementが定義されており，正しいと判断できる。　6　「語の使用の適切さを知っていることも，語を知っていることの一部である」は，TABLE3.1のconstraints on use「使用上の制限事項」より，正しいと判断できる。　(6)　第2段落2文目の後半を抜き出せばよい。　(7)　第3段落の内容が設問文において日本語でまとめられていることがわかり，それぞれの箇所を和訳して記述すればよい。　①　3文目後半these components somehow need to be addressed in instruction and teaching materials.が該当する。　②　4文目vocabulary knowledge is complex and cannot be addressed with a single approach to instruction or learningが該当する。　③　後ろから2文目のthe framework has encouraged scholars to think creatively about how to measure vocabulary knowledge, and to move beyond tests of the form-meaning linkが該当する。　④　最終文のWith more multi-component studies now beginning to appearが該当する。

【29】1　①　エ　③　イ　⑤　ア　⑥　ウ　2　A　ア　B　ウ　C　イ　3　(進歩的な教育は)厳しさが不十分で(,)生徒が大切な事実や技術を学ばない(という批判)　4　the multiplication tables, or the procedures for how to add fractions　5　(1)　ア　(2)　イ　6　・個別に学ばれる知識ではなく教科の広い理解の中で1つ1つが結びつく知識。(35字)　　・個別に学ばれる知識ではなく科目

の広い理解の中で1つにまとまる知識。(33字)　から1つ　　7　ア，エ
○**解説**○　1　①　浅い知識の例として「標準的なQWERTYキーボード上
の文字の位置」。　③　創造的になるため，浅い知識をたくさん暗記
する必要があると説いている部分。「生徒が読み書きできるようにな
るには語彙を学ぶ必要があり…」。literate「読み書きができる，物知り
の」。　⑤　チャンクの説明。「チャンクとは知識の『原子』であり，
学習可能な最小のものである」。atom「原子，それ以上分解できない
もの」。　⑥　アメリカ50州のそれぞれの名前，州の形，等々を暗記
するように教えられる指導主義との対比。「しかし，創造的な知識を
身につければ，その州の誕生につながった社会的・政治的力学につい
て考える方法を理解し…」。　2　ア「私の朗報が，創造性を高める教
育と事実を教えることに矛盾はないということだ」は，Aに入り，「事
実を暗記しても，生徒の創造性が低下することはない。また，事実を
教えるのをやめたからといって生徒がより創造的になることもない」
と続く。　イ　創造的な知識の説明「浅い知識のチャンクを束にして
複雑な全体を形成する」はCに入る。空所Cのあと，アメリカ50州を例
に浅い知識の習得と創造的な知識の習得の差異に触れている。
ウ「しかし指導主義とは異なり，これらの知識は孤立したチャンクで
はなく，豊かな概念的ネットワークでつながっている」。指導主義と
の共通点を挙げている「創造的な知識には，浅い知識，つまり指導主
義で教えられているのと同じ事実，技能，手順が含まれる」のあとの
Bに入る。　3　a common criticism of progressive education「進歩的な教
育に対してのよくある批判」。厳しさが足りず，生徒が重要な事実や
スキルを学ばないという批判。同格のthatに導かれている節を訳出す
る。that it's not rigorous enough「厳しさが不十分である」。that students
don't learn important facts and skills「生徒が大切な事実や技術を学ばな
い」。　4「私はガレージで工作用のパーツを測っているときに，この
ような知識を使う」。「このような知識」が指す内容は前文にある。the
multiplication tables, or the procedures for how to add fractions「掛け算の
表や分数の足し算の手順」を抜き出す。　5　(1)　第8段落の1文目参
照。指導主義では「生徒たちはたくさんの細かい事実を始終詰め込ま
れる」。　(2)　第8段落の終わりから2文目参照。著者が小学校で賞を

もらったとき「50州の州都の名前だけ」覚えた。　6　指導主義法で学ぶものと比べて，即興性法で学ぶ浅い知識のチャンクは，何が特異か」。第8段落2文目後半のthey learn those chunks bundled together in a broader understanding of the subjectを中心に訳出する，「生徒たちは，教科のより広い理解の中で，個別の知識が束ねられた知識のチャンクを学ぶ」。　7　ア　「浅い知識とは，世界についての個別のデータ群である」。第3段落1文目より，正しい。　イ　「創造性のために教えるということは，教科の知識のために教えることをやめなければならないということである」。第5段落参照。創造的になるためには，知識を教える必要がある。　ウ　「科学的専門知識の研究は，イノベーションが断片的な知識の上に成り立っていることを示している」。第7段落1文目参照。科学的専門知識の研究から，科学的創造性は浅い知識の小片ではなく，知識の束に根ざしていることが分かっている。　エ　「創造的知識は，生徒が浅い知識を学ぶ理由を把握することを可能にする」。最終段落より，正しい。

【30】(1)　エ　　(2)　ウ　　(3)　in what they do know　　(4)　文章や段落の構成について考えるとき，重要なメタ認知的な質問を自分にしていること。　　(5)　たとえメタ認知的な質問に正しく答えられなくても，文章を読む前にメタ認知的な質問に答えようとしている人々の方が，学びが豊かになる。　　(6)　イ　　(7)　Whenever I made teaching plans, I asked myself metacognitive questions, "Is the goal clear for students? Can students achieve the goal by carrying out the plan? Is the task appropriate to improve their skills?" By asking these questions, I was able to improve my plans. This is how I made use of metacognition in my life. (56 words)

○**解説**○　メタ認知と学習について12段落から成る700語程度の英文である。抽象的な説明箇所は精読し具体的な例示箇所は速読するなどメリハリをつけて読む。速度を調整しながら，かつ引用箇所もまとめながら読み進める読解スキルが必要である。　(1)　メタ認知には2つの側面があり，1つは計画的にコントロールする側面，もう1つは認知プロセスを監視する側面である。空欄①について。自分自身が知っていることをどのようにすれば分かるのか，背景にある知識をもっと知って

おく必要があるのかという問いかけは，課題解決に向けた計画的な方策をコントロールするためのものであり，自分の認知についての目標設定もこの範疇に入る。空欄②について。他の方法でもこの課題を理解できるか，自分が現在行っていることをなぜ今行っているのかという問いかけは，自分の認知プロセスを監視，点検するためのものであり，課題解決に向けての進捗度合いの確認もこの範疇に入る。以上からエが正解。　(2)　空欄③前文で，「思考についての思考というメタ認知的思考は，専門家だけでなく誰もが必要とする」と言っている。それは，課題解決に向けて自分自身の思考パターンを客観視し，より良い解決方法に到達するために活用する思考であるという文脈的理解から，空欄③後続の「メタ認知的な問いかけを行うことで課題解決に向けた新たなスキル習得につなげていく」という内容に結びついてくる。よって，空欄③には，対比や追加ではなく言い換えのウが妥当となる。以下，ディスコースマーカーの意味を確認のこと。on the other hand「対比」，in addition「追加」，in other words「言い換え」，on the contrary「対比」。　(3)　feel confident in〜「〜に自信を持っている」。「同時に人々は自分たちがまさに知っていることについて確信を持ちすぎてしまう」となる。　(4)　⑤の単数形this は，when we think about composing sentences and paragraphs, we're often asking ourselves crucial metacognitive questionsを指している。複数あるmetacognitive questionsの具体例を指すと考えるのは十分ではない。　(5)　主語はpeople，述語動詞はlearn a lot moreである。who〜before they read some textは，主語people を修飾している関係代名詞節である。even if「たとえ〜でも」。(6)　アは，第3段落1文目及び2文目と一致しない。ウは，第6段落1文目と一致しない。エは，第10段落「優れた旅行写真家になりたいなら写真を撮り始めるときにメタ認知的質問で自問自答してみるだろう」と言っているので一致しない。イは，第3段落最終文に一致する。(7)　自分の経験について書くということだが，複雑に考えるとまとまらなくなるので，ここでは具体的なメタ認知的な疑問文を例示して短時間で簡単に書けばよい。自分の経験としてどうしても思いつかない場合には，経験したことを想像して書いてもよいだろう。解答例では，指導計画作成にあたって，自分にメタ認知的質問を投げかけることで，

指導計画を改善できたという経験を述べている。5行程度で書けとの指示があり，具体的な語数は示されていないが，公式解答用紙の解答欄を見る限り，およそ50〜70語程度でまとめるとよいと思われる。

【31】問1　生徒たちが何を学んだのか，どのように上手に学んだのか，そして，どこで学びにつまずいているのかということ。(52字)
　　　問2　②　　問3　④　　問4　summative　　問5　3　③　　4　①
　　　5　②　　問6　③　　問7　③，④

○ **解説** ○　学習評価についての概念，特に形成的評価(formative assessment)，総括的評価(summative assessment)，診断的評価(diagnostic assessment)の3つの概念について述べられた英文だが，専門用語や概念が出てくる英文では，その定義や具体例について整理しながら読み進めることが内容理解につながる。　問1　下線部を含む文は「よく設計された評価方法は生徒の学習に関する貴重な情報を与えてくれる」の意であり，さらに「その方法により我々は〜を理解する」と続いているので，下線部に後続する英文内のwhat students learned, how well they learned it, and where they struggled.を日本語に訳してまとめる。下線部は名詞句なので体言止め「〜ということ」で締めくくること。問2　空欄1のある第3段落では，学習する過程においてフィードバックを学習者や教師に与えることにより，新しい学習スタイルを適用し形成的フィードバックを受ける機会を創出し，生徒の学習能力を促すことにつながると読み取れる。つまり，学習上のフィードバックがないことが，伝統的評価法であるsummative assessmentの否定的側面であり，すなわち欠点となる。空欄1には，その意味を表すdownsideを選ぶ。問3　空欄2の前では，「自分が作ったスープの味見を行い，そのフィードバックからスープの味を改良したり改善したりする」と述べている。改善を目指してフィードバックを行う評価方法はformative assessmentに他ならないことから，空欄2の前後は表現を変えて同じ内容を述べていると言える。in other words「言い換えれば」が正解。問4　第4段落では，formative assessmentとsummative assessmentの違いについて対比的に説明していることを念頭に置く。料理として出されたスープを客が食し，その客が最終的にそのスープの味の評価結果を

出すことは，教師が生徒の学習結果を数値で評定することと類似しているのでsummative assessmentと言える。otherwise known as〜「別名〜として知られている」。　問5　疑問詞を挿入する問題で，繰り返し同じ疑問詞を使わない前提であることに注意。空欄4について，whereなら「どこで教えるか」となり不可解。また，他動詞teachに目的語the new courseが後続するのでwhatは不可。よって，howを選び，「どのようにその新しい授業を教えるべきか」と考える。as to「〜に関して」。空欄5にもwhereは不可解。whatなら「何の教授法を使うべきか」となり意味を成す。結果として，空欄3にはwhereを当て，「生徒の今の(学習上の)立ち位置がどこかという全体像を得ること」と読み解く。

問6　第6段落では，formative assessmentがa valuable toolであるという書き出しで始まり，後続するmore importantly, crucial, a significant factorの語句から，フィードバックの重要性について説明しているのが見えてくる。assessmentが重要なのではなく，feedbackが重要であることから，③「なぜ学習にフィードバックが重要なのか」を選ぶ。

問7　①「教師が生徒を評価する時，生徒の学習意欲は考慮に入れるべきではない」は第1段落2文目より不一致。　②「総括的評価は教師に人気がある。なぜならばインフォーマルクエスチョンやプレゼンテーションなど様々な形式をとることができるからだ」は第4段落3文目より不一致。　③「形成的評価では，授業が進行している間にフィードバックを与えることで生徒の学習効果が上がる」は第6段落1文目と一致する。　④「診断的評価を実施することで教師は生徒が学習項目に関する知識を現状どの程度持っているかを確認することができる」は第5段落2文目と一致する。　⑤「総括的評価が効果を発揮するには，教師と生徒を含め双方向的であるべきだ」は第3段落と第6段落最終文より不一致。

【32】1　①　イ　　②　ウ　　③　ア　　2　Because the dormant ties were effectively offering a diversity bonus.　　3　According to the passage, a willingness to share one's knowledge and ideas is important to successful collaboration. In addition, according to the study of the medical students, givers thrive in interdependent roles where collaboration matters. Based on these considerations, successful student collaboration is about working together to achieve a common goal by sharing each other's knowledge and ideas. I think there are three key elements to facilitate student collaboration. The first one is establishing tasks and goals that students need to work on collaboratively. The second one is encouraging each student to contribute their own opinions, perspectives, and skills. The third one is encouraging, students to communicate respectfully and listen to each other's perspectives, even if they disagree in order to build consensus. I believe the facilitation including these elements will enhance teamwork, produce results, and lead to successful collaboration. (140語)

○**解説**○ 1 ① 空欄の前後に着目する。空欄直前の文では，医学生を対象とした調査において，1年目は仲間に対して見識を与えようとしていた「与える人」は取り残されたと述べられている。その一方で，空欄直後の文では，2年目になると協調性のある学生たちが追いつき，3年目には追い越したと述べられている。従って，興味深い現象が見られたという意味のイが正解。 ② 同様に，空欄の前後に着目する。空欄直前の文では，与えるアプローチをする人が繁栄するのは鉄則ではなく，もらう態度を取り，成果を分かち合うことを嫌う人の中にも，素晴らしい成果を上げる人がいることが述べられている。その一方で，空欄直後の文では，しかし，エビデンスは与えるアプローチを支持する広範なパターンを示していると述べられている。従って，世の中のことはきっちりカテゴリー通りにいかないという旨のウが正解。
③ 空欄の前の2文に着目する。知識や創造的なアイデアを提供することは複雑な世界に利益をもたらし，長期にわたり効果的な協力体制を作る接着剤のようなものであると述べられている。従って，さらに恩恵があるとするアが正解。 2 第7パラグラフ5〜6文目に対応する記述がある。解答例はほぼ6文目そのままであるが，5文目の情報を適宜使用した解答でもよいだろう。 3 教師として生徒同士の協力を促すために重要だと考える点を，本文に基づいて英語で記述する問題である。解答例にあるように，前半では本文の内容をまとめた上で，それに基づく具体的な方法などを英語で記述する形が書きやすいと思われる。本文で述べられているように，自分の考えやアイデアなどを

他者と共有することの重要性に触れながら，それを生徒たちにどのように促すかを書いていくとよいだろう。

【33】問1　(1)　ウ　　(2)　ア　　問2　(1)　ア　　(2)　エ
○**解説**○ 問1　(1)　第2段落に，多くのアメリカ人は，金持ちになるチャンスは皆に平等に与えられており，金持ちは一生懸命働いた結果であると考えていることが書かれている。したがって，ウの「貧しい人より一生懸命働いたから」が正解。　(2)　第3，4段落では心理学的な実験について書かれている。実験は，裕福で恵まれた立場の人の行動について，ボードゲームやインタビューを通じて検証したものである。よって適切なタイトルはア。　問2　(1)　第1段落の後半に，ノルウェーの氷河の波形がどのようにできたのか記述されている。　(2)　第2段落以降，専門家によって氷河の後退速度を調査するために海底を調査することが有効であることが説明されている。特にノルウェーの調査地域が地球温暖化の計測，予測に有用であることが示されているため，エは適切。

【34】(1)　この(折半法)方法では，学習者にテストを与え，採点時にテスト内の項目を2つのグループに分ける。例えば，50項目あれば，奇数の項目はすべて1つのグループに，偶数の項目はもう1つのグループに分ける。2つのグループの項目の点数を比較し，信頼できるテストであれば，2つの項目のグループのスコアは似ているはずである。
(2)　High content validity indicates that the test fully covers the content of the skill, language, or course for the target. While low content validity suggests that the test does not contain relevant aspects of the subject matter.
(3)　イ　　(4)　オ　　(5)　When evaluating a student's performance, I should be careful about using the criteria of practicality and reliability. This is because I should increase the number of evaluators due to its practicality. Also, I should have common criteria to score the test due to its reliability.
○**解説**○ (1)　split halvesについては，直後の4文にわたり具体的に説明されている。　(2)　内容の妥当性が高いテストと低いテストの違いを説明する。第7段落を簡単にまとめる。テストされる技能，言語，コー

スの内容をカバーしていれば高いと言える。他の構成要素が含まれていたり，学習者が通常とは異なる方法で構成要素を処理する必要があったりする場合，妥当性は低い。　(3)　実用的なテストの条件として「短い，多くの紙や機器を必要としない，実施に多くの人を必要としない，理解しやすい，採点しやすい，解釈しやすい得点や結果を持つ，妥当性を損なうことなく何度も使用できる」などが挙げられている。ア「解釈の容易さ」，ウ「運営と採点のしやすさ」，エ「時間，お金，量力の節約」が空所に当てはまる。　(4)　ア「テストを採点するときはある程度の妥協が必要で，妥当性が失われてもよい」。第1段落には「信頼性，妥当性，実用性の基準の間で何らかの妥協をしなければならない」とある。妥当性が失われてもよいとは述べていないので，誤り。　イ「たとえ あるテストの表面的妥当性が低くても，それが完了するまで使用をやめるべきではない」。第6段落で述べられている「信頼できるテストであっても，表面的妥当性が低いと，そのテストが使用されなくなる可能性がある」に矛盾する。　ウ「実際には多くの制限があるが，すべての要件を満たすためにテストを行う必要がある」。最終段落に「すべての要件を満たし，なおかつ信頼性が高く妥当なテストを作成することは容易ではない。ほとんどのテストは，様々な基準の間で妥協している」とあるので誤り。　エ「生徒の発音を評価したければ，会話コミュニケーション能力のテストが使用されるべきだ」。第4段落参照。「発音テストは発音のテストとしては有効でも会話コミュニケーション能力のテストとしては有効ではない」とあるので誤り。　オ「信頼できるテストとは，別の日，別の状況でもスコアがほぼ同じであることを意味する」。第2段落の内容に合致するので正しい。　(5)　問いは「生徒のパフォーマンステストを3つの基準で評価する場合，何に注意するか。3つの基準のうち少なくとも2つを述べながら自身の考えとその理由を説明しなさい」。解答例は，「実用性」と「信頼性」に触れている。

【35】(1)　④　　(2)　③　　(3)　④　　(4)　②　　(5)　①
○**解説**○　(1)　第1パラグラフの2文目にゼノボットはアフリカツメガエルの幹細胞からつくられたことが述べられている。　(2)　第2パラグラ

フの3文目に着目する。Michael Levinが驚いたのは，ゼノボットは新しい動き方に加え，新たな生殖の方法を見つけ出したことである。

(3)　第3パラグラフの4文目に着目すると，ロボットが何でできているかよりも，人類のために自ら何をするかの方が重要であると述べられている。　(4)　第4パラグラフの5文目に着目すると，C字形だと口の内側に数百の細胞を集めることができると述べられている。なお，細胞を集めるイメージが本文の下にあるFigure 2に示されている。

(5)　第5パラグラフの3文目に着目すると，ゼノボットの活用可能性として，海中のマイクロプラスチックの収集，植物の根系の調査および再生医療などが述べられている。これらに対応しない「細菌兵器(生物兵器)」を意味する①が正解。

【1】次の英文は，Aさんが英語の授業を構想する際に読んだ雑誌の記事(以下，「本文」という。)である。本文を読み，以下の問いに答えなさい。

本文

Sipping her yuzu tea in a buzzy café, 20-year-old university student Marin Minamiya is exactly what you'd expect of a fashionable young Japanese woman. Her hair is long and shiny. Her fingernails are painted a sparkly gold. She laughs easily and punctuates her conversation with breathless, OMG-style exclamations. What you don't expect is this: A few weeks later, she will be wrapped in up to seven layers of clothing, slogging through minus-70-degree temperatures, in an attempt to ski to the North Pole.

Minamiya―bubbly exterior, steely core―is one of Japan's youngest and most high-profile adventurers. 【 ① 】 At 18, she became the youngest woman ever to climb 8,163-meter Mount Manaslu in the Nepalese Himalayas. At 19, she was the youngest Japanese person, man or woman, to climb Mount Everest. When we meet, in February this year, she is in the middle of training for the North Pole trip, the final leg of her attempt at the famously (②) Explorers Grand Slam. To date completed by just 51 people worldwide, this demands that participants reach both poles and climb the tallest mountains on seven continents. If Minamiya reaches the Pole, she will be the youngest Asian to have completed the challenge.

She'll make the attempt on the North Pole in early April, as part of a small group―but exploring can be a lonely life. Minamiya is often not just the only woman in a group but also the youngest overall. Women can be competitive and men prejudiced: One male Japanese climber once said he was insulted just to be introduced to her.

"People are often really surprised when they learn about what I do," she says. "They say, 'Oh my gosh' and can't imagine me climbing a mountain, especially when I'm wearing my normal, everyday clothes. They ask me why

I do it—and I want to tell them the reason, but it's not easy to say in one sentence."

Minamiya's longing to climb started as a way to connect with others. She was an only child, and her father's work as a financial trader meant the family was always on the move. At the age of 12, after time living in Malaysia, Shanghai and the Chinese city of Dalian, Minamiya moved with her family to Hong Kong, where she went to an English-speaking school for largely expatriate children. She had a difficult time there, she recalls: A culture of overreliance on technology meant there was very little human interaction. Every course was taught on laptops, and at lunchtime, Minamiya ate on the first floor while FaceTiming with her best friend, who sat on the eighth.

Things at home weren't any better. Her father was rarely there, and her mother had stayed behind in Japan. Then, when she was 13, her teachers started taking groups of 50 students on trips to the mountainous interior of Lantau, Hong Kong's largest island. On the mountainside, the group had to collaborate, with the participants helping one another navigate across the unfamiliar landscape and coming together to plan the group meal. "For the first time, there was a human bond between us," she says.

Climbing also gave the adolescent Minamiya a sense of perspective, a view of the wider world that she found invaluable. When she reached her first mountaintop with her schoolmates, she looked east across the waters of the South China Sea to the "concrete jungle of Hong Kong." In that moment, she saw the stresses of her preteen life for what they were. "We thought, Oh my gosh, our existence is so tiny. All these daily issues don't (③)."

After that, Minamiya climbed dozens of mountains around Hong Kong, before joining a friend and two teachers on a 14-day climb to the Annapurna base camp in Nepal. There — still only 13 — she glimpsed Mount Everest looming over a valley and vowed to climb it one day. She then completed an arduous ascent in Argentina.

Her parents divorced when she was 17; climbing high kept her (④), giving her a much needed sense of control. "I knew the one thing that would get me back on track was climbing," she says. "It has always been like meditation for me. It's not only about healing—it's about self-empowerment and self-awareness. I just thought, 'I have to get out of here and find myself, through basing myself on a mountain.'"

She experienced a different kind of grounding too. While she was descending Mount Amida in Nagano in March 2015, the snow beneath her crumbled, and she fell 250 meters, head-first. That's nearly as bad as falling off the Eiffel Tower. "I really thought I was going to die," she says, but then adds, "When I was falling, I screamed and prayed to God, saying, 'I don't want to die yet, please help me.'" Right after her prayer, her crampons got caught in the snow, and she stopped falling.

She spent the night in a snow hole she'd dug for herself, before an emergency search team in a helicopter rescued her. 【 ⑤ 】 She cried for days afterward in an empty house; her parents hadn't visited her in hospital. Yet she completed her record-breaking Mount Everest ascent just 14 months later. "The accident made me realize that people die extremely easily," she says. "That made me propel myself even further."

Where does a woman who's reached both ends of the earth propel herself next? Assuming she makes it back from the North Pole, Minamiya's next plan is to sail around the world — this time, she hopes, not alone. She's looking for a companion to sail with "who is definitely committed, has a dream of their own, is excited about life — and basically has the same goal as me, which is to help others reach their full potential." It doesn't seem like an accident that she's choosing an adventure that requires another person to come along for the ride. I hope she finds someone.

(Newsweek, March 17, 2017 一部改)

1　本文の内容に合うように，【 ① 】【 ⑤ 】に入る最も適する英語を次のア～オより一つずつ選び，記号で答えなさい。

ア　Climbing mountains wasn't any feat.

イ　The accident made her vulnerable in a different way.

ウ　Minamiya juggles time spent on expeditions with studying at the university.

エ　Minamiya thought that she had become somebody completely new.

オ　During her teens, she quietly broke a string of records.

2　本文の内容に合うように，（　②　）（　③　）（　④　）に入る最も適する英語を次のア〜エより一つずつ選び，記号で答えなさい。

②　ア　successful　　　　　イ　straightforward

　　ウ　grueling　　　　　　エ　insignificant

③　ア　pose a challenge　　イ　mean a thing

　　ウ　make an impact　　エ　resolve my doubts

④　ア　grounded　　　　　イ　unstable

　　ウ　immature　　　　　エ　ready

3　本文の内容に合うように，次の質問に6語以上の英語で答えなさい。

(1)　Why are people often really surprised when they learn about what Minamiya does?

(2)　When did Minamiya get inspired to climb Mount Everest?

(3)　For the next plan of sailing, what kind of companion does Minamiya hope to find?

4　Aさんは，世界に発信する日本人というテーマでMinamiyaさんを紹介するために，伝えたいことをまとめた。次はその一部である。本文の内容に合うように，（　①　）〜（　③　）に入る英語を書きなさい。ただし，（　①　）〜（　③　）は，異なる英語を使用すること。

＝The person who sends a message to the world＝

Marin Minamiya

◆Background

→　Minamiya moved around Asia with her father's job.

→　When she went to an English-speaking school for largely expatriate children, she could hardly (　①　) with her classmates.

◆Climbing and her

→　To build (　②　) with others, her longing to climb started.

→　When her teachers took groups of 50 students on trips to the mountainous interior of Lantau, she felt there was a human (　③　) between them for the first time.

---

5 次の英文は，Aさんが，Minamiyaさんについてもっと知りたいと思い，読んだインタビュー記事の一部である。この英文において，Minamiyaさんが，最も伝えたいことを以下のア～エの中から一つ選び記号で答えなさい。

I would like to encourage young girls to pursue anything, whatever it is that they want to do. Believe in your potential and believe that it's infinite. All the limitations and barriers out there — if you do think that they're barriers, you put it on yourself. I think it's all in the mind. And don't be afraid to be the only girl in certain situations, and you'll definitely learn to manage, so go for it.

(CNN ENGLISH EXPRESS, October, 2019 一部改)

ア　Know your own limitations.
イ　Turn to others for help.
ウ　What will be, will be.
エ　Never place limits on yourself.

‖ 2024年度 ‖ 静岡県・静岡市・浜松市 ‖ 難易度 ‖

【2】 Read the following passages and choose the most appropriate answer for each question.

By some measures, the book business is doing better than ever.

Ⓐ Last year, readers bought nearly 827 million print books, an increase of roughly 10% over 2020, and a record since NPD BookScan began tracking this data two decades ago.

Ⓑ As book buyers have migrated online, it has gotten harder to sell books by new or lesser-known authors. With the exception of surprise runaway bestsellers ("Where the Crawdads Sing," for example) and books by celebrities or brand-name authors (Matthew McConaughey, James Patterson), most writers fail to find much of an audience. Of the 3.2 million titles that BookScan tracked in 2021, fewer than 1% sold more than 5,000 copies.

The gap points to what is perhaps the most intractable problem in publishing: how to reproduce online the serendipity of walking into a bookstore and discovering new books and authors. Several companies have attempted to tackle the issue, with mixed results. Now, a new app, Tertulia, launched this week, is trying a different approach, by measuring and distilling the online chatter about books to point readers to the ones that are driving discussions.

Ⓒ When bookstores were the main purveyors of books, an interesting cover, a prominent display in Barnes & Noble or a passionate endorsement from an independent bookseller could nudge a reader to pick up something new. But online, the old methods for creating buzz and driving sales no longer work. On the internet, industry experts say, it is easy for readers to click on something they know they want, but they are less likely to encounter something unfamiliar.

"Everyone knows you can sell books online," said John Ingram, chairman of the Ingram Content Group, the largest book distributor and wholesaler in the United States. "The question is, how do you get content in front of people who might be interested in it?"

Ⓓ Several companies have tried. Two years ago, Ingram launched a discovery website, Bookfinity, which offers users customized recommendations after giving them a survey and assigning them a "reader type," including beach reader, cool mom/dad, and spiritual seeker.

Others include Booqsi, a platform that bills itself as a "community-focused, Amazon-free alternative to Goodreads," and Copper, a new author-centric book discovery app that is designed to connect readers with writers (so far, around 500 authors have signed up). Another company, Open Road Integrated Media, markets e-books of older titles. David Steinberger, its CEO, said that in aggregate, it doubles the sales of its clients' titles.

"There's an endless appetite among the tech people and publishing industry people to find the Holy Grail of book discovery, but I don't think anyone has found a tool or an algorithm or an AI platform that does the job for you," said Peter Hildick-Smith, president of the Codex Group, which analyzes the book industry.

The latest arrival in this increasingly crowded niche is Tertulia, a sleek new app that takes a novel approach to online discovery.

Using a mix of artificial intelligence and human curation, Tertulia aggregates book discussions and recommendations from across the web, drawing from social media posts, book reviews, podcasts and news articles to generate reading recommendations tailored to individuals' tastes and interests.

To get personalized recommendations, users answer questions about which genres they like and what types of people they want to hear about books from (options include space explorers, poets, chefs, historians, entertainers and book critics). Users can also sign in with their Twitter accounts, which allows the app's algorithms to sift through their feeds to pull out book recommendations from people they follow.

Each day, Tertulia generates a personalized list of five books. Elsewhere on the app, users can browse lists of notable titles in different genres, which are ranked according to buzz, rather than sales. Currently, Tertulia's "most talked about" lists feature a mix of older and newer titles — on the fiction list, Toni Morrison's "Sula" and Octavia E. Butler's "Parable of the Sower" appear along with recently released novels by Jennifer Egan and Emily St. John Mandel.

By harnessing online conversations about books and refining them into digestible lists, Tertulia's founders hope to replicate the "word-of-mouth" recommendations that once drove sales in brick-and-mortar stores. The name Tertulia, which means gathering in Spanish, refers to the tradition of informal literary salons and artistic gatherings.

"There's Netflix for movies. There's Spotify for music," said Sebastian Cwilich, CEO of Tertulia and co-founder of Artsy, an online fine arts marketplace. "But there really wasn't an equivalent discovery experience for books."

Cwilich — who co-founded the app with Robert Lenne, who specializes in design and digital product development, and Lynda Hammes, former publisher of Foreign Affairs magazine — said the initial idea was to create an app that generated book suggestions based on "vetted voices" of experts, rather than regurgitating what's on the bestseller lists. That idea morphed into a more ambitious one: "What if it was all the world's book conversations, all the book talk?" he said.

Besides being a recommendation engine, Tertulia functions as a vast online bookstore, with roughly 15 million titles. Ingram, a partner and investor in Tertulia, will fulfill and ship orders placed through the app. For now, only paperbacks and hardcovers are available, but the company plans to start selling e-books and audiobooks in the coming months, Cwilich said.

Some are (a) that an app will crack the online discovery problem. Readers are already bombarded with recommendations on social media, endless best-of lists, celebrity book clubs, reviews and other prompts. Tertulia and other new companies face substantial hurdles, like persuading people to download the app and take a survey.

"It's an industry problem," said Kristen McLean, executive director of business development at NPD Books. "But are people on the hunt every day, do they wake up saying, 'I need to find a book discovery tool?' They do not."

Still, some publishers, authors and agents who've gotten an early look at Tertulia say the app is a promising addition to the online retail landscape, particularly if it becomes a hub for intelligent book recommendations that go beyond the usual one to five star rating system.

"What the app might do is drown out the chaos and lowest common denominator opinions with something that resembles actual discourse about books," said the essayist and novelist Sloane Crosley, who was among the 40 authors and agents recruited to test drive the app before its launch. "If Tertulia can bring up the average discourse about books, long may they reign."

(Alter, A., & Harris, E. A. (2022). A new way to choose your next book. *The New York Times*)

1．Where in the passage does the sentence below best fit?

But all is not as rosy as it seems.

① Ⓐ　　② Ⓑ　　③ Ⓒ　　④ Ⓓ

2．What does the underlined word "serendipity" mean?

① the act of finding the book you have really wanted

② the act of finding books you've been pre-ordering and looking forward to

③　the act of finding books of new or lesser-known authors intentionally

④　the act of finding interesting or valuable books by coincidence

3．Fill in the blank (　a　) with the most appropriate word.

①　confident　　②　frightened　　③　grateful　　④　skeptical

4．Which statement is NOT true about the companies' attempts introduced in the passage?

①　Copper is a new writer centric application that connects readers with writers.

②　Bookfinity assigns reader types to users through a questionnaire and recommends books to them.

③　Tertulia allows users to receive a personalized book list without having to answer questions.

④　Ingram intends to focus on e-books and audiobooks in addition to selling paper books.

5．According to the passage, which statement is true?

①　Tertulia's founders regard word of mouth as an instrumental part of selling books online.

②　Industry experts believe that the possibility of encountering something unfamiliar on the Internet is sufficiently high.

③　The lists created by Tertulia are more reflective of sales than topicality.

④　Readers willingly download the app and complete a survey in order to have their books recommended to others.

6．Below is a summary of this passage. Fill in the blank in the summary with the most appropriate sentence.

Most books are sold online, where it's impossible to replicate the experience of browsing in a brick-and-mortar store. (　　　)

①　Readers are eager to experience that again.

②　Bookstores undertake various approaches to that.

③　Book-discovery apps aim to change that.

④　That has become a serious problem for the industry.

【3】次の英文を読み，以下の問1〜問5に答えなさい。

We are highly sensitive to people around us. As infants, we observe our parents and teachers, and from them we learn how to walk, talk, read ― and use smartphones. There seems to be no limit to the complexity of behaviour we can acquire from (　①　) learning.

But social influence goes deeper than that. We don't just copy the [　あ　] of people around us. We also copy their [　い　]. As we grow older, we learn what other people think, feel and want ― and adapt to it. Our brains are really good at this ― we copy computations inside the brains of others. But how does the brain distinguish between thoughts about your own mind and thoughts about the minds of others? Our new study, published in Nature Communications, brings us closer to an answer.

Our ability to copy the minds of others is hugely important. When this process goes wrong, it can contribute to various mental health problems. You might become unable to empathise with someone, or, at the other extreme, you might be so (　②　) to other people's thoughts that your own sense of "self" is volatile and fragile. The ability to think about another person's mind is one of the most sophisticated adaptations of the human brain. Experimental psychologists often assess this ability with a technique called a "false belief task". ⎰（A）⎱

In the task, one individual, the "subject", gets to observe another individual, the "partner", hide a desirable object in a box. The partner then leaves, and the subject sees the researcher remove the object from the box and hide it in a second location. When the partner returns, they will falsely believe the object is still in the box, but the subject knows the truth. ⎰（B）⎱ But how do we know whether the subject is really thinking about the mind of the partner?

Over the last ten years, neuroscientists have explored a theory of mind-reading called simulation theory. The theory suggests that [　う　].

Neuroscientists have found compelling evidence that the brain does simulate the computations of a social partner. They have shown that if you observe another person receive a reward, like food or money, your brain activity is the same as if you were the one receiving the reward.

There's a problem though. If my brain copies your computations, how does it distinguish between my own mind and my simulation of your mind?

In our experiment, we recruited 40 participants and asked them to play a "probabilistic" version of the false belief task. At the same time, we scanned their brains using functional magnetic resonance imaging (fMRI), which measures brain activity indirectly by tracking changes in blood flow.

In this game, rather than having a belief that the object is definitely in the box or not, both players believe there is a probability that the object is here or there, without knowing for certain. The object is always being moved, and so the two players' beliefs are always changing. ☐ (C) ☐ This design allowed us to use a mathematical model to describe what was going on in the subject's mind, as they played the game. It showed how participants changed their own belief every time they got some information about where the object was. It also described how they changed their simulation of the partner's belief, every time the partner saw some information.

The model works by calculating "predictions" and "prediction errors" . For example, if a participant predicts that there is a 90% chance the object is in the box, but then sees that it's nowhere near the box, they will be surprised. We can therefore say that the person experienced a large "prediction error" . This is then used to improve the prediction for next time.

Many researchers believe that the prediction error is a fundamental unit of computation in the brain. Each prediction error is linked to a particular pattern of activity in the brain. This means that we could compare the patterns of brain activity when a subject experiences prediction errors with the alternative activity patterns that happen when the subject thinks about the partner's prediction errors. ☐ (D) ☐

Our findings showed that the brain uses distinct patterns of activity for prediction errors and "simulated" prediction errors. This means that the brain activity contains information not only about what's going on out there in the world, but also about who is thinking about the world. The(③) leads to a subjective sense of self.

We also found, however, that we could train people to make those brain-activity patterns for self and other either more distinct or more overlapping. We did this by manipulating the task so that the subject and partner saw the same information either rarely or frequently. If they became more distinct, subjects got better at distinguishing their own thoughts from the thoughts of the partner. If the patterns became more overlapping, they got worse at distinguishing their own thoughts from the thoughts of the partner. This means that the boundary between the self and the other in the brain is not fixed, but flexible. The brain can learn to change this boundary. ┃ (E) ┃ On a societal level, it may explain why we find it easier to empathise with those who've shared similar experiences to us, compared with people from different backgrounds.

The results could be useful. If self-other boundaries really are this malleable, then maybe we can harness this capacity, both to tackle bigotry and (④) mental health disorders.

> (出典) https://theconversation.com/how-the-brain-builds-a-sense-of-self-from-the-people-around-us-new-reseach-141844　より一部変更

問1　(①)~(④)に入る文脈上最も適当な語を，次のア～カの中から1つずつ選び，記号で答えよ。ただし，同じ記号を複数回用いてはならない。

ア　combination　　イ　observational　　ウ　adaptation
エ　alleviate　　　オ　stimulate　　　　カ　susceptible

問2　[　あ　], [　い　]に入る組み合わせとして，文脈上最も適当なものを，次のア～エの中から1つ選び，記号で答えよ。

ア　あ　thoughts　　い　beliefs
イ　あ　ability　　　い　simulation
ウ　あ　behaviour　　い　minds
エ　あ　brains　　　 い　behaviour

問3　次のア～ウの英文は，本文中の ┃ (A) ┃ ～ ┃ (E) ┃ のどこに入るか，記号で答えよ。

ア　This might explain the familiar experience of two people who spend a lot of time together and start to feel like one single person, sharing the same thoughts.

イ This supposedly requires the subject to hold in mind the partner's false belief in addition to their own true belief about reality.

ウ The subject is challenged with trying to keep track of not only the whereabouts of the object, but also the partner's belief.

問4 [う]に入る文脈上最も適当な英語を，次のア～エの中から1つ選び，記号で答えよ。

ア when I put myself in your shoes, my brain tries to copy the computations inside your brain

イ when I put an object in a box, your brain tries to guess what is inside the box by computations

ウ when you put yourself in my shoes, my brain tries to simulate what is going on in your brain

エ when you put an object in a box, my brain tries to copy the image of the object by computations

問5 本文の主旨として最も適当なものを，次のア～エの中から1つ選び，記号で答えよ。

ア It is not useful to compare the patterns of brain activity when prediction errors are happening with those when they are not.

イ Neuroscientists think it doubtful that if we see others receiving rewards in social situations, our brain shows the same brain activity as when we are rewarded.

ウ We never distinguish thoughts about our own minds from thoughts about the minds of others.

エ Self-other boundaries are flexible, so in some cases we can empathise with others and in other cases we can keep a sense of self.

▌2024年度 ▌佐賀県 ▌難易度 ■■■■■■

【4】 Suppose you (JTE) and an ALT are going to conduct a performance test on writing in "Logic and Expression I" class. Read the **Lesson Outline**, the **Newspaper Article** and **Class Discussion in the 1ˢᵗ class**, and answer the following questions.

Lesson Outline

Can-Do Statement

With some assistance, I can write about my surroundings in coherent English, paying attention to logic and using familiar phrases and sentences.

Lesson Goals

I can write about Japanese school customs and introduce them to someone abroad.

I can share my opinions about why Japanese schools have certain customs.

Lesson Schedule

1st class	Understand the **Lesson Goals**.
	Read the **Newspaper Article** and discuss the topic in class.
2nd class	Learn useful expressions and model sentences to communicate one's ideas effectively.
	Summarize thoughts about the topic (cleaning) based on one's own experiences and research.
3rd class	Share the opinions and ideas with classmates.
4th class	Take the Performance Test. (Area: Writing, Location: Classroom, Duration: 20 min)
5th class	Review and reflect on the test, and rewrite opinions.

Newspaper Article

Japan fans rewarded for stadium clean-ups

Japanese soccer fans have received an award from FIFA for picking up trash in stadiums, following the Samurai Blue's stunning victory against Germany in their World Cup opener in Doha on Wednesday. Japanese supporters filled about 20 45-liter bags with empty plastic bottles, boxes and other kinds of trash.

Volunteers at the Japan-Germany game praised the efforts of the conscientious Samurai Blue fans, who even received a thank-you message via the public address system.

A World Cup organizing committee official expressed appreciation for the actions of the Japanese supporters at a ceremony in Doha on Thursday and said it would be great if such spirits were shared among the people of Qatar and other countries.

A 22-year-old university student from Japan, who collected trash at both the opening match and Japan's game, received flowers and ①commemorative gifts from FIFA.

"I feel strange receiving an award for doing nothing special," he said. "It's part of Japanese culture, and I want to spread it around the world."

A tweet on FIFA's official Twitter account posted after Samurai Blue's victory read, "It's not only three points that Japan have in the bag."

Class Discussion in the 1ˢᵗ class   A: ALT   J: JTE   S: Student

A : Is it true that this kind of behavior, cleaning after the event, is not something special for Japanese people?

S1: I guess it is not special. I wonder why this news has caught so much attention.

A : Why do you think so?

S1: Well, because I have been cleaning at school and home since I was little. I think it is natural for me to clean up after I use something.

J : In Japan, we say, *"Tatsu tori ato wo nigosazu."* It means [A   ]. Do you agree with this idea?

S2: Yes. Actually, I always try to clean after using the classroom or using sports equipment for the person who will use it next.

J : Yes, that's right. Students are taught from a young age to keep what we use clean. For example, we rarely see ②janitors at school in Japan. Instead, students and teachers all participate in cleaning the school.

A : I see. What surprised me when I came to Japan was that the students clean the school. That is one of the unique customs I found in Japanese schools. Why do you think Japanese schools have a cleaning system? What is a good point of students' cleaning at school?

J : [B   ].

A : Interesting. That is why cleaning is conducted as a part of education.

Questions

Q1: Explain ① and ② in English to the students.

Q2: To have the students understand the **Newspaper Article,** make one fact-finding question and one inferential question.

"Fact Finding Questions" : Questions that make the students read what is shown directly in the text.

"Inferential Questions" : Questions that ask the students to make assumptions based on the information in the text.

Q3: Fill in blanks [A] and [B] to complete each sentence.

Q4: You are making the **Instruction** for the **Performance Test** shown on the next page. Answer the following questions.

(1) In the performance test, the students will reply to an email from a girl named Katie in the UK, who read the same newspaper article. Based on the **Can-Do Statement, Lesson Goals,** and **Conditions,** complete Katie's email message in the **Instruction** part [C].

(2) Based on the **Can-Do Statement** and **Lesson Goals,** fill in blanks [D] and [E] in the **Scoring Criteria.**

Performance Test

＊ Students are given the following performance test along with the Scoring Criteria.

---

nstruction

You have received the following email from your friend Katie in the UK, who saw the same news. Please reply to her.

Hi, there! Have you watched the news about Japanese fans cleaning up at Qatar's FIFA World Cup stadium?

[C]

393

Looking forward to hearing from you!

Best wishes,

Katie

Conditions

1 You should clearly write your thoughts and opinions on given topics.

2 You should write reasons and examples to support your thoughts and opinions.

Scoring Criteria

Rank	Knowledge & Skills	Ability to think, make decisions, and express ideas	Proactive attitude toward learning
a	Writes in easily understandable English with excellent choice of vocabulary and expressions	Using both **Conditions**, writes and conveys relevant information, thoughts, and opinions in detail	[D] , based on both **Conditions**
b	[E]	Writes with both **Conditions**	Tries writing with both **Conditions**
c	Does not meet "b"	Does not meet "b"	Does not meet "b"

▌2024年度 ▌長野県 ▌難易度

【5】

1 Directions: You will read two passages. Each passage is followed by an incomplete statement and four options, marked a to d. Choose the best answer for ［ ア ］・［ イ ］ on the basis of what is stated or implied in the passages. Then, mark your answer on your answer sheet.

(1) For birds, understanding other species' neighborhood gossip about an approaching hawk or brown snake can mean the difference between life or death. Wild critters are known to listen to each other for clues about lurking predators, effectively eavesdropping on other species' chatter. Birds, for example, can learn to flee when neighbors emit a distress call meaning "hawk!" The fairy-wren is a small Australian songbird that is

394

not born knowing the "languages" of other birds. However, it can master the meaning of a few key "words." Scientists explain this discovery in a paper published August 2 in the journal *Current Biology*. Andrew Radford is a biologist at the University of Bristol in England and co-author of the study. "We knew before that some animals can translate the meanings of other species' 'foreign languages,' but we did not know how that 'language learning' came about," said Radford.

This passage claims that a certain type of bird ⎡ ア ⎤.

a will be able to comprehend human language

b has an innate habit of fleeing predators

c can understand some "words" of other species

d is born knowing the "languages" of other species

(2) Further light has been shed on the possible dangers of eating ultra-processed food. A new study has revealed that consuming food such as sausages, frozen pizza, ready-to-eat meals, sodas and cakes can increase the risk of cancer, heart disease or an earlier death. Ultra-processed food includes products made in factories from ingredients that are largely or entirely made in a laboratory. They are added with things like preservatives, flavour enhancers, colourings, sugar and fats. The research was conducted on over 200,000 people in the USA over a 28-year period. Researcher Dr Fang Fang Zhang said men who ate a lot of ultra-processed food had a 29 percent higher risk of developing bowel cancer. Ultra-processed foods make up a growing proportion of the food we eat. The WHO says they account for around two-thirds of calories in the diets of American children and teenagers. Dr Zhang said children who ate ultra-processed food gained weight more quickly than those who ate a more nutritious and well balanced diet. She said: "Americans consume a large percentage of their daily calories from ultra-processed foods." She gave advice on how people can look after their bodies better through their diets. She said: "We should consider substituting ultra-processed foods with unprocessed or minimally processed foods in our diet for cancer prevention and for the prevention of obesity and

cardiovascular diseases."

According to this passage, ［ イ ］ .

a several studies have revealed the impact of ultra-processed foods on our health

b people are eating less and less ultra-processed foods because of health risks

c the production of ultra-processed foods is restricted in several countries

d the relationship between obesity and ultra-processed foods remains unclear

2 Directions: You will read the following passages, one with a table and one with a figure. Beneath them, you will see four options, marked a to d. Choose the best answer for ［ ウ ］・［ エ ］ on the basis of what is implied in the passages. Then, mark your answer on your answer sheet.

(1) In the dictogloss activity (Wajnryb, 1990), learners listen to a short text read twice to them while they take notes. In small groups, they reconstruct a written form of the text from these notes. A full description of the steps in the activity is outlined in Table 5.1. Steps 4 and 5 encourage learners to pay close attention to language form (i.e., word forms, word order, spelling, grammar rules, etc.) within the context of meaning-focused listening and group work. Dunn(1993) cautions that expecting learners to reconstruct a formally identical text may result in strange grammar in the reconstruction as the learners try to fit their notes into the text.This problem may be solved through having long texts, encouraging the learners to take non-linear notes, and expecting an interpretive summary rather than an exact reconstruction.

Table 5.1 Steps for a Dictogloss Activity

Step	*Teacher*	*Students*
1 Preparation	Vocabulary study activities to prepare for the text. Discuss the topic (predict vocabulary and content etc). Move into groups	
2 Listening for meaning	Reads the text at normal speed	Listen to the whole text

3	Listening and note-taking	Reads again at normal speed	Take notes listing key words
4	Text reconstruction in groups	Helps groups. Offers guidance	Work in groups to recon-struct an approximation of the text from notes (one learner acts as the writer)
5	Text comparison between groups	Facilitates class comparison of versions from different groups (on OHP or board). Facilitates discussion and correction of errors	Compare group versions of the text. Pay attention to points of usage that emerge from the discussion

According to this passage and Table 5.1, [ウ] in the dictogloss activity.

a   students need to be made aware not only of the language form but also of the content

b   it is important how accurately students can reconstruct the text through group work

c   it is better not to let students predict the content before listening to the text

d   teachers should encourage students to take as many notes as possible

(2)   Using a language assessment involves linking students' assessment performance to the beneficial consequences that we want to help bring about. When we give a language assessment, we present students with some language assessment tasks that they are expected to perform. We then record their performance in some way; we describe it or assign a score to it. Then we interpret these descriptions or scores as telling us something about students' language ability. We then use these interpretations to make decisions, which we intend to help bring about beneficial consequences. Using a language assessment is like making a chain. We create a series of links from students' assessment performance to assessment records, to interpretations, to decisions, to consequences. When we use an assessment in the classroom, we use the information we have obtained to achieve a specific outcome. Each link in our chain therefore includes some information we obtain and an outcome based on that information. These links between information and outcomes are

illustrated in Figure 2.3.

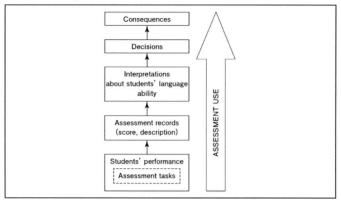

Figure 2.3 Links between assessment performance and consequences (adapted from Bachman & Palmer, Language Assessment in Practice, Oxford University Press)

According to this passage and Figure 2.3, 　エ　 .

a　a series of links is sometimes created by a different procedure than the one shown in the figure, for example, in the reverse direction

b　following the consequences, we make decisions based on the interpretations about students' language ability

c　the most important factor in assessing student performance is the interpretations derived from the assessment records

d　to use a language assessment, we need to relate students' assessment performance to the information-based outcomes we seek

▌ 2024年度 ▌ 高知県 ▌ 難易度 ■■■■□□

【6】次の英文を読んで，(1)〜(8)の問いに答えよ。

The paradox the automobile has thrust upon us is that liberation is bondage. The automobile has made it possible, literally and (ア)figuratively, to go anywhere, to be anyone. The most important freedom has become the freedom to move ― to a new town, a new part of the country, a new life. The car has provided a fast, efficient, adaptable, identifiable engine of forward (and upward) mobility, and as such (イ)it became an important cultural symbol system, a language practically everyone spoke. In some dimension it represented mastery over the truculence of the natural world.

Today, the automobile is mostly thought of as a necessity. Outside the cities it is hard to the point of impossibility (　ウ　) the business of daily living without its help. Jobs, vacations, friendships, family ties ― all seem to depend on the reach provided by the car. It is the needle (　エ　) we have learned to sew together the pieces of our lives, and without it our image of ourselves is tatterdemalion. For all its small tyrannies, the car is still a cornerstone of life, a convenience so taken for granted that its absence in our individual lives is almost beyond comprehension.

However logical and rational these judgments of personal necessity, when they are multiplied one hundred million times (the number of cars in the land) the result is social insanity. At that scale, the sheer force of the automobile's presence commands that we be willing to sacrifice most other needs to its priority. As a collective entity, the automobile threatens to make us its (　オ　). It requires that we plan our cities (or dig them up and rebuild them) around its needs, on pain of death by choking; that we flatten the landscape before it, in the service of speed and directness; that we make unprecedented demands on our natural resources, in the name of economic necessity. We are awakening to the way the automobile has dominated the national business of law enforcement, has concentrated staggering economic power in the auto industries, has reduced us to the barbarity of one driver shooting another over a parking space ― a (カ)contemporary image that suggests the automobile's impact on our assumptions about community. Most immediately, it is poisoning the air around us, while experts dispute the rate at which we are approaching the intolerable.

Overall, it's a standoff. The car has assumed the confusing status of something we can't live with, can't live without.

The trouble with most schemes to deal with the problems created by the automobile is that they underestimate the vastness of their undertaking. The car serves a variety of needs other than transportation and, for all its concrete reality, its greatest powers may be symbolic.

(キ)The automobile provides privacy. Next to the bathroom, it is the nicest, easiest, most acceptable place to be alone. People sing, scream, pick their noses, talk to the radio, and do all manner of other odd and private things within the isolation of their cars. Surely the vast queues of commuters, one to a car, would not suffer their daily bumper-to-bumper indignities if there weren't something (　ク　) about being alone in a car.

The automobile allows an exercise of power. Driving represents a challenge to be overcome; there is a constant parade of tiny decisions that await your action and that certify you as skilled and needed — the master of your ship. It makes perfect sense, therefore, that getting a driver's license has become the rite of passage to the adult world. If you drive, you are competent, responsible, powerful, your own man.

The automobile (　ケ　) the sense of spontaneity in life. A decision involving travel can be made instantaneously if a car is available. Thus spontaneity becomes a proof of freedom: there's no requirement to be bound by schedules of any sort, and the car becomes the ideal transmitter of impulse. As Detroit well knows, buying a particular car is frequently an impulsive decision — logically enough, since the car itself stands for the glorification of impulse.

Above all, the automobile is an instrument of choice. Selecting a car is like facing a keyboard and being asked to pick out an individual melody. Or, if you like, it's like choosing a face to put on for the world. We think of cars as possessing personalities, so they become, to a greater or lesser extent, (　コ　). A Volkswagen has a different cachet from a Pontiac GTO, a Lincoln speaks in a voice different from a Ford's. Because it is practically ubiquitous, the car becomes a badge of identification and is quite knowingly worn as such. Even those who renounce a car are making a statement with the same symbolic language.

Because the automobile trails such a variety of other associations, the attempts to deal with it strictly as a transportation tool miss the mark. They can win minor readjustments in the status quo, but they have little hope of affecting the overall patterns of usage that constitute the affliction. It's the kind of problem that legislation can affect but cannot solve.

(1)　下線部(ア), (カ)に最も意味の近い語を次のA〜Dから一つずつ選

び，その記号を書け。

(ア)　A　approximately　　B　casually　　C　immensely

　　　D　metaphorically

(カ)　A　ancient　　B　future　　C　illegal

　　　D　modern

(2)　下線部(イ)の状況を表す文として最も適切なものを次のA～Dから
一つ選び，その記号を書け。

A　People lost the freedom to express themselves.

B　Many people were obliged to leave their countries.

C　People began to use cars as a matter of course.

D　Some people were disadvantaged by not having a car.

(3)　本文中の(　ウ　)，(　エ　)に入れるのに最も適切な語(句)を次の
A～Dから一つずつ選び，その記号を書け。

ウ　A　discharges　　B　being discharged　　C　to discharge

　　D　has discharged

エ　A　by which　　B　on which　　C　for which

　　D　to which

(4)　本文中の(　オ　)，(　ク　)，(　ケ　)に入れるのに最も適切な語
を次のA～Dから一つずつ選び，その記号を書け。

オ　A　administrator　　B　employer　　C　observer

　　D　servant

ク　A　diligent　　B　functional　　C　jealous

　　D　pleasurable

ケ　A　distorts　　B　impairs　　C　magnifies

　　D　revolves

(5)　下線部(キ)について，その結果として起こる現象として最も適切
なものを次のA～Dから一つ選び，その記号を書け。

A　Small cars that make less noise are getting more popular with people of
all ages.

B　Many people use cars for commuting, which causes traffic jams.

C　More drivers think seriously about what to do to avoid traffic
accidents.

D　Many countries are trying to eliminate crimes committed with stolen cars.

(6)　本文中の(　コ　)に入れるのに最も適切なものを次のA～Dから一つ選び，その記号を書け。

A　fundamentals of our religious life

B　externalizations of our value systems

C　applications of interactive virtual reality

D　origins of democracy in the United States

(7)　本文の内容と一致するように，次の(a), (b)の書き出しに続く最も適切なものを以下のA～Dから一つずつ選び，その記号を書け。

(a)　The car can be compared to the needle because (　　).

A　they are both indispensable for our daily lives

B　the needle is available in most convenience stores

C　there seems to be a huge price gap between them

D　the number of cars is increasing sharply worldwide

(b)　Driving requires continuous decision making, so (　　).

A　obtaining a driver's license is a kind of ritual for entering adulthood

B　many young people are not interested in getting a driver's license

C　the owner of a driver's license can acquire ship handling skills quickly

D　a driver's license can be used as an official identity document in many places

(8)　本文の内容に合う文として最も適切なものを次のA～Dから一つ選び，その記号を書け。

A　The author insists that people should use public transportation more often to protect the environment.

B　The author maintains that the preservation of natural resources is important to keep the economy growing.

C　The author thinks it ridiculous and superficial to try to express one's identity through the choice of cars.

D　The author agrees that a car fulfills various purposes beyond just being a means of transportation.

2024年度 ┃ 愛媛県 ┃ 難易度

402

【7】次の英文とその英文をもとに作成されたプレゼンテーションのスラ
イドを読んで，以下の(1)〜(7)の各問いに答えよ。

Overtourism is a new problem that happens when too many tourists visit a
destination and it becomes overwhelmed. Even though tourism is important
for the economy, overtourism can cause problems for the local community
and environment. Here are some ways overtourism can cause problems.

First, too many tourists can cause too much pressure on the local
infrastructure. For example, if too many tourists visit a place, there may not
be enough places for them to stay or enough food and water to meet their
needs. This can lead to overcrowding, long lines, and higher prices, which can
make it less enjoyable for tourists. Additionally, overtourism can cause
environmental damage, including pollution and waste, damage to natural
habitats, and overuse of resources such as water and electricity.

Overtourism can also negatively affect the local culture and way of life.
When tourism becomes the primary source of income, locals may have to
change their way of life to cater to tourists. This can lead to a loss of
traditional culture, values, and practices, and a decline in the quality of life for
local residents. In extreme cases, overtourism can lead to the displacement of
locals, as they are priced out of their homes and communities by rising
property values and rents.

There are several reasons why overtourism happens. One of the main
reasons is that more and more people are traveling to different places   around
the world. Budget airlines and low-cost travel options have also made it easier
and cheaper for people to travel. Social media and online review sites have
also contributed to the rise of overtourism by promoting popular destinations
and encouraging people to visit.

To address overtourism, we need to adopt a sustainable tourism approach.
Sustainable tourism is about creating a balance between economic growth,
social well-being, and environmental protection. This means that destinations
need to focus on developing tourism that is sustainable and responsible, rather
than just trying to increase the number of tourists. Sustainable tourism also
involves working with local communities to ensure that they benefit from

403

tourism, rather than being negatively impacted by it.

To achieve sustainable tourism, everyone needs to work together. This includes local communities, government agencies, tour operators, and tourists themselves. Local communities need to have a say in the development of tourism in their area and should benefit from the money generated by tourism. Government agencies need to ensure that tourism is developed in a responsible and sustainable way, with rules and policies in place to protect the environment and local communities. Tour operators and tourists need to be aware of the impact of their activities on the destination and take steps to reduce their environmental footprint and support local communities.

In conclusion, overtourism is a serious issue that is causing problems for many destinations around the world. To solve this problem, we need to adopt a sustainable tourism approach that balances economic growth, social well-being, and environmental protection. Everyone needs to work together to create a tourism industry that benefits everyone and protects the environment for future generations.

プレゼンテーションスライド：

1枚目

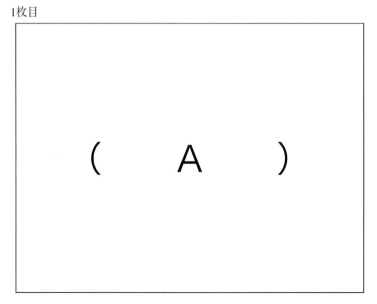

2枚目

1. What is overtourism?

• Overtourism is a new problem that occurs when
  (B   ).

• Although tourism is important for the economy,
  overtourism can cause problems for the local
  community and environment.

3枚目

2. Problems caused by overtourism

• Too much pressure on local infrastructure
  ✓ overcrowding
  ✓ long lines
  ✓ higher prices

• Environmental damage
  ✓ pollution and waste
  ✓ damage to natural habitats
  ✓ overuse of resources

4枚目

3. More problems caused by overtourism

Overtoursim...
• negatively affects local culture and way of life
→(1) a loss of traditional culture, values, and practices.
   (2) a decline in the quality of life for local residents.

• (　　C　　).

5枚目

4. Overtourism is caused by...

(　　D　　)

6枚目

5. Sustainable tourism approach

Sustainable tourism...

- is about creating a balance between economic growth, social well-being, and environmental protection.
- focus on developing tourism that is sustainable and responsible rather than simply （　　E　　）.

7枚目

6. Working together for sustainable tourism

- Achieving sustainable tourism requires the cooperation of all stakeholders.

(1) Local communities should have a say in tourism development and receive benefits from tourism revenue.

(2) Government agencies must ensure responsible and sustainable tourism development through rules and policies that protect the environment and local communities.

(3) （　　F　　）.

8枚目

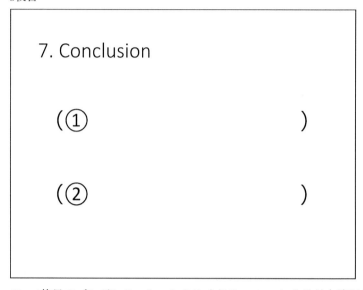

(1) 1枚目のプレゼンテーションスライドの(A)に入る最も適切な
タイトルを，次の1〜4から選び，記号で答えよ。

1 Overtourism: Specific Cases from Around the World for Sustainable
Tourism

2 Overtourism: Causes of Rude Tourists and Their Impact on Local
Residents

3 Overtourism: The Need for Sustainable and Responsible Tourism
Practices

4 Overtourism: The Impact of Popular Destinations to Less Popular Ones

(2) 2枚目のプレゼンテーションスライドの(B)に入る最も適切な
ものを，次の1〜4から選び，記号で答えよ。

1 a large number of tourists are overwhelmed by popular destinations

2 a destination is being overburdened by too many tourists

3 a particular destination attracts a lot of travelers it can handle

4 the number of tourists travelling to a destination increases

(3) 4枚目のプレゼンテーションスライドの(C)に入る最も適切な
ものを，次の1〜4から選び，記号で答えよ。

1　can make it harder for tourists to visit because of the higher cost of tourism

2　can force locals out of their homes and communities due to rising property values and rents

3　can cause a bad reputation and put tourist destinations in financial trouble

4　can result in an increase in the number of people coming to buy properties for profit

(4)　5枚目のプレゼンテーションスライドの(　D　)に入るものとして適切でないものを，次の1～4から選び，記号で答えよ。

1　social media and online review sites promoting popular destinations

2　government measures to encourage people to support the tourism industry

3　budget airlines and low-cost travel options making it easier and cheaper to travel

4　more people traveling to different places around the world

(5)　6枚目のプレゼンテーションスライドの(　E　)に入る最も適切なものを，次の1～4から選び，記号で答えよ。

1　striving to raise the number of visitors to a destination

2　making tourists spend more money on tourism

3　creating more tourist attractions that can be popular

4　diversifying the number of visitors to a destination

(6)　7枚目のプレゼンテーションスライドの(　F　)に入る最も適切なものを，次の1～4から選び，記号で答えよ。

1　Tour operators and tourists should ignore the impact of their activities on the destination

2　Tour operators and tourists should encourage tourism to generate more revenue to local communities

3　Tour operators and tourists should focus on personal enjoyment and help locals earn enough money

4　Tour operators and tourists should minimize their environmental impact while supporting local communities

409

(7) 8枚目は英文の最終段落の内容をまとめたスライドです。筆者の2
つの主張を英語でまとめ，スライドを完成させよ。

┃ 2024年度 ┃ 山口県 ┃ 難易度■■■■■

【8】 Read the following passage and answer the questions from (1) to (5).

1   On the shores of Lake Baringo in Kenya, a slow-motion disaster is
unfolding. For the past decade, the water has been steadily rising,
swallowing homes, shops, health centres, latrines, electricity supplies,
farmland, tourist resorts, and more. Malaria, cholera, typhoid, and
dysentery are increasing. Wildlife is under threat; conflict has broken out
between people and animals and old grievances between neighbouring
groups have resurfaced.

2   Since it started rising, Baringo's surface area has more than doubled, and
it isn't alone. Right across the East African Rift valley, lake water is
creeping over animal and human heads. And where East Africa leads,
much of the rest of the world is following. North America's Great Lakes
have been rising too. Overall, lakes the world over have expanded to
occupy an extra 46,000 square kilometres of space since 1984, roughly the
area of Denmark.

3   The exact cause of the rising waters has long been debated. There are
three possibilities, none of them mutually exclusive. One is natural climate
variability, with greater rainfall the main driver. Another is natural
geological activity: the rift system is tectonically dynamic and shifting
plates under the lakes could conceivably change water levels. The third is
human activity － principally global warming, which increases rainfall, and
land-use change leading to increased water runoff into the lakes and greater
sedimentation, which raises the lake bed and blocks outflow streams.

4   Right now, the finger points firmly at human activity, especially climate
change. A 2021 study of water levels in Kenya's lakes Baringo, Bogoria,
Nakuru, Solai, Elementaita, and Naivasha concluded that changes in
rainfall were sufficient to explain the rises. Even though much of East
Africa is in drought, the rift lakes region has seen increased rainfall.

"Climate change is a major cause of the rising water levels," says Onzere, the co-author of another study that largely attributes Nakuru's 8-metre rise to warming.

5 Not everyone agrees, however. "The preferred scapegoat is always climate change, but I see anthropogenic land use change as the critical factor altering the hydrological cycle," says Sean Avery, an engineer and hydrology specialist at King's College London who is based in Kenya.

6 Tectonic activity also hasn't been ruled out. A recent study of Lake Beseka in Ethiopia, which covers an area about five times its extent in 1972, found that rainfall actually declined over the period. According to the researchers, the most plausible explanation is tectonic activity, which has torn open the lake bed, allowing groundwater to seep in, and has created new basins in which water can collect.

7 Nevertheless, the Kenyan government report is very clear on where it places blame. "The main reason for the rising water levels is climate change," it says.

8 As usual, then, the Global South is bearing the early brunt of climate change. But Western countries largely responsible for emissions aren't immune.

9 A hemisphere away, other bodies of water are also on the rise. In 2013, Lake Michigan in the US was at a record low, but then started rising rapidly and hit record highs in 2021. Nearby lakes Superior, Erie, and Huron also hit record highs; the last of the five North American Great Lakes, Ontario, was well above average too. The waters have receded somewhat since then, but left behind a lot of coastal erosion and flood damage. Some 40 million people live near the shores of the Great Lakes in the US and Canada.

10 At last year's American Geophysical Union (AGU) hydrology conference in San Juan, Puerto Rico, Lauren Fry at the US National Oceanic and Atmospheric Administration's Great Lakes Environmental Research Lab reiterated the cause. Climate change is affecting all three of the factors that control lake levels, she said. These are precipitation over

the lakes, runoff from the land and evaporation.

11 The lakes have risen and fallen quickly in the past, but never quite as fast. There is a historically rapid change in both directions, says Riley Balikian at the Illinois State Geological Survey.

12 Similar surges are forecast in the future. A model presented at another recent AGU conference in Chicago predicted that the Great Lakes could rise by half a metre or more by 2050, exposing people and nature to greater damage from storm surges and flooding.

13 Other models are more circumspect. According to Alexander Vandeweghe at the University of Michigan, it is still unclear how climate change will influence the three drivers of lake levels in North America. "There's significant variability and uncertainty," he says. Some models show large increases, others slight declines. What we can say is that water level variability in the future will be at least as great as it has been in the past, says Vandeweghe.

14 This story of lake-level rise is being repeated across the globe. Last year, a team led by Lian Feng at Southern University of Science and Technology in Shenzhen, China, analysed satellite images of all of Earth's 3.4 million lakes and reservoirs from 1984 to 2019. The team came up with the 46,000-square-kilometre expansion figure mentioned earlier, but found that, if you eliminate lakes that are shrinking, the growth amounts to 167,000 square kilometres.

15 Around half of that involves reservoirs, but the rest is natural lakes. This spells further bad news for the climate. Lakes of all sizes are prolific sources of greenhouse gases because the decomposition of organic matter on their beds produces carbon dioxide, methane, and nitrous oxide. Lakes account for an estimated 20 per cent of global emissions.

16 According to the study, the extra lake area over the course of the study increased carbon emissions by 4.8 million tonnes a year, roughly the same as Kenya's annual emissions.

17 Back in Kenya, fears are growing that the rising waters of Baringo will impose ecological disaster on its neighbour, Bogoria, a world heritage site

and well-known tourist destination. Many of Bogoria's famous hot springs have already been submerged in recent years and it has seen vast flocks of flamingos decimated. But worse is to come if Baringo creeps any nearer. Bogoria is a salty, alkaline lake, which is what makes it attractive to flamingos. Baringo is freshwater. If the two merge, Bogoria's ecosystem will be ruined. The two are in the same basin and used to be 20 kilometres apart, but are now just 13 kilometres from each other.

18 For the foreseeable future, the lakes will carry on getting bigger. "If we continue doing things the way we are doing, it means levels are going to rise," says Onzere. "Only if we have normal temperatures and normal rainfall amounts will the lakes come back to normal." The world isn't just burning, it is drowning too.

(1) Which of the following is NOT true about situation of Lake Baringo in Kenya?

 a Increasing water of the lake has led to the displacement of homes, shops, and other infrastructure.

 b The surface area of Lake Baringo increased more than twice its size because of increasing water of the lake.

 c The water level of Lake Baringo has been rising higher than that of the Great Lakes of North America.

 d It is possible that the water level of Lake Baringo started to rise earlier than in other parts of the world.

 e Increasing water of the lake has resulted in increased cases of diseases and conflict between humans and wildlife.

(2) Which of the following is true about rising water levels?

 a No researcher disagrees that climate change is the main cause of rising water levels.

 b The effects of rising water levels have not been seen to a large extent in the western countries.

 c The three possible causes of rising water are mutually independent of one another.

 d Water levels will no longer fluctuate at least as much as they have in the past.

 e Greenhouse gas emissions are expected to increase as water levels rise.

(3) Why would the merging of Baringo and Bogoria be ecologically disastrous for Bogoria?

 a The hot springs that Bogoria is famous for would release toxic gases if submerged, endangering the wildlife.

 b The rising waters of Baringo would cause flooding in Bogoria, destroying the habitats of the flamingos.

 c The increased salinity of Baringo's water would attract predators that would prey on the flamingos in Bogoria.

 d Baringo's freshwater would dilute the salt content of Bogoria's alkaline water, disrupting the ecosystem.

 e The distance between Baringo and Bogoria would be closer, which could affect the local people's land-based traffic.

(4) You are writing a main idea of this passage. Choose the best option for each blank to complete your writing.

> Rising water levels in lakes around the world, including Lake Baringo in Kenya and the Great Lakes in North America, are causing significant ecological and human impact. (①), with potential factors including natural climate variability, tectonic activity, and human-induced climate change. The consequences include the displacement of communities, the spread of diseases, and conflicts between humans and wildlife. (②).

① a Countries are reluctant to determine the causes

  b The exact causes of the rising waters are debated

  c Governments have been discussing the causes

  d The causes of the rising waters have been overlooked

  e The responsibility for the causes of the problem is not identified

② a In addition to rising water levels, other adverse impacts of climate change, such as wildfires, must also be considered

  b Researchers on climate change should focus on ways to reduce water levels in lakes all over the world

c   Studies, on the other hand, have shown that the water level of the lake will remain constant in the future

d   The situation highlights the global impact of climate change and the urgent need for mitigation measures

e   The effects of climate change differ from country to country, so each country needs to address the issue individually

(5)   You are adding the heading of each paragraph as the chart below. Choose the best option to fill in the blanks ①－③ and complete the chart.

Paragraph	Heading
①~②	Rising water levels in Lake Baringo, Kenya
③	The possible three causes of rising water levels
④	Human activity and climate change
⑤~⑥	(①)
⑦~⑪	(②)
⑫~⑬	Predictions for the future
⑭~⑯	(③)
⑰	Baringo and Bogoria's proximity and ecosystem
⑱	The inevitability of rising water levels

A   Climate change impact on water levels in countries

B   The debate over the cause of rising water levels

C   Another negative impact of rising water levels

	①	②	③
a	A	B	C
b	A	C	B
c	B	A	C
d	B	C	A
e	C	A	B

┃ 2024年度 ┃ 茨城県 ┃ 難易度

【9】次の英文を読み，以下の(1)～(5)の問いに対し最も適する答えをア ～エからそれぞれ1つ選び，その記号を書きなさい。

A little joey pokes a front paw and then its head out of its mother's pouch. Dave White, a zookeeper at Chester Zoo, in England, points up to the mother perched on a branch and beams with pride. He has been watching the baby tree kangaroo develop since it was born the size of a jellybean — first tracking its growth with an endoscope camera placed inside the pouch, and now, seeing the 7-month-old emerge.

White has formed a close connection with the joey and its mother, visiting and feeding them each day. It's the first birth of a Goodfellow's tree kangaroo he's witnessed, and indeed the first time in Chester Zoo's 91-year history that it has bred the species. White says the birth is a sign of hope for the endangered species, which is threatened by hunting and habitat loss in its native Papua New Guinea.

The baby adds to an insurance population of captive animals, and it could provide crucial data on the species and its reproductive process to help inform protection efforts in the wild, he says: "This little, tiny joey can contribute significantly to conservation."

The joey is just one of a series of rare births that Chester Zoo has welcomed in the last eight months. Sumatran tiger twins, a western chimpanzee, a Malayan tapir, a greater one-horned rhino and a triplet of fossa pups have also been born. All those species are threatened with extinction.

With the world facing a crisis of biodiversity as extinctions accelerate at an unprecedented rate, zoos could help to provide crucial protection for endangered species. Chester Zoo's central mission is to "prevent extinction," and those words are emblazoned on staff t-shirts and signs across the site. In 2021, it published a 10-year masterplan laying out its methods for achieving this, including scientific research and education, habitat restoration and its renowned conservation breeding program.

"(The world) is losing species at a phenomenal rate," says Mark Brayshaw, the zoo's curator of mammals. "It's really important that we save species wherever we can."

Brayshaw explains that the breeding program has a range of purposes. Some species are temporarily bred in captivity to protect them from imminent threats or to give them a head start before being reintroduced into the wild. Other times the aim is to preserve a species that is already extinct in the wild, or on the verge of extinction, while some endangered species are bred to help maintain a viable population that could be released in the wild if threats in their native habitats were eliminated.

Other zoos also have conservation breeding programs, but Chester is regarded as a world leader due in part to its wildlife endocrinology laboratory — the only one of its kind at a zoo in Europe. This is where scientists track a species' hormones by analyzing its feces.

"For something like the tree kangaroo, we'll take (fecal) samples every day," explains Katie Edwards, lead conservation scientist at Chester Zoo. "We'll run (tests) about once a month so that we can measure reproductive hormones in our female, and that helps us understand when she's going to be most likely ready for breeding."

Hormone levels indicate when a female starts developing an egg and when she's likely to ovulate. Edwards and her team pair this evidence with visual and behavioral cues observed by zookeepers and put the male and female together at the optimal time for breeding.

Chester's lab is attracting interest from elsewhere. Other zoos in the UK and Europe are sending in fecal samples from animals to inform breeding decisions or diagnose pregnancies, and Chester Zoo is also working with partners to replicate its endocrinology technique in Kenya to help conservation in the wild.

Edwards notes that there's strength in numbers. "If we can collect samples from our tree kangaroos here but also from other individuals across Europe, we can learn a lot more about the species." she says. "The more we can understand about species biology, the better conditions we can provide so that individuals and species can thrive both in human care and also on a larger conservation scale as well."

Conservation breeding in zoos can be a thorny subject. Critics believe that breeding animals for a future in captivity is cruel, as many of these individuals will never be rewilded because their natural habits are too degraded. There has also been research that suggests that breeding programs can sometimes lead to genetic changes that can affect a species' ability to survive in the wild.

But others argue that well-run zoos engage the public in conservation by showcasing the wonders of the planet's wildlife. They allow scientists to study animals closely in a way that for some species would be impossible in the wild. And conservation breeding in zoos has been credited for saving some species from extinction — the first being the Arabian oryx, which was hunted to extinction in the wild by 1972 but was later reintroduced to the desert in Oman, thanks to a breeding program that began at Phoenix Zoo, Arizona.

Plus, zoos like Chester bring in big money for conservation, says Brayshaw. As one of the largest zoos in the UK — boasting more than 27,000 animals from 500 different species of plants and animals — it welcomes around 2 million visitors a year. Ticket sales, visitor spend on site and membership fees make up 97% of the zoo's annual income, he says.

As a non-profit, all of this goes back towards funding the zoo, its staff and conservation efforts. According to the 2021 annual report, around £21 million ($25 million) was spent on conservation that year, 46% of its income, and in 2022 (the report for which has not yet been published) this rose to £25 million ($30 million).

"We put our money where our mouth is," says Brayshaw. "We are lucky. We're a large zoo with a good income that can devote resources to (conservation), and we are effective in doing so." For Jon Paul Rodriguez, chair of the IUCN Species Survival Commission, the hallmark of a good zoo is one that makes a difference to the survival of species in the wild; that is not simply breeding animals to attract more visitors, but it is motivated to protect them in their native habitat. He believes Chester Zoo fulfils these criteria.

"Ultimately, what we all seek is a species that lives in the wild (and is) playing their ecological role." he says. There will be some cases when habitat is restored enough for species to return; there will be others where species will be reintroduced to new habitats; and there will also be cases when species will be stuck in captivity for perpetuity, he says. "But if we don't have those insurance populations, there is no hope at all."

From：CNN 　　：This zoo is breeding hope for endangered species
By Nell Lewis 　　March 28, 2023

(1) According to the statement of Dave White, which is true about Chester Zoo?

ア Chester Zoo helped give birth to baby Goodfellow's tree kangaroos many times.

イ It was really rare to form a close relationship with a little joey.

ウ It took 91 years for Chester Zoo to conserve many kinds of species.

エ Researching the tiny joey can give significant information to help endangered species.

(2) According to the article, which of the following is NOT true as the reasons that zoos are making efforts to prevent extinction?

ア Many species are in danger of extinction because of hunting and habitat loss.

イ The world is losing the variety of plants and animals drastically.

ウ If zoos learn species biology better, the conditions for the conserved animals will be improved.

エ Conservation breeding program is renowned.

(3) According to the article, why is Chester Zoo regarded as a world leader on conservation breeding programs?

ア It has raised the most number of species in the world.

イ It has a special laboratory to research hormones to see when females can have a baby.

ウ It started the conservation breeding program first and has the best knowledge about wildlife endocrinology.

エ It has attracted other zoos in the UK and Europe.

(4) According to the article, why is conservation breeding in zoos a thorny subject?

ア Because zoos can attract many people to conservation.

イ Because zoos are non-profit and can devote a lot of money to conservation.

ウ Because it may make animals' natural habits degraded.

エ Because it enables scientists to research animals in detail.

(5) What did Jon Paul Rodriguez mention in the article?

419

ア Animals should live in captivity and play their own roles.

イ It may be impossible to reintroduce some species to the wild.

ウ Chester is the best zoo in the world.

エ The most important aim to breed animals is that zoos can attract more visitors and protect species in their native habitats.

┃ 2024年度 ┃ 青森県 ┃ 難易度 ┃▇▇▇▅▢▢

【10】 Read the passage below and answer the following questions in English. This passage, which was written in the late 19ᵗʰ century, is a part of a book about American school education.

Some few years ago I was looking about the school supply stores in the city, trying to find desks and chairs which seemed thoroughly suitable from all points of view—artistic, hygienic, and educational—to the needs of the children. We had a great deal of difficulty in finding (1)<u>what we needed</u>, and finally one dealer, more intelligent than the rest, made this remark: "I am afraid we have not what you want. You want something at which the children may work; these are all for listening." That tells the story of the traditional education. Just as the biologist can take a bone or two and reconstruct the whole animal, so, if we put before the mind's eye the ordinary schoolroom, with its rows of ugly desks placed in geometrical order, crowded together so that there shall be as little moving room as possible, desks almost all of the same size, with just space enough to hold books, pencils, and paper, and add a table, some chairs, the bare walls, and possibly a few pictures, we can reconstruct the only educational activity that can possibly go on in such a place. It is all made "for listening" —because simply studying lessons out of a book is only another kind of listening; it marks the dependency of one mind upon another. The attitude of listening means, comparatively speaking, passivity, absorption; (2a).

There is very little place in the traditional schoolroom for the child to work. The workshop, the laboratory, the materials, the tools with which the child may construct, create, and actively inquire, and even the requisite space, have been for the most part lacking. The things that have to do with these processes

420

have not even a definitely recognized place in education. They are what the educational authorities who write editorials in the daily papers generally term "fads" and "frills." A lady told me yesterday that she had been visiting different schools trying to find one where activity on the part of the [3a] preceded the giving of information on the part of the teacher, or where the children had some motive for demanding the information. She visited, she said, twenty-four different schools before she found her first instance. I may add that that was not in this city.

Another thing that is suggested by these schoolrooms, with their set desks, is that everything is arranged for handling as large numbers of children as possible; for dealing with children *en masse*, as an aggregate of units; involving, again, that they be treated passively. The moment children act they individualize themselves; they < 4a > to be a mass and become the intensely distinctive beings that we are acquainted with out of school, in the home, the family, on the playground, and in the neighborhood.

On the same basis is explicable the uniformity of method and curriculum. If everything is on a "listening" basis, you can have uniformity of material and method. The ear, and the book which reflects the ear, constitute the medium which is < 4b > for all. There is next to no opportunity for adjustment to varying capacities and demands. There is a certain amount—a fixed quantity—of ready-made results and accomplishments to be acquired by all children alike in a given time. It is in response to this demand that the curriculum has been developed from the elementary school up through the college. There is just so much desirable knowledge, and there are just so many needed technical accomplishments in the world. Then comes the mathematical problem of dividing this by the six, twelve, or sixteen years of school life. Now give the children every year just the proportionate fraction of the total, and by the time they have finished they will have mastered the whole. By covering so much ground during this hour or day or week or year, everything comes out with perfect evenness at the end—provided the children have not forgotten what they have previously learned. The outcome of all this is Matthew Arnold's report of the statement, proudly made to him by an

421

educational authority in France, (2b); and in one of our own western cities this proud boast used to be repeated to successive visitors by its superintendent.

I may have exaggerated somewhat in order to make plain the typical points of the old education: (2c). It may be summed up by stating that the center of gravity is outside the child. It is in the teacher, the textbook, anywhere and everywhere you please except in the immediate instincts and activities of the child himself. On that basis there is not much to be said about the *life* of the child. A good deal might be said about the studying of the child, but the school is not the place where the child *lives*. Now the change which is coming into our education is the (5)shifting of the center of gravity. It is a change, a revolution, not unlike that introduced by Copernicus when the astronomical center shifted from the earth to the sun. In this case the child becomes the sun about which the appliances of education revolve; he is the center about which they are organized.

If we take an example from an ideal home, where the parent is intelligent enough to recognize what is best for the child, and is able to supply what is needed, we find the child learning through the social converse and constitution of the family. There are certain points of interest and value to him in the conversation carried on: (2d). He states his experiences, his misconceptions are corrected. Again the child participates in the household occupations, and thereby gets habits of industry, order, and regard for the rights and ideas of others, and the fundamental habit of subordinating his activities to the general interest of the household. Participation in these household tasks becomes an opportunity for gaining knowledge. The ideal home would naturally have a workshop where the child could work out his constructive instincts. It would have a miniature laboratory in which his inquiries could be directed. The life of the child would extend out of doors to the garden, surrounding fields, and forests. He would have his excursions, his walks and talks, in which the larger world out of doors would open to him.

Now, if we organize and generalize all of this, we have the ideal [3b]. There is no mystery about it, no wonderful discovery of pedagogy or educational theory. It is simply a question of doing systematically and in a large, intelligent, and competent way what for various reasons can be done in most households only in a comparatively meager and haphazard manner. In the first place, the ideal [3c] has to be enlarged. The child must be brought into contact with more grown people and with more children in order that there may be the freest and richest social life. Moreover, the occupations and relationships of the home environment are not specially selected for the growth of the child; the main object is something else, and what the child can get out of them is incidental. Hence the need of a school. In this school the life of the child becomes the all-controlling aim. All the media necessary to further the growth of the child center there. Learning? certainly, but living primarily, and learning through and in relation to this living. When we take the life of the child centered and organized in this way, we do not find that he is first of all a listening being; ＜ 4c ＞.

Questions

Q1: What does the underlined part (1) refer to ?

Q2: Choose the most appropriate sentence for blanks (2a), (2b), (2c), and (2d).

  (a) that so many thousands of children were studying at a given hour, say eleven o'clock, just such a lesson in geography

  (b) its passivity of attitude, its mechanical massing of children, its uniformity of curriculum and method

  (c) statements are made, inquiries arise, topics are discussed, and the child continually learns

  (d) that there are certain ready-made materials which are there, which have been prepared by the school superintendent, the board, the teacher, and of which the child is to take in as much as possible in the least possible time

Q3: Fill in each blank [3a], [3b], and [3c] with an appropriate word.

Q4: Choose the most appropriate word(s) for blanks ＜ 4a ＞, ＜ 4b ＞, and ＜ 4c ＞.

4a   (a)   begin   (b)   cease

       (c)   decide   (d)   deny

4b   (a)   alike   (b)   demanding

       (c)   interesting   (d)   optimal

4c   (a)   beyond expectations   (b)   no doubt

       (c)   quite the contrary   (d)   second to none

Q5: Based on the text, what does the author mean by the underlined part (5)? You cannot copy the sentences in the passage as they are.

▌2024年度 ▌長野県 ▌難易度▉▉▉▉▉▉▉▉

【11】 ALTが英語教員Bさんに ICT活用について次のような発言をした。それに対する意見を述べるため，Bさんはある文献(以下本文)を読んだ。英文を読み，その後の問いに答えなさい。

> We can see so many technologies moving at such a pace・・・. Students are already tech-savvy. I think that deploying devices is ideal. Students will be active learners by using technology on their own.

ALT

＜文献＞

With the rapid growth of online testing, schools have also rushed to buy educational technology that supports these assessments. Since some states require online assessments, districts have essentially been forced to add large numbers of devices. So far, the emphasis of this type of technological integration has overwhelmingly been on the assessment side, and the instructional side has gotten lost in the process. This has led to devices in schools being [①] somewhat randomly－tossed around with little precision yet done with the hope that it'll enrich current growth far and wide. In many cases, the devices become simplistic instructional add-ons or gap fillers for time, yielding little to no instructional benefit.

We must also question the pedagogical practice of teaching and learning in a traditional format and then assessing digitally. We believe that such assessments require an additional skill set. In cases where assessments are fully digital but are rarely used during the learning process, students are likely to perform at a lower level.

The research is clear. Technology by itself does not, and will not, transform teaching and learning. In fact, like any tool, when used poorly, it can have negative consequences. We believe that

- Simply adding the latest technology to traditional learning environments can have a negative effect on teaching and learning.
- Technology can accelerate great teaching practices, which can in turn support equity and create greater opportunities for all students.
- Technology can amplify poor teaching practices and increase the amount of time students spend on low-level learning tasks.
- Assessing students in an online format but consistently using traditional instructional methods during the learning process can yield lower results. Online assessments require a digital skill set and comfort level that may not be present for students who have learned in a very different fashion.

A 2014 report by the Stanford Center for Opportunity Policy in Education and the Alliance for Excellent Education set out to study the effective use of technology, particularly with students who are most at risk (Darling-Hammond et al., 2014). The report verified that early versions of technology-based instruction that were structured like "electronic workbooks," where students passively moved through a digital curriculum, showed little effect on achievement. The report cited one particular study that evaluated the impact of math and reading software products in 132 schools across 33 districts, which found no significant difference on student test scores between classrooms that used the software and classrooms that didn't (Dynarski et al., 2007). The report also cited another large study that evaluated the effectiveness of students' [②] to a phonics-based computer program, which also found no effect in terms of gains on reading comprehension tests

(Borman, Benson, & Overman, 2009). Time and again, the "digital drill and kill" or use of technology as an electronic workbook shows little to no effect on student learning.

So what does the effective use of technology actually look like? What is worth the investment of time and money? There are three important variables for the successful infusion of technology, particularly with at-risk students who are learning new skills.

Interactive Learning: The interactive use of technology can enhance student learning and, ultimately, achievement by providing multiple ways for learners to grasp traditionally difficult concepts. Interactive learning opportunities have become more robust as adaptive content and systems have evolved in recent years. In these systems, the content levels up and down based on a student's ability; in other words, it adapts to a student's level of need. When leveraged for interactive learning, students become active users — not passive consumers of content.

Use of Technology to Explore and Create: When students are given the opportunity to leverage technology to explore and create, new learning can be accelerated. When this is the case, students are able to create and develop new content rather than absorb content passively. When empowered to explore and create, students also demonstrate higher levels of engagement, more positive attitudes toward school, higher levels of skill development, and self-efficacy.

【 ③ 】 : When students have ubiquitous access, particularly in environments with 1:1 student-to-device ratios, digital experiences can be blended into the learning environment to extrapolate concepts and maximize learning opportunities. In these environments, students can access the "right blend" of direct instruction and technology-accelerated learning. Student voice and choice play an important role while the teacher gives the needed level of direct support.

Technology use is most productive when experiences combine the "structured learning of information with collaborative discussions and project-based activities that allow students to use the information to solve meaningful

problems or create their own products, both individually and collectively"
(Darling-Hammond et al., 2014).

Displaying lesson notes on an interactive whiteboard, answering multiple-
choice questions in an online platform, typing documents that are saved to the
cloud, reading a textbook on a mobile device, or looking up facts online may
make certain tasks more efficient, but they do nothing to challenge or redefine
an outdated pedagogy. Leveraging technology to create a more teacher-centric
environment is detrimental to student learning and undoubtedly fails to create
the personal and authentic learning opportunities students need. Intentionally
designed schools refuse to utilize technology for technology's sake. These
schools purposefully use technology as the right tool, at the right time, to
create the needed access and opportunity.

(出典： LEARNING TRANSFORMED:8 Keys to Designing Tomorrow's
Schools, Today, Sheninger, Eric C., & Murray, Thomas C., 2017　一部改)

1　本文の内容に合うように，[　①　][　②　]に最も適する英語を次
　のア～エより一つずつ選び，記号で答えなさい。

　①　ア　spread out　　　　イ　passed through
　　　ウ　handed in　　　　エ　entered in
　②　ア　regulation　　　　イ　obstacle
　　　ウ　concealment　　　エ　exposure

2　【　③　】にはその後に続く内容を説明する見出しが入ります。
　【　③　】のタイトルとして最も適する英語を次のア～エより一つ
　選び，記号で答えなさい。

　ア　Right Blend of Teachers and Technology
　イ　Right Blend of An Outdated Pedagogy and A Digital Pedagogy
　ウ　Right Blend of Learning and Accessing
　エ　Right Blend of Digital Experiences and Digital Supporting

3　本文の内容に合うように，次の質問に6語以上の英語で答えなさい。

　(1)　According to the author, when are students likely to perform at a
　　lower level?

　(2)　According to the author, how can achievement help enhance learners
　　to grasp traditionally difficult concepts?

(3) Give an example written in this passage of teaching methods that makes certain tasks more efficient but does nothing to challenge or redefine an outdated pedagogy.

4   文献を読んだ英語教員Bさんは文献を基に次のようにALTに伝えました。(①)〜(③)にあてはまる適切な英語を書きなさい。

> I think that deploying technology without considering how to use it effectively for maximum educational benefit will (①) a detrimental effect on student learning. Some reports verified that the "digital drill and kill" or use of technology as an electronic workbook showed little to no effect on student learning and students became passive learners.
>
> The technology itself is not effective. The technology with (②) can be effective. I don't think that students will be active learners by using technology on their own. With technology, we teachers can (③) students to have the personal and authentic learning opportunities they need.

英語教員
Bさん

＜条件＞
・語数は問わない
・(①)〜(③)は全て異なる英語を使用すること

| 2024年度 ‖ 静岡県・静岡市・浜松市 ‖ 難易度 ████████ |

【12】 Questions (1) through (6) are based on the following passages ＜A＞, ＜B＞ and ＜C＞. For each question, choose the most appropriate answer.

＜A＞

In the following conversation, college students are discussing the topic "What is a very important skill a person should learn?" To answer (1) and (2), choose the most appropriate answer from ① to ⑤.

Hiroshi : Hi, everyone. Let's get started discussing the topic "What is a very important skill a person should learn?" Keiko, could you begin?

Keiko : "It is never too late to learn" is an English proverb meaning that people can learn at any stage in life. In other words, life is a process of constant learning, which enables an individual to make

428

continuous progress to try to perfect themselves as a human being. Therefore, I deem the ability to learn is the most important skill of a person in the world today to achieve any accomplishments. We are living in an era of knowledge explosion. There are too many skills to be grasped by a single individual within a comparatively short period of time. Skills considered necessary nowadays include English, computer, driving, etc. It is not very likely for a fresh college graduate to be proficient in all these skills. The most possible occurrence is that a person first chooses his field of profession and then starts to master those required skills in his field.

Another reason for my advocating for the learning ability is that if a person is capable of acquiring new knowledge he must be a smart, trainable, and adaptable person, which is what the rapidly developed society needs. In a society fraught with new difficulties and problems, a quick-witted person, when faced with them, will come up with solutions more easily than those who only know "the skills." That is why I believe the capacity to acquire knowledge carries more weight than "the knowledge" itself.

In short, in a time teeming with many unprecedented events, the problem-solving ability or new knowledge-acquiring skill is the most crucial one for a person who wants to be successful.

Hiroshi : OK. How about Satoru?

Satoru : Two years ago, if you ask a person, "What do you think is the most important skill to be successful in the world?", you will get a variety of answers. If you ask a person who is about my age the same question, presumably, eight out of ten will give the same answer as mine — computer skills are the most important skills a person should learn.

Why do I think computer skills are the most important skills? First, computer skills such as operating a word processing software package or typing are convenient and efficient. For example, I am writing an essay by using a computer. If I do not have computer skills, I cannot make a composition as quickly; maybe I can only write on paper. Another example is that many colleges are offering online classes for students to choose from, which means the students can study in the comfort of their homes and acquire their knowledge by means of using computers.

Secondly, computers are an important tool for teaching and communicating between teachers and students. These days, teachers have an increasing demand on students to turn in their papers or school works online, and the teachers can score them online. If a teacher gives an assignment, they just send an e-mail to the students. Many university students attend classes with computers. In addition, they even play online games through the Internet. Therefore computer skills are important for students to communicate with their teachers and fellow students.

Last but not least, computer skills help people to find good jobs after they graduate. As we open newspapers and search for a good job, we find that computer skills are required skills for nearly every job. Indeed, whether you work as a receptionist, salesperson, warehouse manager and office clerk, you have to operate a computer and therefore computer skills are absolutely necessary for these jobs and most others. Although there are many other important skills for a person to succeed in today's world, based on what I have mentioned earlier, I think my point of view is solid and sound. Having computer skills is one of the most important things in today's world.

Hiroshi : Thank you, Satoru. Your point is that having computer skills are important because (1   ).

(1)   Which statement is the most appropriate for (1   )?

　　①   teachers in college are using computers to give classes to their students

　　②   computers are a means for young students to communicate with each other

③ computer literacy is not required in modern society

④ being able to use a computer is the key to success

⑤ using a computer is only an essential skill for teachers

(2) Which statement is true?

① Keiko thinks that children should autonomously learn a second language.

② Keiko thinks that university students are required to study what is needed by society.

③ Keiko thinks that adults don't have to study hard even after their graduation from high schools.

④ Keiko thinks that the ability to learn new skills is more essential than the skills themselves.

⑤ Keiko thinks that old people must learn again at university.

＜B＞

Read the following passage. To answer (3) and (4), choose the most appropriate answer from ① to ⑤ .

Common European Framework of Reference (CEFR).

In Europe, endeavors to describe language proficiency within a large-scale framework started in the 1970s by the Council of Europe (CoE), a human rights organization, to enhance communication and mobility across Europe (Trim, 2001). Taking a functional-notional approach, van Ek published the *Threshold Level* in 1975, which described what language learners need to be able to do in order to function independently in a second or foreign language environment. This was followed by *Waystage* (van Ek & Alexander, 1977), which described an intermediate proficiency stage. Based on this early work focusing on English and French, the CoE commissioned the development of a framework of language proficiency with the intention to "provide a common basis ... for the description of objectives, content and methods ... of courses, syllabuses and qualifications" (CoE, 2001, p. 1). The resulting CEFR (CoE, 2001) is a language- and context-independent framework describing relevant aspects of language learning and use, language teaching, communicative tasks, curricula, assessment and language policy. The CEFR is a language policy tool that aims to increase transparency, provide a metalanguage for stakeholder communication, and enable mutual recognitions of qualifications and exams across Europe. At its core, the CEFR provides a descriptive proficiency scale system, that depicts relevant horizontal aspects of proficiency (differentiated for receptive, productive and interactive skills as well as for several linguistic competences) on six ascending levels (A1 and A2 describe beginning proficiency, where A2 represents *Waystage* ; B1 and B2 describe independent usage, with B1 corresponding to *Threshold* ; C1 and C2 represent mastery). This proficiency framework and accompanying illustrative scales for language learning, teaching, and assessment was recently updated and widened by the *Companion Volume* (CoE, 2018a), which contains additional descriptors for existing scales, as well as a whole new set of scales for the concept of mediation, amongst other additions.

The CEFR scales are based on over 40 existing proficiency scales (North, 2002) and on expert-derived level descriptions (*Threshold, Waystage*) ; meanwhile, the more recent *Companion* descriptors are mainly based on expert descriptions. The descriptors of the CEFR and its *Companion* were empirically scaled : Teachers (and other language professionals in case of the *Companion*) were asked to estimate the descriptors' difficulty levels, and these estimations were subjugated to statistical analyses, resulting in the six ascending proficiency levels. Nevertheless, the theoretical foundation of the CEFR remains one of its weak points (e.g., Cumming, 2009 ; Hulstijn, 2007). While the CEFR proficiency concept is based on models of communicative competence (e.g., Bachman & Palmer, 1996 ; and Canale & Swain, 1981), the descriptors themselves are based "on professional consensus rather than empirical evidence" (Harsch, 2014, p. 156). North (2007), however, stressed the importance of involving practitioners in the development of such a framework, rather than basing it on SLA theories. Hence, while the levels were derived from expert estimation and quantitative analyses, the ascending order of the levels is not a validated, theoretical description of second language acquisition, nor does it describe proficiency development precisely.

Comparing ILR, ACTFL, and CEFR.

When the CEFR was released in 2001, there were no official correspondences between the ILR, ACTFL, and CEFR scales (Tschirner, 2012). Meanwhile, research was conducted that aimed at aligning the three frameworks (ILR, ACTFL and CEFR). In 2010, ACRFL worked to establish relationships with European testing organizations to explore crosswalks among the three scales. Over several years and multiple meetings, including working groups comprised of users of both scales, cooperative studies were conducted to compare and align the scale systems, with differing outcomes. Tschirner (2012) reported a set of standard setting studies to align ACTFL and CEFR scales, and based on additional studies by the team headed by Tschirner, ACTFL published the following alignment table for the receptive and productive skills :

As Table 1 shows, the alignment is currently uni-directional ; that is, a score on an ACTFL- certified test can be converted to a CEFR level but not the reverse. In addition, one issue with directly comparing different proficiency systems, of course, is that of the tests used within each system. In the US, regardless of language, the only official ILR tests come from the US government (or ACTFL) and the only certified ACTFL tests are administered via ACTFL's testing arm, Language Testing International (LTI). This situation contrasts with CEFR contexts; there is no official body in Europe or elsewhere that would endorse tests that are aligned to the CEFR. Rather, test providers and exam boards develop their own tests and conduct their own CEFR alignment studies. Hence the quality, nature, and difficulty of tests that claim alignment to the CEFR levels vary by language and even country. Although some work has been conducted to align these frameworks, more research and collaboration would benefit language learners who need to transfer a test result from one system to another in order to receive credit for studying abroad or to communicate the language gain made.

Table 1

ONE-DIRECTIONAL ALIGNMENT: Receptive Skills – Reading and Listening		ONE-DIRECTIONAL ALIGNMENT: Productive Skills – Speaking and Writing	
Rating on ACTFL Assessment	Corresponding CEFR Rating	Rating on ACTFL Assessment	Corresponding CEFR Rating
Distinguished	C2		
Superior	C1.2	Superior	C2
Advanced High	C1.1	Advanced High	C1
Advanced Mid	B2	Advanced Mid	B2.2
Advanced Low	B1.2	Advanced Low	B2.1
Intermediate High	B1.1	Intermediate High	B1.2
Intermediate Mid	A2	Intermediate Mid	B1.1
Intermediate Low	A1.2	Intermediate Low	A2
Novice High	A1.1	Novice High	A1
Novice Mid	0	Novice Mid	0
Novice Low	0	Novice Low	0

[based on *The Routledge Handbook of Second Language Acquisition and Language Testing*]

(3) Which statement is true?

① Language learners' proficiency levels described in the CEFR depends on the purposes, situations, and circumstances of the communication.

② The descriptors in the CEFR are reliable because they were created by second language acquisition researchers.

③ The CEFR was revised in 2018, and more than 40 existing standards were replaced with new standards.

④ The CEFR is only applicable for English because English is widely used not only in Europe but all over the world.

⑤ The CEFR serves not only as a teaching tool for language teachers, but also as a qualification for language learners.

(4) If you were estimated to be B1.2 on the CEFR level, what would your proficiency level be expected to be on the ACTFL?

① Intermediate High reader in ACTFL

② Intermediate High writer in ACTFL

③ Intermediate Mid speaker in ACTFL

④ Intermediate Mid listener in ACTFL

⑤ You cannot estimate it using ACTFL assessment

＜C＞

Read the following passage. To answer (5) and (6), choose the most appropriate answer from ① to ⑤.

To be a literate person today means having control over a range of print and electronic media. The ways we write, the genres we create, the authorial identities we assume, the forms of our finished products and the ways in which we engage with readers have been transformed by new technologies in a short space of time, so that students routinely make use of digital technologies to construct written text both in and out of the classroom. Many teachers have therefore enthusiastically embraced these into their writing classes, seeing the integration of new technology-enhanced pedagogies as a means of enlivening instruction, improving students' writing skills and facilitating collaboration and interaction. Technology is, however, a smorgasbord of options and possibilities rather than a single tool, and not all teachers will be familiar with some they are called upon to use. A brief introduction to <u>the key technologies</u> currently found in writing classes might therefore be useful.

Writing, in the sense of making language visible, always involves the application of technology of some kind, and tools influence how we go about it, from cave drawings to Snapchat. What is different today is the pace of change, so that the varieties of outlets, the integration of text with other media and the reach our writing can achieve are unprecedented. In classrooms, many teachers find themselves using commercial course management systems such as *Blackboard* or *Moodle* to present course materials, contact students and read students' online posts. Others have been using asynchronous (delayed) tools such as email or bulletin boards for many years to encourage student writing, and more are recognising the value of supporting students to publish their own websites so they can practice new online literacy skills. Class blogs are now also relatively common ways of encouraging writing and creating a sense of community (Bloch, 2008), while wikis are seen as encouraging collaborative research and writing (Beach et al., 2014). More recently, teachers have turned to mobile technologies to exploit text messaging and micro-blogging and to social media as ways to engage students in authentic writing activities.

One reason for including a chapter on the use of new technologies in this book is because these changes have happened quickly. Until fairly recently, Computer Mediated Communication (CMC) meant email (asynchronous) and instant messaging in chatrooms (synchronous). These had the effect of removing the teacher as the locus of control and encouraging more participation from less confident writers (e.g. Warschauer, 2000). The advent of the web provided teachers with qualitatively different types of instructional possibilities, enabling students to engage in collaborative multimedia authoring rather than only mediated interaction with others. From the mid-2000s, web 2.0 technologies began to redefine the web as a social platform for collaboration, knowledge-sharing and networking, replacing the *informational web* with the *social web* (Pegrum, 2009 : 18). The ever-growing diversity and flexibility of digital media and the ease with which they can be managed has contributed to a massive expansion of options for writing teachers (e.g. Motteram, 2013 ; Thomas et al., 2013). Tools such as wikis, blogs and 3D virtual worlds like *Second Life*, which contains its own language school (Cooke-Plagwitz, 2008), are now common leaning spaces for writing teachers.

But while a survey of 2,500 writing teachers in the United States found that digital technologies were shaping the ways middle and high school students now write and were used widely in classrooms, they also had reservations (Purcell et al., 2013). These teachers saw major challenges in teaching writing in the digital age, including the 'creep' of informal style into formal writing assignments and the need to better educate students about issues such as plagiarism and fair use. Overall, however, these digital technologies do not only open possibilities for more varied, engaging, interactive and collaborative L2 writing instruction, but are the very stuff of everyday life. It is likely that many of our students will be familiar with, if not heavily invested in, at least some of these tools and to not use them in the writing class may actually seem a perverse avoidance. For these reasons, this chapter will explore some of the more commonly used technologies in L2 writing classes.

[based on *Second Language Writing*]

(5) Which statement is NOT true as an example of the underlined part?

① To learn more about the topic in the textbook, students search for newspaper articles on the web and read them.

② To make a video introducing Japanese culture to overseas students, students email them about what they are interested in.

③ To practice gestures for speeches, students make pairs in a class and give feedback when exchanging partners.

④ To practice communicating with others on the Internet, students post comments on the bulletin board.

⑤ To gather evidence to use in debates, students search the Web for texts written from different perspectives on environmental issues.

(6) Which statement is true?

① Purcell et al. (2013) recruited more than twenty-thousand teachers in their survey.

② Some teachers are concerned about students' Internet literacy in technology-based writing classes.

③ Teachers should introduce technology that encourages autonomous English learning to their students.

④ Teachers should actively use technology to improve their own writing skills.

⑤ Technological developments have brought synchronous online meetings into schools, but asynchronous teaching has delayed.

▌2024年度 ▌ 岐阜県 ▌ 難易度 ▰▰▰▱▱▱

【13】 Read the following article and answer the questions below by marking the correct answer on the answer sheet.

1 The earliest Japanese loanword to appear in the Oxford English Dictionary, kuge (court noble), came in 1577. By 2014, a study by Kinjo Gakuin University researcher Schun Doi had found 584 [A] loanwords.

437

2 Since Commodore Matthew Perry's Black Ships forced Japan open to trade in the 19th century, such loanwords have repaid the favor by contributing to the English language. The internet and increased travel now allow people to increasingly catapult their linguistic heritages — and attendant values — into each others' lives.

3 The term "emoji" is a good example. It first appeared in the OED in a 1997 citation from the Nikkei Weekly, but didn't make the dictionary until 2013. The year before last, it was dubbed Oxford Dictionaries' word of the year for reflecting "the ethos, mood and preoccupations of 2015." Oxford says the use of emoji more than tripled compared to 2014, allowing it to beat out words such as "refugee" and "lumbersexual." OED President Casper Grathwohl cited Hillary Clinton's request for people to send emojis in response to a campaign questiom, and the debate over emoji skin tones as signs of how the word moved from teen [B] jargon into the main lexicon. He added that emoji pictograms suit our "obsessively immediate" times perfectly, an example of how Japan's preference for visual communication has hit a nerve overseas.

4 Indra Levy, associate professor of Japanese literature at California's Stanford University, notes that whereas precedents often named a specifically Japanese object ("geisha" or "anime"), the latest loanwords represent a new level of interplay between Japan and the world. She says these words show, "the broadening and deepening of Japan's international influence on 'high popular culture,' by which I mean the vocabulary of daily life — eating, emailing or texting, and consuming — shared by countries around the world that enjoy large middle-class populations."

(1)

5 So how exactly do loanwords "become" English? There's no absolute [C] test. In the formal world of dictionaries, lexicographers pore over traditional media, literature and an expanding myriad of web-based forms. Experts at Merriam-Webster decide a word merits inclusion when usage benchmarks are reached; "A word must be used in a substantial number of citations that come from a wide range of publications over a considerable

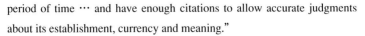

period of time ⋯ and have enough citations to allow accurate judgments about its establishment, currency and meaning."

6   Out in the real world, Doi loosely identifies three phases in the process of migration from Japanese to English. "In the initial stage, words are paraphrased by easily recognizable words or phrases to guarantee that the foreign words employed are understood," he says. "Then, attributive usages appear as a transitional phase. To finish the naturalization process, the loanwords acquire greater productivity and in due course achieve the fully incorporated status."

7   For example, "origami" first appeared in the OED in a citation from Samuel Randlett's 1961 book "The Art of Origami," where it is described as an art of "individually unique, folded paper." (2) In 1972, it was attributed in Celia Fremlin's novel "Appointment with Yesterday" as "origami cut-outs." In 1996, it is printed in The Australian requiring no explanation: "Proteins also need to be folded into shape and this biological origami is not always flawless."

8   It's hard not to notice the rapid penetration of Japanese cultural signifiers into daily discourse. As terms such as "emoji," "umami" and "KonMari" show, Japanese concepts — rather than simple objects (sushi), people (samurai) or practices (karate) — are resonating with the way we live our lives.

9   Vectors for the migration of loanwords include: food, where highly specific terms such as "dashi" (Japanese soup stock) are employed by knowing chefs and "umami" represents a recently discovered fifth flavor; technology, where photographers use the word "bokeh" to describe the soft-focus look provided by expensive lenses; and increasingly in the realms of media, art, lifestyle and fashion.

10   Japanese words are often deployed to demonstrate one's area of expertise. W. David Marx, the author of "Ametora; How Japan Saved American Style," says he was, "surprised to see that jeans fans used the words 'tate-ochi' for that specific fading style of vertical lines."

11   Stanford's Levy believes the embrace of loanwords such as "emoji" and

"KonMari" represents a sea change in relations between Japan and the world, in the sense that these words acknowledge a Japanese expression for phenomena considered to be universal, but that were as yet unnamed in other languages. (　3　)

12 The rapid naturalization of "KonMari" shows the amped speeds at which the process can now occur. The word began simply as the name of the author of a series of books on decluttering by Marie Kondo that took off in the West with the 2014 best-seller "The Life-Changing Magic of Tidying Up."

13 By 2016, in a New York Times magazine feature, a writer was quoting a woman saying she had "KonMaried" her boyfriend. "Having tidied everything in her home and finding she still distinctly lacked happiness," the author writes, "she held her boyfriend in her hands, realized he no longer sparked joy and got rid of him," (　4　)

14 Levy says the popularization of "KonMari" is down to the genius of Cathy Hirano's translation and the marketing strategy of Ten Speed Press. Noting that Kondo's success "represents a popular version of anti-consumerism that can directly speak to any advanced consumerist culture," she also cautions that when it comes to perceptions of Japan, the more things change the more they stay the same.

15 "The fact that the English translation of her work became a best-seller has to do with its unique combination of a lifestyle issue shared across the Pacific," she says, "and the exoticizing subtitle 'The Japanese art of decluttering and organizing." (　5　) "In that sense," she concludes, "despite the deepening of Japan's international influence, exoticism continues to be an important part of how Japan sustains its relevance to the Western world, for better or worse."

(1)　Choose the best meaning of [A] loanwords in the article from below.

① 　a word or phrase with a secret meaning that is used instead of the usual name for something

② 　the English language before about 1150, which is very different from modern English

③　noun, a verb, an adjective or an adverb whose main function is to express meaning

④　a word from another language used in its original form

⑤　a word that has become fashionable and popular and is used a lot in newspapers, etc.

(2)　Choose the best meaning of [B] jargon in the article from below.

①　words that many people find offensive

②　words or expressions that are used by a particular profession or group of people, and are difficult for others to understand

③　a phrase consisted of more than one word

④　a comment that expresses praise or approval of somebody

⑤　a language that somebody learns to speak well and that they use for work or at school, but that is not the language they learned first

(3)　Choose the best word below to fill in the blank [　C　] in the fifth paragraph.

①　litmus　　②　language　　③　mental　　④　proficiency

⑤　written

(4)　Based on the sixth paragraph, which statement is NOT true?

①　There are three stages of transition for a word to become a loanword.

②　At first, a foreign word is paraphrased in simple terms to guarantee that the meaning of the word will be conveyed.

③　The more attractive a word is, the more it is used in its original form without being paraphrased.

④　Attributive usages of a word appear in the transitional stage.

⑤　Loanwords obtain greater productivity in the final stage.

(5)　Based on the seventh and eighth paragraph, which statement is true?

①　English cultures are rapidly spreading into the Japanese language.

②　The term origami is first described in the OED to describe biological structures.

③　Japanese concepts such as emoji are becoming widespread in foreign languages.

④　Japanese words in English are used to refer to simple things rather than cultures or concepts.

⑤ The artistry of origami was critically reviewed in The Australian.

(6) Choose the most appropriate sentence which can be inferred from the ninth to eleventh paragraphs.

① The use of specialized foreign words in romaji writing is spreading in Japan.

② Loanwords can be accepted when there is a universal matter that is not expressed in their first language.

③ Japanese will become the only common language of choice for communication in the world.

④ The use of Japanese as a foreign language will expand only in the area of food.

⑤ The transmission of language across oceans suggests the development of modern information technology.

(7) Choose the most appropriate sentence which can be inferred from the twelfth to fourteenth paragraphs.

① Examples like "KonMari" show how language takes time to be naturalized.

② "KonMari" is a term used only for the topic of romance.

③ The slogan "KonMari" would encourage the further development of a consumerist society.

④ We can use "KonMari" like a verb to describe putting something away and letting it go.

⑤ Hirano and Kondo will continue to work together on their writing.

(8) Choose the most appropriate section from blanks (1) to (5) to insert the following sentence.

> Levy says without the stress on "Japanese art," the book would likely not have become a New York Times best-seller.

① 1 ② 2 ③ 3 ④ 4 ⑤ 5

(9)～(12) Choose the best option from the word bank for the blanks in the following tables.

①	emoji	②	origami
③	Japanese object	④	Western culture
⑤	specific terms in some areas of expertise		
⑥	samurai	⑦	refugee
⑧	bokeh	⑨	life-changing magic

According to Doi, there are 584 loanwords.

・Examples of loanwords:

word	year first appeared in Oxford English Dictionary
kuge	1577
(9)	? (as a citation of a book published in 1961)
(10)	1997

・Use of loanwords:

referring to	Examples of loanwords
(11)	geisha, anime
vocabulary of daily life (i.e., high popular culture)	(10), KonMari
vocabulary of food	umami, dashi
(12)	tate-ochi

(13) Choose the most appropriate title for the article.

① Body language: Know your Japanese from head to toe

② Japanese is affecting the English lexicon in new ways

③ How do this year's English buzzwords translate into Japanese?

④ I know Japanese. Why can't I read signs in Hokkaido?

⑤ The study of Japanese slang is challenging and never stops. Luckily, it's also a lot of fun.

‖ 2024年度 ‖ 神戸市 ‖ 難易度 ▆▆▆▭▭

解答・解説

【1】1 ① オ　⑤ イ　2 ② ウ　③ イ　④ ア

3 (1)　Because they can't imagine her climbing a mountain.

(2)　When she was 13, she got inspired to climb Mount Everest.

(3)　She hopes to find a companion who is definitely committed, has a dream of their own, is excited about life and basically has the same goal as her, which is to help others reach their full potential.　4　①　interact

②　relationships　③　bond　5　エ

○**解説**○ 1 ①　空所の後で「彼女は18歳の時に標高8,163メートルのマナスルに登った最も若い女性となった」「彼女は19歳の時にエベレストに登った最も若い日本人になった」という最年少記録が述べられていることよりオが適切。　⑤　空所の後で「誰もいない家でその後彼女は何日も泣き続けた」とあり精神的に弱くなっていたことが読み取れ，イが適切である。The accidentは前の段落で述べられている250メートルの高さを頭から落ちてしまった出来事を指す。　2 ②　直後のExplorers Grand Slam「探検家グランドスラム」を修飾する空所に当てはまるのはウのgrueling「辛い，過酷な」である。　③　空所の直前にOur existence is so tiny「我々の存在はとてもちっぽけなものである」とありall these daily issues don't（　③　）「これらの日常の問題の全ては大したことではない」といった内容にすることで意味がつながる。よってイのmean a thingが適切である。否定語＋mean a thingで「少しも意味がない」の意。　④　空所直後のgiving her a much needed sense of control「とても必要とされている，物事をコントロールしている感覚を彼女に与えた」とあり，空所は同様の意味であるアのgrounded「地に足のついた」が適切。　3 (1)　設問の答えは第4段落2文目に書かれている。設問文はWhyが使われているため理由を表すBecauseで書き始める。　(2)　設問の答えは第8段落2文目に書かれている。設問文はWhenが使われているため，答えとしてWhen she was 13, と時期を明確に示す。　(3)　設問の答えは最終段落3文目に書かれている。設問文で用いられている疑問文を平叙文にしたShe hopes to find a companion

444

who〜と書き出し，who以下は本文の表現をそのまま用いればよい。
4 ① 空所を含む文については第5段落4文目で言及されている。空
所に入るのは動詞であり，本文のthere was very little interactionはcould
hardly interactと言い換えられる。 ② 空所を含む文については第5
段落1文目で言及されている。as a way to connect with others「他人とつ
ながる手段として」はTo build relationships with others「他人と関係を
築くために」と言い換えられる。 ③ 空所を含む文については第6
段落最終文で言及されており，本文のthere was a human bondがそのま
ま解答となる。 5 Minamiyaさんのインタビューでは，自分の潜在
能力を信じて，恐れず自分のしたいことに挑戦してみるよう応援メッ
セージを彼女が送っていることが読み取れる。このメッセージとして
適切な選択肢はエ「自分自身に制限を設けるな」となる。

【2】 1 ② 2 ④ 3 ④ 4 ③ 5 ① 6 ③
○解説○ 1 挿入文は「しかし，すべてがバラ色というわけではない」。
書籍ビジネスが好調であることを述べたあとの⑧に入るのが適切。そ
して，「書籍の購買層がオンラインに移行するにつれ，新人やあまり
知られていない作家の本が売れにくくなっている」と続く。 2 下
線部を含む文意は「このギャップ(書籍ビジネスが好調だが，新人やあ
まり知られていない作家の本が売れにくくなっている)は，おそらく出
版界で最も難解な問題，つまり書店に足を運び，新しい本や著者を発
見するセレンディピティをいかにしてオンラインで再現するかという
問題を示唆している」。serendipity「偶然の発見」は，④「偶然面白く
貴重な本を見つける行為」と言える。 3 空所後の文意は「読者は
すでに，ソーシャル・メディアでの推薦文，無限のベスト・オブ・リ
スト，有名人のブッククラブ，書評，その他の宣伝文句にまみれてい
る」。オンラインで未知の本を手に取るよう仕向けることの難しさを
述べている。よって「アプリがオンライン上で発見問題を解決するこ
とに『懐疑的な』人もいる」となる。 4 第8段落より，①「Copper
は読者と作家をつなぐ新しい作家中心のアプリである」は正しい。第
7段落より，②「Bookfinityは，アンケートを通して利用者に読者タイ
プを割り当て，本を薦める」は正しい。第18段落より，Tertuliaはアプ

リをダウンロードしてアンケートに答えさせていることから，③は誤り。第6，7，17段落のIngramに関する記述より，④「Ingramは紙の書籍の販売に加え，電子書籍とオーディオブックにも注力するつもりだ」は正しい。　5　第14段落に「Tertuliaの創設者たちは，本に関するオンライン上の会話を利用し，それをわかりやすいリストにまとめ上げることで，かつて実店舗で売上を牽引した『口コミ』による推薦を再現したいと考えている」とある。よって，①「Tertuliaの創設者たちは，口コミはオンラインで本を売るための重要な要素だと考えている」が正しい。　6　要約文として「たいていの本はオンラインで売られていて，そこでは実店舗で見て回る経験を再現することが不可能だ」に続くものを選ぶ。業界をあげて新たな本を発見するアプリに期待を寄せていることが書かれていることから，③「書籍発見アプリは，この状況を変えることを目指している」が適切。

【3】問1　①　イ　　②　カ　　③　ア　　④　エ　　問2　ウ
問3　ア (E)　　イ (B)　　ウ (C)　　問4　ア　　問5　エ
○**解説**○　問1　各空所に入るべき品詞を見極める。　①「…私たちは両親や教師を観察し，彼らから歩き方や話し方…を学ぶ」に続く文なので，observational learning「観察学習」。　②「他人の思考に影響されすぎて『自分』という感覚が不安定で壊れやすくなる」。be susceptible to～「～に影響されやすい」。　③　空所前の文意は，「つまり脳の活動には，そこで何が起こっているかという情報だけでなく，誰がそれについて考えているかという情報も含まれている」。よって，「この組み合わせが主観的な自己意識につながる」となる。combination「組み合わせ」。　④「自他の境界が本当にこれほど柔軟であるならば，私たちは偏見に対処し，精神障害を緩和するためにこの能力を利用できるかもしれない」。alleviate～「～を緩和する」。　問2　第1段落を受けて，空欄あ は，「私たちは周囲の人々の『行動』を真似るだけではない」。空所後の文が「大人になるにつれて私たちは他の人が何を考え，何を感じ，何を望んでいるかを学び…」と続くことから，空欄い は，「彼らの『心』も真似ている」。　問3　ア「このことは，多くの時間を一緒に過ごす2人が，同じ思考を共有するひとりの人間のように感

じ始めるという身近な経験を説明するかもしれない」は，空所(E)に入れ，次の文で「社会的なレベルでは，異なる背景を持つ人と比べて自分と似たような経験を共有した人に共感しやすいと感じる理由を説明できるかもしれない」と続くのが適切。　イ「この場合は，被験者が現実に関する自分の真の信念に加えて，パートナーの偽りの信念を心に留めておく必要があると考えられる」。第4段落の課題に関する英文で「パートナーはその物体がまだ箱の中にあると錯覚するが，被験者は真実を知っている」のあとの空所(B)に入るのが適切。　ウ「被験者は，物体の行方だけでなく，パートナーの信念も追跡し続けなければならない」。第8，9段落の実験「対象物がどこにあるかという情報を得るたびに被験者がどのように自分の信念を変えていくか，また，パートナーが何らかの情報を見るたびにパートナーの信念のシミュレーションをどのように変えたかも描写した」に関する記述であるので空所(C)に入るのが適切。　問4　シミュレーション理論の説明になるよう英文を挿入する。　ア「自分が相手の立場に立つと，自分の脳は相手の脳内の処理を真似ようとするのだ」が適切。put oneself in one's shoes「〜が…の立場になる」。　問5　エ「自己と他者の境界線は柔軟で，他者と協調する場合もあれば自己の感覚を保つ場合もある」は，第13段落の内容より適切。　ア「予測ミスが起きているときと起きていないときの脳活動のパターンを比較するのは有益ではない」は，第11段落の内容に反する。　イ「神経科学者たちは社会的な状況で他人が報酬を受けているのを見た場合，私たちの脳は自分が報酬を受けているときと同じ脳活動を示すかどうかは疑わしいと考えている」は，第6段落の内容に反する。　ウ「私たちは自分の心についての考えと他人の心についての考えを区別することはない」は，第13段落の内容に反する。

【4】Q1　①　Gifts to honor the great behavior of people.　②　People who are employed to clean a building and make minor repairs.　Q2　Fact-Finding question: What did the Japanese fans do at the Doha stadium on Wednesday?　Inferential question: What does the last quote in the article, "It's not only three points that Japan have in the bag"mean?

Q3　A　when you leave a place, leave the place cleaner than you first found it　B　I think the purpose, besides saving the school money by not employing cleaning staff, is to teach the students personal responsibility and to prepare them for the working world　Q4　(1)　I found it interesting that Japanese students clean their classrooms and hallways. I think that's why tidiness is widely accepted as a virtue, particularly in public spaces. You should be proud of it. Do you have other Japanese school customs you would like to introduce to people abroad?　(2)　[D]　Tries writing to communicate relevant information in a detailed description of your thoughts and opinions　[E]　Some errors are present, but the English text is written in a way that does not interfere with comprehension

○**解説**○　Q1　下線部の単語を英語で説明する問題である。①は「記念品」の意であり，下線部直後の「from FIFA」に着目するとよいだろう。②は「用務員」の意であり，下線部を含んだ文とその直後の文に着目するとよいだろう。　Q2　新聞記事の英文について事実質問と推論質問のそれぞれを作成する問題である。それぞれの定義については問題の指示文で与えられており，事実質問はテキストに書かれていることを理解できているかを確認するような質問を作ればよい。推論質問については，解答例にあるような本文の解釈を尋ねる質問の他にも，理由および因果関係を尋ねる質問や，書き手の意図を尋ねる質問などが可能であろう。　Q3　空欄に当てはまる英語を書く問題である。空欄Aについては，直前にある「立つ鳥跡を濁さず」を英語で説明すればよい。空欄Bについては，日本の学校に清掃がある理由や，生徒が清掃を行うことの良さを英語で説明すればよい。　Q4　与えられた単元計画に基づいてパフォーマンステストを行う場合の材料や評価基準等について，英語で記述する問題である。空欄Cについては，本単元の目標と単元計画に着目する。まず，単元の目標としては，日本の学校における習慣を外国人に紹介すること，そしてそれについての自身の意見を述べるということである。また，単元計画では，パフォーマンステストは4時間目にあり，その前に2～3時間目では自身の経験や調査に基づいて考えをまとめる活動を行っていることがわかる。すると，1時間目の授業で行った学校における清掃以外について，生徒たち自

身が考えた日本の学校における習慣について，自身の考えを含めて説明することを求めるような場面設定ができる英文を書く必要がある。空欄Dと空欄Eについては，観点別学習評価における3観点が設定されていることに着目すればよい。空欄Dは主体的に学習に取り組む態度に関するa評価の記述文であり，bに加えて，より場面設定を踏まえたコミュニケーションをしようとしていることを記述するとよいだろう。空欄Eについては，知識・技能に関するb評価の記述文であり，a評価に比べて，正確さや理解しやすさに部分的な課題があるが内容理解はできることを記述するとよい。

【5】1　(1)　c　　(2)　a　　2　(1)　a　　(2)　d

○**解説**○　1　(1)　鳥には，種類の異なる鳥や他の動物が発する，敵の接近を警戒する声を言葉として理解するものが存在する例を示しながら，「異なる種の動物が発する言葉を自分たちの言葉に変換して理解できる動物が存在するが，どのようにしてそのような言語学習ができているのかは分かっていない」と生物学者の説明を引用している。本文には，選択肢a「人間の言葉が理解できている鳥」，b「捕食動物から逃げるのが生得的に備わっている鳥」，d「生まれながらにして他の動物の言葉が分かる鳥」への言及はない。なお，本文3文目のcritterは「生物」の意。　(2)　冒頭文でUltra-Processed Foods「超加工食品」摂取の危険性が本文の主題であることが分かる。続けて「超加工食品」の定義，米国での調査結果と食生活改善への提言について述べている。9文目に「食生活に占める割合が増加している」とあるのでb, c は不適切。13文目に，「『超加工食品』を食べた子どもたちは，栄養バランスのとれた食事を食べた子どもたちより体重の増加が早かった」という研究結果が述べられている。さらに，最終文で，「がんと肥満の予防のために『超加工食品』に代わる食品を摂取するべきだ」と述べられている。これらから「超加工食品」と肥満の関係性は明らかと考えられ，dは不適切。　2　ディクトグロス学習指導法の説明文である。(1)　本文の3文目に「意味重視型のリスニングやグループワークの中で，語順や文法などの形式にも注意するよう，生徒に奨励する」と述べていることから，a「生徒は，形式と内容の両方に注意しなければ

449

ならない」が適切。他の選択肢はTable 5.1の各Stepの内容を確認。
b　Step 4にapproximation「概要」とあるので不適切。　c　Step 1に
predict vocabulary and content とあるので不適切。　d　Step 3にTake
notes listing key words とあり，できるだけ多くメモを取るわけではな
いので不適切。　(2)　学生の言語学習評価の実施プロセスとして，学
生の作業→評点の記録→言語能力の分析→評価内容の決定→プラス効
果がある評価結果という流れを説明している。Figure 2.3 からこのプロ
セスの流れは不可逆的であることが分かるので，a，b は不適切。筆者
の主眼は，この一連のプロセスが連鎖的につながっていることで評価
結果が正当化されるという点にあり，言語能力の分析段階が最も重要
とは言っていないのでc は不適切。本文の最後から2文目と3文目に，
学習評価を実施する際には，われわれがこれまでに得た学生の能力に
関する情報を活用すること，実施プロセスの流れの各段階には，こう
した情報と情報に基づく評価が含まれていることが述べられている。
よって，dが適切。

【6】(1)　(ア)　D　　(カ)　D　　(2)　C　　(3)　ウ　C　　エ　A
(4)　オ　D　　ク　D　　ケ　C　　(5) B　　(6)　B　　(7) (a)　A
(b)　A　　(8)　D

○**解説**○ (1)　(ア)　figuratively「比喩的に」と同じ意味なのはDの
metaphoricallyとなる。　(カ)　contemporary「現代の」と同じ意味な
のはDのmodernとなる。　(2)　下線部(イ)は「自動車は重要な文化の象
徴システム，つまり実質的に全員が話す言語となった」という意味で
ある。要は誰でも自動車を使うようになったということを指しており，
Cが適切と判断できる。　(3)　ウ　it is hardの形式主語itに対応する真
主語to doの部分が空所に入ると考えられるのでCのみが適切である。
なお，to the point of impossibilityは「不可能なくらいに」の意味で形式
主語itとは関係がない。　エ　we have learned to sew together the pieces
of our lives by its needleという文を空所の関係詞で結ぶことになるため
by whichが適切となる。　(4)　オ　空所の後では我々が自動車を走ら
せるための環境を整える必要があることが述べられており，空所では
それをservant「しもべ，使用人」と表現していると考えられる。

ク　下線部(キ)は，車はプライバシーを提供してくれるという意味である。次の文で人々は好きなことができるということが述べられており，空所にはpleasurableを入れてsomething pleasurable about being alone in a car「車に一人でいることについて楽しく感じること」とするのが適切と判断できる。　ケ　空所を含む段落の後半で，自動車を買うことは衝動的な決断であり，気持ちが大きくなる傾向にあることが述べられているため，Cのmagnifies「誇張する」が適切だと判断できる。

(5)　文意より下線部(キ)と同じ段落のthe vast queues of commutersは通勤者の車が連なっての渋滞を示していると考えられる。B以外の選択肢は本文中に述べられていない内容であるためBが正解と判断する。

(6)　空所を含む段落では車を持つこと，選ぶことは自己表現の一種であるといった内容が述べられている。これに基づくとBのexternalizations of our value systems「我々の価値体系の表出化」が適切。

(7)　(a)　Aの内容が第2段落4文目と一致する。　(b)　Aの内容が第7段落3文目と一致する。　(8)　第6～9段落に車の単なる移動手段以外の購入目的や効力が述べられておりDが適切である。

【7】(1)　3　　(2)　2　　(3)　2　　(4)　2　　(5)　1　　(6)　4

(7)　①　Sustainable tourism is the solution to overtourism, which creates a balance between economic growth, social well-being, and environmental protection.　②　Collaborative efforts are needed to achieve sustainable tourism and benefit everyone involved while protecting the environment for future generations.

○解説○ (1)　本文はovertourism「観光公害」の問題点や対応策・解決法についての文章である。プレゼンテーションの1枚目にもってくるべき内容として，作成者が最も主張したい対応策・解決法に関する内容であると判断できる。対応策・解決法にあたるのは第5段落および第6段落で，繰り返し現れるsustainable tourismやresponsibleがキーワードであることがわかる。これに合致する表題として3が適切。　(2)　空所直前のwhenよりovertourismがいつ起こるかについての内容が入ると判断できる。これに合致するのは第1段落1文目である。本文ではoverwhelmed「圧倒される」だが，設問文ではoverburdened「過重負担

451

の」と言い換えられている。　(3)　空所に入るのはovertourismの問題
点となり，本文では第2段落および第3段落が該当する。空所は第3段
落の内容で，選択肢2が第3段落4文目と合致する。be priced out of～
「～は高額すぎて買えない」の意。　(4)　空所にはovertourismが起こ
る原因が入り，原因が述べられているのは第4段落となる。選択肢1は
4文目，3は3文目，4は2文目に合致する記述がある一方，選択肢2は該
当する記述がない。　(5)　空所に合致するのは第5段落3文目のrather
than以下である。strive to doは「～しようと努力する」でtry to doと同
じような意味である。　(6)　プレゼンテーション7枚目の資料の内容
は第6段落の内容と合致する。空所に該当するのは最終文である。本
文のreduceは設問文ではminimize「最小化する」と言い換えられてい
る。　(7)　結論が述べられているのは本文の最終段落であり，2文目
と3文目の内容をそれぞれ記載すればよいことがわかる。本文をその
まま回答するのではなく，要点を短く示すプレゼン資料として適切で
はない2文目のTo solve this problemや3文目のEveryone needs to work
together～といった部分は解答例のように別の言葉で短く書き換えると
よい。

【8】(1)　c　　(2)　e　　(3)　d　　(4)　①　b　　②　d　　(5)　c
○解説○ (1)　バリンゴ(Baringo)湖の状況について正しくないものを選ぶ
問題。cが第2段落の内容に反する。バリンゴ湖の水位が北アメリカの
五大湖より上昇しているという記述はなく，同じような水位の上昇と
いう現象が起こっているという記述があるのみである。　(2)　a　第4
段落と第5段落で，温暖化が主要な原因であるという説にすべての研
究者が同意しているわけではないと述べているので，不適。　b　第9
段落で，北米の五大湖やカナダでも湖岸の浸食や洪水の被害を受けて
いると述べられているので，不適。　c　第3段落2文目に，3つの可能
性は相互に関連していると述べているので，不適。　d　第13段落で，
今後の水位上昇はこれまでよりもはるかに大きくなるだろうとの予測
が述べられているため，不適。　e　第15段落で，湖沼からは，有機
物の分解によって二酸化炭素やメタンガスや亜酸化窒素が発生するた
め，温室効果ガスの発生源であることが述べられている。よって，湖

沼の水位が上昇して面積が拡大するにつれ，温室効果ガスも増えることがわかり，適切。　(3)　バリンゴ湖とボゴリア(Bogoria)湖の関係について述べられているのは第17段落で，その内容と一致しているのはdとなる。　(4)　①　水位上昇と3つの主な原因について述べられているのは第3段落で，第1文がbと一致する。　②　本文全体及び第18段落で，一刻も早く対策を立てなければいけないという主旨が読み取れ，dが正しいと判断できる。　(5)　空所となっている各段落の内容の概要を正しく読み取ることでcが適切な組み合わせだと判断できる。①　第5段落と第6段落では，水位上昇の原因は，人為的土地利用や地殻変動の影響である可能性が述べられているのでBが適切。　②　第7段落～第11段落では，気候変動がケニア，北米，カナダで引きこしている湖沼の水位上昇について述べられているのでAが適切。　③　第14段落～第16段落では，水位上昇により湖沼の面積が拡大することで，湖沼から発生する温室効果ガスの量が増大することが述べられているので，Cが適切。

【9】(1)　エ　　　(2)　エ　　　(3)　イ　　　(4)　ウ　　　(5)　イ
○**解説**○　18段落からなる記事であるが，誰が何を言っているのか，誰からの引用なのかをまとめながら読み進めると解答しやすくなる。

(1)　Dave White氏に関連するのは第1段落から第3段落の箇所である。第3段落最後の文 This little, tiny joey can contribute significantly to conservation. からエを選択。　(2)　動物園が動物の絶滅を防ぐ努力をしている理由として不適切な英文を選ぶ問題。エにConservation breeding program is renowned.とあるが，第5段落後半で2021年に絶滅危惧種保全に向けての施策として10年基本計画(10-year masterplan)を発表したとあり，その中にrenowned conservation breeding programが含まれている。これは保全に向けての方法であって，保全を行う理由というわけではない。　(3)　Chester Zoo as a world leaderについては，第8段落，第9段落で触れられており，その理由として野生生物を対象にした内分泌学研究所の存在があり，ヨーロッパでは唯一の動物園附属研究所となっている。この研究所では，定期的に排泄物を分析しメスの生殖ホルモンの推移を測定調査し，子を産み育てる身体的準備が整う

時期の見当をつけることができると述べているので，イが正解。ウは保全繁殖システムを初めて行ったとあるが，本文中にそのような言及はない。　(4)　保全繁殖が厄介な問題であることへの言及は，第13段落で触れられている。保全繁殖では，捕獲した状態で動物を繁殖させることになるが，自然界で生息していく力が劣化していることもあり，その多くは野生には戻れないとあるので，ウを選択。　(5)　Jon Paul Rodriguez氏については第17段落，第18段落で言及されている。同氏は，動物が自然界で野生として生息し，生態学的役割を果たしていることが最終的に重要であるとした上で，絶滅危惧種の保全のための様々な方策は保険であるものの，そのような方策を行わなければ絶滅危惧種の喪失は避けられないと言っている。　ア　動物は捕獲された状態で生態学的役割を果たして生きるべきとあるが，本文中では，自然界で野生として生息し，生態学的役割を果たして生きるべきであると述べられている。　イ　第18段落の中で，人の手で捕獲された状態で種の保全が永久になされる場合があるかもしれないと述べているが，それはその種を自然界での野性的な生活に戻すことができないかもしれないことと相通じるので，イが適切。　ウ　Jon Paul Rodriguez氏は，Chester Zooが優れた動物園の条件を満たす優良な施設であると認めているが，the best zoo in the worldとは述べていない。　エ　動物を繁殖させる目的は来園者を惹きつけることではないので不適切。

【10】Q1　The underlined part (1) refers to desks and chairs that fit the needs of children artistically, hygienically, and educationally. These types of desks and chairs allow children to work.　Q2　2a　(d)　　2b　(a)　　2c　(b)　2d　(c)　Q3　3a　children　　3b　school　　3c　home　Q4　4a　(b)　　4b　(a)　　4c　(c)　　Q5　The author states that education is trying to improve by moving the focus away from teachers and textbooks to the child himself. In this type of educational system, the child's life and development is at the center of attention rather than the class content itself.

○**解説**○　Q1　下線部が指している内容を英語で書く問題である。直前の文の後半部分に対応する記述があるため，その表現を使用して答え

ればよい。　Q2　空欄に当てはまる英語を選ぶ問題である。空欄2aについては空欄直前に着目すると, 聞くという態度は比較的, 受動的で吸収的であると述べられている。つまり, 従来の教室における伝統的な机やいすは児童や生徒が教師から与えられたものを取り入れることが想定されているということであり, 対応する (d) が正解。空欄2bについては空欄を含んだ文とその直前の文に着目する。直前の文では, 子どもたちが従来の聞く授業で学ぶ場合, 1時間, 1日, 1週間または1年間の期間でより多くの分野を学ぶことができれば, 最終的には全てを均一的に身につけることができると述べられている。この文を受け, 空欄を含んだ文では, このような結果として, 何千人もの子どもたちが決まった時間にそのような地理の勉強をしているようなことが誇らしげに言われていたという意味になる (a) が正解。空欄2cについては空欄直前とコロンでつながっていることに着目する。空欄直前では, 古い教育の特徴的な点を明確にするためにやや強調的な言い方をしたかもしれない, と述べられており, この空欄は古い教育の特徴的な点を説明する内容になっている。よって, 受動的な態度, 機械的な子どもたちの集団化そして画一的なカリキュラムや教育方法を意味する (b) が正解。空欄2dについても空欄直前とコロンでつながっていることに着目する。空欄直前では理想的な家庭環境における会話の中には子どもにとって興味と価値がある点がある, と述べられており, この空欄はそれを説明する内容になっている。そのため, 発言が行われ, 質問がされ, 主題について議論が行われ, 子どもが継続的に学んでいくことを意味する (c) が正解。　Q3　空欄に当てはまる英単語を記述する問題である。空欄3aについては, 直前にあるon the part of theという表現が, 同文中でon the part of the teacherという形で再び用いられていることに着目する。空欄を含んだ関係詞節は「子どもたちの側が教師側の与える情報よりも先行する」の意であり, 空欄に入るのは子どもたちを意味する単語である。空欄3bについては空欄を含んだ文と, 第6パラグラフで述べられていることに着目する。まず, 空欄を含んだ文では, これらの全てを整理して一般化すれば, 理想的な何かを作ることができると述べられている。ここで整理して一般化することというのは, 第6パラグラフで述べられているような, 理想的な家庭におけ

る子どもの主体的な学びができる環境のことである。従って，空欄に
適切なのは家庭と対比される形で学校を意味する単語である。空欄3c
については空欄を含んだ文の直後の文に着目する。子どもたちは最も
自由で豊かな社会生活を送れるようにするために，より多くの大人や
子どもと接触しなくてはならないと述べられており，学校の環境だけ
ではなく，理想的な家庭環境が必要になることがわかる。従って，空
欄に適切なのは学校と対比される形で家庭を意味する単語である。
Q4　空欄に当てはまる英語を選択する問題である。空欄4aについては
空欄の直前に着目すると，子どもたちは活動を始めると個性的になる
と述べられており，集団であることをやめるという意味になる (b) が
正解。空欄4bについては空欄を含んだ文とその直前の文に着目する。
直前の文では全てが聞く授業の場合は教材や方法が画一的にできると
述べられている。この文を受け，空欄を含んだ文では，子どもたちの
耳や，その耳を反映している本が全員に同じような媒体を構成してい
る(つまり，画一的な構成をしている)という意味になる (a) が正解。空
欄4cについては，空欄直前とセミコロンでつながっていることに着目
する。空欄直前では，子どもたちを中心にして，生活を通して学ぶよ
うに組織化した場合には，子どもたちは聞くだけの存在とは思わない
と述べられており，空欄はその直前の内容を受けている内容である。
よって，子どもたちは聞くだけの存在ではない，むしろ真逆である，
を意味する (c) が正解。　Q5　下線部について著者の考えを書く問題
である。内容としては，下線部を含んだ第5パラグラフの内容を整理
して書けばよいのだが，本文の表現を言い換える必要があることに留
意したい。

【11】1　①　ア　　②　エ　　2　ア　　3　(1)　Students are likely to
perform at a lower level in cases where assessments are fully digital but are
rarely used during the learning process.　　(2)　By providing multiple ways
for learners.　　(3)　(解答例)　・Display lesson notes on an interactive
whiteboard.　　・Answering multiple-choice questions in an online
platform.　　・Typing documents that are saved to the cloud.　　・Reading a
textbook on a mobile device.　　・Looking up facts online.　　から1つ

4　①　have

②　traditional teaching　　③　encourage

○**解説**○　1　①　空所の後のtossed around with little precision「ほとんど精度のない検討がされる」と同じ意味の内容が空所＋somewhat randomlyとなることが読み取れる。よってアのspread outが適切。being spread out somewhat randomly「いくぶんランダムに広がる」といった意味になる。　②　studentsがa phonics-based computer program「フォニックス(音声学)をベースにしたコンピュータプログラム」に触れるという内容になると考えられるので，エのexposure「さらされること」が適切。2　空所を含む第8段落の"right blend" of direct instruction and technology-accelerated learningという語句に着目する。direct instruction「直接的な指導」は教師による指導を指すため，教師と技術の正しい融合という意味のアが適切と判断できる。　3　(1)　設問の答えは第2段落最終文に書かれている。設問文はWhenが使われているが，本文のIn cases where～がそのまま解答として用いることができるため，本文の表現をそのまま用いればよい。　(2)　設問の答えは第6段落1文目に書かれている。設問文はHowの疑問文であるため，手段を表すByを用いて本文の表現By providing multiple ways for learners.とする。　(3)　設問の答えは最終段落に書かれている。例を挙げるよう設問で求められており，該当箇所は冒頭から列挙されている5つのうち1つを記述すればよい。　4　①　空所を含む文については第3段落のSimply adding～で言及されている。「考えなしにテクノロジーを導入しても有害な効果をもたらす」という意味であり，空所にはeffectの動詞となるhaveが適切。②　設問2や第8段落で見てきたように，教師による指導とテクノロジーの融合が大きな効果をもたらす。教師による指導はいろいろな表現が考えられるが解答例ではtraditional teachingとしている。　③　冒頭で述べられたALTの発言Students will be active learners by using technology on their own.への反論である。Bは，テクノロジーと併せて，教師は生徒がアクティブ・ラーナーになるように生徒の学びを奨励することができると考えている。よって，encourageが適切である。

【12】(1)　④　　(2)　④　　(3)　⑤　　(4)　⑤　　(5)　③　　(6)　②

○**解説**○ (1)　Satoruの発言の趣旨は，人が世界で成功するうえで最も大切な学ぶべきものは，コンピュータの技術であるということである。空所はそのSatoruの発言の趣旨が入るため④が適切と判断できる。

(2)　Keikoの後半の発言That is why I believe the capacity to acquire knowledge carries more weight than "the knowledge" itself.や，その前後の内容と一致するのが，技術そのものよりも技術を学ぶ能力が大切だとする④である。　(3)　第1段落5文目The resulting CEFR(CoE, 2001)is a language- and context-independent framework describing relevant aspects of language learning and use, language teaching, communicative tasks, curricula, assessment and language policy.より，教師の言語教授に役立つことが読み取れる。さらに，続く6文目The CEFR is a language policy tool that aims to increase transparency, provide a metalanguage for stakeholder communication, and enable mutual recognitions of qualifications and exams across Europe.より，学習者の能力を示す資格としても機能していることが読み取れることから，⑤が適切となる。　(4)　最後の段落の1文目As Table 1 shows, the alignment is currently uni-directional; that is, a score on an ACTFL- certified test can be converted to a CEFR level but not the reverse. にある通り，ACTFLのスコアを基準にCEFRのレベルを出すことは可能だが，その逆は不可能だと述べられている。よってCEFRのレベルを基準にACTFLで評価することはできないため⑤が適切となる。　(5)　下線部の内容は次の第2段落で述べられており，writingの技術を上達させるために役立つオンライン上の資料を集めたり，実際にEメールや掲示板などに書く機会を設けたりするといった例が挙げられている。これを踏まえて選択肢を検討すると，③のみがスピーチでのジェスチャーというwritingには明らかに無関係なことが述べられており，これが不適切だと判断できる。　(6)　第4段落2文目が②の内容と一致する。デジタル世代の中高生が剽窃などの問題を起こさず，教師が適切に指導できるかどうかが課題である旨が述べられている。

【13】(1)　④　　(2)　②　　(3)　①　　(4)　③　　(5)　③　　(6)　②
(7)　④　　(8)　⑤　　(9)　②　　(10)　①　　(11)　③　　(12)　⑤

(13)　②

○**解説**○　The Oxford English Dictionary(OED)とは学術研究者にとって最も権威ある包括的な英語大辞典であり，語源の説明はもとより，語彙の意味が歴史的にどのように変遷してきたか，また，その変遷の過程で初めてその語彙や意味が出現した代表的な例文を逐一掲載している辞典であることを理解しておこう。　(1)　loanword「借用語，外来語」の意。　(2)　jargon「専門用語，隠語」の意。　(3)　litmus test「試金石」。物事の価値などを見極めたり判断したりするための基準を表す。外来語として認められるためには，長きにわたり頻繁に使用されることでその市民権を得るので，絶対的な判断基準がないという意味である。　(4)　第6段落では，「日本語から英語に外来語化するプロセスには3段階あり，初期段階として，外来語は，確実に理解してもらえるように容易にわかる語句で言い換えられ，次に，限定的な使い方がなされる時期を経て，最終的にはより生産的に使われるようになり完全な市民権を得る」と説明されているので③を選ぶ。　(5)　第7段落，第8段落では，日本語の単語が英語に取り込まれた実例を説明している。第7段落で，「折り紙」という日本の文化が英語の語彙に加えられた経緯を分析しているので①は不適切。「折り紙」という語が初めてOEDに載ったときは，紙の芸術として紹介されているので②は不適切。第8段落では，日本文化を表す語彙が日々の話の中で使われるようになり，単なる物ではなく日本文化を表す概念が生活スタイルと共鳴することで，外来語として英語の中に定着するようになったと言っているので④も不適切。The Australian紙では，origamiという語が，幾重にも重ねられた形状を意味する語として使用されているのであって，折り紙の芸術性を論評しているわけではないので⑤も不適切。

(6)　②　「外来語は，自分たちの言語では表現されない普遍的な事象が存在する時に，それを意味する語として受け入れられる」は，第11段落でスタンフォード大学准教授Indra Levy氏の説明「emojiやKonMari(近藤麻理恵氏が考案した片付け法)という日本語由来の外来語は，他の言語ではまだ名前がないが普遍的な現象を表している日本語的表現なのである」と合致している。　(7)　第12段落から第14段落までKonMariという外来語について説明している。第13段落で動詞とし

ての "KonMari" の使用例「家の中のものをすべて整理し，その中には，もはやトキメキを与えてくれないボーイフレンドも含まれた」とあるので④を選択。　①　第12段落でrapid naturalization of "KonMari" と言っているので不適切。　②　第13段落は，恋愛感情を "KonMari" で表現した一例であるので不適切。　③　"KonMari" の成功の背景にはanti-consumerism「反消費主義」があるので，消費主義社会の発展とは反対である。　⑤　近藤麻理恵氏と翻訳者Cathy Hirano氏とが共著したとは書いていない。　(8)「Levy氏が言うに，その本は『日本の芸術』という点を強調しなければ，おそらくNew York Times紙のベストセラー本にはならなかったであろう」。適切な挿入箇所を探るには，① Levy氏の言であること，② "Japanese art" と関連のあること，③ "the book" の指すものを考慮すること。　(1)の第4段落には書籍の言及がない，(2)の第7段落はLevy氏には関係がない，(3)の第11段落には書籍への言及がない，(4)の第13段落では "Japanese art" への言及がない，(5)の第15段落にはそれぞれ触れているので，⑤を選択。　(9)　第7段落参照。origamiが最初にOEDに載ったのは，1961年のSamuel Randlettによる著作The Art of Origamiからの引用としてであったと書かれている。(10)　第3段落に，emojiは，1997年に日経ウイークリーからの引用としてOEDに載ったことが書かれている。第4段落には，Use of loanwordsの表に該当するvocabulary of daily lifeについての記述があり，さらに第8段落ではemojiがKonMariやumamiと併記されている。

(11)　第4段落参照。1文目に該当する記述がある。　(12)　第10段落参照。デニム用語である「縦落ち」(縦に筋が入るよう白く色落ちすること)のように，専門用語が外来語化した例について述べられている。(13)　英文タイトルを問う問題なので，部分的でなく英文全体にわたって論じられている点をカバーしていることが必要。本文では，ある日本語が外来語として英語に定着している現象について論じているところから，②が適切。

学習指導要領・指導法

中学校学習指導要領

実施問題

【1】中学校学習指導要領(平成29年告示)の「第2章　第9節　外国語」に関して，次の(1)，(2)の問いに答えよ。

(1) 次の文は，「第1　目標」の一部を示そうとしたものである。文中の（　①　），（　②　）にあてはまる語句を，それぞれ以下のア～エから一つ選んで，その記号を書け。

> 外国語によるコミュニケーションにおける（　①　）を働かせ，外国語による聞くこと，読むこと，話すこと，書くことの（　②　）を通して，簡単な情報や考えなどを理解したり表現したり伝え合ったりするコミュニケーションを図る資質・能力を次のとおり育成することを目指す。

① ア　思考力・判断力　　イ　知識・技能　　ウ　感性・情緒
　　エ　見方・考え方
② ア　一連の過程　　　　イ　言語活動　　　ウ　技能の活用
　　エ　統合的な学習

(2) 次の文は，「第2　各言語の目標及び内容等　英語　1　目標　(3) 話すこと［やり取り］」を示そうとしたものである。文中の（　①　）～（　③　）にあてはまる語句を，それぞれ以下のア～エから一つ選んで，その記号を書け。

> ア　関心のある事柄について，簡単な語句や文を用いて即興で（　①　）ことができるようにする。
> イ　日常的な話題について，（　②　）や自分の考え，気持ちなどを整理し，簡単な語句や文を用いて伝えたり，相手からの質問に答えたりすることができるようにする。
> ウ　社会的な話題に関して聞いたり読んだりしたことについて，考えたことや感じたこと，その理由などを，簡単な語句や文を用いて（　③　）ことができるようにする。

① ア　話す　　イ　伝える　　ウ　伝え合う　　エ　述べ合う
② ア　概要　　イ　要点　　　ウ　情報　　　　エ　事実

③　ア　話す　　イ　伝える　　ウ　伝え合う　　エ　述べ合う

‖2024年度‖香川県‖難易度■■■■□□

【2】次の文は，平成29年告示の中学校学習指導要領「外国語」の「第2　各言語の目標及び内容等」における「3指導計画の作成と内容の取扱い」の一部である。次の(　①　)～(　④　)に当てはまる語句を書け。

> (1)　指導計画の作成に当たっては，小学校や高等学校における指導との接続に留意しながら，次の事項に配慮するものとする。
> 　エ　生徒が英語に触れる機会を充実するとともに，授業を(　①　)のコミュニケーションの場面とするため，授業は英語で行うことを基本とする。その際，生徒の(　②　)の程度に応じた英語を用いるようにすること。

> (2)　2の内容に示す事項については，次の事項に配慮するものとする。
> 　エ　文法事項の指導に当たっては，次の事項に留意すること。
> 　　(イ)　文法はコミュニケーションを(　③　)ものであることを踏まえ，コミュニケーションの目的を達成する上での必要性や有用性を実感させた上でその知識を活用させたり，繰り返し使用することで当該文法事項の規則性や構造などについて気付きを促したりするなど，(　④　)と効果的に関連付けて指導すること。

‖2024年度‖岡山市‖難易度■■■■□

【3】次の文章は，平成29年告示の中学校学習指導要領の「第2章　第9節　外国語　第2　3指導計画の作成と内容の取扱い」の抜粋で，指導計画の作成に当たっての留意点等を示している。文章中の(　①　)～(　④　)に当てはまる語句を答えよ。

(1) 指導計画の作成に当たっては，小学校や高等学校における指導との接続に留意しながら，次の事項に配慮するものとする。

ア　（　①　）など内容や時間のまとまりを見通して，その中で育む資質・能力の育成に向けて，生徒の主体的・対話的で深い学びの実現を図るようにすること。その際，具体的な課題等を設定し，生徒が外国語によるコミュニケーションにおける（　②　）・考え方を働かせながら，コミュニケーションの目的や場面，（　③　）などを意識して活動を行い，英語の音声や語彙，表現，文法の知識を五つの領域における実際のコミュニケーションにおいて活用する学習の充実を図ること。

(中略)

エ　生徒が英語に触れる機会を充実するとともに，授業を実際のコミュニケーションの場面とするため，授業は英語で行うことを（　④　）とする。その際，生徒の理解の程度に応じた英語を用いるようにすること。

┃ 2024年度 ┃ 岡山県 ┃ 難易度 ■■■□□

【4】次の(1)，(2)に答えなさい。

(1) 次の文は，中学校学習指導要領「外国語」の「各言語の目標及び内容等」の「英語」の「内容」の一部である。（　①　）～（　⑤　）にあてはまる語句を書きなさい。

(3) 言語活動及び言語の働きに関する事項
① 言語活動に関する事項
(略)
カ　書くこと
(ア)　趣味や（　①　）など，自分に関する基本的な情報を語句や文で書く活動。
(イ)　簡単な手紙や（　②　）の形で自分の近況などを伝える活動。

> (ウ) 日常的な話題について，簡単な語句や文を用いて，
> （　③　）などを説明するまとまりのある文章を書く
> 活動。
> (エ) 社会的な話題に関して聞いたり読んだりしたこと
> から（　④　）した内容に基づき，自分の考えや気持
> ち，その（　⑤　）などを書く活動。

(2)　次の文は，中学校学習指導要領解説外国語編の「外国語科の目標
及び内容」の「英語」の「目標」の一部である。①〜⑤に最も適す
る語句を以下の あ〜と からそれぞれ1つ選び，その記号を書きなさ
い。

> (2)　読むこと
>
> > イ　日常的な話題について，簡単な語句や文で書かれた
> > 短い文章の概要を捉えることができるようにする。
>
> （略）
> 「短い文章」は，同様のトピックについての「長い文章」よ
> りも，一般に負荷がかからないため，理解しやすいと考えら
> れる。したがって，「読むこと」の指導では，後述する「概要
> を捉える」ためにも，「聞くこと」ウと同様，生徒にある程度
> の分量でまとまりのある文章を読ませることになるが，その
> 際，中学生にとって長すぎない分量である必要がある。なお，
> 「短い文章」であっても，あまり情報が（　①　）すぎてしまっ
> たり，十分な（　②　）性がなかったりすると，理解しやすい文
> 章とは言えないため，注意が必要である。
> 　「概要を捉える」とは，例えば物語などのまとまりのある文
> 章を最初から最後まで読み，一語一語や一文一文の意味など
> 特定の部分にのみとらわれたりすることなく，登場人物の行
> 動や（　③　）の変化，全体の（　④　）など，書き手が述べてい
> ることの（　⑤　）な内容を捉えることである。

あ　難解　　　　い　大まか　　　う　構想　　　　え　詰まり

お	一貫	か	汎用	き	心情	く	適当
け	正確	こ	偏り	さ	詳細	し	多様
す	あらすじ	せ	最も重要	そ	読みごたえ	た	要点
ち	文章構成	つ	信頼	て	余剰	と	具体的

┃ 2024年度 ┃ 青森県 ┃ 難易度 ▓▓▓▓░░

【5】次の文章は，「中学校学習指導要領(平成29年3月告示 文部科学省)第2章 各教科 第9節 外国語 第1 目標，および第2 各言語の目標及び内容等」の一部である。(A)～(F)に当てはまる語句の組合せとして正しいものを，それぞれ①～⑤の中から一つ選べ。

(1)

第1 目標

(中略)

(1) 外国語の音声や語彙，表現，文法，言語の働きなどを理解するとともに，これらの知識を，聞くこと，読むこと，話すこと，書くことによる(A)において活用できる(B)を身に付けるようにする。

---

① A 言語活動　　　　　　　　　　B 思考力
② A やり取り　　　　　　　　　　B 表現力
③ A 実際のコミュニケーション　　B 技能
④ A 技能統合型の活動　　　　　　B 能力
⑤ A アクティブラーニング　　　　B 知識

(2)

第2 各言語の目標及び内容等

(中略)

2 内容

(中略)

(3) 言語活動及び言語の働きに関する事項

① 言語活動に関する事項

(中略)

ウ 読むこと

466

（ア）　書かれた内容や文章の構成を考えながら
（　C　）したり，その内容を表現するよう（　D　）
したりする活動。

① C　音読　　D　発話
② C　黙読　　D　音読
③ C　速読　　D　発表
④ C　熟読　　D　対話
⑤ C　要約　　D　作文

(3)

第2　各言語の目標及び内容等
（中略）
3　指導計画の作成と内容の取扱い
(1)　指導計画の作成に当たっては，小学校や高等学校におけ
る指導との接続に留意しながら，次の事項に配慮するもの
とする。
（中略）
オ　言語活動で扱う題材は，生徒の（　E　）に合ったものと
し，国語科や理科，音楽科など，他の教科等で学習した
ことを活用したり，（　F　）で扱う内容と関連付けたりす
るなどの工夫をすること。

① E　興味・関心　　F　学校行事
② E　実態　　　　F　小学校
③ E　発達段階　　F　高等学校
④ E　言語能力　　F　総合的な学習の時間
⑤ E　習熟度　　　F　次の単元

2024年度 ┃ 岐阜県 ┃ 難易度

【6】中学校学習指導要領「第2章　各教科　第9節　外国語」について，次の(1)，(2)に答えよ。

(1) 次は「第2　各言語の目標及び内容等　英語　2内容(3)言語活動及び言語の働きに関する事項　①言語活動に関する事項　ウ　読むこと」の一部である。（　A　）〜（　D　）にあてはまる語を，以下の【選択肢】からそれぞれ一つ選び，記号で記せ。

> (ア)　書かれた内容や文章の構成を考えながら黙読したり，その内容を表現するよう（　A　）したりする活動。
>
> (イ)　日常的な話題について，簡単な表現が用いられている広告やパンフレット，予定表，手紙，電子メール，短い文章などから，自分が必要とする（　B　）を読み取る活動。
>
> (ウ)　簡単な語句や文で書かれた日常的な話題に関する短い説明やエッセイ，物語などを読んで（　C　）を把握する活動。
>
> (エ)　簡単な語句や文で書かれた社会的な話題に関する説明などを読んで，イラストや写真，図表なども参考にしながら，（　D　）を把握する活動。また，その内容に対する賛否や自分の考えを述べる活動。

【選択肢】

ア　概要　　イ　内容　　ウ　要点　　エ　音読　　オ　気持ち
カ　発音　　キ　情報

(2) 次は「第2　各言語の目標及び内容等　英語　1目標(5)書くこと」の一部である。

> イ　日常的な話題について，事実や自分の考え，気持ちなどを整理し，簡単な語句や文を用いて<u>まとまりのある文章を書く</u>ことができるようにする。

1　<u>まとまりのある文章を書く</u>とはどのようなことか，記せ。

2　<u>生徒がまとまりのある文章を書く</u>ために，教師が授業を行う際に工夫したり留意したりすることは何か，具体的に記せ。

【7】次の問1〜問5は，平成29年3月に告示された「中学校学習指導要領 第2章　第9節　外国語」の中に示されているものである。[　　]の中に入るものとして最も適切なものを，以下のそれぞれ①〜④のうちから選びなさい。なお，【　　】は抜粋部分を示している。

問1【第1　目標　(2)】

　コミュニケーションを行う目的や場面，状況などに応じて，日常的な話題や社会的な話題について，外国語で簡単な情報や考えなどを理解したり，[　　]表現したり伝え合ったりすることができる力を養う。
① コミュニケーションにおいて
② これらを活用して
③ 言語活動を通して
④ 外国語の背景にある文化に対する理解を深めて

問2【第2　各言語の目標及び内容等　英語　1　目標　(5)　書くこと ア】

　関心のある事柄について，簡単な語句や文を用いて[　　]書くことができるようにする。
① まとまりのある文章を　　② 読み手を意識して
③ 事実や自分の考えを　　　④ 正確に

問3【第2　各言語の目標及び内容等　英語　2　内容　〔思考力，判断力，表現力等〕　(3)　言語活動及び言語の働きに関する事項　① 言語活動に関する事項　イ　聞くこと　(エ)】

　友達や家族，学校生活などの日常的な話題や社会的な話題に関する会話や説明などを聞いて，概要や要点を把握する活動。また，[　　]活動。
① その内容を把握し，適切に応答する
② 自分か必要とする情報を聞き取る
③ その内容を英語で説明する
④ 話し手の意向を正確に把握する

問4【第2　各言語の目標及び内容等　英語　2　内容　〔思考力，判断力，表現力等〕　(3)　言語活動及び言語の働きに関する事項　① 言語活動に関する事項　エ　話すこと[やり取り](イ)】

日常的な話題について，伝えようとする内容を整理し，自分で作成したメモなどを活用しながら[　　]活動。

① 相手と口頭で伝え合う

② 互いに会話を継続する

③ 口頭で要約する

④ 適切に応答したり自ら質問し返したりする

問5 【第2　各言語の目標及び内容等　英語　3　指導計画の作成と内容の取扱い　(2)　エ　(イ)】

文法は[　　]ものであることを踏まえ，コミュニケーションの目的を達成する上での必要性や有用性を実感させた上でその知識を活用させたり，繰り返し使用することで当該文法事項の規則性や構造などについて気付きを促したりするなど，言語活動と効果的に関連付けて指導すること。

① コミュニケーションを支える

② 実際に活用できるようにする

③ 日本語との違いに留意して指導する

④ 英語の特質を理解させる

‖ 2024年度 ‖ 神奈川県・横浜市・川崎市・相模原市 ‖ 難易度 ■■■■□□

【8】次の文は，「中学校学習指導要領(平成29年3月告示)第2章　第9節　外国語　第1　目標」「中学校学習指導要領(平成29年3月告示)第2章　第9節　外国語　第2　各言語の目標及び内容等　英語　3　指導計画の作成と内容の取扱い(1)ア」の記述である。(　　)に当てはまる語句として適切なものを以下の語群から選び，記号で答えなさい。

第1　目標

外国語によるコミュニケーションにおける(1)を働かせ，外国語による聞くこと，読むこと，話すこと，書くことの(2)を通して，簡単な(3)などを理解したり表現したり伝え合ったりするコミュニケーションを図る(4)を次のとおり育成することを目指す。

「中学校学習指導要領(平成29年3月告示)第2章　第9節　外国語　第1　目標」

第2　各言語の目標及び内容等

英語

3　指導計画の作成と内容の取扱い

(1)　指導計画の作成に当たっては，小学校や高等学校における指導との接続に留意しながら，次の事項に配慮するものとする。

ア　単元など(5)や時間のまとまりを見通して，その中で育む(4)の育成に向けて，生徒の(6)の実現を図るようにすること。その際，具体的な(7)等を設定し，生徒が外国語によるコミュニケーションにおける(1)を働かせながら，コミュニケーションの(8)や(9)，状況などを意識して活動を行い，英語の音声や語彙，表現，文法の知識を(10)の領域における実際のコミュニケーションにおいて活用する学習の充実を図ること。

「中学校学習指導要領(平成29午3月告示)第2章　第9節　外国語　第2　各言語の目標及び内容等　英語　3　指導計画の作成と内容の取扱い(1)ア」

＜語群＞

ア　場面　　　イ　四つ　　　ウ　五つ
エ　技能　　　オ　課題　　　カ　見方・考え方
キ　情報や考え　ク　相手　　　ケ　思いや考え
コ　言語活動　サ　内容　　　シ　主体的に学習に取り組む態度
ス　資質・能力　セ　目的　　　ソ　交流活動
タ　主体的・対話的で深い学び　チ　教科書　　ツ　基礎

2024年度　静岡県・静岡市・浜松市　難易度

【9】次の問いに答えなさい。

(1)　「中学校学習指導要領」(平成29年3月)第2章　第9節　外国語　第2　各言語の目標及び内容等　に即して次の文の(①)～(④)に当てはまる語句を書きなさい。

1 目標

英語学習の特質を踏まえ，以下に示す，聞くこと，読むこと，話すこと[やり取り]，話すこと[発表]，書くことの五つの領域別に設定する目標の実現を目指した指導を通して，第1の(1)及び(2)に示す資質・能力を一体的に育成するとともに，その過程を通して，第1の(3)に示す資質・能力を育成する。

(中略)

(5) 書くこと

ア　関心のある事柄について，簡単な語句や文を用いて（　①　）に書くことができるようにする。

イ　（　②　）的な話題について，（　③　）や自分の考え，気持ちなどを整理し，簡単な語句や文を用いてまとまりのある文章を書くことができるようにする。

ウ　（　④　）的な話題に関して聞いたり読んだりしたことについて，考えたことや感じたこと，その理由などを，簡単な語句や文を用いて書くことができるようにする。

(2) 「中学校学習指導要領解説　外国語編」(平成29年7月)第2章　外国語科の目標及び内容　第2節　英語　2　内容　[思考力，判断力，表現力等]　(3)　に即して次の文の(　①　)～(　④　)に当てはまる語句をA～Hから1つずつ選び，その記号を書きなさい。

また，言語活動を行う際は，単に繰り返し活動を行うのではなく，生徒が言語活動の(　①　)や言語の(　②　)を意識して行うことができるよう，具体的な(　③　)等を設定し，その(　①　)を達成するために，必要な(　④　)を取捨選択して活用できるようにすることが必要である。このような言語活動を通じて，生徒の「学びに向かう力，人間性等」を育成することが重要である。

A　目的　　B　場面　　C　めあて　　D　言語材料
E　目標　　F　使用場面　G　課題　　H　既習表現

(3)　英語の授業で教師が中学校3年の生徒と次のようなやり取りを行った。生徒の発言を参考に，教師が質問した英文を9語以上14語以内で書きなさい。ただし，短縮形(I'mやdon'tなど)は1語と数え，符号(, や?など)は語数に含めません。また英文は2文以上になってもかまいません。

〔生徒と英語でやり取りする授業場面〕

教師：Your graduation ceremony will be held next month.

生徒：Yes. I'm very sad. I still want to be here.

教師：You like our school very much. (　9語以上14語以内　)?

生徒：The school trip is. I really enjoyed it.

┃ 2024年度 ┃ 長野県 ┃ 難易度 ▮▮▮▮▮

【10】平成29年3月告示の中学校学習指導要領　外国語　英語　目標　(3)話すこと[やり取り]には次のように示されています。これについて，以下の1・2に答えなさい。

ア　関心のある事柄について，簡単な語句や文を用いて①即興で伝え合うことができるようにする。

イ　日常的な話題について，②事実や自分の考え，気持ちなどを整理し，簡単な語句や文を用いて伝えたり，相手からの質問に答えたりすることができるようにする。

ウ　社会的な話題に関して聞いたり読んだりしたことについて，考えたことや感じたこと，その理由などを，簡単な語句や文を用いて述べ合うことができるようにする。

1　下線部①の「即興で伝え合う」とはどのようなことですか。日本語で書きなさい。

2　下線部②の「事実や自分の考え，気持ちなどを整理」するとはどのようなことですか。日本語で書きなさい。

┃ 2024年度 ┃ 広島県・広島市 ┃ 難易度 ▮▮▮▮▮

解答・解説

【1】(1) ① エ ② イ (2) ① ウ ② エ ③ エ

○**解説**○ 平成29年3月告示の中学校学習指導要領では，「外国語科」におけるコミュニケーション能力の育成が一層重視されるように改訂されたことに着目する。 (1) 目標については，最低限「外国語科」及び「英語科」の両方の目標を全文暗記し，できれば「読むこと」，「聞くこと」などの各領域の目標もおさえておきたい。 (2) 出題の「話すこと[やり取り]」の領域では，コミュニケーション能力の向上という観点から，「即興で」話すことがキーワードの一つとなっている。なお，「話すこと[やり取り]」は，「話すこと[発表]」とともに改訂時に新設された領域である。学習指導要領解説外国語編を参照しながら，具体的な内容を確認しておくこと。

【2】① 実際 ② 理解 ③ 支える ④ 言語活動

○**解説**○ 記述式問題であるため，2017(平成29)年の中学校学習指導要領改訂の経緯や基本方針を理解した上で，正確な文言を覚えておく必要がある。「第9節 外国語」における「第1 目標」，「第2 各言語の目標及び内容等」，「第3 指導計画の作成と内容の取扱い」は，どこを問われても解答できるくらいにしておきたい。学習指導要領では，2017年の改訂から，これまでより一層英語によるコミュニケーション能力の向上が求められるようになり，授業は可能な限り英語で行うことが望ましいとされた。出題文(1)では，まず教師自身が生徒に対して，コミュニケーションの手段として英語を使う姿勢と態度を示し，生徒が積極的に英語でのコミュニケーション活動に取り組めるよう配慮すべきことが述べられている。また，出題文(2)では，実際に使える英語能力を育成する観点から，文法事項は単に知識として覚えるのではなく，コミュニケーションの中で活用しながら定着させることが望ましいことが述べられている。

【3】　① 　単元　　② 　見方　　③ 　状況　　④ 　基本

○**解説**○ 記述式問題であるため，2017(平成29)年の中学校学習指導要領
改訂の経緯や基本方針を理解した上で，正確な文言を覚えておく必要
がある。中学校学習指導要領「第9節　外国語」における「第1　目標」，
「第2　各言語の目標及び内容等」，「第3　指導計画の作成と内容の取
扱い」は，どこを問われても解答できるくらいにしておきたい。過去
問をさかのぼり，出題されていないところを重点的に押さえておこう。
なお，出題の文言以外にも，「資質・能力の育成」，「主体的・対話的
で深い学び」，「五つの領域」，「授業を実際のコミュニケーションの場
とする」等はキーフレーズであるので，中学校学習指導要領解説外国
語編(2017(平成29)年7月)を参照しながら，具体的に何を示しているか
確認しておきたい。

【4】　(1)　① 　好き嫌い　　② 　電子メール　　③ 　出来事　　④ 　把
握　　⑤ 　理由　　(2) 　① 　え　　② 　て　　③ 　き　　④ 　す
⑤ 　い

○**解説**○ 中学校学習指導要領の「第2章　第9節　外国語」の項には必
ず目を通しておくこと。同じ語句，漢字や表現が多く使われているの
で，自分なりに暗記しておきたい。また，学習指導要領と併せて同解
説外国語編を一通り読み，自分では思いつかない漢字や語句，前後か
ら推測できない表現があれば注意して暗記しておこう。

【5】　(1)　③ 　　(2) 　② 　　(3) 　①

○**解説**○ 記述式ではなく選択式であり，選択肢もさほど紛らわしくない。
正確に暗記しておくことで比較的容易に解くことができると思われ
る。　(1) 　外国語科における，何を理解しているか，何ができるか，
という知識及び技能の習得に関わる目標として掲げたものである。本
目標は，「外国語の音声や語彙，表現，文法，言語の働きなどを理解
する」という知識の面と，その知識を「聞くこと，読むこと，話すこ
と，書くことによる実際のコミュニケーションにおいて活用できる」
という技能の面とで構成されている。　(2) 　黙読は声を出さずに読む
ことであるが，読み手が自分に合った速度で読むことができ，確認の

ため繰り返して読んだり，前に戻って読み返したりすることで柔軟な読み方をすることができる。黙読の指導に当たっては，このような特徴を十分に生かすようにすることが大切である。その際，文章全体を通してどのように物語や論述が進んでいるのか，どのように話をまとめているのか等の文章の構成を意識させることが大切である。一方，音読は，黙読とは異なり，声に出して読むことであり，書かれた内容が表現されるように音読するためには，説明文，意見文，感想文，対話文，物語などの意味内容を正しく理解し，その意味内容にふさわしく音声化する必要がある。　(3)　この配慮事項は，言語活動の題材を取り上げるに当たっては，生徒の発達の段階や知的好奇心を踏まえ，言語活動への積極的参加を促せるものとできるよう工夫する必要があることを述べたものである。自分の考えや気持ちなど，実際に相手に伝えたい内容についてコミュニケーションすることにより，主体的に英語を用いてコミュニケーションを図ろうとする態度を養うことが大切である。そのためにも，題材には，他教科等でこれまで学んできた，あるいは現在学んでいることを積極的に活用するなど，カリキュラム・マネジメントの視点から，教科等間で学びのつながりや広がりがあるものとなるよう工夫が求められる。

【6】(1)　A　エ　　B　キ　　C　ア　　D　ウ　　(2)　1　文と文の順序や相互の関連に注意を払い，全体として一貫性のある文章を書くこと。「導入－本論－結論」や「主題－根拠や具体－主題の言い換えや要約」など，文章構成の特徴を意識しながら，全体として一貫性のある文章を書くことができるようにすること。　　2　「①テーマや話題に関する情報やキーワードを，順序を意識しながら，簡単な語句や文を用いてメモさせる。②その内容について，ペアやグループで質問したり，コメントを述べたりする。③やり取りした内容を参考に推敲する」といったように，言語活動を関連付けて段階的な指導を行うこと。
○**解説**○　(1) 学習指導要領の空所補充問題は，選択式でなくても文言の再生ができるようしておくこと。概要と要点の違いなど混同しやすい語について押さえておこう。　　(2) 中学校学習指導要領の内容については同解説に詳述されている。本問は，中学校学習指導要領外国語編

(平成29年7月)に記載されている解説に基づいて解答すればよい。

1　同解説外国語編では，解答例の他に，「出来事や事実を描写したり，考えや感想を述べたりする場合において，よりよく読み手に伝わるよう意識しながら，自分の言いたいことに最もふさわしい表現形式を工夫して書き表すことができるようにすることも必要である」と記されている。　2　その他，まとまりのある文章を書くことに慣れていない生徒には，文と文のつながりを示す語句を効果的に用いながら書くよう指導する，生徒との直接的な対話によって書きたい内容を引き出しながら，書くことへの抵抗感を減らすこと，などが挙げられている。

【7】問1　②　　問2　④　　問3　③　　問4　①　　問5　①
○**解説**○　問1　外国語の目標の3つの柱のうち，「思考力・判断力・表現力等」の育成に関わる目標として示されたものである。　問2　「正確に書く」とは，文構造や文法事項を正しく用いて正しい語順で文を構成することや，伝えたいことについての情報を正確に捉え，整理したり確認したりしながら書くことを示している。文字言語においては，音声言語以上に正確さが重視されることから，特に「正確に」書くとしていることに留意する必要がある。　問3　聞いた内容を英語で説明できる段階までに至ることが，聞いた内容を本当に理解したこととも考えられる。しかし，この事項はあくまでも「聞くこと」であるため，この活動での「説明すること(＝話すこと)」においては，例えばひな形を与えたり，単語のみでの発話を許容したりするなど，「話すこと」の活動に対するつまずきを極力軽減する配慮が必要である。
問4　本項では，まとまった内容を伝えた上で，それを基に相手とやり取りを展開する活動を示している。情報や考えなどを適切に伝え合うためには，自ら対話の流れをつくることが大切であり，会話を継続・発展させるために必要なことを活用することが重要である。
問5　本項では，コミュニケーションを図る上での文法の位置付けについて言及している。文法構造の概念的な理解だけを追求して一方的な教師の説明に終始するのではなく，コミュニケーションの目的を達成する上でいかに文法が使われているかに着目させて，生徒の気付きを促す指導を考えるべきであるとしている。

【8】1　カ　　2　コ　　3　キ　　4　ス　　5　サ　　6　タ　　7　オ
　　　　8　セ　　9　ア　　10　ウ

○**解説**○　外国語科の目標は，「簡単な情報や考えなどを理解したり表現
したり伝え合ったりするコミュニケーションを図る資質・能力を育成
すること」であることを，しっかり理解しておこう。この資質・能力
を育成するために，(1)「知識及び技能」，(2)「思考力，判断力，表現
力等」，(3)「学びに向かう力，人間性等」の3つの柱が設けられている。
学習指導要領を参照し，これらの3つの柱の内容を精読しておくこと。
また，英語の指導計画の作成と内容の取扱いについては，指導計画に
当たっての留意事項について出題されている。生徒の主体的・対話的
で深い学びの実現を目指した授業改善を進めること，外国語科の特質
に応じて効果的な学習が展開できるように配慮すべき内容が示されて
いる。選択肢の数が多く，やや紛らわしいものも含まれているため，
正確に暗記しておくことが求められる。なお，「外国語科」の目標及
び「英語」の目標を，混同せずに覚えておきたい。

【9】(1)　①　正確　　②　日常　　③　事実　　④　社会
(2)　①　A　　②　F　　③　G　　④　D　　(3)　What is your best
memory of your junior high school days (11 words)

○**解説**○　(1)　外国語科の「英語」における「書くこと」の目標に関する
記述の空欄補充である。まず，アからウにかけて目標が高くなってい
くことに留意しておくとよい。①は空欄直前にある「簡単な語句や文
を用いて」に着目したい。小学校外国語科で学んだことを踏まえて，
正確に書けるようになることを目標としている。次に②は，④と対照
的なものであり，小学校外国語では「日常生活に関する身近で簡単な
事柄」であったものが，イでは「日常的な話題」になり，ウでは「社
会的な話題」と広がっていく。最後に③であるが，空欄直後にある
「自分の考え，気持ちなどを整理し」に着目したい。「話すこと [発表]」
や「話すこと [やり取り]」でも同じ表現が用いられている。　(2)　出
題文は，「(3)　言語活動及び言語の働きに関する事項」の解説部分の
一部である。ここで示されている言語活動は，小学校中・高学年の学
びを踏まえて設定されている。小学校からの学びを中学校の言語活動

において繰り返し活用することによって，生徒が自分の考えなどを表現する際にそれらを活用し，話したり書いたりして表現できるような段階まで確実に定着させることが重要である。目的・場面・状況等が設定された言語活動では，生徒は言語の使用場面に応じて，適切な言語材料を取捨選択することが求められる。　(3)　空欄直後に着目すると，生徒は「修学旅行です。本当に楽しかった」と答えている。解答例にあるように，中学校時代の思い出を尋ねるような発話を書けばよい。

【10】1　話すための原稿を事前に用意してその内容を覚えたり，話せるように練習したりするなどの準備時間を取ることなく，不適切な間を置かずに相手と事実や意見，気持ちなどを伝え合うこと。　　2　聞き手が理解しやすいように伝える項目を精選したり適切な順序に並べ替えたりするなど，話す内容をまとめ，コミュニケーションの見通しを立てること。

○**解説**○　出題の「話すこと [やり取り]」の領域は，平成29(2017)年3月告示の改訂中学校学習指導要領において新設されたものである。本指導要領の内容が具体的に何を示しているかは，同解説外国語編において詳細に解説されている。相互参照しながら精読し，理解を深めておく必要がある。　1　今回の改訂によって，外国語科では，より実際的なコミュニケーションスキルを身に付ける指導が重視されるようになった。従って，コミュニケーションに不可欠な「即興で伝え合う」能力の育成が大切となる。　2　コミュニケーションにおいては，流れを大切にしながら伝え合うことが重要であり，限られた時間で意見や考えをまとめて伝えたり，質問や意見に対応したりしていくことが，円滑なコミュニケーションにつながることに留意する。従って，自分が何かを相手に伝える際は，ポイントをしぼってわかりやすく簡潔・明確にまとめなければならない。

【1】 高等学校学習指導要領に関する次の各問いに答えなさい。

(1) 次の文は,「高等学校学習指導要領(平成30年告示)第2章　各学科に共通する各教科　第8節　外国語　第1款　目標」の全文である。文中の(　)に当てはまる語句を,以下の選択肢からそれぞれ1つずつ選び,記号で答えなさい。

> 　外国語によるコミュニケーションにおける見方・考え方を働かせ,外国語による聞くこと,読むこと,話すこと,書くことの言語活動及びこれらを結び付けた(　①　)的な言語活動を通して,情報や考えなどを的確に理解したり適切に表現したり伝え合ったりするコミュニケーションを図る資質・能力を次のとおり育成することを目指す。
>
> (1) 外国語の音声や語彙,表現,文法,言語の働きなどの理解を深めるとともに,これらの知識を,聞くこと,読むこと,話すこと,書くことによる実際のコミュニケーションにおいて,目的や場面,状況などに応じて適切に活用できる(　②　)を身に付けるようにする。
>
> (2) コミュニケーションを行う目的や場面,状況などに応じて,日常的な話題や社会的な話題について,外国語で情報や考えなどの概要や要点,詳細,話し手や書き手の意図などを的確に理解したり,これらを活用して適切に表現したり伝え合ったりすることができる力を養う。
>
> (3) 外国語の背景にある文化に対する理解を深め,聞き手,読み手,話し手,書き手に配慮しながら,主体的,(　③　)的に外国語を用いてコミュニケーションを図ろうとする態度を養う。

ア　総合　　イ　表現力　　ウ　積極　　エ　自律　　オ　統合
カ　技能　　キ　対話　　ク　判断力

(2) 次の文は,「高等学校学習指導要領(平成30年告示)第2章　各学科に共通する各教科　第8節　外国語　第3款　英語に関する各科目に

わたる指導計画の作成と内容の取扱い」の一部である。文中の
(　)にそれぞれ当てはまる語句の組合せとして正しいものを，以
下の選択肢から1つ選び，記号で答えなさい。ただし，同じ番号に
は，同じ語句が入るものとする。

> 1　指導計画の作成に当たっては，小学校や中学校における指
> 　導との接続に留意しながら，次の事項に配慮するものとす
> 　る。
> 　(1)　単元など内容や時間のまとまりを見通して，その中で
> 　　育む資質・能力の育成に向けて，生徒の(　①　)の実現
> 　　を図るようにすること。〈以下省略〉
> 　〈(2)(3)省略〉
> 　(4)　多様な生徒の実態に応じ，生徒の学習負担に配慮しな
> 　　がら，年次ごと及び科目ごとの(　②　)を適切に定め，
> 　　学校が定める卒業までの指導計画を通して十分に段階を
> 　　踏みながら，外国語科の(　②　)の実現を図るようにす
> 　　ること。
> 　(5)　実際に英語を使用して自分自身の考えを伝え合うなど
> 　　の言語活動を行う際は，既習の語句や文構造，文法事項
> 　　などの学習内容を(　③　)指導し定着を図ること。
> 　(6)　生徒が英語に触れる機会を充実させるとともに，授業
> 　　を実際のコミュニケーションの場面とするため，授業は
> 　　英語で行うことを(　④　)とする。その際，生徒の理解
> 　　の程度に応じた英語を用いるようにすること。
> 　〈(7)(8)(9)(10)省略〉

ア　①　有機的・横断的で深い学び　②　目標　③　簡潔に
　④　必須
イ　①　主体的・対話的で深い学び　②　目的　③　繰り返し
　④　必須
ウ　①　有機的・横断的で深い学び　②　目的　③　簡潔に
　④　基本
エ　①　主体的・対話的で深い学び　②　目標　③　繰り返し

④　基本

(3)　「高等学校学習指導要領(平成30年告示)解説　外国語編　英語編　第1章　総説　第2節　外国語科改訂の趣旨及び要点」からの抜粋ではない文の組合せとして正しいものを以下の選択肢から1つ選び，記号で答えなさい。

---

①　高等学校の授業においては，依然として外国語によるコミュニケーション能力の育成を意識した取組，特に「話すこと」及び「書くこと」などの言語活動が適切に行われていないこと，「やり取り」や「即興性」を意識した言語活動が十分ではないこと，読んだことについて意見を述べ合うなど複数の領域を結び付けた言語活動が適切に行われていないことといった課題がある。

②　中学校における学習を踏まえた上で，五つの領域別の言語活動及び複数の領域を結び付けた統合的な言語活動を通して，五つの領域を総合的に扱うことを一層重視する必履修科目として「論理・表現Ⅰ」を設定し，更なる総合的な英語力の向上を図るための選択科目として「論理・表現Ⅱ」及び「論理・表現Ⅲ」を設定した。

③　小学校及び中学校との接続及び発信能力の育成の強化を図る観点から，「話すこと[やり取り]」の領域を設定するとともに，語，文法事項などの言語材料を言語活動と関連付けて，実際のコミュニケーションにおいて効果的に活用できる技能を身に付けるようにすることとした。

④　指導計画の作成と内容の取扱いについて，文法事項の指導は，実際のコミュニケーションにおいて正確に用語や用法の区別などができるよう，指導の中心とすることを明記した。

⑤　「話すこと[やり取り]」,「話すこと[発表]」及び「書くこと」の指導に当たっては，目的や場面，状況などに応じたやり取りや発表，文章などの具体例を示した上で，生徒がそれらを参考にしながら自分で表現できるよう留意するこ

> とを明記した。

ア　①と③　　イ　①と④　　ウ　①と⑤　　エ　②と③
オ　②と④　　カ　②と⑤

┃ 2024年度 ┃ 宮崎県 ┃ 難易度 ■■■□□

【2】次の文は，「中学校学習指導要領(平成29年告示)」及び「高等学校学習指導要領(平成30年告示)」で示されている外国語科の目標の一部である。話すこと[発表]の活動を行う際，生徒が聞き手に配慮しながらコミュニケーションをとることができるようにするために，指導する上で大切だと思うことを，5行程度の英文で書きなさい。

> 「中学校学習指導要領(平成29年告示)」第9節　外国語　第1　目標
> (3)　外国語の背景にある文化に対する理解を深め，聞き手，読み手，話し手，書き手に配慮しながら，主体的に外国語を用いてコミュニケーションを図ろうとする態度を養う。

> 「高等学校学習指導要領(平成30年告示)」第8節　外国語　第1款　目標
> (3)　外国語の背景にある文化に対する理解を深め，聞き手，読み手，話し手，書き手に配慮しながら，主体的，自律的に外国語を用いてコミュニケーションを図ろうとする態度を養う。

┃ 2024年度 ┃ 新潟県・新潟市 ┃ 難易度 ■■■□□

【3】次の文章は，平成30年告示の高等学校学習指導要領の「第2章　第8節　外国語　第2款　第4　論理・表現Ⅰ　2内容　(3)①言語活動に関する事項」の抜粋である。文章中の(　①　)～(　④　)に当てはまる語句を答えよ。

> イ　話すこと[発表]
> (ア)　関心のある事柄や学校生活などの日常的な話題について，使用する語句や文，発話例が十分に示されたり，

（　①　）のための多くの時間が確保されたりする状況で，情報や考え，気持ちなどを適切な理由や（　②　）とともに話して伝える活動。また，発表した内容について，質疑応答をしたり，意見や感想を伝え合ったりする活動。

（イ）　日常的な話題や社会的な話題に関して聞いたり読んだりした内容について，使用する語句や文，発話例が十分に示されたり，（　①　）のための多くの時間が確保されたりする状況で，（　③　）的な手順を踏みながら，意見や（　④　）などを適切な理由や（　②　）とともに伝える短いスピーチやプレゼンテーションをする活動。また，発表した内容について，質疑応答をしたり，意見や感想を伝え合ったりする活動。

▮ 2024年度 ▮ 岡山県 ▮ 難易度 ▮▮▮▮▮▯

【4】次の(1)，(2)に答えなさい。

(1)　次の文は，高等学校学習指導要領「外国語」の「各科目」の「英語コミュニケーションⅢ」の「内容」の一部である。（　①　）～（　⑤　）にあてはまる語句を書きなさい。

> (3)　言語活動及び言語の働きに関する事項
> 　①　言語活動に関する事項
> 　　(略)
> 　イ　聞くこと
> 　　(ア)　日常的な話題について，インタビューやニュースなどから（　①　）な情報を聞き取り，話の（　②　）や話し手の意図を（　③　）する活動。また，聞き取った内容について，（　④　）をしたり，意見や感想を伝え合ったりする活動。
> 　　(イ)　社会的な話題について，複数のニュースや（　⑤　）などから話の（　②　）に注意しながら（　①　）な情報を聞き取り，概要や要点，詳細を（　③　）する活

484

動。また，聞き取った内容について，（　④　）をし
たり，意見や感想を伝え合ったりする活動。

(2)　次の文は，高等学校学習指導要領解説外国語編の「総説」の「外
　　国語科の目標」の一部である。（　①　）～（　⑤　）に最も適する語
　　句を以下の あ～と からそれぞれ1つ選び，その記号を書きなさい。

> (2)　コミュニケーションを行う目的や場面，状況などに
> 　応じて，日常的な話題や社会的な話題について，外国
> 　語で情報や考えなどの概要や要点，詳細，話し手や書
> 　き手の意図などを的確に理解したり，これらを活用し
> 　て適切に表現したり伝え合ったりすることができる力
> 　を養う。

(略)

　本目標での「コミュニケーションを行う目的や場面，状況
など」とは，コミュニケーションを行うことによって達成し
ようとする際の目的や，話し手や聞き手を含む発話の場面，
コミュニケーションを行う（　①　）との関係性やコミュニケー
ションを行う際の環境などを指す。母語でコミュニケーショ
ンを行うときと同様に外国語で行う場合にも，読んだ情報を
他の情報と比べるなど，目的に応じて情報を（　②　）したり，
（　①　）に応じた話の内容，構成，表現などを選択するともに，
伝える内容を自らが的確に理解し，自分の言葉として表現し
たりできるようにする必要がある。このように，「目的や場面，
状況など」に応じた言語の（　③　）を考えることで，「思考力，
判断力，表現力等」が育成される。

　本目標での「日常的な話題」とは，生徒の日々の生活に関
わる話題のことであり，「社会的な話題」とは，社会的な話題
や社会で起こっている出来事に関わることである。取り扱う
話題の種類については中学校と大きな違いはないが，高等学
校では，より深く多面的・（　④　）な考察が求められているこ

とから，英語に関しても使用すべき語彙や表現などが（　⑤　）することが必要であることに留意しなければならない。中学校で扱った話題と同じ話題を扱う場合でも，生徒の発達の段階に応じて，生徒がその話題を自分のこととして捉え，主体的に考えることができるような，具体的で適切な設定が望まれる。

あ	配慮	い	多角的	う	認識	え	高度化
お	精査	か	探究	き	協働	く	尊重
け	ペア・ワーク	こ	一時的	さ	多様化	し	運用
す	相手	せ	手段	そ	社会生活	た	客観的
ち	操作	つ	学校生活	て	部分的	と	場合

┃2024年度┃青森県┃難易度 ■■■□□

【5】次の文は，高等学校学習指導要領(平成30年3月告示)の「第2章　各学科に共通する各教科　第8節　外国語　第2款　各科目　第4　論理・表現Ⅰ　1　目標」の一部である。文中の（　1　），（　2　）に当てはまる言葉を書け。ただし，同じ番号には同じ言葉が当てはまる。

(3)　書くこと
　ア　日常的な話題について，使用する語句や文，事前の準備などにおいて，多くの支援を活用すれば，基本的な語句や文を用いて，情報や考え，気持ちなどを（　1　）を工夫して文章を書いて伝えることができるようにする。
　イ　日常的な話題や社会的な話題について，使用する語句や文，事前の準備などにおいて，多くの支援を活用すれば，（　2　）したことを活用しながら，基本的な語句や文を用いて，意見や主張などを（　1　）を工夫して文章を書いて伝えることができるようにする。

┃2024年度┃愛媛県┃難易度 ■■■■□

486

【6】 次の問1～問5は，平成30年3月に告示された「高等学校学習指導要領　第2章　第8節　外国語」の中に示されているものである。[　　]の中に入るものとして最も適切なものを，以下のそれぞれ①～④のうちから選びなさい。なお，【　　】は抜粋部分を示している。

問1 【第1款　目標(1)】

　　外国語の音声や語彙，表現，文法，言語の働きなどの理解を深めるとともに，これらの知識を，聞くこと，読むこと，話すこと，書くことによる実際のコミュニケーションにおいて，目的や場面，状況などに応じて[　　]を身に付けるようにする。

① コミュニケーションを図る資質・能力

② 適切に活用できる技能

③ コミュニケーションを図ろうとする態度

④ 適切に表現したり伝え合ったりすることができる力

問2 【第2款　各科目　第1　英語コミュニケーションⅠ　3　内容の取扱い(2)】

　　中学校における学習との接続のため，既習の語句や文構造，文法事項などの学習内容を繰り返したり，特にこの科目の学習の初期の段階においては[　　]指導し，定着を図るよう配慮するものとする。

① 国語科や地理歴史科，理科など，他の教科等で学習した内容と関連付けたりして

② 五つの領域別の言語活動および複数の領域を結び付けたりして

② 情報や考えなどを表現したり伝え合ったりして

④ 中学校における基礎的な学習内容を整理したりして

問3 【第2款　各科目　第3　英語コミュニケーションⅢ　2　　内容〔知識及び技能〕　(1)】

　　「英語コミュニケーションⅠ」の2の(1)と同様に取り扱うものとする。ただし，指導する語については，「英語コミュニケーションⅡ」の2の(1)で示す語に[　　]を加えた語とする。

① 400～600語程度の新語　　② 600～850語程度の新語

③ 700～950語程度の新語　　④ 500～750語程度の新語

問4 【第2款　各科目　第4　論理・表現Ⅰ　1　目標(3)書くこと　イ】

　　日常的な話題や社会的な話題について，使用する語句や文，事前

の準備などにおいて，[　　]，聞いたり読んだりしたことを活用しながら，基本的な語句や文を用いて，意見や主張などを論理の構成や展開を工夫して文章を書いて伝えることができるようにする。

① 多くの支援を活用すれば

② 一定の支援を活用すれば

③ 支援をほとんど活用しなくても

④ 辞書を効果的に活用すれば

問5 【第3款　英語に関する各科目にわたる指導計画の作成と内容の取扱い　2(8)】

　　生徒が身に付けるべき資質・能力や生徒の実態，教材の内容などに応じて，視聴覚教材やコンピュータ，情報通信ネットワーク，教育機器などを有効活用し，生徒の興味・関心をより高めるとともに，英語による情報の発信に慣れさせるために，キーボードを使って英文を入力するなどの活動を効果的に取り入れることにより，[　　]を図るようにすること。

① 指導の効率化や言語活動の更なる充実

② 外国語科の目標の実現

③ 実際のコミュニケーションにおいて活用する学習の充実

④ 英語を用いて課題解決

┃ 2024年度 ┃ 神奈川県・横浜市・川崎市・相模原市 ┃ 難易度 ┃

【7】高等学校学習指導要領(平成30年3月)第2章第8節「外国語」について，次の問1〜問4に答えなさい。

問1　第2款の第1「英語コミュニケーションⅠ」における次の記述を読み，高等学校学習指導要領解説(平成30年7月)外国語編で示されている，「話すこと[やり取り]」における生徒への支援として，最も適当なものをア〜オの中から選びなさい。

第2款　各科目

　第1　英語コミュニケーションⅠ

　　1　目標

　　　(3) 話すこと[やり取り]

　　　　ア　日常的な話題について，使用する語句や文，対

488

> 話の展開などにおいて，多くの支援を活用すれば，基本的な語句や文を用いて，情報や考え，気持ちなどを話して伝え合うやり取りを続けることができるようにする。

ア　語彙や表現の正確な使用方法を身に付けることができるよう，使用する語彙や表現を限定すること。

イ　会話の展開の仕方や，会話がうまく続けられないときの対処法は安易に提示せずに，生徒自身で考えさせるようにすること。

ウ　ティーム・ティーチングによる教師同士のやり取りや，モデルとなる生徒同士のやり取りを見せたり，ペアを何度も変えてやり取りを続けることで，やり取りに慣れさせたりすること。

エ　中学校において学習した，会話を継続させるために必要な表現などは繰り返し活用することがないよう，常に新しい表現を指導すること。

オ　英語が苦手な生徒に失敗させることのないよう，話す内容を覚えたりそのまま読んだりするための原稿を用意させるようにすること。

問2　第2款の第1「英語コミュニケーションⅠ」における次の記述を読み，[　1　]〜[　3　]の空欄に入る語句として，正しい組合せをア〜オの中から選びなさい。

> 第2款　各科目
> 第1　英語コミュニケーションⅠ
> 　2　内容
> 　　〔思考力，判断力，表現力等〕
> 　　(2)　情報を整理しながら考えなどを形成し，英語で表現したり，伝え合ったりすることに関する事項
> 　　　具体的な課題等を設定し，コミュニケーションを行う[　1　]などに応じて，情報を整理しながら考えなどを形成し，これらを論理的に適切な英語で表現することを通して，次の事項を身に付けることがで

きるよう指導する。

ア　日常的な話題や社会的な話題について，英語を聞いたり読んだりして，情報や考えなどの[　2　]，詳細，[　3　]の意図などを的確に捉えたり，自分自身の考えをまとめたりすること。

イ　日常的な話題や社会的な話題について，英語を聞いたり読んだりして得られた情報や考えなどを活用しながら，話したり書いたりして情報や自分自身の考えなどを適切に表現すること。

ウ　日常的な話題や社会的な話題について，伝える内容を整理し，英語で話したり書いたりして，要点や意図などを明確にしながら，情報や自分自身の考えなどを伝え合うこと。

① 資質や能力　　② 目的や場面，状況　　③ 言語や文化
④ 概要や要点　　⑤ 話し手や書き手　　⑥ 書き手や読み手

	1	2	3
ア	①	③	⑤
イ	①	④	⑥
ウ	②	③	⑤
エ	②	④	⑤
オ	②	④	⑥

問3　第2款の第1「英語コミュニケーションⅠ」における次の記述を読み，[　1　]〜[　3　]の空欄に入る語として，正しい組合せをア〜オの中から選びなさい。

第2款　各科目
第1　英語コミュニケーションⅠ
3　内容の取扱い
(1)　中学校におけるコミュニケーションを図る[　1　]を育成するための[　2　]な指導を踏まえ，五つの領域別の言語活動及び複数の領域を結び付けた[　3　]な言語活動を通して，[　2　]に指導するものとする。

① 資質・能力　　② 態度　　③ 基礎的　　④ 総合的

⑤ 統合的　　　　⑥ 対話的

	1	2	3
ア	①	④	⑤
イ	①	⑤	④
ウ	①	⑥	④
エ	②	④	⑤
オ	②	⑥	③

問4　次の1〜5の記述のうち，第3款の1「指導計画の作成に当たっての配慮事項」について，高等学校学習指導要領解説(平成30年7月)外国語編で示されている内容として，適当なものの組合せをア〜オの中から選びなさい。

1　主体的・対話的で深い学びについては，1単位時間の授業の中で毎回実現を図るようにすること。

2　自分自身の考えを伝え合うなどの言語活動を行う際には，新出の語句や文構造，文法事項などの言語材料に重点的に焦点を当てて，短時間で集中して指導すること。

3　生徒が英語に対する苦手意識から抜け出すためには，教師が英語で発話する際にはできるだけ日本語の意味を付け加える必要があること。

4　言語活動の題材には，他教科等で学んだ内容を積極的に活用するなど，カリキュラム・マネジメントの視点から，教科等間で学びのつながりや広がりがあるものとなるよう工夫すること。

5　指導計画の作成や授業の実施に当たり，生徒が生きた外国語に触れる機会を一層充実させるため，積極的にネイティブ・スピーカーや英語が堪能な地域人材などの協力を得る等，指導体制の充実を図ること。

ア　1，2　　イ　1，4　　ウ　3，4　　エ　3，5　　オ　4，5

2024年度 ▎北海道・札幌市 ▎難易度 ■■■■■

【8】平成30年3月告示の高等学校学習指導要領　外国語　論理・表現Ⅰ　目標　(1)　話すこと[やり取り]には次のように示されています。これについて，以下の1・2に答えなさい。

> ア　日常的な話題について，使用する語句や文，対話の展開などにおいて，多くの支援を活用すれば，基本的な語句や文を用いて，情報や考え，気持ちなどを話して伝え合ったり，①<u>やり取りを通して必要な情報を得</u>たりすることができるようにする。
>
> イ　日常的な話題や社会的な話題について，使用する語句や文，対話の展開などにおいて，多くの支援を活用すれば，ディベートやディスカッションなどの活動を通して，聞いたり読んだりしたことを活用しながら，基本的な語句や文を用いて，意見や主張などを②<u>論理の構成や展開を工夫して話して伝え合</u>うことができるようにする。

1　下線部①の「やり取りを通して必要な情報を得」るとはどのようなことですか。日本語で書きなさい。

2　下線部②の「論理の構成や展開を工夫して話して伝え合う」とはどのようなことですか。日本語で書きなさい。

▌2024年度 ▌広島県・広島市 ▌難易度 ■■■■■

【9】「高等学校学習指導要領(平成30年3月告示)第2章　各学科に共通する各教科　第8節　外国語」について，次の(1)，(2)の問いに答えなさい。

(1)　次の文は，「第1款　目標」の英訳版の一部抜粋である。文中の　　A　　～　　D　　に当てはまることばを，以下のア～エからそれぞれ1つずつ選び，記号で書きなさい。

> To develop students'　A　competencies, such as accurately understanding and appropriately expressing and exchanging information, thoughts, etc., as outlined below through the language activities of listening, reading, speaking and writing in a foreign language and　B　language activities which combine these skills.
>
> (1)　To deepen students' understanding of foreign language sounds, vocabulary, expressions, grammar and functions, and acquire the

skill of using this knowledge in actual communication through listening, reading, speaking and writing appropriately in accordance with the [①], [②] and [③].

(2) To foster the ability to accurately understand the overview, main points, details of information and ideas, and a speaker's or writer's intention, etc., about everyday and [C] topics in the foreign language, and appropriately express and exchange information and ideas about these topics in accordance with the [①], [②] and [③] in which communication takes place.

(3) To cultivate a willingness to communicate proactively and [D], deepening understanding of the culture behind the foreign language and considering the listener, reader, speaker or writer.

A　ア　advanced　　　イ　communicative　　ウ　grammatical
　　エ　international
B　ア　interacted　　　イ　integrated　　　ウ　interpreted
　　エ　interrupted
C　ア　abstract　　　　イ　public　　　　　ウ　social
　　エ　technical
D　ア　autonomously　　イ　courageously　　ウ　inquisitively
　　エ　reluctantly

(2) 文中の下線部の空所①～③には，それぞれ同じことばが入る。①～③に入ることばの組み合わせとして最も適当なものを次のア～エの中から1つ選び，記号で書きなさい。

	①	②	③
ア	goals	procedures	situations
イ	goals	scenes	regulations
ウ	purposes	procedures	regulations
エ	purposes	scenes	situations

【10】 次に示すものは，高等学校学習指導要領(平成30年3月告示)第2章第8節外国語第1款目標の一部である。これを読んで，以下の問い(1)，(2)に答えなさい。

外国語によるコミュニケーションにおける見方・考え方を働かせ，外国語による聞くこと，読むこと，話すこと，書くことの言語活動及びこれらを結び付けた統合的な言語活動を通して，情報や考えなどを的確に理解したり適切に表現したり伝え合ったりするコミュニケーションを図る資質・能力を次のとおり育成することを目指す。

(1) 外国語の音声や語彙，表現，文法，言語の働きなどの理解を深めるとともに，これらの[①]を，聞くこと，読むこと，話すこと，書くことによる実際のコミュニケーションにおいて，目的や場面，状況などに応じて適切に活用できる[②]を身に付けるようにする。

(2) コミュニケーションを行う目的や場面，状況などに応じて，[③]な話題や[④]な話題について，外国語で情報や考えなどの概要や要点，詳細，話し手や書き手の意図などを的確に理解したり，これらを活用して適切に表現したり伝え合ったりすることができる力を養う。

(3) 外国語の背景にある[⑤]に対する理解を深め，聞き手，読み手，話し手，書き手に配慮しながら，主体的，[⑥]に外国語を用いてコミュニケーションを図ろうとする態度を養う。

---

(1) [①]～[⑥]にそれぞれ当てはまる語句を答えよ。

(2) 次の表は，英語コミュニケーションⅠのある授業の学習指導案における生徒の活動の流れを示したものである。あなたが教師として統合的な言語活動を取り入れた授業を計画した場合，(ア)～(ウ)にはどのような活動が考えられるか。それぞれ簡潔に英語で述べよ。

【Teaching Plan】
Aim: Students understand what they listen to about other students' plans on summer vacation.

Time (50 min.)	Activities	Point of Evaluation
5 min.	Students listen to the model conversation about plans on summer vacation between the Japanese teacher and the ALT.	
☐ min.	(ア)	
☐ min.	(イ)	
☐ min.	(ウ)	
10 min.	Students confirm what they listened to about other students' plans on summer vacation through interaction with the teacher.	Students understand what they listened to.

‖ 2024年度 ‖ 群馬県 ‖ 難易度 ▮▮▮▮▮▮

解答・解説

【1】(1) ① オ ② カ ③ エ (2) エ (3) オ

○**解説**○ (1) 高等学校学習指導要領本文の空所補充問題である。選択肢には紛らわしい語句も含まれているため，各項目が具体的にどのようなことを示しているか，同解説外国語編・英語編で確認し重要語句を整理しておくこと。 (2) ～的という語句，目標と目的，基本と必須，総合と統合など紛らわしい語句には注意し，また公正，多様，明確など空所補充の対象になりそうな語句を意識してみるとよい。5つの領域である「聞くこと，読むこと，話すこと[やり取り]，話すこと[発表]，書くこと」において，自分ならどのような教授法を取り入れて授業を作るかという問題意識を持ちながら，学習指導要領及び同解説を読み込んでおこう。 (3) 紛らわしく書き換えられているので要注意。②では「論理・表現Ⅰ」，「論理・表現Ⅱ」，「論理・表現Ⅲ」がそれぞれ「英語コミュニケーションⅠ」，「英語コミュニケーションⅡ」，「英語コミュニケーションⅢ」であれば正しい。④について正しくは「文法事項の指導については，用語や用法の区別などが中心とならないよう，実際のコミュニケーションにおいて活用できるようにするための効果

的な指導を工夫することを明記した」である。出題の高等学校学習指導要領解説外国語編・英語編における「外国語科改訂の趣旨及び要点」の項には，これからの外国語教育を実施していく上での目標，科目構成，指導内容の方向性，各科目の目指す目標，学習指導上の留意点などが記載されている。その趣旨を理解した上で，自分の教育方針や教授法とのすり合わせを行いながら，要点を整理していくとよい。

【2】It is important for students to make themselves understood by the audience. They should use simple words or phrases when they make a draft. When they are giving a speech or a presentation, they should speak clearly, using eye contact and gestures. It is also effective for them to ask the audience for questions and seek feedback after speaking. (59 words)

○**解説**○ ここ数年来，英語教育においては，「話すこと[やり取り]」や「話すこと[発表]」に比重が移ってきている。よって，普段から生徒がコミュニケーションスキルを身に着けるための授業作りについて考えておくと，スムーズに自分の意見をまとめやすくなる。英文を書く際には，論理的に内容を整理して書いているか，文法的な間違いがないか，という点にも注意すべきである。難しく考える必要はなく，自分が生徒に対して具体的にどのような作業をさせたいかに思いを巡らせ，内容のアウトラインをまとめてから英文に仕上げることになる。解答例では，指導上の大切なポイントとして聴衆に理解してもらうことを挙げ，その具体的な方法として，簡単な表現を使うこと，はっきりと発音すること，非言語的な要素にも注意を払わせること，質疑応答やフィードバックを取り入れさせることの4つを挙げている。make oneself understood「自分の言うことを理解してもらう」。

【3】① 準備 ② 根拠 ③ 段階 ④ 主張
○**解説**○ 昨年度まで，学習指導要領に関する問題は，中学校は記述式，高等学校は選択式で出題されていた。しかし，本問のように，今年度は高等学校も記述式となり，やや難易度が上がった。今後もこの出題形式が踏襲されると思われる。したがって，科目段階別の目標や言語活動については，空所に文言が再生できるようにしておくことが求め

られる。高等学校学習指導要領解説外国語編・英語編(2018(平成30)年
7月)には，巻末資料として，科目段階別(英語コミュニケーションⅠ・
Ⅱ・Ⅲおよび論理・表現Ⅰ・Ⅱ・Ⅲ)の目標や言語活動がわかりやすく
一覧表にまとめられているので，ぜひ活用されたい。なお，2018(平成
30)年3月告示の高等学校学習指導要領から，外国語科の従来の4領域の
ひとつ「話すこと」の領域が，「話すこと[発表]」と「話すこと[やり
取り]」の2つの領域に分けられた。出題の「話すこと[発表]」ではス
ピーチやプレゼンテーション能力，「話すこと[やり取り]」ではディス
カッションやディベート能力の育成を目標としている。

【4】(1)　①　必要　　②　展開　　③　把握　　④　質疑応答
　⑤　講演　　(2)　①　す　　②　お　　③　し　　④　い　　⑤　え
○**解説**○　高等学校学習指導要領の「第2章　第8節　外国語」の項には必
ず目を通しておくこと。同じ語句，漢字や表現が多く使われているの
で，自分なりに暗記しておきたい。また，高等学校学習指導要領と併
せて同解説外国語編・英語編を一通り読み，自分では思いつかない漢
字や語句，前後から推測できない表現があれば注意して暗記しておこ
う。また，学習指導要領等をプレゼンテーション，ディベート，論理
的表現と英語的思考法の指導方法と関連させて読むことで，問題意識
を持ちながら理解を深めることができる。

【5】1　論理の構成や展開　　2　聞いたり読んだり
○**解説**○　選択肢ではなく記述式であり，確実に暗記しておくことが求め
られる。　1「論理の構成や展開を工夫して文章を書いて伝える」と
は，情報や自分の考えや気持ちなどを論理的に伝えるために，モデル
などを活用して論理の構成や展開の仕方を学んだ上で，論理に矛盾や
飛躍がないか，理由や根拠がより適切なものとなっているかなどにつ
いて留意しながら，文章を書いて伝えることである。　2「聞いたり
読んだりしたこと」とは，教師や他の生徒による発話，様々な映像や
音声の教材，教科書などから得た情報や考えなどのことである。この
中には，外国語科だけではなく，他教科の授業などを通した学習にお
いて聞いたり読んだりしたことも含まれる。

【6】問1 ② 問2 ④ 問3 ③ 問4 ① 問5 ①

○**解説**○ 学習指導要領に関しては，毎年，同様の形式で出題されている。第1款の目標，第2款の各科目の目標，内容，内容の取扱いについては出題の頻度が高い。それらについては，選択肢がなくても空所補充問題が再生できるくらいまで読み込んでおきたい。かなりの分量になるので，「外国語の目標」の科目段階別一覧表や「外国語の言語活動の例」の科目別一覧表をうまく活用したい。　問1　外国語科における「何を理解しているか，何ができるか」という「知識及び技能」の習得に関わる目標として掲げられたものである。　問2　中学校の学習から本科目における学習への円滑な移行のため，中学校で学習した語句や文構造，文法事項などを繰り返し活用するような言語活動を扱ったり，初期の学習段階で，中学校の基礎的な学習内容を整理したりするなどの工夫をすることが大切であることが示されている。

問3　「700語」とは，「英語コミュニケーションⅢ」で新たに指導する語数の下限を示し，「950語」とは扱う一定の目安となる語数を示しており，950語程度を上限とするという趣旨ではないことに留意する。問4　この目標では，使用する語句や文，事前の準備などについて支援することを示しており，使用する語句や文における支援とは，まとまった文章を書く際に有用な語句や文を提示するなどの配慮のことである。　問5　例えば，生徒がコンピュータを活用して英文を書くことにより，添削などの指導面において効率化が図られるなど，教育機器を効果的に活用し，言語活動をより充実させることが求められる。また，今後生徒が社会生活を送る上で，コンピュータ上でやり取りをする機会が更に増えることなどを考慮し，教育機器の効果的な活用を工夫していくことが重要である。

【7】問1 ウ 問2 エ 問3 ア 問4 オ

○**解説**○ 問1　アは「使用する語彙や表現を限定」，イは「対処法は安易に提示せずに，生徒自身で考えさせるようにすること」，エは「繰り返し活用することがないよう，常に新しい表現を指導すること」，オは「話す内容を覚えたりそのまま読んだりするための原稿を用意させるようにすること」が不適切である。　問2　1　「思考力，判断力，表

現力等」を育むためには，目的や場面，状況のあるコミュニケーションが不可欠である。　2　直後にある「詳細」に着目すれば，より大きな理解である「概要や要点」であることがわかる。　3　直後にある「…の意図」に着目すれば，「話し手や書き手」であることがわかるだろう。　問3　1　直前にある「コミュニケーションを図る」に着目すれば，「資質・能力」であることがわかる。　2　「コミュニケーションを図る資質・能力」を育むための指導方法であり，言語活動を通して指導するということを踏まえると，「総合的」であることがわかる。　3　直後の「…な言語活動」に着目したい。「統合的」という用語は「統合的な言語活動」という形で用いられており，2の「総合的」と混同しないようにしたい。　問4　1は「1単位時間の授業の中で毎回実現を図るようにすること」，2は「新出の語句や文構造，文法事項などの言語材料に重点的に焦点を当てて，短時間で集中して指導すること」，3は「できるだけ日本語の意味を付け加える必要があること」が不適切である。

【8】1　相手から自分に必要な情報を引き出すために質問をしたり，質問に対する応答を受けて更に質問したりするなどして，必要な情報の交換ができること。　2　論理的に伝え合うために，モデルなどを通して論理の構成や展開の仕方を学んだ上で，自分の意見における論理に矛盾や飛躍がないか，理由や根拠がより適切なものとなっているかなどについて留意しながら伝え合うこと。

○**解説**○　出題の「話すこと [やり取り]」の領域は，平成30(2018)年3月告示の高等学校学習指導要領で新設されたものである。本指導要領の内容が具体的に何を示しているかは，同解説外国語編・英語編において詳述されている。これらを相互参照しながら精読し，理解を深めておく必要がある。　1　「論理・表現Ⅰ」では目標イにあるように，ディベートやディスカッションなどの活動を行うことになっており，それらの活動を想像しながら考えるとよいだろう。やり取りの内容を深めていくためには，一方的に情報を伝えるだけでなく，双方向的に質問を行ったり，質問に対する解答を踏まえてさらに質問をしたりすることが求められている。　2　ここでもディベートやディスカッション

などの活動を想像しながら，例えば，ディベートを論理的に展開させるために必要な指導をイメージすると思い浮かびやすくなるかもしれない。やり取りのモデルを提示したり，やり取りを行う際には意見が論理的であるかを確認させたりする必要があるだろう。

【9】(1) A イ　　B イ　　C ウ　　D ア　　(2) エ
○**解説**○ 外国語科の目標に関する問題である。高等学校学習指導要領「外国語科」と「英語科」の英訳版については，文部科学省のウェブサイトに公開されている。本問では，代表的なキーワードやキーフレーズが出題されているので，どのように訳されているか日本語版と対照しながら確認しておきたい。なお，本問では全て選択肢が与えられているため，英訳版を見たことがなくても，日本語版の学習指導要領を踏まえれば解答できるだろう。　(1)　空欄Aは空欄直後のcompetenciesに着目すればよく，「コミュニケーションを図る資質・能力」と対応するイが正解。次に，空欄Bは空欄直後のlanguage activities which combine these skillsに着目すればよく，「これらを結び付けた統合的な言語活動」と対応するイが正解。さらに，空欄Cは空欄前後にあるeveryday andとtopicsに着目すればよく，「日常的な話題や社会的な話題」に対応するウが正解。最後に，空欄Dは空欄直前にあるa willingness to communicate proactively andに着目すればよく，「主体的，自律的に外国語を用いてコミュニケーションを図ろうとする態度」に対応するアが正解。　(2)「目的や場面，状況など」に対応する英語表現を考えればよい。目的については，goalsとpurposesの違いが分かりにくいかもしれないが，場面と状況に対応する英語がわかれば正答を選ぶことができる。

【10】(1)　①　知識　　②　技能　　③　日常的　　④　社会的
⑤　文化　　⑥　自律的　　(2)　ア　Students share their plans with other students about their summer vacation.　　イ　Students take notes on what they shared about their plans on their summer vacation.　　ウ　In pairs or groups, students verbally summarize what they heard based on their notes.
○**解説**○ (1)　頻出の問題である。目標の(1)は，外国語科における「何

を理解しているか，何ができるか」という「知識及び技能」の習得に
関わる目標，(2)は，外国語科における「理解していること・できるこ
とをどう使うか」という「思考力，判断力，表現力等」の育成に関わ
る目標，(3)は，外国語科における「どのように社会や世界と関わり，
よりよい人生を送るか」という「学びに向かう力，人間性等」の涵養
に関わる目標として掲げられたものである。科目別の目標や言語活動
例などからもよく出題されるので，空所補充形式に対応できるように
準備が必要。　(2)　高等学校学習指導要領では，英語コミュニケーシ
ョンⅠ「聞くこと」の言語活動の一つとして，「日常的な話題につい
て，話される速さが調整されたり，基本的な語句や文での言い換えを
十分に聞いたりしながら，対話や放送などから必要な情報を聞き取り，
話し手の意図を把握する活動。また，聞き取った内容を話したり書い
たりして伝え合う活動」が示されている。解答例では聞く→メモを取
る→話すという流れで組み立てられている。夏休みについて英作文を
課し，休み明けには，友達の作文を読む→(感想を)書くなど，様々な
場面をとらえて統合的な活動を盛り込むようにする。

中学校

【1】次の教材を使って，中学3年生を対象に外国語指導助手(ALT)と Team-Teachingで授業を行う場合，あなた(JTE)は，教材の主題と結びつけた導入(Oral Introduction)をどのように行うか。JTE，ALTの発言及び生徒の予想される発言を英語で書け。ただし，(   )には発話者を記入し，その際，JTE，ALT及び生徒はそれぞれJ，A及びSで表すこと。(生徒は，S1，S2，S3…の順で表記すること。)

Shinji : Hi there, have you ever lived in the countryside?

Nancy : Yes, I have. I grew up in a small village surrounded by fields and forests. I loved the peace and quiet, the fresh air, and being close to nature. It was a great place to grow up. How about you?

Shinji : I have lived in an urban area since I was born. I can have access to more entertainment options. For example, I always go to shopping malls, movie theaters, and restaurants.

Nancy : Sounds good. We have local markets and shops that sell fresh produce and homemade goods.

Shinji : Oh, I want to go there.

Nancy : But it is far from here and there are less public transportation options in the countryside.

Shinji : I've never worried about public transportation. But there are a lot of people living around my house and they use cars, so the roads are always very busy. The air is also polluted.

Nanc : Both lifestyles have their advantages and disadvantages, right?

Shinji : That's true. It depends on which lifestyle suits you better.

┃ 2024年度 ┃ 山口県 ┃ 難易度 ┃

【2】次の各問いに答えなさい。なお，それぞれの問いは，中学校の英語の授業での活動を想定している。

(1) 第2学年の授業で，自分の町のお気に入りの場所とその理由につ

いてペアで対話する活動をさせるために，活動の導入として，英語
教師と外国語指導助手(ALT)がモデルとなる会話を行いたい。次の2
つ(条件)を踏まえ，（　①　），（　②　）に適する英文を書き，二人の
対話文を完成させなさい。

(条件)

・(　　)内にアルファベットが書いてある場合は，その文字が先頭
　に来る単語から始まる文を書くこと。

・一文～二文の英文で書くこと。(語数は問わない。)

英語教師	外国語指導助手（ALT）
（① W　　　　）?	
	The park near my house.
Why do you like that park?	
	Because I can walk my dog there and play with him. I can also see my friends who have dogs too.
That's nice!	
	How about you? Tell me about your favorite place and why you like it.
OK. (　　②　　).	

(2)　第3学年の授業で，ディベートをさせるにあたり，モデルとして
生徒に提示する(英語のメモ)を作成する。論題に対して賛成側，反
対側の立場を一つ選び，(英語のメモ)内のどちらかの(　　)に○を
書き入れなさい。また，「主張」にその理由を英語で書きなさい。
その際，次の3つ(条件)を踏まえること。

(条件)

・理由を二つ書くこと。

・理由には接続詞のifを用いた文を一文入れること。

・一文～二文の英文で書くこと。(語数は問わない。)

(英語のメモ)

論題	Boxed lunches are better than school lunches.	
立場	(　　) I agree.	(　　) I disagree.
主張		

(3)　第3学年の授業で，将来なりたいものについて，理由やその職業
でしたいことを入れてスピーチをさせる際，関係代名詞を用いた文

503

を使わせたい。モデルとして提示する文章を英語で書きなさい。その際，次の2つ(条件)を踏まえること。

(条件)

・45語程度の英語で書くこと。文の数は問わない。

・I'mのような短縮形は1語として数え，符号(, や . など)は(例)のように書き，語数に含めないこととする。

(例) 符号をつける場合の書き方：～ __a__ __boy__ , __Tom__ .

▌ 2024年度 ▌ 鳥取県 ▌ 難易度■■■■■

【3】「中学校学習指導要領　外国語(平成29年告示)」の「第2章　各教科　第9節　外国語　第2　各言語の目標及び内容等　英語　1　目標　(1)　聞くこと」には，「ア　はっきりと話されれば，日常的な話題について，必要な情報を聞き取ることができるようにする。」「イ　はっきりと話されれば，日常的な話題について，話の概要を捉えることができるようにする。」と示されています。

　これらを踏まえて，聞くことの指導について，中学校3年生に対する外国人指導助手(ALT)とのティーム・ティーチングの授業を構想する場面を想定し，次の(1)・(2)の各問いに答えなさい。

(1)　次の英文は，ALTが授業の中で行うモデルスピーチの内容です。これについて，①～③の各問いに答えなさい。

> In April of 2023 I visited a friend who works in a military base in the beautiful prefecture of Okinawa. During my visit, I was surprised by many wonderful things. Okinawa has amazing beaches and a unique culture. Even in April, I could swim in the ocean. It was the clearest water I've ever experienced. My friend showed me Okinawa's culture, such as Shima-Uta music at Okinawa and taco-rice. If I live in Japan in the future, I want to live in Okinawa.

①　ALTと授業の打合わせをする際に，ALTにどのような点に留意して上記のモデルスピーチを話してほしいと伝えるとよいですか。小学校学習指導要領の目標との違いを踏まえて日本語で簡潔に答えなさい。

②　生徒が話の概要を捉えることができるよう，モデルスピーチを

聞かせる前にどのような指導をするとよいですか。日本語で簡潔
に答えなさい。

③ 「聞くこと」の上記のモデルスピーチ原稿をより生徒にとって
身近な内容となるようにしたいとき，どのような表現を加えると
よいですか。15語以上20語以内(1文でなくてもよい)の英語で答え
なさい。なお，どこに付け加えるか分かるよう，挿入する前後の
語を明記すること。

(2) 「中学校学習指導要領外国語(平成29年告示)」では，外国語の5つ
の領域にわたってコミュニケーションを図る資質・能力をバランス
よく育成することや，領域統合型の言語活動が重視されています。
そこで，「話すこと[やり取り]」「話すこと[発表]」「書くこと」のい
ずれかの領域を1つ取り上げ，「聞くこと」の領域と統合した言語活
動をするとき，どのような活動を行うとよいですか。日本語で簡潔
に答えなさい。

| 2024年度 | 名古屋市 | 難易度 |

【4】あとの英作文は，「中学校の思い出を英語で残し，仲間とこれまで
の歩みを振り返ろう」という単元の途中で生徒が書いたものです。次
の問いに答えなさい。

1 この英作文を書いた生徒が，英作文をよりよくするためにアドバ
イスをしてほしいと言っています。あなたなら，どのように誤りを
修正しますか。英作文に書き込む形で生徒に伝えなさい。

単元のゴール

中学校の思い出について，事実や自分の考え，気持ちなど
を整理し，これまでに学んだ表現を用いてまとまりのある英
文を書くことができる。

Chorus Contest

The chorus contest was my fovorite memory.

We practiced every day for a month.

It was difficult for us to singing the different parts.

We could sings well at the end.

I remember will our beautiful harmony and our victory!

Aya

comment

2 単元のゴールに向けて，生徒がさらに意欲的に取り組んでいける
ように，あなたならどのようにコメント欄に記入して返却しますか。
50語程度の英語で書きなさい。

3 あなたは，生徒に単元のゴールを達成させるために，英作文を返
却後に全体に対してどのような指導を行いますか。具体的な指導場
面を2つ日本語で書きなさい。

2024年度 ┃ 岩手県 ┃ 難易度■■■■■

【5】次の問いに答えなさい。

中学校学習指導要領(平成29年3月)の外国語科の目標は「外国語によ
るコミュニケーションにおける見方・考え方を働かせ，外国語による
聞くこと，読むこと，話すこと，書くことの言語活動を通して，簡単
な情報や考えなどを理解したり表現したり伝え合ったりするコミュニ
ケーションを図る資質・能力を次の通り育成することを目指す。」で
ある。小学校学習指導要領(平成29年3月)，高等学校学習指導要領(平
成30年3月)においても，下線部が共通して明記され，小学校，中学校，
高等学校を通じて，外国語によるコミュニケーションにおける見方・
考え方を働かせた言語活動の充実が求められている。中学校指導にお
いて，言語活動の充実を図る上で，特に必要なことについて「小学校
における指導」と「高等学校への橋渡し」の二つの観点を踏まえ，日
本語で書きなさい。

2024年度 ┃ 岩手県 ┃ 難易度■■■■■

【6】 第2学年「Work experience」の単元について，次のように構想し，授業を行った。後の(1)～(6)の問いに答えなさい。

○全7時間計画　　　○新出言語材料　不定詞

＜単元の課題＞

　シンガポールの中学生と，お互いのことをもっと知るために，将来の夢について伝え合おう。

＜評価規準（話すこと［発表］）＞

知識・技能	思考・判断・表現	主体的に学習に取り組む態度
［知識］不定詞の特徴やきまりを理解している。 ［技能］自分の将来の夢についての思いや考えなどを，不定詞を用いて伝える技能を身に付けている。	お互いのことをもっと知るために，自分の将来の夢についての思いや考えなどを，簡単な語句や文を用いて伝えている。	お互いのことをもっと知るために，自分の将来の夢についての思いや考えなどを，簡単な語句や文を用いて伝えようとしている。

＜指導と評価の計画＞　　　　　　　　　　　　　　　　※○は記録に残す評価

時間	主な学習活動	評価の観点 知技	思判表	主体態
1	・外国語指導助手(ALT)の話を聞いて，単元の課題をつかむ。 ・既習表現を用いて，将来の夢についてペアで伝え合う。（試しの活動）			
2	・不定詞の用法を理解する。 ・自分の好きなことやしたいこと等をペアで伝え合う。			
3～5	・不定詞の用法を理解する。 ・教科書本文を読み，内容を理解する。 ・教科書本文についての言語活動に取り組む。			
6	・メモをもとに，将来の夢についてペアで伝え合う。 ・メモを見直し，グループで再度伝え合う。	○		
7	・オンラインで，シンガポールの中学生とお互いに将来の夢を伝え合い，感想を述べる。	○	○	○
後日	・パフォーマンステスト	○	○	○

(1)　1時間目において，教師(T)と外国語指導助手(ALT)，生徒(S1～S5)との間で次のようなやり取りを行った。以下の①～③の問いに答えなさい。

ALT : I have a sister in Singapore. She is a junior high school student.

　S1 : We know her. She is fourteen years old, right?

ALT : Yes. She sent me an email last week. Her English class had speeches about their futures. She said it was very interesting. Now, she and her friends want to know about the dreams for the future Japanese students have. Do you have your dreams

---

for your future?

　S2 ： Yes, I do.

　　T ： Oh, that's nice. (ア)You had a work experience last month, right?

ALT ： How was it?

　S2 ： I learned a lot. I'm thinking about my future. I want to know my friends' dreams.

ALT ： The students in Singapore also have their own dreams for the future. Are you interested in those?

　S3 ： Yes!

　　T ： Okay. What will you do?

　S4 ： We talked with the students in Singapore online before. How about having a presentation about our dreams online?

　S5 ： That's a good idea. We can know each other more.

　　T ： Great! Then, please tell each other about your dreams for the future.

① このように授業を英語で行う目的を日本語で2つ書きなさい。

② 単元の導入の際に，このようなやり取りをする指導上の意図を日本語で書きなさい。

③ 下線部(ア)のように，教師が話した指導上の意図を日本語で書きなさい。

(2) 3時間目において，教科書本文の内容(登場人物Kenの職場体験レポート)について，次のように教師(T)と生徒(S)の間でやり取りを行った。後の①，②の問いに答えなさい。

＜教科書本文＞

I went to an elementary school for my work experience. I helped a teacher with an English class. I enjoyed singing and talking with the students in English. The class was very fun. When we were talking in English, one student asked me a question but I couldn't answer it. Then the teacher helped us and we could enjoy communication in English. I think that teaching is hard work because teachers have to

> pay attention to many students and they have a lot of things to prepare for each class. But I enjoyed working with the students. I want to try it again.

＜教師(T)と生徒(S)の実際のやり取り＞

> T : Ken went to a work experience. He had a speech about it in his English class. This is Ken's report of his work experience.
> (イ)Where did Ken go for his work experience? What did he do there? What did he think of his work experience? Please read his report by yourselves. Then share your ideas in pairs. Okay?
> S : Okay.
> ・・・(After students share their ideas)・・・
> T : (ウ)Now, let's read the text aloud together.

① 下線部(イ)のように，教師が質問した指導上の意図を日本語で書きなさい。

② 下線部(ウ)の活動後，複数の領域を統合した言語活動につなげたい。教師はどのような活動を設定するとよいか。日本語で書きなさい。

(3) 6時間目において，メモを使用して伝え合う活動をさせる意図を日本語で書きなさい。

(4) 6時間目の「将来の夢について伝え合う活動」において，評価規準に照らし合わせて，知識・技能を評価した。この時間で知識・技能について記録に残す評価を行った理由を日本語で書きなさい。

(5) 7時間目において，オンラインで発表する利点を日本語で書きなさい。

(6) 7時間目において，本単元の学習を踏まえて，教師として生徒に発表させたい文を50～60語の英語で書きなさい。なお，英文は1文でなくてもよい。

S:　Hello.

Thank you.

| 2024年度 | 群馬県 | 難易度 |

高等学校

【1】高等学校学習指導要領(平成30年告示)において，外国語の各科目の指導計画の作成にあたっては，「<u>コミュニケーションの目的や場面，状況など</u>を意識して活動を行い，英語の音声や語彙，表現，文法などの知識を五つの領域における実際のコミュニケーションにおいて活用する学習の充実を図ること。」(抜粋)とされている。あなたなら下線部を意識して具体的にどのような指導を行うか，200語程度の英語で述べよ。

| 2024年度 | 山梨県 | 難易度 |

【2】次の教材を使って，高校1年生を対象に外国語指導助手(ALT)とTeam-Teachingで授業を行う場合，あなた(JTE)は，教材の主題と結びつけた導入(Oral Introduction)をどのように行うか。JTE，ALTの発言及び生徒の予想される発言を英語で書け。ただし，(　　)には発話者を記入し，その際，JTE，ALT及び生徒はそれぞれJ，A及びSで表すこと。(生徒は，S1，S2，S3…の順で表記すること。)

While animals may not pay much attention to the color of food, for humans it is of great importance. If a plate contains different kinds of foods with similar colors, it does not appear as delicious as one with a mixture of foods with bright colors.

Although most kinds of foods have one overall color (e.g. milk is white, strawberries are red, broccoli is green, etc.), many types have two. The bread, rice, eggs and sugar sitting on supermarket shelves are either white or brown.

The same is true of the fish caught in the oceans, which contain either white or red meat. Among fruits grown by farmers, grapes are either green or purple.

However, it is not as easy to find one type of food that comes in three different colors, but there is a vegetable possessing such a characteristic. The vegetable is the bell pepper, which, Iike a set of traffic signals, has three distinct colors: green, yellow and red. Have you ever wondered why consumers have a choice of such colors? To find out, the place to look is the peppers' price label. You will see that green peppers are the cheapest and red peppers the most expensive.

So what is the reason for the difference in price? Green peppers are picked before they mature so they taste slightly bitter but contain vitamins A and C. As for yellow peppers, they are picked when they are semi-ripe and contain more nutrients than green peppers but not as many as the red variety. For instance, they have almost twice as much vitamin C as their less mature versions. Red peppers, however, contain the highest amount of nutrients (ten times as much vitamin A as green peppers). They also taste sweet since they are fully matured when picked although the longer growth time results in higher prices than the other two colors.

So like tree leaves changing color in the fall, green bell peppers mature into a yellow (or orange) color and then turn red. For consumers, these peppers picked at different stages of growth allow them to enjoy their different flavors and benefits for health. However, to do so, they must decide how much they are willing to pay for the color.

┃ 2024年度 ┃ 山口県 ┃ 難易度 ■■■■■■

【3】国の「GIGA スクール構想」により，鳥取県立高等学校全日制課程では，令和4年度入学生から年次進行で，指定する端末(Chromebook)を生徒が1人1台ずつ購入し，授業などで活用しています。英語の学力を高めるために，英語の授業，及び英語の授業外で，タブレット端末をどのように活用していくか考えていくことが必要となります。次の英文を読み，各問いに答えなさい。

From a small start - just a simple e-mail requesting used book donations - Room to Read, an organization pursuing quality education for all children around the world, has grown into a well-known nonprofit organization. It has established over 14,000 libraries, distributed over eleven million books, and built more than 1,500 schools, improving the lives of over six million children in Asia and Africa. These figures are updated regularly and show what a big difference those involved are actually making. The successful growth and sound management of this nonprofit project has been greatly supported by the lesson John Wood, who is the founder of Room to Read and used to be the executive at Microsoft, learned in the competitive business world. Room to Read is still growing in the strong belief that education is crucial in breaking the cycle of poverty and taking control of one's life.

(東京書籍　*PROMINENCE English Communication* Ⅲ　を参照)

(1) この英文を題材として，書くことや話すことの言語活動をどのように行うか，日本語で書きなさい。

(2) (1)で述べた言語活動を行うにあたって，Chromebookなどの端末の活用方法について，日本語で説明しなさい。その際，学び合いや協働学習の視点も述べること。

(3) (2)で述べた活用方法に対して，どのような効果が得られるか，日本語で説明しなさい。

▌2024年度 ▌鳥取県 ▌難易度■■■■■

【4】平成30年3月告示の高等学校学習指導要領　外国語　英語コミュニケーションⅡ　目標　(2)　読むこと　イ　には，「社会的な話題について，使用される語句や文，情報量などにおいて，一定の支援を活用すれば，必要な情報を読み取り，概要や要点，詳細を目的に応じて捉えることができるようにする。」と示されています。このことを踏まえ，次の1・2に答えなさい。

1　ある学校で，科目「英語コミュニケーションⅡ」を設置し，授業において，本時の目標を「携帯電話に関する英文を読んで，その要点を捉えることができる。」と設定し，次の〈教材〉を用いて指導することとします。この〈教材〉における英文の要点はどのようなことですか。日本語で書きなさい。

〈教材〉

　In one of my classes today we discussed the question of how our lives would be without a phone and I actually felt quite sad to hear how some kids these days cannot survive without their mobiles. Personally, I think nowadays we are controlled by our technology and pressurised to keep up. So let's see some of the points that came up in the debate and see if our generation really is addicted to electronic connections rather than true communication.

　It is true that everything works at a fast pace these days, due to the quick access we have to pretty much anything and anyone. For example, you can contact someone who lives on the other side of the world within seconds. This is great if you think about how connected we can stay to the people who are far away from us; however, on the contrary, can we be too connected to the people who are close to us? An argument arose about the fact that it is easier to message someone from your sofa than to meet them in person and talk. On one hand, it is easier and nice sometimes to casually chat to a friend this way. However, it is also lazier and rude to prefer to talk to someone on your phone rather than meeting up, if you are able to, in my opinion. Social skills are important to have and if you are not going to put effort into real-life communication, then you are not going to progress in this ability.

　Another point was that phones are very handy to look up something that you are wondering about. For example, if you don't know a word in another language, you can quickly and simply access a translator to help you out. This can be very helpful in many situations, but it can also make a person dependent on the internet to help with anything. This factor slightly takes away the diversity of learning a language and conversing with people, as you are able to access everything you need via the web.

　All in all, this question is very interesting to consider for oneself as we become day by day more dependent on technology. We should just be aware of how much we really need to be connected via our phones while considering the benefits and damage it can cause us.

(https://learnenglishteens.britishcouncil.org/blogs/science-and-technology/what-would-your-life-be-without-phone　© British Council)

2　1で示した本時の目標を達成するために，この〈教材〉を用いた授業において「読むこと」の言語活動を設定し，指導することとします。その言語活動をどのように展開しますか。具体的な言語活動の展開とその際の指導上の留意点について，日本語で書きなさい。

言語活動の展開	指導上の留意点

解答・解説

中学校

【1】(J): Good morning, everyone. Last night, I watched a TV program introducing country life. Have you ever lived in the countryside?

(A): Yes, I have. I lived in a small town in the countryside for several years before moving to the city.

(J): That sounds interesting. What was it like?

(A): It was very peaceful and quiet. There were also some great local festivals and events that brought the community together.

(J): Oh, I see. Everyone, do you have any questions about living in the countryside?

(S1): Did you miss anything from city living?

(A): Well, one of the biggest challenges was access to services. There were limited options for healthcare and shopping, and transportation could be a bit tricky.

(J): Do any of you have any experiences living in the countryside?

(S2): I grew up in a rural area, and I loved it. There were always plenty of outdoor activities to do.

(S3): I lived in a small town for a while, and I enjoyed the slower pace of life. But, I did miss having more options for entertainment.

(S4): I have never lived in the countryside, but it sounds peaceful and relaxing.

(J): It's interesting to hear about everyone's experiences and ideas. Living in the countryside can have both advantages and disadvantages, depending on your lifestyle preferences. Here is the dialogue between two people. Let's explore more about this topic and learn from each other's experiences.

○**解説**○ 設問文の教材は田舎と都会のメリット，デメリットはどちらにもそれぞれあり，自分にあった生活様式を選ぶのがよいという結論で締めくくられている。この主題に結びつく導入として，JTEとALTで

515

田舎に住んだことがあるかについて日常会話のようなやり取りをする。その後でEveryone, do you have any questions about living in the countryside?やDo any of you have any experiences living in the countryside?と生徒に対して問いかけをし，発言の機会を与えていることがわかる。生徒の発言としては1～2文の短い文で簡潔な表現での発話としている。またALTは生徒S1の質問にもしっかり回答していることもうかがえ，最後にJTEが教材の紹介をして導入を終わらせている。

【2】(1) ① Where(What) is your favorite place (in your town)?
② My favorite place is the library because I like reading books. So I often go there and borrow many books. (2) (I agree.) First, if you bring a boxed lunch, you don't have to eat foods that you don't like. Second, you don't have to serve school lunches, so you can save time and have a longer lunch break. (36語) (3) I want to be a tour guide and visit many countries in the world. I have wanted to go abroad since I started learning English. I think I can see many people, so I want to talk with them in English. It will be interesting. (45語)

○**解説**○ (1) 第2学年の活動であることを踏まえ，第2学年の文法事項や語彙を意識して，①には「お気に入りの場所をたずねる英文」，②には「お気に入りの場所を理由とともに答える英文」を書く。 (2) 同じく，第3学年の活動であることを踏まえ，第3学年の文法事項や語彙を意識して書く。解答例では，論題「学校給食より弁当のほうがよい」に賛成(I agree.)の立場で意見を述べている。反対(I disagree.)の立場では「給食のほうが栄養バランスがよい」，「温かいものが提供される」，「親の作る手間が省ける」等が理由として挙げられる。 (3) 45語程度とあるので，3～4文くらいを目安とする。

【3】(1) ① 小学校の外国語科で「ゆっくりはっきりと」話されたことを聞き取ることを練習してきた経験があることから，過度に遅くなく自然な速度に近い音声で話すよう依頼する。 ② 一語一語聞くのではなく，概要を捉えさせるために，これから話すALTのスピーチのタイトルを考えるようにするというリスニングポイントを与える。

③　挿入直前の語…Okinawa　　I've heard Okinawa has original cultures which are quite different from my hometown. I really wanted to feel those cultures. (20 words)　　挿入直後の語…During　　(2)　・「話すこと[やり取り]」…聞いたことを踏まえて，より詳しく尋ねたいことをALTに質問する。　　・「話すこと[発表]」…それぞれが旅行をして一番良かった場所やその理由をペアやグループで発表し合う。　　・「書くこと」…聞いたことを参考にし，自分自身が一番印象に残っている旅行先の紹介文を書く。　から1つ

○**解説**○ (1)　①　小学校の外国語科における「聞くこと」の目標ウを踏まえるとよい。「ゆっくりはっきりと話されれば，日常生活に関する身近で簡単な事柄について，短い話の概要を捉えることができるようにする」とある。「はっきりと」は中学校の目標にも依然として残っているが，「ゆっくり」がなくなっていることに着目するとよいだろう。　②　「概要を捉える」ことができるようにするための指導上の留意点を記述すればよい。中学校学習指導要領解説外国語編に示されている通り，概要を捉える際には，一語一語や一文一文などの細かな理解に固執するのではなく，話全体を大まかに捉えさせるような指導が不可欠である。そのため，解答例にあるように，スピーチのタイトルやトピックを事前に与えることが考えられる。　③　モデルスピーチの内容に，生徒がより関心を抱くような工夫が求められている。解答例のように，いわゆる異文化理解的な観点で書くこともできるが，様々な別解が可能であろう。例えば，沖縄の地理や歴史など他教科で学ぶことや，修学旅行等の学校行事を踏まえ，中学校3年生が沖縄について知っているであろうことを含めることもできる。　(2)　モデルスピーチの内容を踏まえた，具体的な産出型の言語活動を答えることが求められている。どの技能および領域を選択したとしても，モデルスピーチのトピックである旅行について，友達やALTとコミュニケーションさせることを基本にするとよい。その際，生徒がモデルスピーチを真似するだけの活動にはならないように留意したい。

【4】 1

Chorus Contest

The chorus contest was my favorite memory.

We practiced every day for a month.

おしい！ It＋be動詞＋for ～＋to不定詞の特徴は？

It was, difficult for us to singing the different parts.

We could sings well at the end.

助動詞の後ろは？

I remember will our beautiful harmony and our victory!

語順　will の使い方

Aya

2　Great job with your details! Practicing every day is hard, but I can see this contest was a very good memory. Try using words like "and" and "but" to connect sentences. I also want to know how you chose the song which that you sang. I'm looking forward to reading more of your work. (54 words)

3　・生徒と直接的な対話によって書きたい内容を引き出しながら，書く活動への抵抗感を減らしたり少しずつでもその内容を表現できるように支援していく。　　・それぞれの英作文をグループ内で読み合うことで得られる気付きを自分の英作文の中に活かせるように支援していく。

○**解説**○　「書くこと」について，具体的な指導場面を踏まえて生徒へのフィードバックの方法を説明することが求められている。　1　英作文の誤りを修正することが求められているため，生徒の英作文のスペリングや文法的なミスについて指摘をすればよい。その際，解答例にもあるように，生徒が前向きに捉えられるような形で指摘をしたい。2　指定されている単元のゴールを踏まえて，生徒へのコメントを英語で書くことが求められている。単元のゴールにある「事実や自分の考え，気持などを整理し，これまでに学んだ表現を用いてまとまりのある英文を書く」が達成できるようなコメントを書くとよいだろう。特に，「自分の考え，気持などを整理」と「まとまりのある英文」という点に課題があるので，どこを修正すればよいのかが具体的にわかるように書きたい。本問も1と同様に，生徒が前向きに捉えられるようにするため，書かれている内容や，既に達成されている点について

は褒めるなどの工夫をしたい。なお，公式解答の4文目のthe song which that you sangには，関係代名詞が重複している。the song that you sangの誤りと思われる。　3　英作文の返却後にクラス全体に対して行う具体的な指導について，日本語で書くことが求められている。1および2で記入した修正やコメントを踏まえて考えていくとやりやすいかもしれない。そもそもトピックが中学校の思い出であることから，中学校3年生であることが想定される。しかし，生徒によっては基本的なスペルや文法的なミスがあり，また，「まとまりのある英文」を書くことに課題がある生徒がいる可能性が示されているため，スモールステップで少しずつでも英作文を改善していけるような働きかけを書けばよいだろう。

【5】中学校は小学校と高校をつなぐ校種であることから，次のようなことに留意することでより一層の活動の充実が図られると考える。まず，小学校での学びを把握し，音声を中心とした言語活動からスタートさせることである。その上で，音声から文字，そして読む活動，書く活動へとつなげていく。次に高校では統合的な言語活動が求められているため，聞いて理解するだけで終わらせず，聞いた内容について話したり，書いたりする活動へつなげていくことが大切である。

○解説○　見方・考え方を働かせる必要のある言語活動をキーワードとして，小学校および高校と連携できるような中学校の指導について説明することが求められている。小学校の外国語活動および外国語科は「聞くこと」および「話すこと」による音声中心の学習であり，「読むこと」および「書くこと」の文字指導については慣れ親しみに留まっていることを踏まえ，音声言語から文字言語への円滑な接続を支援することが重要である。また，高校においては，高等学校学習指導要領に「五つの領域別の言語活動及び複数の領域を結び付けた統合的な言語活動を通して」とあるように，複数領域を統合した活動が求められている。従って，中学校の後半においては，「聞くこと」または「読むこと」を通して理解したことについて，「話すこと[やり取り]」，「話すこと[発表]」または「書くこと」で自分の考えなどを表現する言語活動も必要になる。

【6】(1) ①　・生徒が英語に触れる機会を充実させるため　　・授業を実際のコミュニケーションの場面とするため　②　コミュニケーションを行う目的・場面・状況を明確に設定し，単元の課題に気付かせるため　③　扱う題材と，日常生活や学校行事との関連を想起させることで，言語活動への積極的な参加を促すため　(2) ①　文章の概要を捉えることができるようにするため　②　教科書本文の内容理解を通して感じたこと，考えたこと，自分の経験や学んだこと等をペアで話したり，英語で書いたりする活動　(3)　メモやキーワードを頼りに話す活動を繰り返すことで，簡単な語句や文を用いて即興で話す力や，事実や自分の考え，気持ちなどを整理し，まとまりのある内容を話すことができる力を育成するため　(4)　本言語活動が，本単元の言語材料(不定詞)の使用を指定しなくても，当該言語材料が必然的に使用されるような文脈であるため　(5)　英語話者との実際のコミュニケーションを可能とし，聞き手に配慮しながらコミュニケーションを図ることができる力が育成できるため　(6)　I want to be an English teacher. I like talking with my friends and teachers in English. Communication in English is very fun. I went to an elementary school for work experience. I was very happy to learn a lot of things. I found that I have many things to do to be a teacher. I'll study harder. (58語)

○**解説**○ (1)　指導の目的や意図については，学習指導要領に基づいて解答すること。　①　現行の「中学校学習指導要領　第2章　第9節　外国語　第2　各言語の目標及び内容等　3　指導計画の作成と内容の取扱い　(1)　エ」の項に，「生徒が英語に触れる機会を充実するとともに，授業を実際のコミュニケーションの場面とするため，授業は英語で行うことを基本とする。その際，生徒の理解の程度に応じた英語を用いるようにすること」と示されていることを踏まえる。　②　コミュニケーションを図る際には，その目的や場面，状況等に応じて情報を整理したり吟味したりする必要がある。本活動でも，誰に，どのような目的で話すのか等を明確にすることで，生徒が積極的に取り組めるようにする。　③　現行の「中学校学習指導要領　第2章　第9節　外国語　第2　各言語の目標及び内容等　3　指導計画の作成と内容の取扱い　(1)　オ」においても「…国語科や理科，音楽科など，他の教

科等で学習したことを活用したり，学校行事で扱う内容と関連付けたりするなどの工夫をすること」と示されている。　(2)　①　下線部(イ)は，本文の内容理解に関する質問である。教師は生徒に文章から読み取るべきポイントを示している。　②　自分の職場体験について話す，Kenにメールを書く等，読むことから話すこと，書くことへつなげることが可能である。　(3)　学習指導要領における話すこと[発表]の領域の目標の一つである「関心のある事柄について，簡単な語句や文を用いて即興で伝え合うことができるようにする」を踏まえると，「メモを使用して伝え合う」という箇所が「即興で話すこと」につながることが分かる。よって，「即興で話すこと」について触れて解答する。　(4)　to不定詞では，これから起こる未来のことを表せる。6時間目の学習活動において，to不定詞を活用すれば，将来自分のしたいことやその目的を表現できる。したがって，指導の計画から，6時間目が，評価規準「[知識]不定詞の特徴やきまりを理解している」，「[技能]自分の将来の夢についての思いや考えなどを，不定詞を用いて伝える技能を身に付けている」を評価できる初時である。次時(7時間目)でも同評価を計画していることから，複数回で同観点の比較もできる。　(5)　(1)の①の解説を参照。授業が実際のコミュニケーションの場となるという点を挙げて解答する。　(6)　まとまりのある文章になるよう，文構成や文のつながりを意識して書かせるよう指導する。モデル文を提示したり，ペアからフィードバックを受けたりしながら推敲を重ねる方法もある。

高等学校

【1】 I believe placing an explicit focus on the purpose, setting, and situation for each language activity through pre-activity activation and post-activity reflection will effectively raise students' awareness.

　I will use a smartphone shopping role-play activity as an example. After assigning the roles of shopper and salesperson, I will have students write down what their goal for the interaction is, e.g., buy a cheap flip phone, understand the shopper's wants, etc. Next, I will have students share their ideas to help them improve their goals and then move to what information or vocabulary may be needed-after all, most people shop for a smartphone after doing some research first. Finally, I will check what register each role should take: more formal for the salesperson, and less so, yet polite, for the shopper.

Hopefully, with students' attention purposely directed towards these qualities, they will be able to have a more realistic interaction. However, I will also have students reflect on what they kept in mind during their conversation. For example, if the student were the salesperson, they would think about whether they adjusted their manner of speech to include more formal modes of dialogue including modal verbs, such as "could" and "would." (199 words)

○**解説**○ 高等学校学習指導要領解説外国語編・英語編(平成30年7月)には，外国語教育における学習過程について，「①設定されたコミュニケーションの目的や場面，状況等を理解する，②目的に応じて情報や意見などを発信するまでの方向性を決定し，コミュニケーションの見通しを立てる，③目的達成のため，具体的なコミュニケーションを行う，④言語面・内容面で自ら学習のまとめと振り返りを行うといった流れの中で，学んだことの意味付けを行ったり，既得の知識や経験と，新たに得られた知識を言語活動で活用したりすることで，『思考力，判断力，表現力等』を高めていくことが大切になる」と示されている。これを踏まえ，解答例では，スマートフォンショッピングのロールプレイ活動を例にとり，現実に即した実践的な力が身に付くように生徒を支援することを挙げている。

【2】(J): Good morning, class. The other day, a friend of mine gave me an instant curry as a souvenir from a trip to Ibaraki, but it was a little different from ordinary curry. What do you think the difference is?

(A): Umm, is it a super hot curry?

(J): No, it isn't. Everyone, can you guess what the difference is?

(S1): Is it a different color from regular curry?

(J): That's right! Do you know there is a blue curry?

(A): Yes, I have seen it introduced on a TV program, but that curry did not look tasty at all. Everyone, have you ever seen unusually colored curry before?

(S2): Yes, I have. In fact, I have eaten a pink curry before. It was delicious, but before eating it, I didn't want to eat it. I didn't have an appetite.

(J): I agree. I actually had a blue curry yesterday and it took me a while to get it into my mouth.

(A): The color of food is important for us, right? It can affect our perception of how tasty food looks.

(J): Absolutely. We've talked about curries in unusual colors like blue and pink, and the color affects our appetite. It's not only our appetite that is affected by color. OK, let's read a passage about a specific type of vegetable and find out more about it.

○**解説**○ 設問文の教材には，食べ物の色が人間に与える影響や，色によって値段や栄養価，味が変わる野菜であるbell pepper「ピーマン」について述べられている。この教材に結びつく導入として，JTEとALTで通常のカレーとは異なるインスタントカレーをお土産にもらったことについてやり取りをする。JTEはEveryone, can you guess what the difference is?とクイズ形式にして生徒を巻き込む問いかけをし，発言の機会を与えていることがわかる。生徒の発言としては高校1年生レベルの短い文で簡潔な表現での発話としている。ALTやJTEは青いカレーは食べるのに少し抵抗があるといった食べ物の色についての教材の内容と関連のあるコメントをし，最後にJTEが教材の紹介をして導入を終わらせている。

【3】〈解答例1〉…(1) John Wood になりきって，Room to Read について英語でプレゼンテーションする活動。 (2) それぞれが考えたプレゼンテーションを自分で録画し，ドライブ上に保存し共有させ，感想をドライブ上で述べる。 (3) 授業で行うプレゼンテーションでは1度しか他人のものが見れないが，ドライブ上に保存することで何度も繰り返し視聴できる。 〈解答例2〉…(1) 教育に困難がある国の現状を調べ，自分たちに何ができるかのポスターを英語で作成する。(2) オンラインでRoom to Read の職員に発表する機会を作り，作成したポスターについて発表する。 (3) 遠隔地の人であっても，自分

が考えたことを英語で伝える機会を持つことができる。また，そこで撮影した動画を学校のホームページに載せることで，他生徒も端末を使ってそれを視聴できる。

○**解説**○ ここでは，(1)〜(3)について2種類の解答例が挙げられている。(1) 題材となっている英文は，世界中のすべての子どもたちに質の高い教育を提供することを目指す団体，Room to Readの活動紹介と「貧困の連鎖を断ち切り，自分の人生をコントロールするためには教育が不可欠だ」とする創設者John Woodの信念に触れている。解答例の他にも，団体や創設者についてさらに詳しく調べた内容を発表する等が考えられる。 (2) 他の生徒の活動をいつでも共有できるなど，Chromebookの特長を生かした活用方法を解答する。 (3) メールツールやビデオ会議ツールなどにより，活動の幅が広がり，それにより得られる効果も大きい。解答例は「何度も視聴できる」，「遠隔地の人と交流できる」等を挙げている。

【4】1 携帯電話によるつながりがもたらす利益と損害を考慮しながら，実際にどれだけ携帯電話でつながる必要があるかを認識するべきであること。

2

言語活動の展開	指導上の留意点
○国内外の高校生のコミュニケーションツールの利用状況調査に関する記事について教師とＡＬＴが行う対話を聞き、これから読む内容を推測する。	
○〈教材〉の英文を読む目的を把握する。	・英文を読んだ後に、英文の要点について感想や自分の意見を交流することを説明し、読む目的を意識させる。
○英文を読み、ワークシートに示された表に事実と書き手の意見を整理する。	・机間指導を行い、生徒が事実と書き手の意見を区別して読めているかを確認する。
○表に整理した内容についてグループ内で説明し合う。	・生徒の学習状況に応じて、事実が書かれている文と意見が書かれている文のそれぞれの特徴や用いられている語句

	（the fact, in my opinion など）に気付くことができるように助言する。 ・各段落に書き手の意見やその根拠となる文があることに気付くことができるように助言する。
○書き手の意見やその根拠となる文を意識して、もう一度英文を読み、要点を捉える。	
○英文の要点をグループで説明し合う。 ○各グループで説明し合った内容をクラス全体で共有し、要点を捉える。	・生徒の学習状況に応じて、書き手の意見や根拠のキーワードやキーフレーズに気付かせたり、"What does the writer cite as benefits(damage)?" と問うたりして、検討のための手掛かりを与える。
○英文の要点について感想や自分の意見をクラス全体で交流する。	・生徒が述べた感想や意見に対して、なぜそう思うのか発問するなどして、理由や根拠を述べるように促す。

○**解説**○ 具体的な授業場面における言語活動を想定した問題である。

1 主に第4パラグラフに書かれている内容をまとめればよい。この英文は論証型で明快な論理構成になっており、第1パラグラフが導入、第2および第3パラグラフが本論、そして、第4パラグラフが結論になっている。 2 高等学校学習指導要領平成30(2018)年3月告示外国語科において、科目「英語コミュニケーションⅡ」の「読むこと」の目標は、「ア 日常的な話題について、使用される語句や文、情報量などにおいて、一定の支援を活用すれば、必要な情報を読み取り、文章の展開や書き手の意図を把握することができるようにする」及び「イ 社会的な話題について、使用される語句や文、情報量などにおいて、一定の支援を活用すれば、必要な情報を読み取り、概要や要点、詳細を目的に応じて捉えることができるようにする」と示されている。文中の「必要な情報」とは概要や要点を捉えるために必要となる情報のことであり、「要点」とは、書き手が伝えたい主な考えなどの読み落としてはならない重要なポイントのことである。これらを踏まえて、教材の要点を捉えるために必要となる情報を理解させることが求められている。英文を読む目的を(可能であれば、場面および状況も)導入した上で、英文の要点を理解できるように、英文中の情報を読み取らせていくことが基本となる。今回の英文は論証型であるため、書き手

の主張を正しく理解できるように，書き手の意見とその根拠となる事実を区別しつつ，英文中の情報を理解させるような流れにするとよいだろう。その際，個別最適な学びとして生徒1人1人に英文を読んで考えさせる場面に加え，協働的な学びとして生徒同士に意見交換などを行わせる場面なども取り入れられるとなおよい。

●書籍内容の訂正等について

　弊社では教員採用試験対策シリーズ（参考書，過去問，全国まるごと過去問題集），公務員試験対策シリーズ，公立幼稚園・保育士試験対策シリーズ，会社別就職試験対策シリーズについて，正誤表をホームページ（https://www.kyodo-s.jp）に掲載いたします。内容に訂正等，疑問点がございましたら，まずホームページをご確認ください。もし，正誤表に掲載されていない訂正等，疑問点がございましたら，下記項目をご記入の上，以下の送付先までお送りいただくようお願いいたします。

> ① 　書籍名，都道府県（学校）名，年度
> 　（例：教員採用試験過去問シリーズ　小学校教諭 過去問　2025年度版）
> ② 　ページ数（書籍に記載されているページ数をご記入ください。）
> ③ 　訂正等，疑問点（内容は具体的にご記入ください。）
> 　（例：問題文では"ア～オの中から選べ"とあるが，選択肢はエまでしかない）

〔ご注意〕

○ 電話での質問や相談等につきましては，受付けておりません。ご注意ください。

○ 正誤表の更新は適宜行います。

○ いただいた疑問点につきましては，当社編集制作部で検討の上，正誤表への反映を決
　定させていただきます（個別回答は，原則行いませんのであしからずご了承ください）。

●情報提供のお願い

　協同教育研究会では，これから教員採用試験を受験される方々に，より正確な問題を，より多くご提供できるよう情報の収集を行っております。つきましては，教員採用試験に関する次の項目の情報を，以下の送付先までお送りいただけますと幸いでございます。お送りいただきました方には謝礼を差し上げます。

(情報量があまりに少ない場合は，謝礼をご用意できかねる場合があります)。

◆あなたの受験された面接試験，論作文試験の実施方法や質問内容

◆教員採用試験の受験体験記

送付先	○電子メール：edit@kyodo-s.jp ○FAX：03-3233-1233（協同出版株式会社　編集制作部 行） ○郵送：〒101-0054　東京都千代田区神田錦町2-5 　　　　　　協同出版株式会社　編集制作部 行 ○HP：https://kyodo-s.jp/provision（右記のQRコードからもアクセスできます）	

　※謝礼をお送りする関係から，いずれの方法でお送りいただく際にも，「お名前」「ご
　　住所」は，必ず明記いただきますよう，よろしくお願い申し上げます。

教員採用試験「全国版」過去問シリーズ⑥

全国まるごと過去問題集
英語科

編　集	©協同教育研究会
発　行	令和6年1月10日
発行者	小貫　輝雄
発行所	協同出版株式会社
	〒101-0054　東京都千代田区神田錦町2‐5
	電話　03－3295－1341
	振替　東京00190－4－94061
印刷所	協同出版・POD工場

落丁・乱丁はお取り替えいたします。